SPIRITUALITY

THE CLASSICS

Christian Spirituality: The Classics is a unique and comprehensive guide to thirty key Christian spirituality texts. Ranging from Origen and Augustine to Jonathan Edwards, Thérèse of Lisieux and Thomas Merton, it offers a view of the texts which is founded in scholarship, but which also presents them as living documents that invite—even compel—contemplative reflection and existential response.

Each chapter briefly describes the classic text's author and audience, gives a synopsis of its contents, suggests some of its influence in history, and then explores aspects of the text's meaning for readers today. Key themes include: What is the meaning of life? How can human beings find truth? How can they discover who they really are? How can they live together in peace? How can they live more fully in God's presence in this world and be united with God in the world to come?

The scholars who have written these chapters are all experts on their respective topics, but they wear their learning lightly. Anyone wishing to discover the riches of Christian spirituality will find this the ideal introduction and should be able to progress to a deeper understanding of the texts themselves.

Arthur Holder is Dean, Vice President for Academic Affairs, and John Dillenberger Professor of Christian Spirituality at the Graduate Theological Union in Berkeley, California. He is president of the Society for the Study of Christian Spirituality for 2009.

CHRISTIAN SPIRITUALITY

THE CLASSICS

Edited by
Arthur Holder

Routledge
Taylor & Francis Group

LONDON AND NEW YORK

First published 2010 by Routledge
2 Park Square, Milton Park, Abingdon, Oxon OX14 4RN

Simultaneously published in the USA and Canada by Routledge
711 Third Ave, New York, NY 10017

Routledge is an imprint of the Taylor & Francis Group, an informa business

Typeset in Aldus and Scala Sans
by Florence Production Ltd, Stoodleigh, Devon

British Library Cataloguing in Publication Data
A catalogue record for this book is available from the British Library

Library of Congress Cataloging in Publication Data
Christian spirituality: the classics/edited by Arthur Holder. p. cm.
Includes bibliographical references and index.
1. Spirituality. 2. Christian literature. I. Holder, Arthur G. BV4501.3.C496 2009
248—dc22   2009001055

ISBN13: 978–0–415–77601–1 (hbk)
ISBN13: 978–0–415–77602–8 (pbk)
ISBN13: 978–0–203–87472–1 (ebk)

CONTENTS

CONTRIBUTORS

Mark S. Burrows is Professor of the History of Christianity at Andover Newton Theological School in Newton, MA, past President of the Society for the Study of Christian Spirituality, and co-editor of *Minding the Spirit: the study of Christian spirituality* (Johns Hopkins University Press 2005).

Douglas Burton-Christie is Professor of Christian Spirituality at Loyola Marymount University, Los Angeles. He is author of *The Word in the Desert: scripture and the quest for holiness in early Christian monasticism* (Oxford University Press 1993), and founding editor of *Spiritus: a journal of Christian spirituality*.

Steven Chase is Associate Professor of Christian Spirituality at Western Theological Seminary in Holland, MI, and President-elect of the Society for the Study of Christian Spirituality. The most recent of his books on Christian contemplation, mysticism, and spirituality is *The Tree of Life: models of Christian prayer* (Baker Academic 2005).

Joann Wolski Conn is Professor Emeritus of Religion at Neumann College in Aston, PA and past President of the Society for the Study of Christian Spirituality. She is the author of "Therese of Lisieux: far from spiritual childhood," which appeared in *Spiritus: a journal of Christian spirituality* (2006).

Lisa E. Dahill is Assistant Professor of Worship and Christian Spirituality at Trinity Lutheran Seminary in Columbus, OH. She co-chairs the "Bonhoeffer: Theology and Social Analysis Group" of the American Academy of Religion and is a translator of Bonhoeffer's works.

Elizabeth A. Dreyer is Professor of Religious Studies at Fairfield University in Fairfield, CT. She is general editor for the series *Called to Holiness: spirituality for Catholic women* (St. Anthony Messenger Press, 2008–9) and author of *Holy Power, Holy Presence: rediscovering medieval metaphors for the Holy Spirit* (Paulist 2007).

Mary Frohlich, RSCJ, is Associate Professor of Spirituality and Director of the Master of Arts in Theology program at Catholic Theological Union in Chicago, and past President of the Society for the Study of Christian Spirituality. Her publications include *The Intersubjectivity of the Mystic: a study of Teresa of Avila's "Interior Castle"* (Oxford University Press 2000).

Dana Greene was Professor of History at St. Mary's College of Maryland and Dean of Oxford College of Emory University. She is the author of *Evelyn Underhill: artist of the infinite life* (Crossroad 1990).

Nonna Verna Harrison is Assistant Professor of Church History at Saint Paul School of Theology in Kansas City, MO. She has written four books and many articles on the Cappadocian fathers, theological anthropology, patristic spirituality, and Orthodox theology.

Timothy Hessel-Robinson is Alberta and Harold Lunger Assistant Professor of Spiritual Resources and Disciplines at Brite Divinity School in Fort Worth, TX.

Jennifer Hockenbery is Associate Professor of Philosophy at Mount Mary College in Milwaukee, WI. She has written on Augustine, Hildegard of Bingen, Luther, and Nietzsche. She is married to a Lutheran pastor and has three children.

Arthur Holder is Dean, Vice President for Academic Affairs, and John Dillenberger Professor of Christian Spirituality at the Graduate Theological Union in Berkeley, California. He is President of the Society for the Study of Christian Spirituality for 2009 and editor of *The Blackwell Companion to Christian Spirituality* (Blackwell 2005).

John D. Jones is Professor of Philosophy at Marquette University in Milwaukee, WI. He has published a number of articles on Dionysius, focusing on how he has been interpreted in the Eastern Orthodox, Latin Scholastic, and Neoplatonic traditions.

David J. Kangas teaches in the Philosophy Department at Santa Clara University. He is on the editorial board and translator for *Kierkegaard's Journals and Notebooks* (Princeton University Press) and author of *Kierkegaard's Instant* (Indiana University Press 2007).

Elisabeth Koenig is Professor of Ascetical Theology at the General Theological Seminary of the Episcopal Church in New York City.

Theresa Ladrigan-Whelpley is a doctoral candidate in the Christian Spirituality area at the Graduate Theological Union in Berkeley, California. She currently serves as the Director of Resident Ministry at Santa Clara University in Santa Clara, CA.

Bo Karen Lee is Assistant Professor of Spirituality and Historical Theology at Princeton Theological Seminary. Her doctoral dissertation was entitled "Sacrifice and Desire: The Rhetoric of Self-Denial in the Mystical Theologies of Madame Jeanne Guyon and Anna Maria van Schurman."

Bruce H. Lescher is Associate Academic Dean of the Jesuit School of Theology of Santa Clara University, located in Berkeley, CA. He is co-editor of *Exploring Christian Spirtualty: essays in honor of Sandra M. Schneiders, IHM* (Paulist Press 2006).

Maria Lichtmann has written two books on Gerard Manley Hopkins as well as *The Teacher's Way: teaching and the contemplative life* (Paulist Press 2005). She and her husband reside in Boone, NC and teach at Appalachian State University.

Elizabeth Liebert, SNJM, is Professor of Spiritual Life at San Francisco Theological Seminary, a member of the Christian Spirituality Doctoral Faculty at the Graduate Theological Union, and past President of the Society for the Study of Christian Spirituality. She is the author of *The Way of Discernment: spiritual practices for decision making* (Westminster/John Knox 2008).

John A. McGuckin is a Priest Theologian of the Romanian Orthodox Church and Professor of Byzantine Theology at Columbia University and Union Theological Seminary, New York. He has published extensively in the fields of early Christian theology and New Testament interpretation.

John J. O'Keefe is Professor of Theology at Creighton University in Omaha, NE. He has published widely on the history and theology of ancient Christianity, most recently in the area of early Christian interpretation of the Bible.

David B. Perrin, OMI, is Professor of Religious Studies, President, and Vice-Chancellor of St. Jerome's University in Waterloo, ON, Canada. A past President of the Society for the Study of Christian Spirituality, he is the author of *Studying Christian Spirituality* (Routledge 2007).

Suzette Phillips is a Sessional Lecturer at Saint Paul University, Ottawa, and Newman Theological College, Edmonton, and a mental health therapist. Her doctoral thesis, "Re-reading *The Way of a Pilgrim*: a research project utilizing contemplative psychology," explores the text's psycho-spiritual insights.

Darleen Pryds is Associate Professor of Christian Spirituality and Medieval History at the Franciscan School of Theology and the Graduate Theological Union. Her research centers on the tradition of lay preaching in medieval Italy. She is interested in online resources such as social networking programs and micro-blogging that can be used as forms of preaching today.

Philip Sheldrake is Honorary Professor at University of Wales, Lampeter and Moulsdale Fellow, St. Chad's College, Durham University. A past President of the Society for the Study of Christian Spirituality, he has written extensively on the history and theology of Christian spirituality, most recently *A George Herbert Reader* (SCM Press 2009).

Luther E. Smith, Jr. is Professor of Church and Community at the Candler School of Theology at Emory University in Atlanta, Georgia. He is editor of *Howard Thurman: essential writings* (Orbis 2006).

Timothy J. Wengert is the Ministerium of Pennsylvania Professor of Church History at The Lutheran Theological Seminary at Philadelphia. He has published extensively on Martin Luther, Philip

Melanchthon, and the Lutheran Confessions and is co-editor with Robert Kolb of *The Book of Concord* (Fortress 2000).

Ulrike Wiethaus is Director of Religion and Public Engagement and Professor of Religion and American Ethnic Studies at Wake Forest University. She is the author of *Ecstatic Transformation: transpersonal psychology and the work of Mechthild of Magdeburg* (Syracuse University Press 1996).

Wendy M. Wright is Professor of Theology at Creighton University and holds the John C. Kenefick Faculty Chair in the Humanities. A past President of the Society for the Study of Christian Spirituality, she is the author of *Heart Speaks to Heart: the Salesian spiritual tradition* (Orbis and Darton, Longman & Todd 2004).

ACKNOWLEDGEMENTS

The Divine Comedy by Dante Alighieri, translated by John Ciardi. Copyright 1954, 1957, 1959, 1960, 1961, 1965, 1967, 1970 by the Ciardi Family Publishing Trust. Used by permission of W.W. Norton & Company, Inc.

EDITOR'S
INTRODUCTION

> A vital aspect of the special power of spiritual classics is the fact that they are *committed texts*. Spiritual classics, rather like scriptural texts, offer a particular interpretation of events, people, or teachings. Every spiritual classic has a specific "take" on the tradition it promotes. In interpreting a spiritual classic, we unavoidably engage with this commitment. We cannot bypass the claims to wisdom—indeed, to a vision of "truth"—embodied in such texts.
>
> Philip Sheldrake

The chapters in this volume provide comprehensive introductions to thirty classics of Christian spirituality. While these texts are undeniably important as historical-cultural artifacts and as literature, they are presented here as *living wisdom documents* that invite—even compel—contemplative reflection and existential response. These are texts that can make a difference in a person's life. (Indeed, that is one way of defining what it means to be a "spiritual classic": any text claiming a religious truth that has made a profound difference in the lives of generations of readers across time and space.) The ultimate goal of the volume is to *let the texts speak* in such a way that readers are invited to respond from the depth of the heart.

The thirty classic texts treated here represent much of the diversity within Christian spiritual traditions. The authors of these texts include women and men; Catholics, Protestants, and Orthodox; monks, clergy, and laypeople; mystics and reformers. What all these authors have in common is a deep conviction that the God revealed in Jesus Christ has spoken (and continues to speak) words of loving wisdom and truth to a world that needs to listen and respond. Other texts could have been included, and not every text here will be received as a genuine "classic" by every reader. But these thirty texts are likely to be of interest to almost anyone who wants to discover the riches of Christian spirituality.

The scholars who have written these chapters are all experts on their respective topics, but here they are addressing not other specialists but a more general readership. Each chapter briefly describes the classic text's author and audience, gives a synopsis of its contents, suggests some of its influence in history, and then explores aspects of the text's meaning for readers today. The contributors to this volume have not presumed that their readers are necessarily committed to any particular Christian tradition, or even to the Christian faith at all. The only assumption is that readers are interested in the ultimate questions encountered in these texts: What is the meaning of life? How can human beings find truth? How can they discover who they really are? How can they live together in peace? How can they live more fully in God's presence in this world and be united with God in the world to come?

What this volume provides, then, is some background information about these spiritual classics and a selection of interpretive keys for reading these texts in a way that invites deep transformation. It is left up to the readers—ideally not just as individuals but as participants in reading communities—to decide how each classic text might make a difference in their lives. Of course the hope is that those who read *about* these spiritual classics will then want to read (or perhaps reread) the texts for themselves, and perhaps to do further study about the texts and their authors. For this purpose, bibliographical sections at the end of each chapter list the best available editions or translations of the classic text, along with suggestions for further reading.

There is a story in the Acts of Apostles (8:26–40) that tells of an encounter between Philip the evangelist and an Ethiopian eunuch who is reading the Book of Isaiah. Philip asks: "Do you understand what you are reading?" To which the eunuch answers: "How can I, unless someone guides me?" After Philip explains that Isaiah is talking about Jesus, the eunuch's life is changed forever. "Look," said the eunuch, "here is water! What is to prevent me from being baptized?" In their own modest way, the contributors to this volume hope to serve as guides for readers who want to understand Christian spiritual classics not only as historical texts but as invitations into a more abundant life.

Arthur Holder

FURTHER READING

Holder, A. (ed.) (2005) *The Blackwell Companion to Christian Spirituality*, Malden, MA and Oxford: Blackwell Publishing, provides a comprehensive overview of the subject, including six essays on the history of Christian spirituality in various periods as well as the essay by Philip Sheldrake on "Interpretation" that is the source of the quotation at the beginning of this introduction.

Perrin, D.B. (2008) *Studying Christian Spirituality*, New York and London: Routledge, is an excellent introduction to the discipline of Christian spirituality as an interdisciplinary field encompassing theology, history, and the human sciences.

Sheldrake, P. (2007) *A Brief History of Spirituality*, Malden, MA and Oxford: Blackwell Publishing, is a reliable survey of major figures and movements in Christian spirituality from the New Testament to the present.

Tyson, J. (1999) *Invitation to Christian Spirituality: an ecumenical anthology*, contains selections from spiritual texts by a wide range of authors, including twenty-five of the thirty authors whose works are discussed in *Christian Spirituality: The classics*.

ORIGEN
(c.185–c.253)
Commentary on the Song of Songs

JOHN J. O'KEEFE

In the opening prologue of his *Commentary on the Song of Songs*, Origen issues a warning about content: it will seem to be erotic, and readers with inadequate spiritual training will likely find themselves assaulted by temptation. Invoking Paul's comparison between those who are ready only for milk and those who can now move on to solid food (1 Cor 3), Origen explains that readers who interpret the Song carnally are still drinking "milk" and should avoid this text altogether. Such readers, "not knowing how to hear love's language in purity and with chaste ears" (p. 22) will twist and distort the sacred meaning and fall deeper into carnality and passion. On the contrary, the spiritually minded reader—one who has long practice in religious discipline—will see past the erotic overlay of "kisses," "mouths," and "bridal chambers" to the true meaning of the text. The Song of Songs is a figural (non-literal) tale narrating the desire of the soul and the church for intimacy with God. It is not a poetic narrative celebrating sexual love between a bride and a bridegroom.

Although Origen was among the first theologians to attempt a thoroughly Christian reading of the Song of Songs, every ancient commentator shared his convictions about the true meaning of the book. No Christian commentary on the Song written before the modern period would have suggested that the Song of Songs celebrates human love. The love described by the Song is divine love, and the union depicted is spiritual union.

Sophisticated modern readers of these ancient commentaries may find themselves puzzled. On the one hand, such readers are generally comfortable with non-literal reading. Fundamentalist efforts to understand the creation narrative in the Book of Genesis as a literal description of God's creation of the world fail before the more compelling conclusions of modern science. On the other hand, the Song of Songs suffers from no such deficiency. There is no scientific or historical counter-narrative to the Song's tale of nuptial intimacy. Indeed, a literal interpretation of the eroticism of the Song seems much more plausible to modern readers than the ancient attempt to spin the book into something esoteric and spiritual.

For Origen and other ancient interpreters, however, reading the Song of Songs literally was impossible. Such a reading created for them the same kind of cognitive dissonance that reading the creation narratives literally creates for many modern people. Understanding the source of this ancient dissonance and Origen's role in helping to resolve it will assist us in coming to a deeper appreciation not only of Origen's great commentary on the Song of Songs, but also of the entire ancient Christian interpretive project.

AUTHOR AND AUDIENCE

Condemned at the Second Council of Constantinople in 553, three hundred years after his death, Origen's legacy is difficult to assess. History has denied him the title "saint" and the church's posthumous rejection of some of his key theological teachings ensured that many of his greatest works were lost. Indeed much of Origen's work survives only in Latin translations, and these are often incomplete. Origen's *Commentary on the Song of Songs,* which once ran to ten books in the original Greek, now endures as four books in the Latin of Rufinus, one of Origen's admirers. In spite of this, Origen's impact on the developing Christian tradition was massive.

One of the oldest accounts of the life of Origen remains among the most controversial. In the *Ecclesiastical History,* written in the early years of the fourth century, the church historian Eusebius of Caesarea glides past a troubling detail. According to Eusebius, Origen took far too literally Jesus's claim in Matthew 19:12 that there are some who have "made themselves eunuchs for the sake of the kingdom of heaven." While ancient religious sensibility would have received word of Origen's extreme asceticism—self-castration—with less scandal, or even, in some circles, quiet admiration, this particular act of youthful excess dogged Origen his entire life and gave ammunition to his many critics.

Although troubling to modern readers, this story of Origen's ascetical excess tells us a great deal about the complex forces that were shaping emerging Christianity in the middle part of the third century. Before the conversion of the emperor Constantine in the early fourth century, the Christian church labored under the continuous threat of persecution by the Roman Empire. For the most part, persecution occurred sporadically and locally. The popular perception that generations of early Christians hid in the catacombs of Rome exaggerates and distorts the reality. Nonetheless, some persecutions were especially cruel. Origen's father Leonides suffered martyrdom *c.*201 CE during the reign of Septimius Severus, and Origen himself was imprisoned and tortured during the persecutions promulgated by the emperor Decius (250–1 CE). Origen's death shortly after this persecution was certainly hastened by the injuries he sustained at the hands of the church's enemies.

The pervasive possibility of persecution and even martyrdom led many in Origen's generation toward an even more rigorous embrace of ascetical practices that had long helped Christians define themselves as a counterculture in Roman society. Among these, sexual renunciation and sexual control figured prominently, not so much as hatred of the body, but as an expression of the future heavenly life where, as Jesus says, "in the resurrection they neither marry nor are given in marriage" (Mt 22:29). Origen's self-imposed membership in the company of "eunuchs for the kingdom" is best understood within this wider context of emerging Christian identity and helps explain why Origen's *Commentary on the Song of Songs* deliberately eschews the erotic.

Persecution, of course, can be more than bodily. Almost from its inception the Christian church was accused of being a weak and silly religion. To many observers, Christianity possessed nothing of value. While the church shared much in common with ancient Judaism, it lacked the latter's antiquity, which the Romans respected. Its core belief in a resurrected enemy of the state struck many intellectuals within the empire as beyond laughable. In the second century the Christian community of Alexandria emerged as a center of intellectual response to the perception that Christian faith could not be reconciled with the collective knowledge and wisdom of the dominant culture. Origen spent his early life in Alexandria, where he absorbed and continued the intellectual project of Clement, a pioneer in the church's effort to reconcile Greek thought and Christian revelation. The Greek celebration of things spiritual and intellectual over things carnal and material posed significant challenges for Christian interpreters.

At the heart of the Christian response to charges of intellectual inadequacy was the figural and non-literal reading of the scriptures. Although a literalist in youth, upon his discovery of this Alexandrian Christian style, Origen used it to construct an edifice of non-literal biblical interpretation. Origen's genius was not so much in discovering a method of interpretation, but in his ability to deploy it with such effect. Commenting on nearly every book of the Bible in extreme detail, Origen paved the way for generations of Christian intellectuals seeking to give an accounting for their faith. Origen's *Against Celsus* survives as one of the greatest of all early Christian works of apologetics, and his book *On First Principles* has often been called the first serious work of Christian systematic theology. While not a philosophical tract, Origen's *Commentary on the Song of Songs* frequently reflects this larger intellectual project.

Origen's strong interest in "the intelligible world" and his Platonic propensity toward intellection can leave the impression that he lacked passion. This would be false. From Origen derives the Christian idea that human beings possess a set of "spiritual senses" by which they are able to perceive God and move toward union with God. Language so characteristic of medieval mysticism about love's wounds has roots in Origen's commentary: "and the soul is moved by heavenly love and longing ... it falls deeply in love with [the Word's] loveliness and receives from the Word himself a certain dart and wound of love" (p. 29). Writing, perhaps autobiographically, in one of his sermons on the Song of Songs, Origen exclaims, "God is my witness ... I have often perceived the bridegroom drawing near me" (p. 280). Passages like these reveal a man of deep desire that is often difficult to discern behind the relentless power of his intellect.

SYNOPSIS

Good commentary, whether ancient or modern, follows the contours of the text it seeks to illuminate. Thus a commentary, as commentary, defies summary. Origen's *Commentary on the Song of Songs* is no exception. Readers who wish to appreciate fully the genius of Origen's interpretation can do so only by engaging directly the actual words of the commentary itself. Nonetheless, some discussion of the framework of Origen's method will certainly help modern readers understand his interpretation with greater acumen.

In the prologue to the commentary, Origen informs us that the Song of Songs is one of three texts written by Solomon. According to Origen, Solomon also wrote the book of Proverbs and the book of Ecclesiastes. With this trilogy, Solomon first sought to explore the topic of moral wisdom (Proverbs). He then moved on to the study of "natural" learning (Ecclesiastes) where readers are taught how to distinguish "the useless and the vain from the profitable and the essential" (p. 41). Third and finally, Origen explains, Solomon wrote the Song of Songs as a way to access the "inspective" by which we "go beyond things seen and contemplate somewhat of things divine and heavenly, beholding them with the mind alone, for they are beyond the range of bodily sight" (p. 40). Indeed, in the Song of Songs Solomon "instills into the soul the love of things divine and heavenly, using for his purpose the figure of the Bride and the Bridegroom" (p. 41). He also teaches us that "communion with God must be attained by the paths of charity and love" (p. 41). Only the creation narratives in the book of Genesis and the first chapters of Ezekiel offer similar deep insight into the spiritual destiny of all beings capable of contemplating God.

According to Origen, the Song of Songs is an eschatological text (that is, a text dealing with last or ultimate things). Unlike other scriptural books, which also narrate various aspects of our earthly life, the Song of Songs is literally a text from heaven that allows readers to understand and to contemplate the nature of the love that binds the Son of God to the Father, a love that all Christians are invited to share. Thus, the erotic nuptial imagery that energizes the literality of the Song morphs, in Origen's interpretation, into an eschatological account of the union of soul and church with God's own life. Every trace of the bodily character of the Song is reoriented to this other, spiritual, purpose. As Origen himself writes, the Song of Songs is "a drama" sung "under the figure of the bride, about to wed and burning with heavenly love toward her bridegroom, who is the Word of God." "And deeply indeed did she love him," he continues, "whether we take her as the soul . . . or as the Church" (p. 21).

Understanding ancient interpretation

For Origen, the Song of Songs is a pure allegory. That is, its meaning is entirely spiritual. To understand what Origen meant by this, modern readers need some familiarity with basic assumptions governing ancient biblical interpretation. First, the historical method that dominates modern interpretation had not been invented. No ancient interpreter sought to apply exegetical tools in an effort to recover things such as original historical context or the perspective of the original authors. For the ancients, every book in the Bible, indeed every word on the page, witnesses in some way the drama of salvation that God had accomplished for humanity through the life, death, and resurrection of Jesus. The technical term to describe this drama is the word "economy." This word comes from the Greek *oikonomia* and means variously "household management" or "the inhabited world." Modern "economics" traces to the former while the theological use of the term traces to the latter. In theological parlance, the "divine economy" refers to God's plan to redeem the world in Christ. For the ancients, the Bible contained a record of that plan.

Teasing out the divine economy in the words of the sacred scriptures, however, is not an obvious exercise, precisely because that meaning is not generally discernable at the literal level. Thus, the story of the Exodus is literally about the deliverance of the Jews from bondage in Egypt, not a coded account of Christ's redemptive work and the salvific character of baptism, which is how the church traditionally understands the Christian significance of Exodus. In order to access the deeper spiritual meaning of the Bible, Christian interpreters relied upon techniques of figural interpretation, where what the text literally says is shown to be not what the text actually means. Ancient interpreters, including Origen, commonly referred to this method as "spiritual interpretation."

In some forms of the spiritual interpretation, the connection between the literal narrative and the spiritual interpretation is easy to discern. The aforementioned example of the Exodus illustrates: slavery in Egypt is understood as a reference to slavery to sin and death, and the crossing of the Red Sea as reference to deliverance from slavery to freedom through the cleansing waters of baptism. Literal slavery and literal crossing connect readily to spiritual slavery and spiritual crossing. Modern scholars who study ancient interpretation commonly call this technique "typology." A second common method used in the uncovering of spiritual meaning was "allegory." Allegories often appear completely arbitrary to modern readers because there are no obvious clues in the literal text that suggest the resulting allegorical interpretation. Thus, when they read in Song 1:1 about the "kisses of his mouth," modern readers move with difficulty to Origen's suggestion that "the plural 'kisses,' is used in order that we may understand that the lighting up of every obscure meaning is a kiss of the Word of God bestowed on the perfected soul" (p. 61). However, from Origen's point of view, this meaning is really there as the spiritual core of the text. What allows the theologically sensitive reader to see it is the life of prayer and a thorough knowledge of the totality of the divine economy.

To make this more concrete, a reference to contemporary fiction might be helpful. Readers of C.S. Lewis's *The Lion, the Witch and the Wardrobe* easily recognize the Christian allegory suspended below the literal narrative about the land of Narnia. The allegory is really there—put there by the mind of Lewis himself. For Origen, the allegorical layer of the Bible was really there, put there intentionally by God. By doing this, God forces the Christian reader to ponder mysteries that the literal text cannot approach. The allegory of the Song of Songs invites the reader to "come higher" toward the contemplation of God.

Most ancient interpreters believed that the biblical text operated simultaneously at two levels, the literal and the spiritual, with the spiritual providing dramatically more assistance in the acquisition of Christian wisdom. For Origen, however, the Song of Songs, uniquely among all the books of the Bible, possessed only spiritual meaning. Thus, Origen believed that the Song of Songs was a kind of textual artifact of God's transcendent perfection.

An example of Origen's method

To understand fully how Origen interpreted the Song, consider the example of chapter two, verses one and two: "I am the flower of the field and the lily of the valleys; as the lily among the thorns, so is my neighbor among the daughters" (p. 176). The biblical text here differs from that found in modern English translations because Origen, like all ancient commentators except Jerome, relied upon the ancient Greek version of the Bible known as the Septuagint. Modern translations follow instead the ancient Hebrew version known as the Masoretic Text.

The exact wording of the text, however, does not affect the method that Origen used to understand it. In this passage, Origen explains that the word "flower" represents Christ speaking to his church about God's gift to the Gentiles. "Fields," in contrast to "valleys," are cultivated places. "So," Origen writes, "we can take the field as meaning that people which was cultivated by the Prophets and the Law, and the stony, untilled valley as the Gentiles' place" (p. 176). However, Christ (the flower) could not prosper in the field (among the Jews) because of the limitations of the Law, so he became a "lily" among the gentiles. The reference to "lilies" reminds Origen of the "lilies of the field" in Matthew 6 that wear clothing greater than Solomon. The "lily of the valleys" is thus the Word of God clothed in flesh and sojourning among the Gentiles (p. 177). Following the same logic, "the neighbor among the daughters" refers to the church, "the neighbor" which comes either from the Gentiles (one possible meaning of "daughters") or as it struggles against heretics (another possible meaning of "daughters") (p. 178).

This is a single example, but others like it form the entirety of Origen's commentary on the Song of Songs. Modern readers who are unfamiliar with the basic principles of ancient interpretation often get lost in this sea of allegory. Indeed, for many, the oddness invites dismissal. Origen, however, differed from his contemporaries only in the genius of his interpretation. No ancient Christian reader would have balked at the ease with which Origen connects images of flower, fields, and lilies to Christ, Jews, and Gentiles. Even the ancient Jewish community, which would certainly have rejected the Christological core of Origen's interpretation, would not have been troubled by the claim that the Song of Songs was an allegory.

INFLUENCE

Origen's reading of the Song of Songs as an allegorical narrative of the union of church and soul with God influenced all subsequent commentary on the book before the rise of modern criticism. Gregory of Nyssa (d.c.395), Ambrose (d.397), and Gregory the Great (d.604) all followed Origen's paradigm in their own interpretation of the Song. Through the fourth-century author Apponius, Origen was also an indirect influence on the Venerable Bede (d.735). The tradition continued throughout the Middle Ages with hundreds of commentaries on the Song of Songs, including Bernard of Clairvaux's exegetical sermons, that witness powerfully to the impact of this small biblical book on the entire monastic project.

As noted above, Origen was condemned at the Second Council of Constantinople in 553. The reasons for this condemnation defy easy summary, but one of the key theological problems that plagued Origen's and subsequent "Origenist" theology was a tendency to construe salvation as only spiritual. The critics of Origen and his legacy charged, with some justification, that the Origenist position had been overly influenced by Neoplatonism, and that it denigrated both the psychosomatic unity of the human person and the doctrine of the resurrection of the body. In his defense, one might say that Origen had little patience for Gnostic arguments about the evils of the flesh. However, for Origen, the flesh, while not evil, served primarily as a temporary vessel for souls moving toward a reintegration with God at the level of intellectual contemplation. Origen's *Commentary on the Song of Songs* reflects these priorities. Origen the Platonist manages to remove the passion from one of the most passionate books in the Bible.

One of the great achievements of medieval exegesis of the Song of Songs was the reintegration of passion and eros into the interpretation. Curiously, medieval authors did not achieve this reintegration by attempting to recover the carnal eroticism of the Song that seems so obvious to modern readers. Instead, they were able to do this by introducing the language of eros into the spiritual quest itself. The allegorical center of the Song as a narrative of the soul's journey to God remains intact, but, in a surprising way, the allegorical became the literal, adding an erotic dimension to the spiritual journey that is generally absent from modern spiritual discourse. Perhaps for this reason many modern readers continue to be attracted to the passionate imagery of spiritual longing and desire that so marks the work of someone like Bernard of Clairvaux.

READING THE TEXT TODAY

While many modern readers of the Song of Songs may find the allegorical interpretation of Origen intriguing, they are also likely to think it is somewhat odd. Most contemporary commentaries on the book have abandoned the notion that the Song sings allegorically about the soul's love for God. Instead, they state without hesitation that the Song of Songs is a collection of erotic love poems. Some argue theologically that the Song's collection of imagery celebrating human love affirms the sacramental potential of marital union. Where Origen and the tradition of interpretation he inspired labors to sever the cords that moor the Song of Songs to bodily eros, modern readers shift the conversation, arguing that these very cords bind God more closely to the physical world, filling it with value.

Some modern interpreters suggest that focusing interpretation of the Song of Song on human love is overly anthropomorphic. A careful consideration of the Song's imagery suggests that the beauty and the fecundity of the creation provide a strong subtext of meaning. Thus, the Song of Songs, along with the book of Genesis and parts of the book of Job, stands out among all of the books of the Bible as one the most promising for ecological reflection.

Because the modern erotic and ecological interpretations of the Song of Songs appeal more viscerally, it can sometimes be difficult for modern readers to labor through the complexity of a text like Origen's commentary. There are, however, several reasons that recommend such an effort.

Reconciling faith and reason

First, by reading Origen's commentary, contemporary readers become exposed to the thought process of one of Christianity's most influential thinkers. Origen believed that faith and reason could be reconciled. While Christians today who are not biblical fundamentalists take this for granted, it is easy to forget that this assumption has a history. Origen's interpretive method, using allegory and other forms of figural reading, was the means by which he brought about the reconciliation of Greek and Hebrew wisdom.

Access to an interpretive world

Second, although difficult, Origen's *Commentary on the Song of Songs* provides modern readers with access to the interpretive world of the early church. While historical criticism dominates modern biblical interpretation, the methods perfected and deployed by Origen dominated ancient interpretation. All ancient readers of the Bible believed that it contained hidden meanings, put there by God, which could only be accessed by the rigorous application of non-literal interpretation. Indeed, one could argue, the entire superstructure of Christian theology was constructed using the same interpretive techniques as Origen. Without allegory and typology, not only would it be impossible to read the Song of Songs as a veiled narrative about the soul's longing for God, it would also be impossible to understand Isaiah's *Immanuel* as a reference to Christ or *Melchizedek* as prototype of Christian priesthood. For the ancients, interpretation in the style represented by Origen in his *Commentary on the Song of Songs* was the primary means by which the Old and the New Testaments were joined together as a single revelation.

Multivalent meaning

Third, perhaps the greatest insight of ancient interpretation—and in this it differs significantly from its modern counterpart—was that the meaning of the Bible is multivalent. No single reading could ever capture the superabundance of meaning that God has embedded in the words of the sacred text. As long as a reading did not contradict the fundamental doctrinal positions of the church, it could be a legitimate reading. Thus, the modern reader who appreciates and reverences the modern recovery of the sensuality of the Song of Songs—both human and non-human—may, by reading Origen, be challenged to grow in spiritual wisdom. It may well be that God's word is big enough to hold all of these meanings. The Song of Songs simultaneously and without contradiction can be about humanity's deep desire for God, deep love for each other, and deep love for the world.

TRANSLATION

Origen (1956) *The Song of Songs: commentary and homilies,* trans. R.P. Lawson, New York: Newman Press.

FURTHER READING

Astell, A.W. (1990) *The Song of Songs in the Middle Ages,* Ithaca and London: Cornell University Press, traces the reception and transformation of Song of Songs as Christian allegory.

Dawson, D. (1992) *Christian Figural Reading and the Fashioning of Identity,* Berkeley and Los Angeles: University of California Press, studies how Origen used interpretation as a spiritual project.

King, J.C. (2005) *Origen on the Song of Songs as the Spirit of Scripture: the Bridegroom's perfect marriage-song,* Oxford: Oxford University Press, provides a fresh new reading of the text.

O'Keefe, J.J. and Reno, R.R. (2005) *Sanctified Vision: an introduction to early Christian interpretation of the Bible,* Baltimore: Johns Hopkins University Press, explains early Christian interpretive practices including significant discussion of Origen.

Trigg, J.W. (1983) *Origen: the Bible and philosophy in the third-century church,* Atlanta: John Knox Press, offers an excellent introduction to Origen's life and contribution.

ATHANASIUS
(c.295–373)
The Life of Antony

DOUGLAS BURTON-CHRISTIE

The figure is gaunt and lifeless, the full weight of his body tearing at the nails in his hands and feet, his flesh torn to shreds by what appear to be staples, his head hanging limp like a thing hardly attached to his body. Mathias Grünewald's fifteenth-century Isenheim Altarpiece presents one of the most powerful and disturbing images of Christ to be found anywhere in Western art. It is a difficult image to take in. This is also true of the two other figures who are central to the altarpiece. One of them, appearing on a side panel, is a hideous figure whose flesh is covered with putrid sores, whose stomach is distended, and whose limbs appear ready to fall from his body altogether. He is suffering from a dreaded and often fatal bacterial disease known as St. Antony's Fire that had been ravaging Europe for five hundred years. The other figure is St. Antony of Egypt, a saint who was believed to have a particular power to secure healing for those suffering from the disease. He is depicted as enduring his own torment, being pummeled, clawed, and torn at by a host of gruesome, demonic beings.

The confluence of these three figures in Grünewald's altarpiece— Christ, St. Antony, and the anonymous victim of St. Antony's Fire —creates an almost overwhelming vision of human suffering. Gazing at these figures, one cannot avoid a feeling of uncertainty about whether relief from this suffering is actually possible. It seems too acute, too potent; how could anything or anyone ever fully overcome it? Yet the altarpiece is in truth an emblem of hope, a sign that redemption and healing are possible, even for those living, like the victims of St. Antony's Fire, on the very edge of despair. In the context in which the altarpiece was first created, as part of a hospital complex where victims of the disease were treated, it was crucial that neither Christ nor St. Antony be seen as standing aloof from the suffering and anxiety that marked the lives of those living in the hospital. Rather they needed to be seen as empathizing with suffering, even participating in it. The depiction of St. Antony in the Isenheim Altarpiece, being hounded and torn to pieces by a host of gruesome creatures, reveals a figure who is nothing if not exposed, vulnerable, helpless. Like Christ, and like the victims of St. Antony's Fire, the saint could be seen to have traveled deep into an awful place of doubt and agony. He could meet these lonely souls in their suffering; perhaps he could even kindle in them a sense that they too could discover God's presence amidst and beyond their affliction.

The image of St. Antony in the Isenheim Altarpiece was inspired, as were countless other depictions of the saint in medieval Europe, by the fourth-century masterpiece, *The Life of Antony*. From its earliest appearance, the tale of the solitary monk searching for God and struggling against demons in the Egyptian desert resonated deeply in the Christian imagination. It continued to do so long after it appeared, becoming subject to myriad adaptations and interpretations, each age striving to give fresh meaning to the story.

AUTHOR AND AUDIENCE

The Life of Antony is generally believed to have been written by Athanasius, who was born at the end of the third century in Alexandria, Egypt. As a young man he was baptized, along with his mother, and taken under the guidance of the bishop Alexander. Athanasius's education included a basic introduction to the principles of classical rhetoric and to Stoic and Middle Platonic philosophy. He also gained a deep familiarity with scripture, and with the work of some of the great figures of the Alexandrian Christian tradition, such as Origen and the bishop known as Dionysius the Great. His gifts must have been considerable, for already by the age of thirty Athanasius was a deacon and principal secretary to Bishop Alexander at the

Council of Nicea in 325. Three years later, Alexander died and Athanasius was elected bishop (and patriarch) of Alexandria.

Athanasius's close association with Alexander helped draw him into one of the most significant and controversial doctrinal disputes of the early church. Athanasius became a fierce defender of the Nicene position and and equally fierce opponent of Arianism. For the rest of his life, he remained embroiled in the disputes arising from the Arian controversy, which became increasingly political. Athanasius, caught amidst the shifting allegiances of the Roman authorities, was exiled from his episcopal see no fewer than five times. Between the years 346 and 356, Athanasius enjoyed a period of relative calm and stability as patriarch of Alexandria. However, in February 356, Emperor Constantius's strident support of the Arian position and his long-simmering disatisfaction with Athanasius finally boiled over and he moved to arrest him. Somehow, in spite of the large number of troops engaged against him, Athanasius managed to escape into the desert, where he was sheltered by his monastic supporters. It was there, in hiding during his third exile, that Athanasius wrote *The Life of Antony*.

Athanasius ostensibly wrote *The Life of Antony* in response to a request from some "monks abroad" to learn more about Antony so that they might imitate him and "emulate his purpose." The story of Antony was thus composed, as one early commentator noted, as a kind of monastic rule in narrative form. But it seems clear that Athanasius also had other interests in composing the life of this saint, for Antony, in perfecting the ascetic life, also works to confound the Arians and defend Nicene "orthodoxy." *The Life of Antony* became important not only for its eloquent expression of the values of the emerging Christian monastic culture, but also for its theological depth and polemical force.

SYNOPSIS

The Life of Antony is regarded as one of the earliest and most important examples of the literary genre known as hagiography, or the life of a saint, a genre that would become increasingly significant in the history of Christian spirituality. It was likely influenced both by the Greco-Roman genre of the *encomium* that praises the life of the hero or sage, and key biblical and Christian themes such as the temptation in the wilderness. It does not purport to relate the biography of the hero dispassionately, but rather tells the story in a way meant to inspire others to imitate the saint, just as the saint is portrayed as one who has successfully imitated Christ. *The Life of Antony* is presented in ninety-four short chapters that trace the story of the monk from his childhood, to his decision to disengage himself from the pressures and obligations of life in society and embark on a life of ascetic practice, to his long sojourn in the Egyptian desert and the trials and triumphs he experienced there, to his dealings with those who came to visit him in his solitude and his dramatic journeys to Alexandria in times of crisis, and finally to his death and burial. In addition to the biographical materials that sketch the outline of Antony's life, the text also contains long passages of a more didactic character, in which Antony functions as a teacher of the principles of monastic life (although this teaching is generally believed to reflect Athanasius's vision of monastic spirituality as much as it does Antony's). *The Life of Antony* presents a compelling portrait of an exemplary monastic saint whose life and teaching, Athanasius claims, had already begun to inspire others to follow him and "make the desert a city."

Call

The opening chapters of the text depict a young Egyptian man, raised as a Christian, living quietly at home with his parents. Athanasius says that "he could not bear to learn letters," placing an accent on Antony's simplicity and lack of sophistication; this would become important later in the story, when Antony confounds his more learned pagan opponents with his wisdom. He is described as being different from other children, and one senses that Antony already enjoys a rich inner life. This childhood prefiguring of what is to come in the saint's life eventually became a staple of hagiographical literature. Here it is related in a simple, naïve fashion that invites the reader to sense Antony's sincerity and his proclivity toward the spiritual life. Antony's parents die when he is still relatively young, between eighteen and twenty years of age. Although Athanasius makes no attempt to reflect on the effect of this loss on Antony, it is difficult to escape the sense that this event weighed heavily on Antony and opened him to the momentous experience that was soon to come.

Athanasius narrates this experience with great care and delicacy, allowing the reader to feel something of the shift in awareness Antony experienced as he first began to open himself to the transforming power of God in his life. He notes how, following the death of his parents, Antony had become preoccupied with stories from the Acts of the Apostles about how the apostles forsook everything to follow Christ. It was in this state of mind that Antony wandered into a church one day and heard the Gospel being read, "If you would be perfect, go, sell what you possess and give to the poor, and you will have treasure in heaven" (Mt 19:21). Athanasius relates that for Antony, "it was as if by God's design he held the saints in his recollection and as if the passage were read on his account" (2). His response was immediate and dramatic. He sold the land he had received from his parents and gave the proceeds to the poor, keeping only a few things for his sister. But he continued searching, and when he again entered the church, he "heard in the Gospel the Lord saying, 'Do not be anxious about tomorrow'" (Mt 6:34). Hearing this, Antony made a complete and final break with his old life, selling his remaining possessions, placing his sister in the company of some "trusted virgins," and devoting himself from that point forward to "the discipline."

Ascetic life

This opening section of the text describing Antony's call or conversion is crucial to everything that follows. It is clear from Athanasius's account that Antony takes up "the discipline" or "the ascetic life" primarily in response to a profound religious experience. One might even say that all that unfolds in *The Life of Antony* represents the monk's effort to live into that experience, to give it room to grow within him, to realize its full meaning. The next part of the text in fact takes up the question of what, precisely, it will mean for Antony to live into this call and give practical expression to it in his life. In chapters three through fourteen, we encounter Antony as he begins to practice the discipline—embarking on a life of fasting, prayer, scripture reading, sexual abstinence, and solitude. We are told that he is not the first to embark upon this path, and that he apprentices himself to those elders who have had some experience with the ascetic life. Still, as the story unfolds, it becomes clear that Antony is a pioneer.

Athanasius conveys this most strikingly through his narration of two related themes: Antony's solitude and his struggle with the demons. By the late third century when Antony lived, there were already many Christians (and non-Christians) living in Egypt who were embarked on experiments in ascetic living. Most of these ascetics lived in or near the villages in the Nile Valley, where Antony himself began his ascetic life. But after a while he moved to some abandoned tombs situated some distance away from the village. Then, after spending some time in this place practicing the discipline, he crossed the river toward "the mountain" and took up residence in a "deserted fortress." It is in these places of stark solitude that Antony experienced the series of profound and powerful encounters with demons that would transform him. The temptations, playing on the insecurities and anxieties of the monk (having to do with food, sex, financial security, and mortality), are noteworthy for their violence and severity. At one point Athanasius tells us that Antony was "whipped with such force that he lay on the earth, speechless from the tortures" (8).

Life in Christ

Central to this experience of temptation for Athanasius is Antony's gradual awakening to a sense of security grounded in God's presence. Athanasius signals this through a repeated allusion to Christ as the fundamental source of Antony's power against the demons. After Antony survives his first serious trial, Athanasius notes that "this was Antony's first contest against the devil—or, rather, this was in Antony, the success of the Savior" (7).

In another instance, after Antony survives a series of bruising encounters with the demons, who seem to be able to penetrate into the depths of his cell, he looks up to see the roof being opened, "as it seemed, and a certain beam of light descending toward him." It is difficult to miss the allusion to the Nicene Christ, "God from God, light from light, true God from true God." Antony's strength is in his gradual transformation that takes place *in Christ*.

This transformation leads to what is perhaps the axis of the text when, after nearly twenty years in solitude, Antony's friends finally came to tear down the fortress door and beckon him forth. Antony emerges from his long struggle luminous, balanced, and whole, a person possessed of the power to heal, to cast out demons, and to reconcile those who are alienated from one another. He is, in effect, another Christ.

The remainder of the text presents us with a portrait of this mature monk, secure in his identity in Christ, teaching his disciples how to live the ascetic life, confounding the heretics and pagans, and engaging members of the Egyptian Christian community as a sage and prophet. Much of this takes place far from the Nile Valley, in a place known simply as "the Inner Mountain." It is here that Antony fled once it became apparent to him that he would have no peace living so close to the towns and villages along the Nile. Yet, in Athanasius's portrait of him, even in the stark solitude of the Inner Mountain, Antony remained alert and alive to the concerns of those living far away. He participated in the life of the community from the depths of his solitude; his intimacy with God was understood to be so profound that neither time nor space could prevent the healing power of the monk from pouring forth on behalf of the community.

INFLUENCE

The story of Antony soon became widely known within the world of early Christianity. Already by the year 380, Gregory of Nanzianzus had mentioned it in his panegyric on Athanasius. Episodes and motifs from *The Life of Antony* appeared in such influential texts as the First Greek *Life of Pachomius* (c.400), Cyril of Scythopolis's *History of the Monks of Palestine* (c.440), and Gregory the Great's *Dialogues* (c.590). It became a model for many subsequent hagiographical texts, such as Jerome's *Life of Paul* and Sulpicius Severus's *Life of Martin of Tours*. By the end of the fourth century, at least two Latin versions of *The Life of Antony* had been made, ensuring that it would become influential not only in the Greek-speaking Christian East, but also in the Latin West. In fact, it was in a Latin text, the *Confessions of Augustine*, that *The Life of Antony* would receive perhaps its most important and enduring tribute in the early Chrstian world. Augustine claims that it was the experience of hearing the story of Antony narrated to him by his friend Ponticianus that emboldened him to make the final break with his old way of life and become a Christian.

It seems that many others during this period also fell under the spell of this tale, seeing in the Egyptian monk Antony a model for the life they themselves hoped to lead.

The influence of *The Life of Antony* on the subsequent history of Christian monasticism is less easy to discern. Christian monasticism for the most part followed a a more communal model than the solitary ideal laid out by Antony's life. Pachomius, Basil, and Benedict would each give eloquent expression to this communal form of monasticism, helping to ensure its lasting impact in both the Christian East and West. By its very nature, the solitary path depicted in *The Life of Antony* was a more difficult and rare path to follow. Nor was it easily accessible to those who wished to document it. Still, the vocation of the solitary monk persisted in Christian monasticism, and in nearly every subsequent generation one can find examples of hermits or solitaries who trace their own vocation back to Antony's witness.

The story of Antony has also reverberated profoundly in the Christian artistic imagination. From the fourth through the twelfth centuries, the image of Antony appears in a variety of forms, including stone crosses, frescoes, sculpted portals and capitals in churches, illustrated manscripts, and mosaics. In the later artistic tradition, stories from *The Life of Antony*, especially stories concerning Antony's temptations, would receive an astonishing number of renderings, in works by artists as diverse as Martin Shongauer, Pieter Huys, Lucas Cranach, Jacobo Tintoretto, Hieronymous Bosch, Mathias Grünewald, and Paul Cézanne. The nineteeenth century witnessed the publication of *La Tentation de Saint Antoine*, a phantasmagoric literary work from the pen of the great Gustave Flaubert. *The Life of Antony* has continued to inspire artistic responses in the twentieth and twenty-first centuries, with compelling depictions of the saint's life by Max Ernst, Salvador Dali, and many others, and more recently a staged, musical version of Flaubert's *Tentation*.

READING THE TEXT TODAY

Athanasius's portrait of Antony's call, his solitary struggle in the desert, and his gradual emergence as a holy man, prophet, and sage, has made *The Life of Antony* irresistible for generation after generation of readers. The story of Antony captures the sense of radical relinquishment and heroic struggle that has always been central to Christian spirituality, while also offering a vision of how spiritual growth and transformation can take hold across a lifetime. Above all, it suggests that for those seeking to follow Christ (whether or not they are called to a monastic vocation), a life of depth, authenticity, and intimacy with God is truly possible. There are three themes highlighted by the text that help account for its enduring status as a spiritual classic: honoring spiritual experience, the pursuit of self-knowledge, and solitude and community.

Honoring spiritual experience

One of the enduring questions in the history of Christian spirituality is how to acknowledge, make sense of, and attribute value to spiritual experience. A powerful spiritual experience that remains opaque or uninterpretable is, for all intents and purposes, lost to the person in whose life it unfolds. Similarly, rushing to attribute meaning to an experience before it has had time to gestate can do violence to it, leaving one with a thin and superficial sense of its meaning. In *The Life of Antony*, we are given a model of how to attend to and honor a powerful spiritual experience in such a way that it can unfold and reveal its meaning on its own terms. In the dramatic terms expressed in this text, we see this most forcefully expressed in the movement from Antony's initial sense of call to his subsequent solitary sojourn in the desert. The text does not make this connection explicit, but it does make clear that something powerful, perhaps even disturbing, takes place for Antony in that period during which his parents die and he hears the scripture being addressed to him in church. He responds to these experiences as honestly and fully as he can when they occur. But it is only over time, in the solitude of the desert, that he has the opportunity to enter fully into these experiences. One could argue that his break with his old life and entry into the desert was in some sense born of a need to enter more deeply into his own experience, to give it room to grow and gestate within him. The struggle that ensues in the desert can only truly be understood if one sees it as arising in response to the powerful experience Antony had early in his life.

The pursuit of self-knowledge

There are many different ways to interpret the struggle with the demons that Antony endures while living in the desert. But it is difficult to overstate the importance of the journey toward self-knowledge that these struggles help to clarify. In the dramatic terms framed by *The Life of Antony*, the movement into the desert is itself what provokes the demons (it is their home) and in turn provokes the monk to discover who he is. Athanasius, in keeping with the rest of the early Christian monastic tradition, astutely portrays the demons as part of the monk's own inner life, a way of understanding his deepest anxieties, doubts, and fears. In part it is the experience of solitude that reveals these things to the monk. In the desert, he cannot evade them or distract himself from them, but must face them honestly—which, according to Athanasius, Antony does. Doing so gradually purifies him, frees him to live without fear. Athanasius makes it clear that Antony does not accomplish this on his own, but does so only to the extent that he becomes a co-worker with Christ. It is Christ *in* him, gradually coming to occupy the center of the monk's consciousness, who frees him from fear and enables him to dwell simply and fully in God's presence. Still, the struggle in solitude is real and harrowing. Although Athanasius never leaves any doubt that his hero will overcome the onslaught of the demons' temptations, neither does he attempt to soften the impact of the experience upon the monk. The lesson is clear: one becomes purified and arrives at authentic self-knowledge and knowledge of God only by facing and entering into the most vulnerable places in one's soul.

Solitude and community

Still, a question can legitimately be raised: does this portrait of solitary struggle give an adequate account of *Christian* spirituality? Isn't it too solipsistic, too oriented toward the self to the exclusion of all else, including community? Not a few readers of *The Life of Antony* have answered this question in the affirmative. But the text provides a complex and compelling sense of the necessary reciprocal relationship between solitude and community. When Antony emerges from his long years of solitary struggle, the reader senses intuitively that it is precisely those long years in solitude that now enable Antony to function in the community as a healer, exorcist, and mediator. Later in the story, when Antony has retreated far into the Red Sea desert and has taken up residence in the Inner Mountain, this relationship between solitude and community becomes even more sharply defined. Antony enters into the life of the community not only by directly addressing its needs and concerns as these are presented to him in person, but also through the sheer force of his visionary and spiritual power. He dwells hidden and remote in the Inner Mountain, yet he is fully and powerfully engaged with the rest of the community. And members of the community feel his presence profoundly.

More than a thousand years later, in a very different historical-cultural context, the Isenheim Altarpiece evoked a similar sense of St. Antony's healing presence. One wonders whether those victims of St. Antony's Fire, struggling amidst agonizing pain and perhaps wavering between despair and hope, found solace from gazing upon the image of a human being who, like them, had passed through a crucible of suffering? It remains one of the most important and enduring questions posed by *The Life of Antony*: whether an honest and simple descent into the depths of one's own soul can have redemptive power for others?

TRANSLATION

Athanasius of Alexandria (1980) *The Life of Antony and the Letter to Marcellinus*, trans. R.C. Gregg, Mahwah, NJ: Paulist Press.

FURTHER READING

Anatolios, K. (1998) *Athanasius: the coherence of his thought*, London and New York: Routledge, is a fine introduction to the theological vision of Athanasius, with a probing discussion of themes in *The Life of Antony*.

Brakke, D. (1998) *Athanasius and Asceticism*, Baltimore: Johns Hopkins University Press, is an outstanding treatment of Athanasius's social, ecclesial, and intellectual worlds, with an excellent chapter on *The Life of Antony*.

Colegate, I. (2002) *A Pelican in the Wilderness: hermits, solitaries and recluses*, Washington, D.C.: Counterpoint, is a brilliant survey of the phenomenon of solitude across a range of traditions, times, and places, with a brief but illuminating discussion of St. Antony.

Cowan, J. (2004) *Desert Father: a journey in the wilderness with St. Anthony*, Boston: Shambala, is a personal account of an encounter with St. Antony that examines the cultural and religious influence of the saint.

Rubenson, S. (1995) *The Letters of St. Antony: monasticism and the making of a saint*, Minneapolis: Augsburg Fortress, is a significant contribution to the understanding of St. Antony that treats the respective witnesses of *The Life of Antony*, the *Letters*, and the *Sayings*.

3

GREGORY OF NYSSA
(c.335–c.395)
The Life of Moses

NONNA VERNA HARRISON

Gregory of Nyssa was convinced of the limitless capacities of human freedom. He says in *The Life of Moses* that people make choices at every moment and can choose what they will become. "We are in some manner our own parents," he writes, "giving birth to ourselves by our own free choice in accordance with whatever we wish to be" (II.3). As he explains throughout the book, people either choose to be trapped in a vicious circle by their own compulsions toward impulses such as greed, anger, or sensual pleasure, or they break the cycle and ascend toward God, toward sharing in God's infinite life.

Gregory invents vivid, memorable metaphors to explain what he means. For instance, he compares those trapped in the vicious circle of desire to the Israelite slaves in Egypt who were making bricks (II.59–62). They took clay, put it in a brick mold, took it out again, and then took more clay. So however much they toiled, they were always looking for more clay, and their brick mold always ended up empty. Gregory explains that when people work only for material things, symbolized by clay, they repeat themselves over and over, yet their quest is futile. On the other hand, when they seek God, they receive more and more divine life, and that same life expands their capacity so they can hold still more. This means that with God, people's potential is unlimited, since they are called to a process of unending growth in the divine.

Gregory describes a spirituality of unlimited freedom and unlimited potential. These concepts resonate with people today. So it is no surprise that his works, especially *The Life of Moses* which is quite accessible, have been rediscovered and have become popular in recent years. For contemporary readers, the place and time in which he lived may be more surprising. He lived in the fourth century in Cappadocia, a mountainous region in what is now northeastern Turkey, which was part of the Roman Empire. Then the social structure was very hierarchical. The circumstances of a person's birth determined what they could do in life. Rich and poor, free persons and slaves, men and women all had prescribed social roles. Yet, whatever their circumstances, Gregory challenged them to remake themselves from within, with God's help. He looked deeper than all the stereotyped categories and recognized that all people are made in the image of God, and all have been created with the goal of becoming like God and sharing the divine life. In his *Fourth Homily on Ecclesiastes*, he used the concept of the divine image in Genesis 1 and the unity of all humankind to critique the very idea of slavery. He did this even though the institution of slavery was built into the economic system in which everybody in the fourth-century Mediterranean world lived.

AUTHOR AND AUDIENCE

Gregory was born *c.*335 into a large, wealthy family. His father, a teacher of Greek literature and culture, died when Gregory was young. He was one of ten children. His oldest brother, Basil of Caesarea, was sent to Athens for a splendid university education, then came back and taught the rest of the family as well as many others. Basil became the organizer of Cappadocian monasticism, a leading bishop, and an ecclesiastical statesman. His oldest sister Macrina, who became the center of the family, emerged as an abbess, strong personally and spiritually. She taught her siblings Scripture, Christian theology, and asceticism. Basil's friend from the university, the son of another wealthy, devout Cappadocian family, was Gregory of Nazianzus, a brilliant preacher, writer, and theologian, who also became Gregory of Nyssa's friend. Basil and the two Gregories were collaborators in the fourth century's great theological tasks: defending the full divinity of Jesus Christ in the Arian controversy, articulating the doctrine of the Trinity, and bringing together Christianity and the best of classical Greek culture. Together, they are known as the three "Cappadocian fathers."

Each of the three had a different personality and different talents. Basil became archbishop of the region, and in 372, for political reasons, he appointed the two Gregories, who were close to him, to be bishops of newly created sees. Unlike Macrina, Basil, and Gregory of Nazianzus, Gregory of Nyssa had begun his adult life by marrying and beginning a lay career as a teacher. But his brother appointed him bishop of Nyssa. So he went there and stayed, pretty much for the rest of his life. He served as a small town pastor, prayed, and studied. Basil asked him to write an essay *On Virginity* to inspire the monastic movement, and he did. Somehow he also learned much more Greek philosophy than his brother had taught him.

After Basil's death in 380, Gregory continued his brother's theological work, but in his own voice. He became a speculative systematic theologian, using innovative concepts, rigorous logic, and vivid metaphors to argue for the full divinity and humanity of Christ, and to articulate the doctrine of the Trinity, addressing the theological controversies of the day in a number of works. Besides this, he reflected deeply about what it is to be human in *On the Soul and the Resurrection* and *On the Creation of Humanity*. These works of theological anthropology also address issues of spiritual life, the human relationship with the divine.

Toward the end of his life (in 386), he focused on writing essays about spirituality organized around his interpretations of Scripture. He wrote about the Psalms, the Beatitudes, and the Lord's Prayer. Today the best known of these writings is *The Life of Moses*. It is structured as a long letter, a reply to a request from a younger man named Caesarius for guidance in the spiritual life (II.319). It was no doubt an open letter. It would have been of interest to members of the monastic communities Basil had founded, and to other Christians serious about their own sanctification. Also noteworthy is Gregory's *Commentary on the Song of Songs*, a series of fifteen homilies covering the same themes as *The Life of Moses* but at greater length.

SYNOPSIS

Gregory's approach in *The Life of Moses* is to study the biography of Moses as recounted in Exodus, Numbers, and Deuteronomy. Unlike modern biblical scholars, however, he is not attempting to discover the original historical setting and cultural context in which the events narrated took place, or in which the narratives were first written or read. Rather than trying to dig behind the stories to find out what they presuppose but do not tell explicitly, he begins from the stories themselves. He studies the life of Moses looking for examples that Christians in his own time can follow in order to live virtuously. Like any good preacher, he seeks to build a bridge between the biblical text and his audience.

After a preface that explains his purpose in writing, his method of approaching his subject, and some major themes, Book I retells the story of Moses. Here, Gregory combines material from different biblical books into a single narrative. Book II is much longer and is the real focus of the *Life*. It goes through the same story again in sequential order and gives Gregory's interpretations of each event. He uses methods of interpretation with roots in the New Testament and branches throughout the centuries leading up to his time. In methodology and in some details, he is influenced especially by Alexandrian interpreters, the Jewish philosopher Philo of Alexandria (first century), and the Christian scholar Origen (second to third century). Like his predecessors he uses allegory, which is essentially a method of building bridges between different events in Scripture and between the Biblical text and the community of readers in his own time. He looks for things that will serve his aim and will benefit his audience. Primarily, this means teachings about virtue. But like his Christian predecessors, Gregory finds references to Christ and the church in the Hebrew Bible. For example, he is the first to see the burning bush as a symbol of Christ's virgin birth (II.19–21). Of course, he sees Christ and the church as essential in leading people to virtue, too.

Gregory lived before the church had a wide variety of saints to use as moral examples. So he writes about some saints but finds most of his examples in the Bible. Besides Moses, he writes about Abraham, David, and the bride in the Song of Songs. Significantly, he sees Moses and the bride as progressing through essentially the same pattern of growth toward perfection.

The book's full title is *The Life of Moses, or Concerning Perfection in Virtue*. Gregory's goal—perfection in virtue—means moral excellence. To achieve it requires sustained effort through the vicissitudes of life, and consistent practice in doing good. It also requires struggle against misdirected impulses and emotions within oneself—what Gregory called "passions." Much of the book discusses various virtues and passions. Yet it is essential to remember that besides constituting much of the divine image and likeness that defines people's *humanity*, virtues are, first of all, *divine* attributes. They include goodness, steadfastness, wisdom, justice, and love. So, to share in virtues is to participate in God. A choice to act virtuously is a choice to join one's will to the divine will, and thus to become united with God. Moses was perfected in virtue only after his three encounters with God. His example shows that a pure life of virtue leads to a vision of God and union with him, but virtue can only be fully actualized with God's help. Thus, virtue and communion support each other. This is why *The Life of Moses* is a mystical treatise, not only a moral treatise.

The human person

Like Plato and many early Christians, Gregory distinguishes between the mind and the senses. Through bodily senses, people perceive earth and sky, the material world, and everything in it. The mind reasons and chooses freely; it receives input from bodily senses, but also has its own kind of perception. It is able to perceive other people as spiritual beings, to perceive angels and ultimately God. In antiquity and in the Middle Ages, people took their capacity for spiritual perception for granted. Yet many today do not know it exists. So it needs to be awakened through faith and prayer. Gregory encourages his readers to focus their attention on spiritual realities and not only on material realities.

To be sure, Gregory believed that body and soul are profoundly interconnected and belong together. He affirmed the resurrection of the body, its eternal union with the soul. Yet he encouraged people to take care in choosing which has priority. When one puts God first, one arrives at an inner harmony that includes the body. When one is pulled in different directions by fleshly desires grounded in pleasure, anger, or greed, there is inner conflict. So what is perceived by the mind has priority over what the senses perceive, though ultimately they belong together.

Like other Christians of his time, Gregory uses a Platonic distinction among three capacities of the soul. The first is the mind.

The second is called *thumos*, a word hard to translate. *Thumos* means assertiveness, which can be anger but can also be the energy behind perseverance and courage. (The English translation of the *Life* calls it the "spirited" part of the soul, which can be confusing. In English, "spirit" has a different meaning.) The third is desire, either for worldly things or for virtues and God. Gregory compares these three capacities to a door frame. Desire and assertiveness are the pillars on each side of the door, and mind is the beam on the top. This illustration shows that the three capacities belong together. The mind needs the support of the two more emotional capacities. As Gregory says elsewhere, they are necessary in spiritual life, to enable a person to love God and fight against evil. Yet the emotions need the mind to hold them in place, to keep them from moving in the wrong directions (II.96–7). When these emotional impulses are used rightly, they become virtues. When they are used wrongly, they become passions.

Moses's three theophanies

Moses encountered God three times, according to Gregory. The three encounters follow a sequential order that marks his progress in spiritual life. The first theophany was at the burning bush (II.23–5). According to Gregory, it is a breakthrough from sense perception to the mind's perception of God. Like a good Platonist, Moses recognizes that everything he perceives with his senses comes and goes, whereas God is "always the same, never increasing nor diminishing, immutable . . . standing in need of nothing else, alone desirable, participated in by all but not lessened by their participation" (II.25). So God is true Being and radiant light; other things actually *exist* less fully and less truly than God, and their existence derives from that of God. Significantly, this Platonic theophany comes near the beginning of Moses's journey; it is not the culmination at the end.

The second theophany takes place atop Mount Sinai. There, Moses recognizes that God surpasses the Platonic concept of the divine that he apprehended at the burning bush. He leaves behind "everything that is observed, not only what sense comprehends but also what the intelligence thinks it sees." That is, he goes beyond the division between sense perception and the mind's perception, because God transcends both. Led by its desire to understand, his mind "gains access to the invisible and the incomprehensible, and there it sees God . . .

because that which is sought transcends all knowledge, being separated on all sides by incomprehensibility as by a kind of darkness." Gregory adds that this is a "luminous darkness," and that God's being is "unattainable not only by humans but also by every intelligent creature," even angels (II.263).

Since God's being is incomprehensible, Moses leaves aside the worldview he received in his first theophany. So he also leaves aside any idea that because God is unchangeable, change is bad, and to attain God's likeness is to be free from change. In his third theophany, any concept of the goal as freedom from change is turned upside down. Created beings are always changing anyway, so such a goal would be unattainable. Instead, Gregory proposes that change itself can be transformed into the driving force enabling ascent to God. In the spiritual life, one moves from a vicious circle into a continual upward movement toward God and into God.

Moses discovers this as he turns away from what he has already received and continues to seek closer communion with God. Moses is called to stand behind a rock as God passes by, then to look through a hole in the rock and see God's back. Gregory interprets the back as the back of a guide (II.219–20). A hiker following on a narrow trail will see only her guide's back. If she faces her guide, she has turned around and is going in the wrong direction. Moses has learned that his task is to follow God continually. In this way, he will ascend higher and higher.

Eternal progress

In his third theophany, Moses has discovered the principle of eternal growth and eternal progress in God. This principle is Gregory's distinctive concept, at the heart of his spirituality.

For change to become good, people must go forward continually; if they stand still they will slide backward. Desire for God is what impels them forward. In eternal growth, one is inspired by what one can see of God to look beyond it toward what one cannot see. Though God is unknowable, one strives to go further toward God, even into God. Then, by God's grace, one receives more of the divine life. Then desire is rekindled, so one is continually moved to go onward. As the desire increases, the gift increases, and with it the capacity to receive expands too. Because God is infinite, and humans are finite at every point in time, unending growth in God always remains a possibility. Once they are engaged in this dynamic of growth, people are filled to capacity at each moment but can always receive more of God. They are always satisfied, yet never satiated, always desirous of more. So those who are making progress are in a paradoxical situation. They are always at rest, since they are firmly fixed in the good, and they are always in motion, ever moving upward into the divine.

Gregory adds that while God is the infinite good, evil is always finite. This means that however destructive it is now, evil will eventually come to an end. Gregory says that people may explore all the possibilities of evil and eventually exhaust them all. Yet they will keep moving, and they will have nowhere left to go but back toward the good, toward God, who is inexhaustible. It follows from the logic of Gregory's theological system that in the end, everybody will be saved. He does not hesitate to draw this conclusion. Yet this does not mean cheap grace. People may have to go through long periods of suffering after death to be cleansed from their sin and impurity (II.82). In his book *On the Soul and the Resurrection*, he compares the process of purification to a rope caked with huge amounts of mud being pulled through a small hole to remove the dirt—a painful process indeed, though not eternal.

Down from the mountain

Moses has been transformed by his visions. Through communion with God, he has become perfect in virtue. Then he is "able to help others to salvation, to destroy the tyranny which holds power wickedly, and to deliver to freedom everyone held in evil servitude" (II.26). He preferred to perish with the Israelites if God would not forgive their sins, so God forgave them (II.319). Moses is known by God and has become God's friend (II.320).

INFLUENCE

Gregory of Nyssa influenced Pseudo-Dionysius (late fifth or early sixth century), who also speaks of the journey of Moses, divine unknowability, and God manifest in darkness. The profound Byzantine theologian Maximus the Confessor (580–662) drew upon Gregory's theology of the human person. A later Byzantine, Gregory Palamas

(1296–1359), developed Gregory's distinction between God's inner nature and God's outward presence, self-manifestation, and activity.

Gregory's spirituality also influenced his near-contemporary the Syrian Pseudo-Macarius, who later influenced John Wesley. However, Gregory himself has reached a broad audience in our own time, probably because major themes in his theology and spirituality resonate with the concerns of people today.

READING THE TEXT TODAY

A number of themes in Gregory of Nyssa's spirituality address difficulties people face in the contemporary world.

Human freedom

The first theme is his emphasis on human freedom. Today, everybody wants to affirm their freedom. People struggle to win freedom for themselves and for others. Yet they secretly wonder whether they are truly free. External circumstances, such as social, economic, or political conditions, often limit the choices they really have. Inner compulsions such as addictions limit them even more. Gregory shows that exercising human freedom is truly a spiritual task. It takes courage in the face of obstacles to affirm that one has real choices and to make creative or life-transforming decisions. It also takes responsibility and discipline to use the freedom one has in ways that bring greater freedom. The alcoholic who chooses to stay sober for one day will have more choices the next day.

The need for virtue

Gregory would address the dilemma of how to use freedom amid constraints by pointing to the need for virtue. Virtues such as courage, responsibility, discipline, moderation, and wisdom not only make people more free, they are goals one can choose to seek. These virtues will make people more fully human, bring them closer to God, and equip them to help other people. When outward circumstances severely limit freedom, people can still choose what virtues they will seek to exercise, and what attitudes they will choose to cultivate. When they are transformed for the better on the inside, they move toward human life's true goals, and, given the opportunity, they are more ready to change their external circumstances.

Image and likeness

Another theme that speaks to people today is Gregory's emphasis on humans as the image and likeness of God. In various writings, he declares that all people have real dignity, including women, the poor, slaves, and the homeless disabled, who were despised in the fourth century. People today are often dehumanized by government agencies, large corporations, and automated systems. There are also large groups of people who are despised in today's society, such as the homeless, undocumented immigrants, or persons with AIDS. Gregory brings today's people the message that they, and all their neighbors, have real value. Churches sometimes tell people they are worthless sinners. But Gregory argues on Christian and Biblical grounds that people are created with the capacity to do good, and that God will help them learn to do it. This is good news indeed.

Participation in the vastness of God

Eternal growth is another theme that speaks to people today. Gregory gives readers a sense of the unlimited vastness of God, who is the source of all good, and invites them to participate in God more and more, without end. People sometimes think that eternal life in heaven would be a repetitive bore. Gregory shows that there is always more to God than people can imagine. However much one knows, there is more to discover, more that is always new and always astonishing.

Boundless human potential

God shares Godself with humankind. This means that human potential is boundless, another appealing theme. Yet Gregory does not allow this idea to provoke empty arrogance or flights of fancy. The infinite potential belongs to God, and humans can share it only by doing God's will, being friends of God, and giving God all the glory. God's will for Moses was to serve Israel, his people, not to acquire empty glory for himself.

The reality of evil

The tragedies of the twentieth and twenty-first centuries may, however, lead people to doubt Gregory's assertion that evil is finite. Yet reading the story of Moses shows that Gregory takes the reality of evil and the need for struggle seriously. Maybe he can help people today find the courage to believe in a God who is entirely good and is greater than all the evils in the world. Given the challenges the world faces today, people everywhere certainly need the help of such a God.

Universal salvation

Finally, there is Gregory's belief in universal salvation. Most churches have not accepted the idea, although some twentieth-century theologians of the Protestant, Catholic, and Orthodox churches have affirmed it as a hope or possibility. Gregory appears to them as an early witness for their perspective. Importantly, he also shows how it can be affirmed without "cheap grace." His position resonates with many who find it hard to understand how a just God could punish any finite human sin, however great, with eternal and therefore infinite torment. Yet like Gregory they may accept the need for a finite period of purification after death. And this purification could prove painful.

Yet Gregory also strongly affirms human freedom, and it is difficult to see how this is fully compatible with universal salvation. If God will save everybody, do they remain free to say no? Can people still choose to reject communion with God? Could the doors of hell be locked from the inside? Ultimately, the answers to such questions remain a mystery. Yet Gregory can still suggest that, however long it takes, people may explore all other options and then return to God. In the end, each person may choose God's inexpressible beauty.

TRANSLATIONS

Gregory of Nyssa (1978) *The Life of Moses*, trans. A.J. Malherbe and E. Ferguson, New York: Paulist Press, provides an excellent introduction with informative footnotes and contains the paragraph numbers cited above.

Gregory of Nyssa (2006) *The Life of Moses*, trans. A.J. Malherbe and E. Ferguson, San Francisco: Harper San Francisco, reprints the translation above but lacks introduction, footnotes, and paragraph numbers.

FURTHER READING

Coakley, S. (ed.) (2003) *Rethinking Gregory of Nyssa*, Oxford: Blackwell, offers contemporary theological essays on Gregory.

Laird, M. (2004) *Gregory of Nyssa and the Grasp of Faith: union, knowledge, and divine presence*, Oxford: Oxford University Press, is an excellent study of Gregory's mystical theology.

Louth, A. (2007) *The Origins of the Christian Mystical Tradition: from Plato to Denys*, rev. edn, Oxford: Oxford University Press, places Gregory in context.

Ludlow, M. (2000) *Universal Salvation: eschatology in the thought of Gregory of Nyssa and Karl Rahner*, Oxford: Oxford University Press, is a model of clarity and insight.

Meredith, A. (1999) *Gregory of Nyssa*, London and New York: Routledge, includes an extensive introduction that surveys Gregory's life and work, along with contemporary translations of some of his writings.

Norris, R.A. (ed.) (2009) *Gregory of Nyssa: homilies on the Song of Songs*, Atlanta: Society for Biblical Literature, provides a fine translation of this commentary by Gregory which is the best companion to *The Life of Moses*.

4

AUGUSTINE
(354–430)
The Confessions

JENNIFER HOCKENBERY

> All my empty dreams suddenly lost their charm and my heart began
> to throb with a bewildering passion for the wisdom of eternal truth.
> . . . My God, how I burned with longing to have wings to carry me
> back to you, away from all earthly things, although I had no idea
> what you would do with me!
>
> (Augustine, *Confessions* III.4)

Confessions is ultimately a love story written to arouse the reader to
fall in love with God. Written over sixteen centuries ago by an African
rhetorician turned doctor of the church, the words of Augustine's love
for God and God's love for him are still inspiring and alluring. As best
as he is able Augustine lays his own heart open for the reader. He
bares his desires, both illicit and sacred, and tells his virtues and vices.
In trying to see and explain himself clearly he attempts to see and
explain the divine lover who first loved him. As he writes he hopes
to ignite in each reader a flaming passion for God who is Truth, Light,
Health, Wealth, Goodness, and Delight.

The simple, passionate writing of Augustine is surprisingly relevant
to the concerns of the twenty-first-century reader. The fourth-century
Roman Empire was a time when people faced many of the same
issues as they do in contemporary modern society. Cities were largely

multi-cultural marketplaces where people of different ethnicities, cultures, and religions were bound by shared goals of prestige and financial success. Underneath those Roman market place values was tension, not unlike that experienced in society today, between groups who disagreed radically on the major questions of human life. Unlike later medieval theologians who expected a mostly monolithic audience of catholic Christians, Augustine was writing to this broad and diverse Roman audience. He used allusions and allegories that would appeal to skeptics as well as Gnostics, to Christians as well as polytheists, to people in the villages of North Africa and to scholars in Rome and Milan. In so doing he also addresses the complex audience of the contemporary world that includes atheists, agnostics, fundamentalists, Protestants, Roman Catholics, Eastern Orthodox, and believers of many non-Christian religions.

Assuming a diverse audience, Augustine poses the difficult question of whether there is any real truth that can be universally acknowledged and understood. Augustine answers this question in the *Confessions* by claiming that not only is there such Truth but that Truth tenderly calls to those who seek, question, and wonder. The *Confessions* is the story of Augustine's odyssey in pursuit of Truth and the joyful realization that the Truth is also pursuing him.

Augustine was an accomplished professor of rhetoric with a skill so great, he claims, that he was able to seduce his listeners to desire things of little value. In the *Confessions* his hope was to use his skill to seduce the reader to Goodness itself. Indeed, Augustine's passion is infectious. The reader sees her heart laid open in Augustine's words and on fire for that Truth which is God.

AUTHOR AND AUDIENCE

Born in the North African city of Thagaste in 354, Augustine was the middle child of a polytheist father and a Christian mother. While there is no reliable evidence of his family's ethnicity, Augustine felt it was important to note that he was an African writing in Africa for Africans. Growing up in fourth-century Roman North Africa, Augustine was exposed to Christianity in a provincial form. He was taught to read the Latin Bible literally, believing without questioning. Outside the church, middle-class Roman values ruled. Augustine's academic prowess was recognized when he was young. His parents saved money for him, and him alone of his siblings, to go to school in Carthage in order that he might study law. While studying in Carthage, the teenage Augustine excelled in his classes, fell in love, fathered a child, enjoyed the theater, and had a coterie of good friends. By Roman standards, indeed by most cultural standards, he had achieved the good life. Yet, at age 19, while reading Cicero, he fell in love with Wisdom, simultaneously finding his life empty of real value. He became consumed with the desire to obtain the Wisdom that might enlighten his life and bring him joy and comfort.

Swollen with academic pride, he rejected the simple Latin Bible and joined the Gnostic Manichees who claimed to be a Christian sect for intellectuals. This group rejected the Old Testament and the Nicene Creed of the catholic Christians and adhered to the Book of Mani. They used rational arguments to point out inconsistencies in catholic Christianity, a belief system that they deemed childishly populist. However, after nine years as a "hearer" of the Manichean sect, Augustine reasoned his way beyond their esoteric teachings and found that even their bishops could not answer his questions. This rejection of Manichaeism led, at first, only to despair that he would ever find any real truths to which he could adhere. However, unlike some Academics, Augustine found he was unable to embrace agnostic skepticism, finding it philosophically untenable. Ultimately Augustine was converted back to the Christianity of his mother, a journey that he describes in the middle books of his *Confessions*.

After his conversion, Augustine was baptized with his son Adeodatus in 387. Having taught rhetoric in Carthage, Rome, and Milan, Augustine returned to Thagaste to live and study in a quiet community, renouncing the honor and prestige of the academy. However, against his will, he was ordained as a priest in 391 and then as bishop of Hippo in 396. Forced into a public role, Augustine used his rhetorical skills in the pulpit to inspire North African Christians not only to believe but to seek greater understanding of what they believed. In his hundreds of books, treatises, letters, and sermons, Augustine set out and philosophically explained much of the doctrine of the Western church in opposition to the major heresies of his age such as Pelagianism, Donatism, and various forms of Gnosticism. In 430 as Vandals invaded Hippo, Augustine died quietly of old age, still confessing his sins and urging his followers to believe in order to seek understanding.

SYNOPSIS

> For my part I declare resolutely and with all my heart that if I were called upon to write a book which was to be vested with the highest authority, I should prefer to write it in such a way that a reader could find re-echoed in my words whatever truths he was able to apprehend. I would rather write in this way than impose a single true meaning so explicitly that it would exclude all others, even though they contained no falsehood that could give me offence.
>
> (*Confessions* XII.31)

The *Confessions* is a prayer that seeks to praise God and to excite readers to raise the same praise. In order to do this, the work is written for every level of reader. The Latin is simple but passionate. The allusions are to the Psalms, the Gospels, the philosophies of Aristotle and Plato, the works of Homer and Virgil. Augustine knew and intended that each reader would find something different in his work, but he hoped each would find the love of God.

The prayer that is the *Confessions* is divided into two parts. The first nine books of the *Confessions* track Augustine from the beloved infant of Monica to a baptized Christian mourning his mother's death. The first six books explain his journey as he wanders, like the Hebrews, or perhaps more like Aeneas, until God grabs him and successfully converts him as he describes in books seven through nine. The final four books reveal his dialogue with God concerning specific difficult theological and philosophical issues. Perhaps most importantly, he uses the last three full books for an exegesis of the first chapter of Genesis in an attempt to explain how to approach scriptures' simple profundity. Thus, in order to excite the reader's heart to God, Augustine begins by telling the story of how God found him, but finishes by teaching the reader how to read the Word of God in order that she might be refreshed and renewed not by the humble writings of Augustine but by scripture.

Augustine's odyssey

The *Confessions* begins with an exclamation of the greatness of God and the poverty of the human soul that is restless without the Divine.

Augustine is simultaneously diagnosing the human condition and praising the Doctor who will cure the soul. Augustine begins by telling the story of his own childhood in order to describe the human condition. Augustine explains that like all babies he was born an erotic creature who was not blessed and happy, but needy and dependent. From the womb, humans come full of want and remain so throughout their lives, restless, anxious, and hungry until they come to rest upon the breast of Truth.

The first chapters reveal Augustine as a boy and man like many others. He prefers playing ball to doing arithmetic and listening to stories to learning Greek. He cherishes his mother, has good friends, likes sex, and wants to be a success. Most of all, he wants to be thought of as a great and intelligent man. Yet, Augustine has the ability to look deeply into his desires and find that he does not always act in his own best interest. Indeed, he is horrified to realize that often he chooses vice simply because it is vice. In giving his own story, Augustine provides new insight into the Bible's account of the human condition. Perhaps the ancient or modern reader does not understand why Adam stole the forbidden fruit or why it was forbidden. But the reader can see in Augustine's account of a few boys raiding a pear tree the truth that people sometimes choose to do what is wrong, not for the pleasure of the vice, but simply because it is forbidden. Through Augustine's account of his life, the reader recognizes the all-too-human confusion about the nature of true satisfaction.

The next chapters of the *Confessions* detail the wanderings of Augustine as a young adult looking for wisdom. Augustine explains that Cicero set him on fire for truth with his exhortation for philosophy. But Augustine also explains that rather than a truly philosophical quest of searching and discerning, he simply joined the first group who claimed to give wisdom. The Manichees promised full understanding of theology, ethics, and science. This sect promised Augustine that their teachings could withstand the rational questioning that other faiths could not. Thus, Augustine believed. Yet later, Augustine came to realize that many of their tenets were demonstrably false. Their cosmology did not accurately reflect what he saw in the night sky. Their ethics felt hollow as they renounced their duties to care for the bodies of those who were not members of their group. Their theology did not adequately answer his most difficult questions about the origin of good and evil both in the world and in himself. Augustine left the Manichees heartbroken for having wasted time believing things that were false.

Augustine was determined to escape the monstrous danger of bad faith. But if wrong faith is Scylla then skepticism is Charybdis. Unable to assent to anything he could not prove for himself, and unhappy with his inability to know anything substantial, Augustine despaired. The usual Roman assumptions that financial success and good reputation are suitable human goals led Augustine only to emptiness. His unhappiness led him to renew his search.

In the midst of reading the philosophical works of the Platonists, Augustine suddenly discovered a Light shining upon his mind and lifting him. He recounts that the Light spoke to him proclaiming that there is Truth. Suddenly, Augustine found he was unable not to believe. The Light who is God pulled Augustine on to her lap and gave Augustine renewed hope in the search. He swayed back toward catholic Christianity, universal in its teachings compared to the esoteric Gnostics. Listening to the sermons of Ambrose, Augustine realized that his choices were not simply blind faith or skepticism. Rather, he discovered the path of believing in order to understand. Ambrose taught him that while faith is required, questioning and reasoning can and must accompany believing. Having converted, Augustine was baptized. His full conversion allowed his mother to finally find peace. After her death Augustine returned to Africa to study, pray, and write. He tells no more of his history after this point in the *Confessions*.

Augustine's exegesis

The last four books take the reader beyond Augustine's life story into theology and Scripture. Augustine left the church as a teenager because he found Genesis both too simple in style and too difficult to understand. He could not believe that God made the world in seven days, for he had been taught by the natural scientists of his time that the universe had always existed. Moreover, he was confused by the idea that humans were in the image of God because this anthropomorphism seemed primitive to him. He was afraid of being simple in his thinking, thus he refused to read Genesis. As a Christian, he returns to the book that once repelled him in order to interpret it for himself and for the reader.

Augustine's exegesis is lovely as well as scholarly. It is as appropriate today in the midst of controversies over evolution and intelligent design as it was in the fourth century. He insists that Moses wrote the work to be read at many levels with many different meanings. He also insists the work is not cosmological in nature. The work does not dispute natural science nor does it forbid further inquiry. Instead, Genesis proclaims that the world is of God, made by God, and loved by God. There are many ways to interpret the *how* of creation, but the obvious point of Moses is that creation is good. Indeed, creation is so good that God was able to dwell within it in the person of Jesus. This contradicts all who declare hatred of the body, hatred of the earth, and hatred of their neighbor. Augustine insists that Genesis has important truths to tell. Furthermore, it is a perfect place to start the further journey of a soul pursing wisdom.

Most importantly, Augustine wants to make clear that the searcher is never alone. God will help the seeker, for God has promised in the person of Jesus that whoever asks will be answered. Augustine ends the *Confessions* with this promise that the love of God will come to the aid of all who are in need.

INFLUENCE

When Augustine left his post as a professor of rhetoric in Milan, he believed he was giving up prestige and academic honor for a humble life. Ironically, he became arguably the most influential theologian in the Western church. Alfred North Whitehead famously said that all the history of Western philosophy is but a footnote to Plato. He also remarked that the only innovation in philosophy after Plato was the Christian concept of the Incarnation, the idea that Eternal Being-itself could and did enter the space–time continuum and interact with creatures here in love while yet remaining the eternal Creator. Arguably, this doctrine was first and best philosophically explained in the West by Augustine.

Augustine's breadth, depth, and authority demanded that his writings profoundly influence most Western Christian thinkers. Most notably, Thomas Aquinas and Martin Luther both claimed to use Augustine's thought to argue the positions that would become authoritative in Roman Catholicism and Protestantism respectively. In the thirteenth century, Thomas's respect for Augustine's ideas allowed him to incorporate Aristotle's philosophy into the theology of the church, for Augustine justified both reading the ancients and inquiring further into faithfully believed doctrines. Moreover, Thomas used Augustine's works to justify many important theological and philosophical points that are now authoritative for most Roman Catholics. In the sixteenth century Martin Luther, as an Augustinian monk, proclaimed that Augustine was superior to Thomas. Many argue that from Augustine Luther discovered the insights upon which he built the arguments for the Reformation. There are clearly marks of convergence and divergence among all three of these thinkers, but Augustine's influence is certainly foundational in the works of the two later theological giants.

Indeed, after a study of Augustine, it becomes evident that almost every Western Christian thinker owes heavy debt to the African saint, including those who do not mention Augustine's name. For example, the visionary Hildegard of Bingen in the twelfth century begins each of her works by explaining that she has learned her insights by the illumination of the Light of Christ. Her account of her visions, like the accounts of many medieval visionaries, is faithful to Augustine's account of the living Light in book seven of the *Confessions*, although she never alludes to Augustine's writings. Clearly by the High Middle Ages, Augustine's epistemology, illumination theory, was considered the obvious and only answer to the question of how it is that humans know. The view that insight is a gift from the divine radically influenced the way philosophy and theology were done in medieval Europe. Ironically, even the father of modern philosophy, René Descartes, who claimed to depart from medieval ideas in order to create a new method for inquiry, was accused of stealing the foundation of his ideas from Augustine's own discussion of the path from doubt to certainty in the *Soliloquies*.

While Augustine saw himself as a seeker who learned only by the light of God, many throughout history have used his insights to grow in the understanding of their Christian beliefs. Because he influenced so many, even the thinker who has never read Augustine may be surprised to find that she recognizes many of his thoughts.

READING THE TEXT TODAY

Postmodern thinkers often believe that place, time, and culture weave a web around individuals that makes communication between people in radically different eras difficult if not impossible. Thus for some readers it strains credulity that the Latin work of a Roman rhetorician living in North Africa in the fourth century could truly be meaningful today. Indeed, finding an ideal translation of the work is not easy. Translating Augustine's Latin into English requires the same rhetorical genius as that which penned the original. The Latin is straightforward, for Augustine was trying to imitate the same style he found so effective in scripture. He wanted both the unlearned and the academic to find profundity. But his simple Latin contains important features that are hard to convey in modern English. For example, because Augustine is in intimate dialogue with God many translators prefer to use the intimate "thou." However, the twenty-first-century reader may find this style formal and difficult, the opposite of the effect that Augustine and the translator intended. As another example, Augustine quoted Scripture as well as ancient writers with ease and without citation, hoping to delight and comfort the reader with familiarities. Translations that halt the text to tell the reader whence each quote comes, as if the text is an academic paper, undermine the very nature of what he was trying to do as a populist. And yet, the contemporary reader unfamiliar with his allusions does benefit from seeing the breadth from which Augustine draws. Finally, Augustine's descriptions of God are poetic and varied. He did not hesitate to denote God with the feminine and neuter pronouns as well as the masculine in his Latin prose. However, no translator has been so bold in the English. And yet, although difficulties abound, almost any translation, if given time, will transfix the reader who will find herself in the presence of a great genius and great friend.

This very fact denies the skepticism of many postmoderns. Augustine can be read and understood. His words travel over 1600 years into languages that had not yet been spoken when he was penning his Latin with ox blood. And they hit their mark. This truth was exactly the truth Augustine hoped to impart. With the grace of God, understanding happens. Augustine's voice from another time, another place, and another culture still speaks to the reader and still gives the hope of understanding.

The twenty-first-century question

At the beginning of the twenty-first century, the most pressing philosophical question is "Can any universal truth be known well enough to comfort and guide us?" Across universities, churches, governments, and cultures, postmodern people are told that parochial truths are all that are available. Each must choose his or her own values using a utilitarianism that must define even the concept of "utility" relatively. The impact of the discussion is everywhere evident. The consumer is skeptical of science, no longer believing that scientists can uncover universal empirical truth. So rather than trust the family doctor, the consumer blindly rushes to magazine advertisements and internet sites. The teenager is skeptical of organized religion, so rather than go to the church of her parents, she seeks a gang or a cult. The politically minded do not trust the mainstream media, but are eager to believe what is read on a blog or heard on talk radio. As individuals struggle to find the truth, they are caught in stranger and stranger myths or become paralyzed into apathy by the fear of error. There has emerged thus a strange combination of fundamentalism, relativism, and nihilism: a simultaneous uprising of skeptics who believe truth cannot be known and neo-Gnostics who believe they alone know the truth.

Augustine's insight

This is not a uniquely twenty-first-century problem. Augustine and his colleagues also fluctuated from cults to skepticism to nihilism. When Augustine finally hears a voice that calls him to a new and hopeful path, the voice also calls to the reader today. Augustine's *Confessions* announces that there is an objective truth that transcends time, culture, and personality. Moreover, this truth is gracious and seeks the human seeker. Augustine, like many in the twenty-first century, reached a period of despair in which he believed that each seeker was so caught in her own web of belief, in her own language game, her own cultural trappings, that she could never communicate with those who were different from her, much less find some common recognizable truth. Augustine almost settled for the Roman (and modern) goals of comfort and financial success, except that he found this to be ultimately unsatisfying. Muddled in despair, he was surprised to find that the truth he sought came to look for him. He did not need to climb the ladder of knowledge to find this truth, for the truth grabbed him by the hair and turned him toward the light. The light bulb flashed; insight came. He recognized that he was not alone but loved. This insight that God ultimately personally cares for individuals allowed Augustine to ask questions and pursue answers with real hope for real understanding. While two people alone might never be able to understand each other, two people aided by the teacher who is Christ have new hope that wisdom will teach them.

When reading the *Confessions*, the reader must recognize that Augustine did not give all the answers to his questions, including his difficult questions about why humans sin, why there is evil, and what is time. Rather, he presented a method of searching for answers that is imbued with hope that answers can be given. He agreed with the skeptics that reason alone cannot provide a wide enough foundation for knowledge. But rather than despair, he urges seekers to begin with belief and to use reason to inquire deeper into this faith. Rational inquiry is important for testing the veracity of faith as well as for developing deeper understanding. The method ultimately works, according to Augustine, because God aids the seeker. The seeker can trust that faith and reason when used together will not lead the searcher further astray, but that Truth itself will come to the aid of the one searching for truth. This is an important message to all those who believe in a personal and loving God, for it not only allows but insists upon conversation and inquiry in order to deepen one's understanding of God, one's self, and ultimately reality.

TRANSLATION

Augustine (1961) *The Confessions*, trans. R.S. Pine-Coffin, New York, NY: Penguin Books.

FURTHER READING

Brown, P. (1967) *Augustine of Hippo*, Berkeley, CA: University of California Press, is an engaging biography and an excellent introduction to Augustine generally.

Miles, M. (1992) *Desire and Delight: a new reading of Augustine's "Confessions"*, New York, NY: Crossroad, is a readable modern guide to the *Confessions*.

O'Connell, R. (1969) *Augustine's "Confessions": the odyssey of soul*, Cambridge, MA: Belknap Press of Harvard University Press, gives a close reading of the text.

5

(PSEUDO) DIONYSIUS THE AREOPAGITE
(late fifth century)

The Divine Names and *Mystical Theology*

JOHN D. JONES

St. Gregory Palamas described Dionysius as "the most prominent of the theologians after the apostles." St. Thomas Aquinas explicitly cites Dionysius nearly 2,100 times. He only cites the Bible, Aristotle, and Augustine more frequently. Both St. Gregory and St. Thomas regarded the writings of Dionysius as fully compatible with Christianity although they often gave conflicting interpretations of his writings. In contrast to both Palamas and Aquinas, Martin Luther had a quite different assessment: "Dionysius is most pernicious; he platonizes more than he Christianizes."

The body of writings known as the *Corpus Dionysiacum* is enigmatic in a variety of ways. The actual identity of its author is unknown. The texts are written in a notoriously difficult style of Greek. The author delights in using complex and often obscure forms of expression. Interpreting and translating the texts has always been challenging and fraught with controversy, especially since the author draws freely from a wide range of Christian and pagan Neoplatonic sources.

In the Western Christian tradition today, the *Corpus Dionysiacum* is primarily an historical artifact. But in the Eastern Orthodox tradition, it has remained a formative source for the living theology of the Church. Regardless of the importance, or lack thereof, which people today might attach to the *Corpus Dionysiacum*, it exercised profound influence on the development of Christian theology and philosophy. The *Celestial Hierarchy* was a primary source for Christian teaching about angels; the *Ecclesiastical Hierarchy* played a similar role for Christian teaching about the nature of the Church and its sacramental life. Indeed, it was Dionysius who introduced the word *hierachia* ("hierarchy") into Greek. *The Divine Names* profoundly shaped Eastern and Western Christian theological and philosophical discourse about God. The very brief work entitled *The Mystical Theology* has been an enduring classic in the world's mystical literature.

AUTHOR AND AUDIENCE

Around 532 CE there are citations of a body of writings purportedly written by Dionysius the Areopagite, mentioned in Acts 17:34. In addition to the four works mentioned above, the *Corpus Dionysiacum* also contains ten letters. All of the works are from a "presbyter Dionysius" to various individuals. The treatises are all addressed to Timothy, a fellow presbyter. The letters are addressed to various individuals including John of Patmos (John the Evangelist). In *The Divine Names* 3.2, the author indicates that he was present at the Dormition ("falling asleep") of the Theotokos (Virgin Mary), perhaps the key historical reference in the corpus by which the author identifies himself as having lived in the first century.

Although the genuineness of the corpus was challenged from the start, both John of Scythopolis and, especially, St. Maximus the Confessor defended the corpus as authentic. Consequently it enjoyed a profound authority for Christian theologians. The next substantive challenges to the authenticity of the corpus did not arise in the West until the Renaissance. The pseudonymous character of the author was decisively validated by the research of Joseph Stigylmayer and Hugo Koch in the nineteenth century, who both showed the unmistakable influence of the writings of Proclus, a fifth-century Neoplatonist, on the corpus. Accordingly, it is now commonly accepted that the corpus was written after 487 AD, and possibly later if one accepts the view that the author knew of the writings of Damascius the Diadochus, the last head of Plato's Academy. The actual identity of the author remains a mystery—one which will likely never be solved. Today the author is most frequently referred to as pseudo-Dionysius. While some scholars have proposed that the author is a Neoplatonist (for example, Damascius), most scholars have accepted the view that the author is a Christian—likely a Syrian monk. There is, however, considerable scholarly disagreement over the depth of his commitment to Christianity and the extent to which it conforms to a Neoplatonic worldview.

Without knowing the identity of the author, it is impossible to determine the original audience of the work. Evidence internal to the corpus suggests a rather narrow audience. Each of the letters is written to a specific person. The author identifies himself as a hierarch (bishop) writing for the most part to a fellow hierarch (Timothy). The author mentions that *The Divine Names* is written to Timothy in order to clarify the teachings of Hierotheus (most likely a fictional mentor of Dionysius) for Timothy (*The Divine Names 3.2*). In several places, Timothy is cautioned not to discuss matters with others who are not prepared for them (cf. *The Divine Names* 1.8). Regardless of his intended audience, his writings became widely known throughout the Christian East and, subsequently, in the Latin West.

SYNOPSIS

Affirmative and negative theology

In addition to the extant works listed above, Dionysius refers throughout his writings to several other works that are lost or, more likely, fictitious. The *Theological Outlines* and the *Symbolic Theology* contained his Trinitarian theology and Christology, while the latter contained a discussion of the application of names from sensible and material things to God. Dionysius, however, briefly presents his Trinitarian theology and Christology in *The Divine Names* 2. He gives a condensed version of his symbolic theology in *Epistle* 9. These two missing works were to form part of a trilogy, of which *The Divine Names* is the middle work that concerns the intelligible names of God—that is, the names of God's causal powers.

Dionysius assigns these three works to affirmative (*kataphatic*) theology (*Mystical Theology* 3). Affirmative theology begins with the consideration of God as Trinity, proceeds through the consideration of God's intelligible causal names, and ends with the consideration of God in terms of material names and symbols. The mystical or negative (*apophatic*) theology found in *Mystical Theology* 4–5 reverses this procession. It begins with the denial or removal of all material names of God. Ascending upwards, discourse is increasingly constricted until after all ascent, discourse, and intellection cease, and one is "wholly united to the ineffable." Thus *Mystical Theology* 3 presents the relation of affirmative and negative theology in terms of a procession from and reversion to God. In *Mystical Theology* 3, Dionysius suggests that these two theologies are carried out separately.

A more complex relation, however, is suggested in *Epistle* 9:

> There is a twofold tradition or teaching (*paradosis*) of those who discourse about God: The one is ineffable and mystical; the other, manifest and more knowable. The one is symbolic and perfective; the other, philosophical and demonstrative. The ineffable is intertwined with what can be uttered. The one persuades and receives the truth of what is said; the other, by means of untaught initiations into the mysteries, acts and establishes [us] in God.
>
> (Dionysius, *Epistle* 9.1)

Mystical theology, thus, is not simply a negative moment within discourse, e.g., the denial of propositions or terms. It is fundamentally anagogical and mystagogical; it leads a person through symbols and mysteries to union with God. For Dionysius, theology is fundamentally a hymning or celebration (*hymnologia*): "we are shaped by the ineffable realities for expressions of the sacred hymns and by these hymns for seeing the divine light commensurately given to us and for hymning/celebrating the good-giving-source of every manifestation of sacred light" (*The Divine Names* 1.3). Moreover, this celebration is liturgical in character. Mystical theology establishes humans in God through "initiations into the mysteries," of which the Eucharist is the mystery of mysteries (*Ecclesiastical Hierarchy* 3.1).

Dionysius describes the task of *The Divine Names* as "the unfolding of the divine names, establishing holy things for the holy in accord with the divine tradition" (*Divine Names* 1.8). The phrase "holy things for the holy" (*ta hagia tois hagiois*) is taken from the Divine or Eucharistic Liturgy of the Orthodox Church. The phrase only occurs in Christian writings prior to Dionysius, and always with a eucharistic significance. Hence, while *The Divine Names* and *Mystical Theology* are frequently read as separate works detached from the

Celestial Hierarchy and the *Ecclesiastical Hierarchy*, it seems more likely that they should be read in the context of those works.

Interpreting *The Divine Names* and *Mystical Theology*

Given the pseudonymous character of these works, the often obscure writing style, and the fact that Dionysius draws from many different sources, *The Divine Names* and *Mystical Theology* have received a number of different, and often conflicting, interpretations. Three of the most prominent are (1) these works reflect a fundamentally Neoplatonic worldview onto which elements specific to a Christian worldview have been grafted—teachings on the Trinity, the Incarnation, the sacraments, etc.—and which can effectively be disregarded or taken in a more or less minimalist fashion. A second interpretation, found particularly in the Latin West, is that these words are fundamentally Christian in orientation and basically compatible with the scholastic philosophy and theology propounded by Sts Albert the Great and Thomas Aquinas. The third interpretation is that these works should be located in the context of the Greek patristic and Byzantine theology characteristic of the Eastern Orthodox tradition. In addition to these frameworks for reading Dionysius, various contemporary thinkers have also drawn on *The Divine Names* and *Mystical Theology* in connection with various problems in contemporary theology and philosophy of religion. The interpretation here focuses on *The Divine Names* and *Mystical Theology* primarily in the context of the Greek patristic and Byzantine tradition.

Dionysius's understanding of God

"The divinity is cause of all, but itself nothing" (*The Divine Names* 1.5). This refrain dominates Dionysius's antinomical or paradoxical hymning of God: God is fundamentally hidden and mysterious, yet fully manifest and present to finite beings. In *The Divine Names* 2, Dionysius sets forth his understanding of God in terms of a distinction between the divine unity and the divine differentiation. The divine unity is the beyond-beingness or "supersubstantiality" (*hyperousiotês*): to it applies whatever belongs to the preeminent denial. The three "persons" or hypostases of the Trinity are differentiated within the divine unity. The divine unity is thus the inner life of the Trinity, fundamentally hidden and unknowable to created beings. Coined by Dionysius, the term *hyperousiotês* is fundamentally apophatic because the term *ousia* (being or essence) is not properly said of the divine unity. Nevertheless, although Dionysius never uses the Nicene formula of the Son as *homoousios* ("of one essence") with the Father, he leaves no doubt that the Father, Son, and Holy Spirit are all fully and equally divine.

In contrast, the divine differentiation refers to the divine causal powers by which God produces and is manifest to all beings; it also refers to the incarnation of Christ. All of the intelligible names applied to God refer to these divine powers: "if we would name the hidden-ness (*kruphiotês*) beyond being either 'God,' or 'being,' or 'life,' or 'light,' or 'logos,' we understand nothing other than the powers— whether being producing, life producing or wisdom producing —which are brought forward out of it into us" (*The Divine Names* 2.7). God is differentiated and multiplied in these powers, although not divided. In the Eastern Christian tradition, the divine names refer to the uncreated divine energies, which are distinct although undivided from the divine "essence" and the persons of the Trinity. God is not absolutely simple in the sense this is understood in the Western tradition. These differentiated divine powers are united in God since they belong in common to the persons of the Trinity, and because whatever participates in these powers participates in God wholly and completely. In contrast, for those who read Dionysius as a Neoplatonist or in the context of the Western Scholastic notion of God as absolutely simple (whatever is said of God is identical to the divine essence), the divine powers refer to the procession of creatures from the One or God, and not an uncreated procession of God or the One into creatures.

How is the differentiation of God in the divine powers related to the divine differentiation of Christ? Dionysius is not completely clear on this. But he does write that the divinity of Christ, the second person of the Trinity, is the cause of all things and the source of their perfection (*The Divine Names* 2.10). It is noteworthy that Dionysius does not talk about the incarnation of Christ with reference to the Fall. It is very likely that, as with some other patristic authors, he views the Incarnation as embedded in the very meaning and purpose of creation.

Dionysius thus offers an antinomical or paradoxical understanding of God: God is nothing (radically hidden from and beyond all finite characteristics and comprehension), yet as cause of all, God is manifest in the world through his uncreated divine powers. However, the various causal powers are distinct but undivided from the divine "beyond beingness" and the persons of the Trinity. This antinomical or paradoxical understanding of God is reflected repeatedly in the constant "to and fro" movement of *The Divine Names:* God is nothing, yet cause of all. He is known to no created intellect, yet known by them. Beings cannot participate in him by "nature," yet they participate in him through his energies or powers (*The Divine Names* 7.3, 11.6).

The divine names

These names refer to God's causal powers or energies; they refer to the Trinity in relation to creation. Dionysius discusses a selection of these names in *The Divine Names* 4–13. He draws upon the Neoplatonic model of abiding (*monê*), procession (*proodos*), and reversion (*epistrophê*) in his understanding of these causal powers. The preeminent divine name is "the good" or "goodness" since this divine power, while remaining in itself, extends to whatever exists, might exist, or transcends existence (*The Divine Names* 4). The good is not simply a final cause. It is the productive cause of all things in which God "comes out of himself" producing a cosmos or ordered totality and returns all things to himself. So too, all things are and have being from the divine power or name of being (*The Divine Names* 5); all things live by participating in the divine power of life (*The Divine Names* 6).

While the divine mystery or hiddenness (*kruphiotês*) is utterly unknown and unparticipated in by any being, the divine powers allow all things to participate in God in order to be whatever they are. This participation is "analogical" or according to the *logos* ("underlying principle") of each thing. Dionysius calls the *logoi* of things as they exist in God, the paradigms of all things (*The Divine Names* 5.8). Hence, all things are an image or icon (*eikon*) of God.

In addition to the names mentioned above, Dionysius also discusses many other divine names including beauty, light, love (*The Divine Names* 4), wisdom, intellect (*The Divine Names* 7), power, justice, salvation, redemption (*The Divine Names* 8), great, small, sameness, difference (*The Divine Names* 9), almighty, "Ancient of Days," Eternity, Time (*The Divine Names* 10), Peace (*The Divine Names* 11), "Holy of Holies" (*The Divine Names* 12), Perfect and One (*The Divine Names* 13). It is worth noting that there is no scholarly consensus on why he discusses the divine names in this particular order.

God as Trinity

There has been much discussion about the relation of Unity and Trinity for Dionysius. But it seems that for him, God is a Triune Unity. The more difficult issue is whether he follows a more radical Neoplatonic view that God in some sense transcends both Unity and Trinity—a view that one finds, for example, with Meister Eckhart.

God as Creator

Both the Neoplatonic and Christian traditions agree that the first cause produces all beings *ex nihilo* ("out of nothing") since there is only one ultimate cause of all beings. But the Christian tradition emphasizes the freedom of God's creation. St. Gregory Palamas and St. Thomas Aquinas both read Dionysius as adhering to a doctrine of free creation of the world. But this reading is not without difficulties. For example, Dionysius does not discuss the will (*thelêma*) as one of the divine names. He likens God's production of beings to that of the sun which produces without choice (*The Divine Names* 4.1). On the other hand, he calls the divine paradigms or *logoi* for things "divine wills" (*thelêmata*) (*The Divine Names* 5.8) and he certainly thinks that humans have free will, which suggests that God does as well.

Language about God

Language about God is both affirmative (kataphatic) and negative (apophatic). Dionysius's understanding of negative language about God is particularly complex since he has two senses of negation. First, although there are positive names for the divine powers, humans must deny these names of God in light of their transcendent and unlimited character. God is good and beautiful (affirmative discourse) but his goodness and beauty infinitely transcend any finite beauty that humans can understand (negative discourse). Apophatic discourse in this sense is a kind of corrective to affirmative discourse since the affirmative names still apply. But there is a more radical apophatic discourse that denies all names of God, including the intelligible divine names. One might regard this as a kind of mystical apophasis, since such discourse aims to close off intellectual awareness of God in order to be led to union with him through "sightless intellects" (*Mystical Theology* 1.1). This second sort of apophatic discourse effectively leads the finite mind away from any sort of analogy between God and beings. Noting these two senses of apophatic discourse is far more common in the Eastern Christian interpretation of Dionysius than in the Western Christian interpretation.

The *Mystical Theology*

This very brief work describes the ascent to God through a mystical contemplation that abandons all cognitive activity. The first three chapters of this work describe this mystical (that is, secret or hidden) union as an apophatic "knowing beyond knowing" or "unknowing knowing" and contrast it with the kataphatic knowledge of God found in *The Divine Names*. Dionysius illustrates this mystical ascent to God with Moses's ascent of Mount Sinai in which, having been purified and abandoning everything, "he comes to be in the wholly imperceptible and invisible belonging to nothing, neither himself or another" (*Mystical Theology* 1.3). The last two chapters of the *Mystical Theology* exemplify this theology in an extended series of negations that deny God is anything sensible or intelligible.

The *Mystical Theology* has been given various and conflicting interpretations. On a Neoplatonic reading, mystical theology aims at a "transnoetic" or trans-intellectual union with God that abolishes any identity or difference between the soul and God. Dionysius, thus, would understand mystical union with God (or the One) in the tradition of Plotinus and Meister Eckhart. Thomas Aquinas, however, argues that Dionysius is merely describing the highest form of natural knowledge of God that humans can have in this life since, for Aquinas, beatitude for the saints and angels consists in a knowledge of the divine essence. Within the Eastern Orthodox tradition,

Dionysius is understood as "describing" the ascent to a vision and union with God in which humans never know the divine essence but, in a manner that transcends all intellection and perception, participate in the life and energies of Christ and, thus, the Trinity. The Eastern Orthodox tradition locates Dionysius in the understanding of mystical union with and deification in God that one finds, for example, in Sts Gregory of Nyssa, Maximus the Confessor, and Gregory Palamas.

INFLUENCE

The entire *Corpus Dionysiacum* exercised an extraordinary influence in the West until roughly the beginning of the Renaissance. With numerous translations and commentaries, it enjoyed a tremendously authoritative status among Western authors such as John Scotus Eriugena, St. Albert the Great, Marcilius Ficino, Meister Eckhart, Nicholas of Cusa, and the author of the *Cloud of Unknowing*. Questions about the genuineness of the author, the decline of Scholastic theology, and the rise of Protestantism all contributed to Dionysius's waning influence. In the contemporary Western Christian tradition, his writings are viewed primarily in the context of historical scholarship.

By way of contrast, the *Corpus Dionysiacum* still exercises a formative influence within Eastern Orthodox Christianity. Dionysius is commemorated as a saint on October 3 and his writings belong to the Holy Tradition of the Church. His influence has extended beyond many Byzantine writers such as Sts Maximus the Confessor, John of Damascus, and Gregory Palamas to Orthodox theologians in the twentieth century including Vladimir Lossky, Christoph Yannaras, and Alexander Golitzin.

READING THE TEXT TODAY

The way in which people appropriate *The Divine Names* and *Mystical Theology* for themselves depends, of course, on how they interpret these works and how they make sense of their own lives. But Dionysius challenges the highly secularized ways of thinking found in contemporary life. At some point, one has to deal with this text from *The Divine Names* and decide whether Dionysius in fact means what he says:

Hereafter, when we have come to be indestructible and immortal and have attained a most blessed and Christ-formed condition, "we shall" as the writings say, "be always with the Lord" (1 Thes 4:17) and shall be filled with his visible theophany in the holy contemplations which shall illumine us with the most brilliant splendors as the disciples were in that most divine transfiguration. We shall share in the unity beyond intellect in the unknown and blessed emissions of the rays that are beyond every light . . . we shall be "equal to the angels and will be sons of God, by being sons of the resurrection" (Lk 20:36).

(*The Divine Names* 1.4)

Transfiguration and deification

If Dionysius means what he says in the above text, then his writings are fundamentally Christological and, thus, Trinitarian in orientation: human lives have deification in Christ as their final end. Moreover, by noting that in their deification humans will be filled with the visible theophany of the Lord as were the disciples on Mount Thabor, he aligns himself with the Eastern Orthodox Christian teaching that Christ's transfiguration revealed the uncreated light of his divinity. This deification is not merely "moral" in nature but deeply ontological. Humans have the capacity to be transfigured in Christ; the process of deification begins in this life although its fullness is never realized until the second coming of Christ.

God is present, but utterly mysterious

For Dionysius, the entire cosmos is suffused with the uncreated energies of God, the Trinity. All things come from God and find fulfillment only in being returned to God. Everything that exists is an image or ikon that expresses God's presence in the world since everything that exists, no matter how corrupted by evil, manifests the presence of divine goodness, beauty, and love. Yet God is utterly mysterious and inaccessible to any created intellect.

An invitation to faith and worship

Humanity's basic response to God, for Dionysius, is one of hymning and worship. Philosophical, scientific, or other sorts of rational reflection about the world are embedded in a liturgical experience of God and the world. Dionysius would be perplexed by a fundamentalist divorce of reason from faith and worship. He would be equally perplexed by a conception of philosophy, theology, or science in which reflection about God, humanity, and the world is divorced from faith and worship.

Dionysius would be utterly astounded at a secular viewpoint in which God is taken to be absent from the world and can enter it only to the extent that he can justify himself to human reason. Dionysius's writings, thus, are profoundly out of synch with a purely secularized worldview. Within this secular framework, Dionysius remains at best the remnant of a religious outlook that has been surpassed. Put bluntly, his works cannot be read and understood on their own terms within a secular framework. Either Dionysius will be discarded or a secular mindset has to be fundamentally transformed.

Read in their entirety, Dionysius's writings invite readers to experience God, themselves, and the world in a profoundly sacramental, liturgical, iconographic, and mystical context. His world is part and parcel of the sacred tradition, faith, and liturgy of the Church and of the Greek patristic and Byzantine Fathers. Most likely he would say that the ability to read and understand him fully depends upon a willingness to enter into that sacred tradition.

TRANSLATIONS

(Pseudo) Dionysius the Areopagite (1987) *The Complete Works*, trans. C. Luibheid, New York: Paulist Press.

(Pseudo) Dionysius the Areopagite (1980) *The Divine Names and Mystical Theology*, trans. with introductory study, J.D. Jones, Milwaukee: Marquette University Press.

FURTHER READING

Golitzin, A. (1994) *Et Introibo ad altare Dei: the mystagogy of Dionysius Areopagita, with special reference to its predecessors in the Eastern Christian tradition*, Thessalonika: George Dedousis's Publishing Company, is a detailed study of Dionysius in the context of the Eastern Christian tradition.

Louth, A. (1989) *Denys the Areopagite*, Wilton, CT: Morehouse, is a very readable general introduction to the works of Dionysius.

O'Rourke, F. (1992) *Pseudo-Dionysius and the Metaphysics of Aquinas*, New York: E.J. Brill, provides a detailed treatment of Aquinas's interpretation of *The Divine Names*.

Perl, E. (2008) *Theophany: the Neoplatonic philosophy of Dionysius the Areopagite*, New York: State University of New York Press, locates Dionysius in the Neoplatonic tradition of Plotinus and Proclus.

Rorem, P. (1993) *Pseudo-Dionysius: a commentary on the texts and an introduction to their influence*, Oxford: Oxford University Press, provides chapter-by-chapter commentary on the works of Dionysius as well as a discussion of his extensive influence on medieval Christian theology.

6

BENEDICT OF NURSIA
(c.480–c.547)

Rule

THERESA LADRIGAN-WHELPLEY

"Listen carefully, my child, to the master's instructions and attend to them with the ear of your heart. This is advice from a father who loves you; welcome it, and faithfully put it into practice" (Prologue.1). So begins Benedict of Nursia's *Rule*, a brief document yet one of the most influential spiritual works in the history of Western monasticism. As this opening invitation suggests, Benedict of Nursia wrote his *Rule* as a loving father sharing his wisdom so that it might transform the hearts and lives of others. The Latin word *regula* ("rule") connotes a guidepost or railing—structures that offer direction and support for travelers on a journey. Thus Benedict's *Rule* is less a program of prescriptive mandates and more a meal to be digested or a map to be interpreted by those seeking to live with God in the midst of a community.

Written in the sixth century for the monastery Benedict established in Monte Cassino shortly before his death, the *Rule* has endured as a living document for almost fifteen hundred years. Today the *Rule* guides the spiritual lives of Benedictine monks and nuns, as well as many other Christian and non-Christian seekers. In a world where the trends of today are outmoded before tomorrow dawns, how has this brief document held the attention of so many for so long? Perhaps the answer lies in the nature and genre of the *Rule* itself. Not so much a document to live *by* as a text to live *through*, the *Rule* deals with the mundane details of human days: what and with whom one eats; how much and when one prays; how and for what one works; where and why one sleeps. It also explores honestly the details of everyday human emotions: joys, fears, virtuous motivations, tendencies toward control, rank, privilege, and power. In all this, the *Rule* does not accuse or condemn but acknowledges human gifts and limitations, and the need for both discipline and freedom in the journey toward God. As Benedict says: "we intend to establish a school for the Lord's service . . . we hope to set down nothing harsh, nothing burdensome. The good of all concerned, however, may prompt us to a little strictness in order to amend faults and safeguard love" (Prologue 45–7).

AUTHOR AND AUDIENCE

All that is known about Benedict of Nursia is derived from Gregory the Great's *Dialogues* (c.593–4), written almost fifty years after Benedict's death. Gregory (the first monastic pope) describes Benedict as a "man of God" and a moral exemplar. In book two of his *Dialogues*, Gregory draws implicit parallels between Benedict's life and the life of Christ, sketching Benedict as one who casts out demons, cures the sick, and raises the dead. Though the historicity of Gregory's *Dialogues* can be questioned, his account reflects the cult of Benedict in the late sixth century. Furthermore, Gregory claims that his knowledge of Benedict comes from the second and third abbots of Monte Cassino, as well as the abbot of the monastic community Benedict founded at Subiaco. Gregory's hagiography therefore serves as the primary source of reliable information about Benedict's life and death, even though the *Dialogues* were more concerned with establishing Benedict's holiness than verifying his historical context.

Benedict was born in Nursia, a town of southeastern Umbria in central Italy. In the late fifth and early sixth centuries, the growing Christian churches in and around Rome were struggling with the preservation of orthodoxy, while the political order throughout Italy was becoming destabilized following the fall of the Western Roman Empire in 476. Thus large portions of Italy were characterized by political, social, and ecclesiological unrest throughout much of Benedict's lifetime. Gregory reports that Benedict left this "world" and his father's "house and wealth" at a young age to live in solitude for three years in a cave at Subiaco, forty miles outside Rome. Following this time of purification, Benedict experimented in the monastic life and eventually established twelve monasteries with twelve monks each at Subiaco, and a larger monastery at Monte Cassino. It was here, eighty miles southeast of Rome at Monte Cassino, that Benedict wrote his "little rule for beginners" (73.8).

Benedict did not intend his *Rule* as a foundational text for Western monasticism. Rather, it was simply offered as *a* rule among many others, compiled from the collective wisdom of monastic tradition. Scholars who have studied the more than two dozen extant rules written for use within localized monastic communities in the Latin West note that all of them draw upon earlier Christian sources such as the writings of Jerome, Ambrose, Augustine, and Cassian. Even a casual reader of Benedict's *Rule* would notice that he references the received tradition, commending the Scriptures, the writings of the "holy catholic Fathers," and the rule of "our holy father Basil" (73.4–5). Furthermore, research has revealed the extent to which Benedict's *Rule* draws upon the earlier anonymous *Rule of the Master* in both composition and form. However, though he was dependent on monastic tradition and never intended for his work to be used in monasteries beyond his own, Benedict's *Rule* has become the most influential rule in the history of Western monasticism and the contemporary practice of monastic life.

SYNOPSIS

Benedict's *Rule* is divided into seventy-three chapters with a significant introductory prologue. The prologue prepares the reader to receive the *Rule* as an invitation to grow in relationship with Christ through the practices of daily life. "The Lord waits for us daily to translate into action, as we should, his holy teachings" (Prologue 35).

More than twenty scriptural references underwrite this prologue, signaling how significant a place Scripture holds within the *Rule* and within Benedict's understanding of the way toward God: "let us set out on this way, with the Gospel for our guide, that we may deserve to see him who has called us to his kingdom" (Prologue 21). In fact there are over three hundred citations or allusions to Scripture throughout Benedict's *Rule*, much in keeping with the tradition of desert monastics for whom Scripture itself was the rule of life.

Cultivation of virtue

Chapters one through seven offer an overview of the virtues necessary for living out the cenobitic (communal) form of monasticism. Three cardinal virtues—obedience, silence, and humility—are discussed in keen detail, and particular attention is given to the monk's disposition of heart in the practice of these virtues. If a monk complies with the requests of the abbot and follows the commandments of Scripture yet maintains a hardened and grumbling heart, "his action will not be accepted with favor from God" (5.18). But if the monk cultivates a humble heart, obedient to the *Rule* and to the abbot who holds the place of Christ in the monastery, he will "arrive at that perfect love of God that casts out fear" (7.67–9). The role of abbot is significant for Benedict; as a shepherd and a teacher, he leads his monks on the road to eternal life. However, the abbot's role in the monastery does not position him outside the guidelines of the *Rule*. Rather he is subject to the discipline of the *Rule* alongside his monks. The abbot must lead his monks toward all that is good and holy "more by example than by words . . . if he teaches his disciples that something is not to be done, then neither must he do it" (2.12–13). Thus Benedict emphasizes that all members of the community must cultivate a virtuous heart; as the virtuous heart grows, so too will right speech, right action, right relationship within the community, and ultimately, right relationship with God.

Adaptability and moderation

Although these first seven chapters closely parallel the content and form of the earlier *Rule of the Master*, Benedict makes some noteworthy deletions and additions. For example, in chapter two Benedict omits portions of the Master's commentary on the teaching office of the abbot and adds two verses on the significance of the abbot's role as a spiritual guide for monks. Through such modifications, Benedict highlights the need for pastoral accommodation to the temperament, character, and intelligence of each monk and grants the abbot a degree of flexibility in adapting the *Rule* to the needs of his community. In this way Benedict reveals his unique commitment to adaptation and moderation, even within a disciplined practice of the *Rule*.

Rhythms of the monastic day

In chapters eight through twenty, Benedict lays out the importance of liturgical prayer and provides clear guidelines for its practice. Eight periods of daily prayer are specified: vigils, lauds, prime, terce, sext, none, vespers, and compline. Benedict even goes so far as to recommend specific psalms, scripture readings, and responsorials for many of these prayer periods. Then, in later chapters, Benedict specifies particular times for eating and drinking (41), for talking and for keeping silent (42), for manual labor and for *lectio divina* or prayerful reading (48). The rhythms of the monastic day are spelled out in great detail, with prayer, work, eating, and reading all present in measured proportions. However, all elements of the monastic day are not equivalent or commensurable, for it is the monk's attention to prayer, to the divine office or the Work of God, that orders all the rest. In chapter forty-three, Benedict gives the instruction: "on hearing the signal for an hour of the divine office, the monk will immediately set aside what he has in hand and go with utmost speed . . . Indeed, nothing is to be preferred to the Work of God" (43.1–3).

Community structures and standards

Chapters twenty-one through sixty-seven detail the structures of common life within the monastery, including the sleeping arrangements for monks, the distribution and preparation of food and clothing, the care for the sick and the elderly, the reception of guests, the process of determining community rank and leadership, and the general regulations for the admission and dismissal of monks. Thus an in-depth engagement with the ordinary details of human life makes up the bulk of Benedict's *Rule*. The monks are offered guidelines not only for how and when to pray to God, but also for how to seek God within their individual and communal practices of eating and talking, arriving and leaving, welcoming and leading.

Benedict shows a keen understanding of human nature. For example, in his discussion of sleeping arrangements Benedict notes that the beds of the younger and the older monks ought to be interspersed so that they might quietly encourage one another since "the sleepy like to make excuses" (22.8). In his discussion of kitchen service, Benedict notes that unless ill, no one should be excused from doing the dishes, for mutual service "increases reward and fosters love" (35.2). Concerning the distribution of goods within the monastery, Benedict specifies that it is not favoritism but a consideration of need and weakness that should determine the use of resources. In fact, Benedict calls for particular attention toward the sick and the elderly, who "should be treated with kindly consideration" (37.3) and given the allowance to eat four-footed animals or any meal before the regular hours, as well as a more moderate form of labor that "will keep them busy without overwhelming them" (48.24).

In the chapter on community rank, Benedict reveals an acute awareness of the human tendency to garner position and privilege. He decrees that "nowhere shall age automatically determine rank" (63.5), but a monk's rank will be determined by his date of entry into the monastery and his virtuous character, as well as the judgment of the abbot. Furthermore, Benedict dictates that the assisting deans of the monastery be chosen for their "virtuous living and wise teaching, not for their rank" (21.4). The monk who serves as an artisan is not to "become puffed up by his skillfulness in his craft, and feel that he is conferring something on the monastery" (57.2); those appointed as cellarers (distributors of food) or porters or readers are also to receive this appointment with humility, offering their gifts for the good of the community.

Benedict is particularly attentive to how the monastic community is built through its construction of boundaries. Those who come seeking to join the monastic life must be subject to trial. An inquirer should be refused entry for four or five days to test his resolve, and then when admitted be carefully watched to learn whether he "truly seeks God and . . . shows eagerness for the Work of God" (58.7). If he is received into the monastery, he is brought before the whole community to offer three vows: stability, fidelity to the monastic life, and obedience (58.17).

When a monk chooses to leave the community and later wishes to return, Benedict suggests that he be received back with the same rank as the last one to enter. If he repeats this course, Benedict advises that he be received back even a second or a third time, though again at the lowest rank. Thus structure and discipline are essential, and community values must be practiced publicly, but a good measure of generosity and reasonable accommodation ought to be included for those who need it.

In his guidelines concerning the reception of guests, Benedict again is quite clear: "All guests who present themselves are to be welcomed as Christ, for he himself will say: I was a stranger and you welcomed me" (53.1). This posture of hospitality is to be extended to all, with pilgrims, the poor, and those who share the faith receiving particular consideration. A monk visiting from another monastery is also to be openly welcomed and his criticisms carefully considered, for "it is possible that the Lord guided him to the monastery for this very purpose" (61.4). Thus for Benedict the boundaries of the monastic enclosure are firmly fixed, but permeable.

The final chapters (68–73) comprise the longest contiguous stretch of material unique to Benedict. These six chapters highlight Benedict's keen understanding of the most ordinary challenges of human communities: murmuring, gossiping, holding a grudge, and political infighting. His treatment of these challenges underscores the way in which all the structures and standards of the *Rule* are "nothing less than tools for the cultivation of virtue" (73.6). The monk's practice of obedience to his abbot, humility in his work, quiet in his heart, attention in his prayer, moderation in his food and drink, simplicity in his clothing, and hospitality in his residence will grow a heart that seeks and welcomes God in the stranger, the superior, the brother, and the self.

INFLUENCE

Benedict's monastery at Monte Cassino was destroyed in the period following the Lombard invasions into Italy in the late sixth century. How is it that Benedict's *Rule* came to live beyond the bounds of its original community? The *Rule* first appeared in use alongside other monastic rules in seventh-century Gaul and eighth-century Northumbria, France, and Italy. In the late eighth and early ninth centuries, Charlemagne sounded a call for uniformity in Christian practice as a means of strengthening his emergent empire. During this period a French monk, Benedict of Aniane, worked to unite monasteries throughout France and Germany under the common observance of Benedict's *Rule*. Though the Viking and Saracen invasions during the late ninth century resulted in the destruction of many of these monasteries, the unifying vision of Benedict of Aniane paved the way for the founding of Benedictine monastic confederations in the early tenth century.

The first and most significant of these confederations emerged in 910 with the establishment of Cluny in central France and its dependent houses, all of which were united under a single ruling abbot. Men's and women's monastic confederations like Cluny flourished in the tenth century and contributed much to the artistic, literary, liturgical, and political landscape of the time. Yet because their practice increasingly diverged from Benedict's *Rule*, reforming movements attempted to reclaim a more ascetic monastic life. The earliest of these reforming movements was that of the Camaldolese, founded in the early eleventh century by Romuald, an Italian monk who sought to join Benedict's *Rule* with the eremitical or solitary life. The Cistercians, a reforming community also founded in the eleventh century and committed to the strict interpretation of Benedict's *Rule*, were characterized by the independent governance of their monasteries and greater simplicity within monastic practice.

With the establishment of new mendicant orders such as the Franciscans and Dominicans in the thirteenth century, the depopulating impact of the Black Death and the Hundred Years War in the fourteenth and fifteenth centuries, and the rising critique of the monastic establishment in the wake of the Protestant Reformation in the sixteenth century, Benedictine monasticism significantly declined. Many monasteries were closed or expropriated, and it was not until the nineteenth century that monasteries following Benedict's *Rule* began to re-emerge in England, France, Germany, and Italy, along with new foundations in the United States. Following the Second Vatican Council, which urged all Roman Catholic vowed religious communities to return to the spirit and charism of their founders, monastic engagement with Benedict's *Rule* grew significantly. Both male and female monastic communities began reading portions of the *Rule* aloud within their community's daily office, and commentaries on the *Rule*'s application to both monastic and lay life proliferated.

READING THE TEXT TODAY

Today, tens of thousands of men and women throughout the world profess to live their lives according to Benedict's *Rule*. These men and women are associated with over two thousand Roman Catholic,

Anglican, and ecumenical Benedictine monasteries on six continents. How has this *Rule* remained relevant across fifteen hundred years and within cultural, social, political, and theological contexts Benedict never could have imagined? Though much of the *Rule* lays out the mechanics of life within the monastery, it reads more as a piece of wisdom literature than as a juridical document. This has facilitated its application beyond the enclosure of the monastery, the boundaries of denomination and gender, and the limitations of time and culture. Its mission is not merely to form the perfect monk but to cultivate the heart of the human person who seeks and welcomes God. Perhaps due to Benedict's keen attention to the transformation of the human heart and his generous provision for adaptation, a growing number of contemporary seekers are experimenting with how Benedict's *Rule* can be lived today, not only by monks and nuns within the monastery, but also by lay persons within the wider world. In many Roman Catholic and Anglican Benedictine monasteries, male and female laity and clergy from many Christian denominations are making a discerned commitment as Oblates of St. Benedict—non-vowed associates of monastic communities who are committed to practicing Benedict's *Rule* within their everyday lives.

Spirituality of sustainable hospitality

One Benedictine value celebrated by both vowed monastics and oblates today is that of hospitality. Benedict's injunction to receive all guests as Christ demands an openness to the other and a permeability within one's sense of home that is not easily realized. This value of hospitality is particularly challenging when its regular practice threatens to compromise other significant monastic values, such as faithfully practicing the divine office, keeping a fast between meals, or restraining one's speech within the home. Yet Benedict does not issue such a radical challenge without offering concrete strategies to support its attainment. He specifies in chapter fifty-three of the *Rule* that the superior may break his fast for the sake of a guest, and a brother may break his silence to greet a guest humbly. Though Benedict advises the abbot and the monks to make specific accommodations for guests, he is not impractical or careless about the provisions required for a sustained commitment to hospitality. Welcoming the stranger does not eclipse one's commitment to other community values such as regular prayer, work, and reading. Benedict's *Rule* invites all those who follow it to consider how the sustained practice of one's most radical values requires both discipline and flexibility. Hospitality to strangers can only be realized within a holistic, boundaried structure that makes room for the balanced practice of all of life's valued commitments.

Spirituality of mutual obedience

Benedict's *Rule* begins and ends with a call to obedience: to the abbot, to one's superiors, and to one's fellow monks. This repeated refrain can sound discordantly today, however, for Benedict, obedience is not a dictatorial tool employed to maintain monastic hierarchical organization. More ascetical discipline than managerial strategy, the practice of obedience is a means by which the monk cultivates an openness and responsiveness to a voice that is not his own, and in so doing grows a heart attuned to the voice of God. The Latin word for obedience (*oboedire*) means "to hear" or "to listen towards." Thus obedience for Benedict is the practice of leaning in with the ear of one's heart to listen for what God may be saying through one's brother or sister or mother or father or friend. It is the practice of openly receiving and responding to another's perspective, counsel, or request with the understanding that God is present there. Though Benedict notes that this type of obedience should be shown in a particular way to the abbot, or to one who demonstrates "goodness of life and wisdom in teaching" (64.2), he goes on to specify that obedience must not be unidirectional, but mutual. "Obedience is a blessing to be shown to all, not only to the abbot but also to one another as brothers, since we know that it is by this way of obedience that we go to God" (71.2–3). For contemporary practitioners of Benedictine spirituality, the practice of mutual obedience prophetically challenges understandings of authority within many ecclesiastical, governmental, and familial hierarchies today.

Spirituality of twelve-step humility

The longest chapter of Benedict's *Rule* is devoted to the virtue of humility. In this chapter, Benedict employs the metaphor of a ladder to describe the twelve steps one must ascend in order to progress in the cultivation of humility. Though the language and tone of this chapter may read harshly to contemporary sensibilities, this twelve-step process parallels many of the principles and practices of modern recovery movements. For example, in the second step of humility Benedict calls for the surrender of one's will to God, a practice recommended in the early stages of most modern twelve-step recovery movements. Furthermore, Benedict sets the fifth step of humility as a thorough examination of conscience and confession to the abbot of "any sinful thoughts entering his heart, or any wrongs committed in secret" (7.44). Likewise, most twelve-step recovery programs describe the fifth step as a thorough accounting of past wrongs to God, oneself, and another person, and a commitment to reconciliation. Within a contemporary culture accustomed to recovery movements as a source of practical spirituality, Benedict's twelve-step program of humility may find growing resonance. Through Benedict's *Rule*, humility can be engaged as a staged process that requires an honest reassessment of one's relationship with God, oneself, and one's community and an active engagement in one's virtuous transformation.

Spirituality of rooted time

Within the practice of Benedictine monasticism, time is devoted each and every day to balanced prayer, labor, reading, and rest. There is no option to accrue vacation time or amass billable hours; rollover minutes cannot be stockpiled for use on a rainy day. For Benedict, time is simply the substrate upon which daily rhythms of life are grown. Though the *Rule* designates specific periods of work, study, and prayer each day, these time periods hold their value alongside one another and cannot be profitably extracted, categorized, and banked in concentrated form. Furthermore, since the cadence of prayer sets the rhythm of the day, all of a Benedictine's daily practices are re-ordered through the transforming matrix of prayer. For monks and nuns and oblates today, living according to Benedict's *Rule* means cultivating an awareness that "the divine presence is everywhere" (19.1): in one's labor and rest, in conversation and silence. A Benedictine engagement with time resists compartmentalization into commodified categories of sacred and secular, quality time and ordinary time, so that all of one's day may be transfigured in the light of God.

TRANSLATION

RB 1980: the Rule of St. Benedict in Latin and English with notes (1981), ed. T. Fry, Collegeville, MN: Liturgical Press.

FURTHER READING

Casey, M. (2005) *Strangers to the City: reflections on the beliefs and values of the Rule of St. Benedict*, Brewster, MA: Paraclete Press, explores salient themes present within the *Rule* and their application for today.

de Vogüé, A. (1994) *Reading Saint Benedict: reflections on the Rule*, trans. C. Friedlander, Kalamazoo, MI: Cistercian Publications, is a detailed commentary by one of the most respected Benedictine scholars.

de Waal, E. (1995) *A Life Giving Way: a commentary on the Rule of St.. Benedict*, Collegeville, MN: Liturgical Press, offers an accessible reading of the *Rule* from the perspective of an Anglican lay woman.

Stewart, C. (1998) *Prayer and Community: the Benedictine tradition*, Maryknoll, NY: Orbis Books, provides a general overview of the history, tradition, and practices of Benedictine monasticism.

Swan, L. (2007) *The Benedictine Tradition: spirituality in history*, Collegeville, MN: Liturgical Press, is a compilation of essays exploring the contributions of significant figures in the history of Benedictine monasticism.

7

GREGORY THE GREAT
(c.540–604)
Book of Pastoral Rule

ARTHUR HOLDER

A contemporary proverb says: "Different strokes for different folks."
That is, people are not all the same. Despite their common humanity,
they have different likes and dislikes, different needs, different hopes
and dreams. In order to love all people equally, it is necessary to treat
them in different ways.

This comes as no surprise to anyone caring for a variety of other
people: the parent with several children, the physician with many
patients, the politician with multiple constituencies, or the pastor
whose congregation comprises people of different genders, ages, tem-
peraments, and personal histories. All of these are in positions of
authority that require them to practice discernment concerning the
particular individuals in their care. How should they approach these
weighty responsibilities? How can they be sensitive to the diverse
needs of different people—especially when the people themselves
do not always know what they really need? And how can those in
charge of others' welfare avoid the dangers of self-importance and
inflated ego?

These were the questions that Gregory the Great addressed in the
work that he himself referred to as *Liber regulae pastoralis* (*Book of
Pastoral Rule*), which since its translation into Old English in the ninth
century has also been known from its opening words as *Pastoral Care*.
Gregory wrote particularly for his fellow bishops, but the terms he

used for the person in authority were quite varied: priest, preacher, pastor (literally, shepherd), teacher, and (most frequently of all) *rector*. Like the word *regula* in the book's title, the Latin word *rector* is derived from the verb *rego* ("I rule"). It is usually translated into English as "ruler" or "governor," but it may be understood somewhat more generically as "the person in charge."

The most recent English translation renders *rector* as "spiritual director," but that is perhaps both too "churchy" and too individualistic. Gregory's *rector* bears responsibility for bodies as well as souls, and for an entire congregation as a group—if not, like that pope himself, for a whole nation. The need to balance individual particularity with corporate welfare is evident in Gregory's admonition:

> [T]he discourse of the teacher should be adapted to the character of his audience so that it can address the specific needs of each individual and yet never shrink from the art of communal edification. For, if I may say so, what are the minds of an attentive audience if not the taut strings of a harp, which a skillful musician plays with multiple techniques so as to produce a beautiful sound? . . . And so every teacher, in order to edify all by the single virtue of charity, ought to touch the hearts of his audience with the same common doctrine but by distinct exhortations.
>
> (Gregory the Great, *Pastoral Rule* III, prologue)

AUTHOR AND AUDIENCE

Born *c.*540, Gregory was the son of an old aristocratic Roman family. His father was in minor clerical orders; his great-great-grandfather was Pope Felix III. He received the best education available and was marked for a career in administration. While still in his early thirties, he was appointed prefect of the city, which was the highest secular office in Rome. But when his father died a year or two later, Gregory gave up his political career to become a monk. With his inheritance he founded six monasteries in Sicily and converted his family home in Rome into a monastery dedicated to St. Andrew, where he and his fellow monks followed a rule much like that of Benedict. Gregory always looked back on this period of monastic seclusion as the happiest time of his life and lamented the loss of contemplative leisure that accompanied his call into the "secular business" of pastoral care.

From his monastic retreat, Gregory was called in 579 to be one of the seven deacons of Rome, and then sent as papal ambassador to Constantinople on an unsuccessful mission to obtain the emperor's help against the invading Lombards. During this period he began to write his *Moralia* on the Book of Job; as a sickly man who suffered from stomach troubles throughout his adult life, Gregory obviously identified with Job, the biblical man of misery par excellence.

When Pope Pelagius II died in 590, Gregory was chosen to succeed him—the first monk named to the papacy. Gregory actually wrote a letter begging the emperor to intervene and deliver him from being made pope, but Gregory's brother intercepted the letter. When Gregory's friend John, the archbishop of Ravenna, admonished him for attempting to decline his election as pope, Gregory sent John the *Pastoral Rule*, a treatise ostensibly written in defense of his action. But Gregory had apparently conceived the work some years before, because the *Moralia* written during his stay in Constantinople contains an outline of the book's third part, along with the author's stated intention to return to the topic at a later time.

Despite the demands of his ministry, Gregory was a prolific writer. Works written during his papacy were the *Homilies on Ezekiel*, *Homilies on the Gospels*, the *Dialogues* relating the lives and miracles of Italian saints including St. Benedict, a *Commentary on the Song of Songs*, and many letters. But the *Pastoral Rule* is generally recognized as the book that best encapsulates his vision of Christian life and ministry.

SYNOPSIS

The *Book of Pastoral Rule* contains four parts of uneven length. Part I describes the spiritual burdens of leadership and the high qualities required of those who undertake it. Part II deals with the pastor's life and conduct, especially in regard to the necessary balance between action and contemplation. Part III, which is by far the longest, advises the *rector* how to preach to different sorts of people. Part IV briefly admonishes the preacher that it is necessary to "return to oneself" by meditating on one's own infirmities in order to avoid the sin of pride.

Part I: The burden of leadership

Borrowing a phrase from Gregory of Nazianzus, Pope Gregory extols the care of souls as "the art of arts," demanding even more skill than the work of a physician (I.1). No one should undertake so high a calling without the requisite expertise, which can only be acquired through study and training. But what has been learned through study must then be applied in practice: "No one does more harm in the Church than he who has the title or rank of holiness and acts perversely" (I.2). Just as Jesus fled from the crowds who would have made him king (Jn 6:15), Christians must prefer adversity to prosperity, and humiliation to the world's accolades.

The heaviest burden of the pastoral office is that the leader is distracted by external affairs so that the mind loses concentration, foregoes self-examination, and soon falls into sin. No wonder many possessing the virtues necessary for leadership prefer to withdraw into contemplative solitude rather than to make themselves useful by preaching to their neighbors! But let such people (and Gregory clearly counts himself among them) consider Christ the only-begotten Son who "came forth from the bosom of the Father into our midst so that he might benefit the many" (I.5).

The qualifications for leadership are many. The pastor must be dead to fleshly passions, fearless in adversity, generous in giving, quick to forgive, and patient in adversity. But Gregory lays particular stress on the prospective leader's "practice and experience of prayer" (I.10). For how can someone hope to be an effective intercessor on behalf of others without first being on familiar good terms with the Judge?

Part II: The pastor's life

As the first monastic pope, Gregory worked tirelessly to advance the cause of monasticism within the church. Thus it is not surprising that he held up an ascetic ideal for the clergy to follow. The pastor's life ought to transcend that of the ordinary faithful, he said, as much as the shepherd's behavior outshines that of the sheep. Let the spiritual leader be "pure in thought, exemplary in conduct, discerning in silence, profitable in speech, a compassionate neighbor to everyone, superior to all in contemplation, a humble companion to the good, and firm in the zeal of righteousness against the vices of sinners" (II.1).

To illustrate, Gregory developed elaborate allegorical interpretations of the sacred vestments of Aaron the high priest. Often the allegories are based on small details in the biblical text, as when Gregory explains why Aaron's vestments were adorned with both little bells and pomegranates (Ex 28:33–4). The vestments represent good works, the little bells are the sound of preaching, and the pomegranates with their many seeds covered by a single rind suggest the multitude of the faithful who differ in merit but are enclosed together within the church. Thus the pastor's good character must be proclaimed both in deeds (vestments) and in words (bells) while carefully observing the unity of the faith (pomegranates).

Appealing again to biblical examples, Gregory urged his readers to strive for a right balance between ministry to the neighbor and contemplation of God: Paul was caught up to the third heaven (2 Cor 12:2–3) but came down to counsel married people about their sex lives (1 Cor 7); Jacob saw angels on a ladder ascending to heaven and descending to earth (Gn 28:12); Moses moved in and out of the tabernacle as he shuttled between God and the people (Ex 33:7–11). Above all, the Truth himself (that is, Jesus) prayed on the mountain but worked miracles in the cities (Lk 6:12–19). "And so he established the way of imitation for good [rulers], so that in contemplation they will already desire the highest things; but they will also show compassion for the necessities of the infirm" (II.5).

Gregory's vision of pastoral ministry assumes an intimate personal relationship between pastor and people. Pastors must behave in such a way that the people willingly disclose their secrets "as a crying child seeks its mother's breast" (II.5). Fundamentally, clergy and laity are equals as sinners in need of divine grace. When people tell them that they are virtuous or wise, pastors should believe rather what they know to be true from their own self-examination. Even when exercising discipline, let pastors remember that they are the equals of those they must correct. (However, Gregory also warns against over-familiarity, advising pastors to demonstrate authority externally while subjugating themselves internally.) Therefore the *rector* will act "as a mother with respect to kindness and as a father with respect to discipline" (II.6).

Generally speaking, spiritual affairs are the concern of the clergy while secular affairs should be left to the laity; nevertheless, clergy must provide for the physical needs of the flock or their preaching will fall on deaf ears. Gregory himself exercised a public ministry that included providing food for the poor and negotiating with invading armies. He must have known firsthand the temptation to curry favor with his people, but he advised that the pastor "should not desire to please others, but should focus on what ought to please them" (II.8). It is good for preachers to be loved, but not for their own sake. If they seek to please others, let it be in order to win their hearts for Truth.

Part III: Preaching to all sorts and conditions

Gregory devotes fully two-thirds of *Pastoral Rule* to advising preachers how to address different sorts of hearers, classified in thirty-six pairs of contrasting types. Some dyads are based on conditions of birth or circumstance: men/women, old/young, poor/rich, servants/masters, healthy/sick, married/unmarried. Other pairs describe varieties of temperament, such as bold/modest, lazy/hasty, or humble/proud. The last eight sets of types have to do with different kinds of sinners: those who have experienced sins of the flesh, and those who have not; those whose sins are minor but frequent, and those whose sins are only occasional but more serious; those who have not even begun to do good works, and those who begin but do not complete them. While warnings of divine punishment abound, Gregory's emphasis is on redemptive grace: "God does not enjoy our torments. Instead, he heals the diseases of our sins with medicinal antidotes" (III.30).

The approach to the very first pair of types sets the pattern for much that follows. Men "should be compelled to a heavier burden so that they can engage in great things," while women receive "a lighter burden so that they may be converted by gentleness" (III.2). Gregory's view of women as the weaker sex (a common cultural assumption in his time) will not receive approval today. Similarly, many people today will question his uncritical acceptance of the hierarchical nature of both society and the church. Nevertheless, even in more egalitarian societies there is wisdom in the general tenor of Gregory's advice, which anticipates the well-known adage that the preacher should "comfort the afflicted and afflict the comfortable." Nor does he lack a concern for social justice, as when he notes that "when we minister what is necessary to the indigent, we bestow not what is ours, but what rightly belongs to them" (III. 21).

After giving direction about the proper approach to each type of person, Gregory usually cites supporting moral exhortations from the Bible and then provides illustrations taken from scripture, from nature, or from everyday life. This concentration on the interplay of scripture and common human experience probably made *Pastoral Rule* more useful to generations of Christian preachers than if Gregory had adorned the text with topical references or sophisticated learned allusions.

Gregory was well aware of the subtleties of human psychology. He worried about good deeds becoming a source of pride, about vices masquerading as virtues, about the cure for one vice providing fuel for another. Above all, he was alert to the dangers of self-deception, which can lead the angry to imagine that their wrath comes from righteous zeal, or the fearful to avoid bold action under the guise of humility. As much as he favored the analogy of pastor-as-physician-of-the-soul, Gregory saw this medicinal practice as more art than science. For his *rector*, there was no substitute for empathy, intuition, and prayer.

Gregory ends part III with reflections on some complicating issues. When preaching a sermon to a diverse audience, the preacher cannot be as direct as when giving private counsel: "the greatest good should be praised in a way that does not ignore lesser goods" (III.36). If a person suffers from two vices at once, the pastor will sometimes need to tolerate one vice in order to deal with another that presents the more immediate danger. Some more elevated truths (perhaps Gregory is thinking of the mystical passages in scripture) are not suitable for a popular audience but should be reserved for those who are mature in faith. And finally, let the preacher remember that deeds speak louder than words; the flock should be able to follow the footprints of one's action, not just the sound of one's voice.

Part IV: Perfection in imperfection

Here Gregory warns against "the hidden joys of self-display" with which the devil often tempts the preacher after a sermon delivered particularly well. The remedy is self-examination and reflection on one's own sinful human nature. Whenever the prophet Ezekiel was taken up in contemplation, the Lord addressed him as a "son of man" (Ez 2:1), as though to remind him that even when contemplating heavenly things, he was still human. "For almighty God perfects, to a great extent, the minds of [rulers] but leaves them partially imperfect, so that when they radiate with extraordinary virtues, they may lament with disgust their own imperfections" (IV).

Gregory concludes by asking his reader John to pray for him because he is like a poor painter who has sketched an idealized portrait, or someone who has pointed others toward the "shore of perfection" but is himself shipwrecked by sin.

INFLUENCE

Gregory's correspondence indicates that in his own lifetime the *Pastoral Rule* was being read with appreciation in Spain, Africa, and Gaul. Emperor Maurice in Constantinople had it translated into Greek. Augustine of Canterbury is said to have carried a copy with him when, at Gregory's command, he left St. Andrew's monastery in Rome for his missionary journey to England in 597. The book also played a major role in Charlemagne's church reforms, being recommended by that Frankish emperor's counselor Alcuin as "a mirror of the life of a bishop and a medicine for all the wounds inflicted by the devil's deception." Later in the ninth century, Archbishop Hincmar of Rheims described a custom by which bishops received copies of Gregory's book at their consecrations and were admonished to follow it in their living, teaching, and pronouncing of judgment.

But perhaps the most famous medieval admirer of *Pastoral Rule* was King Alfred the Great, who numbered it among "the books most needful for all men to know." Alfred translated the text (which he called *The Shepherd's Book*) into a West Saxon dialect and ordered that copies should be sent to all the bishops in his kingdom. While he clearly understood that Gregory's work was intended primarily for the clergy, Alfred's vocabulary choices indicate that he also viewed the book's *rector* as a model for kings and nobles in their teaching roles. As one of the earliest extant texts written in Old English, Alfred's preface to his translation continued to be read in schools long after Gregory's work had fallen out of favor among modern practitioners of pastoral care, who were more inclined to consult the writings of psychologists than those of an early medieval pope.

Since the 1980s, some theologians (especially in neoconservative Protestant and evangelical circles) have sought to retrieve Gregory's

Pastoral Rule as a vital resource for pastors, preachers, and Christian counselors today. Foremost among these advocates is Thomas Oden, who has argued that modern pastoral theology has abandoned its Christian heritage out of misguided over-reverence for the disciplines of psychology and psychiatry. In *Care of Souls in the Classic Tradition* (1984), Oden offered a detailed exposition of *Pastoral Rule* in which he praised Gregory for demonstrating a practical insight into human nature that anticipated much of the wisdom found in modern psychology.

READING THE TEXT TODAY

Preachers, pastors, counselors—indeed, anyone in a helping profession —will recognize Gregory as a skilled fellow practitioner of the healing arts. Reading the *Pastoral Rule* today makes one aware that human nature has remained much the same through centuries of societal change, technological development, and scientific advance. Several of Gregory's favorite themes have particular resonance for people in the contemporary world.

Action and contemplation

Gregory never resolved the tension between his desire for monastic seclusion and the call to serve his neighbors. (In his view, ministry in the church was a form of *secular* work because it took place in the world and for the sake of the public good.) In the end, he decided that resolution was impossible in this earthly life. Like Augustine and John Cassian before him, Gregory redefined the monastic ideal by combining it with a pastoral ideal. Thus contemplation and action became not two separate lifestyles, or two stages in a person's personal history, but poles between which the Christian man or woman continually oscillates back and forth.

In contemplation, one is dazzled by God's wisdom and beauty; in action, one shares that wisdom and beauty with others. Like breathing out and breathing in, both contemplation and action are necessary. But this side of heaven, action demands the greater part of everyone's time and energy. Glimpses of the contemplative vision are unpredictable, brief, and incomplete—yet it is those glimpses that provide the power to love and the strength to persevere. This is good news for people overwhelmed by the demands of a busy, multitasking, goal-oriented culture. They do not have to withdraw completely from the distractions of life; they simply need to look for God *within* and *beyond* the distractions.

An affirmation of diversity

Implicit in Gregory's detailed advice about how to counsel various types of people is an affirmation that diversity in the human family is a good thing. Differences among people are not the problem. In fact, many of those differences are part of God's plan for creation. It takes all kinds of people to make a world, or to make a church. To care for another person is to meet that person where they are and as they are. Before anyone can be of help to someone else, it is necessary to *see* that person as God sees them—and to *love* them as God does.

This does not mean that Gregory advocated tolerance for sinful behavior. Like the psalmist (Ps 139:21–2) he could even speak of hating God's enemies, but he explained that "to hate God's enemies with a perfect hatred is to love what they were made to be but to reprove what they do" (III.22). In other words, hate the sin but love the sinner. There is nothing worth preserving about differences that arise from sin, because vices ultimately destroy the God-given individuality that is what the person was "made to be."

The process of spiritual transformation

In his *Homilies on Ezekiel*, Gregory observed that "no one reaches the summit all of a sudden" (II.3.3). Growth in faith, hope, and love is a lifelong process of transformation. In preaching and teaching, as well as in giving counsel and advice, the pastor's aim is to stir up the fire of love in a person's heart. In the beginning of the Christian life, one may be motivated to repent out of fear of hellfire and the consciousness of the all-seeing "Judge within." But Gregory believed that for the mature in faith, "good should be loved of its own accord, not pursued by compulsion of punishment" (III.13).

Because he looks for inner transformation and not just external obedience, Gregory is concerned with the inner realities of the human soul in all its complexity. He speculates about hidden motives. He appreciates the power of internal conflicts. He never underestimates the human capacity for self-deception, avoidance, and denial. In all of this, it can be said that he takes human experience very seriously as the arena of divine action. But for Gregory "experience" was not so much a matter of feelings and emotions (although those are important signs of movement in the soul) as of discipline and training. The spiritual life is an ongoing experiment with grace.

Leadership as servanthood

Gregory's emphasis on leadership as service rather than the exercise of control speaks forcefully to an era that has seen so many abuses of power by leaders in politics, business, and even the church. For Gregory, the defining characteristic of leadership is not talent or vision or expertise, but humility. Only humility can keep the leader focused on service to others rather than on self-gratification. And this humility comes from recognizing the leader's common humanity with those who are being served.

Gregory observes that a pastor who hears the confession of others' sins may sometimes suffer from the same temptations. But, he says, "the shepherd has nothing to fear because God, who weighs all things precisely, rescues the shepherd from his own temptations in proportion to the compassion he suffers for the temptations of others" (II.5). For any leader, a key to maintaining integrity is empathy for the other person as God's beloved creature standing at every moment, like the leader, in need of grace. This was the approach to leadership that inspired Gregory to adopt for himself the title that summed up both his pastoral theology and his life's work: "servant of the servants of God."

TRANSLATIONS

Gregory the Great (2007) *The Book of Pastoral Rule*, trans. G.E. Demacopoulos, Crestwood, NY: St. Vladimir's Seminary Press, is the translation cited here.

Gregory the Great (1978) *Pastoral Care*, trans. H. Davis, Mahwah, NJ: Paulist Press, is an older translation but with excellent notes.

FURTHER READING

Cavadini, J.C. (ed.) (1996) *Gregory the Great: a symposium*, Notre Dame, IN: University of Notre Dame Press, includes articles on Gregory's exegesis, spirituality, and teachings on contemplation and authority.

Markus, R.A. (1997) *Gregory the Great and His World*, Cambridge: Cambridge University Press, is an excellent biography that places Gregory in the context of late antique Christianity.

Oden, T.C. (1984) *Care of Souls in the Classic Tradition*, Philadelphia: Fortress Press, commends Gregory's *Pastoral Rule* as a helpful guide for Christian pastors today.

Straw, C.E. (1988) *Gregory the Great: perfection in imperfection*, Berkeley: University of California Press, explores the binary oppositions that govern Gregory's approach to human psychology and spirituality.

BERNARD OF CLAIRVAUX
(1090–1153)

On Loving God

MARK S. BURROWS

Judging from the literature of the period, the twelfth century was an age of love. Songs of troubadours and minnesingers, the emergence of the "romance" among court poets, and an outpouring of sermons and commentaries on the Song of Songs by monastic theologians: such diverse sources celebrate love as central to human experience, extolling its joys and honoring its sorrows, plumbing the depths of its anguish and measuring the heights of its delight. The trajectory of this literature reaches its apogee with Dante's *Divine Comedy*, an epic masterpiece narrating a pilgrim's journey through the pit of Hell, up the terraces of Mount Purgatory, and into the heavenly sphere of Paradise. At the end of this epic journey, the pilgrim surveys the heavenly realm with an often uncomprehending awe, and in his confusion finds himself in the presence of one whom Dante describes as an "elder in the robes of heaven's saints" whose eyes were "filled with the divine / joy of the blest, his attitude with love / that every tender-hearted father knows." He identifies himself as Bernard of Clairvaux, the saint who becomes his final guide into heaven's mysteries. Dante opens the final canto with Bernard's prayer, the last speech the pilgrim "hears" before the entire scene turns from the mediation of language to interior reflection and the immediacy of pure vision. These words lead the pilgrim—and, by inference, the reader—into an understanding of love, which Dante describes as "a beauty which was joy in the eyes of all the other saints" who found themselves in paradise.

Love, beauty, and joy: these themes shaped the concerns of secular singers and monastic theologians alike during Bernard's generation. The theologians taught that love is the power removing human beings from fleshly attachments, beckoning them to embrace a genuine freedom of soul and body on the journey toward final beatific vision. Bernard frames his theological vision in the language of desire, that impulse of yearning that binds intellect and affect, soul and (finally) body, on the long pilgrimage of love which carries one into God's very being. Bernard's monologue as Dante constructs it in this final scene offers a glimpse into the depths of Bernard's thought, and an apt introduction to his treatise *On Loving God*.

AUTHOR AND AUDIENCE

Bernard was born in 1090 into a noble family in Fontaines-les-Dijon and educated by the canons of St. Vorles de Châtillon, a formation that prepared him for monastic life by grounding him in Latin grammar and rhetoric. During his boyhood, a reform of Benedictine monastic life emerged at Citeaux, a movement which came to be known as the Cistercian Order. These "white monks" (a name derived from their choice to wear undyed robes) sought to follow Benedict's *Rule* rigorously by committing themselves to manual labor, prizing simplicity of life, and shaping their common life through a strict regimen of prayer and silence.

Bernard arrived at Citeaux in 1113 along with thirty companions, all intending on joining this order. Within two years he became abbot of a new foundation at Clairvaux, a position he held until his death. In that capacity he founded and had oversight of sixty-eight monasteries. The "mellifluous doctor," as he came to be known, died on August 20, 1153, was declared a saint in 1174, made a "doctor of the church" by Pius VIII in 1830, and characterized as "the last of the fathers" by Pius XII in an encyclical issued on the eighth centennial of his death.

In response to a request by the abbot of the Grand Chartreuse, Bernard wrote a "Letter on Love" which he appended to *On Loving God*. The text takes the form of an epistle responding to Haimeric, "cardinal-deacon and chancellor of the see of Rome." Bernard announces in the prologue that he will address himself to a single question: namely, what it means to love God, since this subject "tastes sweeter to the mind, is treated with more certainty, and is listened to with greater profit" than all others. Bernard fashions the text not primarily to instruct but rather to persuade, entice, and inspire; transformation of life is what he is after here, not information that might satisfy human curiosity or provide arguments for debate.

Bernard intended this text for monks, though the story of its textual transmission during the centuries after Bernard's death suggests that it quickly gained a wider readership. The text reads as a devotional treatise, reflecting his temperament as a poetic theologian who understood theology as arising from an essentially meditative engagement with God.

SYNOPSIS

The treatise opens with the question "Why and how should God be loved?" immediately answering that "*God* is the reason God is to be loved" and going on to suggest that "[t]he proper measure [of this love] is to love *without measure*." These questions frame the whole: "How is God to be loved for God's own sake?" shapes his discussion in chapters 1–13, before he turns in chapters 14–17 to the question "Why?"

Seeking God continuously and eagerly

Bernard begins by asking about the "merit" by which God "ought to be loved," a "great" merit because God gives nothing less than God's very self to those who are undeserving. Citing Rom 5:10 ("While we were still enemies, God reconciled us to himself."), Bernard reminds his readers that "God loved freely, and even enemies," such that any merit in this relationship belongs to God and not to humankind. The *experience* of this love, he suggests, has the power to transform the life of those who engage it.

Bernard insists that a *proper* response to the question "Why is God to be loved?" must address not only those Christians but also the "unfaithful" (*infideles*), those who did not share this faith. This is so, first, because all receive "the chief gifts" of bread, sun, and air needed by the body; and, second, because each enjoys the "nobler gifts" of "dignity, knowledge, and virtue" which pertain to the soul. He defines "dignity" as free will, "knowledge" as the recognition that human dignity is not "of [our] own making," and "virtue" as the natural ability to "seek continuously and eagerly for [our] maker and, when [we] find him, [we] adhere to him with all [our] might." The latter is a crucial argument: every person is capable of "seeking" and "adhering to" God, not by faith but on account of their created nature. One is to seek God through the experience of love, because love is humanity's origin and end.

Bernard refuses to view virtue as moral agency, nor does he assume it to be a special privilege of Christians. This reaching out for humanity's "maker"—the literal expression he uses is "the one by whom we are"—expresses a natural human ability. Bernard justifies this assertion with a cluster of biblical citations, mostly from the Psalms. He relies upon such texts because these were authoritative for Christians as well as Jews and "pagans," a veiled reference to Muslims, thereby underscoring the universality of the call to love God. His approach seeks to lure the "infidels" into his argument, since all persons are able to love God naturally.

Bernard concludes this discussion of gifts by praising "Jesus and him crucified" (1 Cor 2:2). The reality of the Incarnation awakens a greater love than natural "virtue" alone can inspire: "Easily they love more who realize they are loved more," he concludes. He illustrates this with a series of scriptural images that describe what it is to "languish with love" (amore langueo, in the Vulgate rendering of Sg 2:5), portraying what "the church sees" in images taken primarily from Jesus's passion and death. Such vignettes have the power to awaken love out of gratitude, provoking the faithful to cry out: "Cushion me about with flowers, pile up apples around me, for I languish with love" (here citing Sg 2:5; see chapter 7).

Memory and presence

Then Bernard asks an unexpected question: "Whence the pomegranates?" Such a query might puzzle contemporary readers, coming at this juncture. What provokes this association is the reference to "apples" in Sg 2:5, which he explains by pointing to Sg 6:11, one of the six passages in the Song of Songs mentioning pomegranates. This intertextual reference reflects a common interpretive practice of his day, since Bernard presumed that every scriptural detail held meaning and insisted that what was difficult to understand offered greater satisfaction for the one who discovered a concealed meaning. In this context, he reasons that "apples" must refer to the pomegranates mentioned later, which "chang[e] their natural taste and color for that of Christ's blood." Such a reference testifies to God's "charity which surpasses all knowledge," because pomegranates are the "fruits of the passion which [the bride] had picked from the tree of life" (7).

The following discussion (7–10) explores the experience of those who devote themselves to loving God. The first steps of love steer the faithful into ever deeper invitations—and mysteries—of love. Desire leads toward a "presence" known fully only after the final resurrection: when the yearning soul enters this "kingdom of heaven," it joins itself again to the body and in this manner experiences God's love directly and fully. In the meantime, souls live in this life by the longing described as a "memory of [God's] sweetness," because "remembrance" is what "consoles the present generation during its pilgrimage" until the time when we are able to "indulge in the feast of God's presence" (10).

Languishing in love

Bernard goes on to argue that Christians come to know "signs of the resurrection" already during their lifetime, an experience he describes in terms of the flowers (Sg 2:12) that blossom "in a new summer under the power of grace." His allegorical reading of such evocative texts beckons readers to loosen their critical hold and enter the "play" of interpretation. Only in this way do they recognize such flowers as a foretaste of the harvest to come, the savor of "fruit" that "comes forth in the end at the future general resurrection and . . . will last forever." Here again, a text from the Song of Songs provides both the metaphor and the meaning for his understanding of the Christian life: "Winter is over, the rain is past and gone; flowers appear in our land" (Sg 2:11–12). Here as elsewhere in his writings the Song of Songs emerges as the central textual reference, providing the experiential and imaginative framework for his call to "love" as the heart of the Christian life.

Throughout the treatise, Bernard emphasizes the importance of "languish[ing] in love," a holy dissatisfaction preventing the faithful from clinging to this life or the "things" of this world. He grounds this monastic commitment with Sir 24:29: "Who eats me will hunger for more." Languishing and hungering are the marks of how one is to love God; satisfaction, in a full sense, lies beyond this life. This insight provokes a lengthy discussion of "the wicked [who] walk round in circles, naturally wanting whatever will satisfy their desires, yet foolishly rejecting that which would lead them to their true end" (19). Here he contrasts the "law of cupidity," rooted in the needs and demands of avarice, with the search for God: "You are good, O Lord, toward the souls that seek you." Thus, he concludes that humankind's "true end" is "not in consumption but in consummation," a theme with a distinctive monastic tone (cf. 19).

At the heart of this text (cf. 23–30) one finds a treatise within the treatise in which Bernard discusses the four "degrees" [*gradi*] of love. The first of these, "carnal love," calls humans to *love themselves for their own sake*, in the process bringing them to realize that a proper self-love frees them to love others. The second brings them to *love God for their own sake* (i.e., "not without reward"). The third calls them to *love God for God's own sake*. And, finally, this path of love beckons them to *love themselves for God's sake*, an experience in which they come to know love as "a mountain, God's towering peak." This most intense, mystical form of love leads to a self-forgetting, freeing the soul from fleshly demands. Bernard concedes here that such love is "rare," and something experienced—if at all—"but once and for the space of a moment" (27). This is what he elsewhere calls a "departure" or "ecstasy" (*excessus*), an experience that might be considered properly "mystical."

Bernard closes the treatise (30–3) by returning to the question of "presence" introduced in his discussion of pomegranates. Here, he inquires about souls "separated from their bodies" at death but not yet fully joined to God. Once again, longing stands at the center of human experience: even in this *post mortem* state the soul remains related to the body through "a natural affection," a lingering attachment preventing the soul from abandoning its desire to be rejoined to the body even while it yearns for union with God. The body remains not only the "site" where love first takes hold of the affections, but also the necessary context for the soul's final embrace of God.

He appends to this treatise the "Letter on Charity" earlier written for the Carthusians, where he points to desire as the spiritual matrix of growth in love: "since we are carnal . . . our cupidity must begin with the flesh and, when this is set in order, our love advances by fixed degrees, led on by grace until it is consummated in the spirit" (39). The trajectory he traces, from carnality to union with God, shapes his approach to the "journey" of love, informing a person's entire life and operative even beyond death. The soul's joining with the body at the final resurrection "does not mean the substance of the flesh will not be present, but that all carnal necessity will disappear [and] the love of the flesh will be absorbed by that of the spirit" (40). Only at this juncture do humans find the perfect rest they desire.

INFLUENCE

While this treatise enjoyed early and widespread popularity among Cistercian and other monastic communities, its transmission carried it quickly beyond the cloisters. It circulated in more than sixty extant manuscripts, often included within collections of devotional texts. Thomas Aquinas relied extensively on it, drawing particularly on Bernard's notion of the "love of self" as the necessary condition of loving God. The Scholasticism that triumphed in the century following the abbot's death, however, turned from the experiential-contemplative style of this text, favoring treatises shaped by logic and argument as these became central to the teaching and learning of emerging universities. Such spiritual texts found traction in the later Middle Ages, though the new lay readership favored spiritual manuals that addressed practical questions facing living in "the world." For similar reasons, early Protestant reformers were generally indisposed to this kind of literature, and leaders of Catholic reform and the so-called "Counter Reformation" turned to sources more congruent with their pedagogical concerns and pastoral needs. In the early modern period, its influence is noticeable in Francis de Sales's *Introduction to the Devout Life* (1608), though Bernard's meditative approach seems inadequate to meet the spiritual aspirations of early modernity.

This treatise emerged from comparative obscurity and began to find a broader readership only in the twentieth century, recovered as a classic of spiritual theology by a new generation of readers interested in monastic spirituality specifically and in mysticism generally. Its visibility had much to do with the retrieval of classical theology in the *ressourcement* ("return to the sources") movement of Catholic theology, and thanks to the prodigious scholarship of theologians such as Étienne Gilson and Jean Leclercq. In recent generations, *On Loving God* has consistently found an appreciative reception among Protestant and Roman Catholic readers committed to understanding theological questions from the vantage point of spiritual questions and concerns. Such readers recognize here a voice that is both relevant and alluring, inviting them to give themselves over to "discovering [in their own experience] how sweet the Lord is" (26). In their hands this treatise has come to be read as a manifesto of spiritual freedom, a guide to the contemplative experience of the divine, and an invitation to loving God as a path of true self-discovery.

READING THE TEXT TODAY

The questions Bernard raises in this treatise seem in certain respects distinctly modern. This has much to do with the parallels between Bernard's world and the world today: first, he acknowledges the religious pluralism of his context, a reality that shaped his spiritual understanding of theological truth claims; second, he is conscious of living in a society oriented toward consumption, and recognizes the moral and spiritual challenges this brought with it; and, third, he points to seeking as the very shape of love, locating desire—humanity's as well as God's—as the very ground of faith.

Spirituality and religious pluralism

Bernard introduces this treatise by addressing the reality of religious pluralism. He argues that all persons, regardless of their religious affiliation, have the innate capacity to love God, not because of religious conviction but rather on account of the "natural" gifts of "dignity, knowledge, and virtue" with which all were created. Although Bernard wrote in an age that was at best intolerant toward the *infideles* standing outside the church's boundaries—and this would have been a broad group that included Jews, Muslims, and those the church declared "heretics"—and while his own convictions and actions often mirrored such negative views, the momentum of his argument respecting the essential dignity of all persons pushes in another direction: it suggests that because all have this natural capability, all share a common capacity and responsibility. When he moves from such an appreciation to a comparison between religions, he speaks confidently of the superiority of Christianity as measured by its deeper awareness of divine love (7): "Easily they love more who realize they are loved more," he argues, pointing to the Incarnation as a more convincing incentive to love than other religions offered. He voices this conviction in a claim that betrays the largely uninformed polemics of his age: he simply assumes that "the Jew and pagan are not spurred on by such a wound of love" (an allusion to Sg 2:5 and 4:9 in the Latin of the Vulgate).

The underlying shape of his argument, however, is important: he does not deny the truth claims rooted in other religions, but rather presses the point that Christianity is most suited to evoking love for God. The biblical revelation known to Christians, according to Bernard, offers the most eloquent unveiling of divine love, a witness he ascribes primarily to "the Father's only son," "the Lord of majesty," and the "author of life." As a revealing of this love, he views the Incarnation as a deep truth Christians come to know experientially: they are "wounded in love," as he puts it (*vulnerata caritate ego sum*, here citing Sg 2:5 in its Vulgate rendering), when they "behold" the example of Christ who embodied divine love in his own "wounds." Making this story of crucified love their own brings them to "languish with love" (again, Sg 2:5), an experiential encounter with God by which they enter into the vulnerability of this love. His apologetic thus finds its shape in the spiritual experience of a love which wounds the soul, not in a truth claim arrived at through abstract argument. Through the experiential evidence of this love, Christians come to "admire and embrace in [God] that charity which surpasses all knowledge," God's love calling forth their own: "love is God and the gift of God [which is to say that] love gives love" (35).

Desire as the heart of human experience

Bernard roots his entire theological project in the nature and function of desire: "[God] makes you desire; [God] is what you desire." Desire lies at the heart of human experience—of self, other, and world—and yet he suggests that this capacity is one that can only be finally and fully satisfied "in God." To illustrate his argument he offers a vivid image of those he calls "the wicked," who are "tired out but never satisfied." Describing them in functional rather than religious terms, he suggests that they are those who "walk round in circles, naturally wanting whatever will satisfy their desires, yet foolishly rejecting that which would lead them to their true end, which is not in consumption but in consummation" (19). The "desire to experience all things" lies at the root of humanity's insatiable cupidity, an unending appetite that is bent on consuming what lies outside the self, luring persons into what he envisions as "a vicious circle, leading us ever more deeply into the thicket of restlessness and not satisfying our desire for the peace we find through final union with God" (i.e., "consummation"). In a poignant aside he asks "Who can have all things?" (18), knowing that if left to their own natural desires, humans will seek an unbridled form of life which will lead to exhaustion, frustration, and even violence.

Bernard suggests that an unguided desire makes one susceptible to an insatiable appetite, a "have-it-all" attitude that is as morally reckless as it is spiritually fruitless. To illustrate this point, he suggests that love develops by degrees, beginning with the love of the self "for the self's own sake," citing Jesus' command to "love your neighbor as you love yourself" (Mt 22:38; Lv 19:18). But he expands on this simple mandate because of his conviction that "love is not imposed by a precept; it is planted in nature": love is an intrinsic dimension of human life, not an extrinsic duty. His warning against an "immoderate" or disordered expression of self-love suggests that such love places people under obligation to others' needs, not out of duty but rather because others share a common nature with them: God "promises to give what is necessary to [those] who withhold from [themselves] what [they] do not need and love [their] neighbor." A proper restraint turns one from the tendencies of avarice and cupidity, and invites one to practice generosity toward others. Love leads to a proper humility and consequent frugality, freeing a person to share with others out of their own excess and at the places of others' needs. Spiritual insight leads to ethical engagement.

Seeking and finding

Such restraint allows readers to recognize that what they *require* for physical health and spiritual growth may be quite different from what they *desire*. To illustrate this point Bernard suggests that everyone's possessions belong to a community of need, interpreting ownership in decisively communal terms. Freedom from greed invites one to love others "in God," as he puts it: humans are not made to be alone, and they discover what it means to love God first by loving their neighbor as they love themselves. In this act of turning their generosity toward others they discover what it means to believe that God loved them not because of what they *deserve* but rather on account of their *need*.

Bernard illumines his theological approach throughout this treatise in experiential categories. Thus, he contends that human life is one of seeking, longing, or "languishing" in love. Addressing God as "you [who] are so good to the soul who seeks you," he concludes that "you wish to be found that you may be sought for, and sought for to be found" (22). Echoing a theme central to Augustine's theological anthropology, Bernard identifies seeking as a form of finding because it already ushers the soul into the generosity of divine love: seeking and finding form a circle in human experience, a realization known to both lover and beloved who find their roles reciprocated in the give-and-take of love. What is decisive in this approach is his important suggestion that desire—humanity's as well as God's—is the experiential reality that grounds human nature, informs the life of faith, and leads finally to the pathway of peace.

TRANSLATIONS

Bernard of Clairvaux (1995) *On Loving God*, trans. R. Walton, Kalamazoo, MI: Cistercian Publications, is the translation used here.

Bernard of Clairvaux (1988) *Selected Works*, trans. G.R. Evans, Mahwah, NJ: Paulist Press.

FURTHER READING

Dumont, C. (1999) *Pathway of Peace: Cistercian wisdom according to Saint Bernard*, Kalamazoo, MI: Cistercian Publications, offers a masterful approach to the theological themes treated in Bernard's writings, with attention to the ongoing relevance of his thought.

Gilson, É. (1990) *The Mystical Theology of Saint Bernard*, trans. A.H.C. Downes, Kalamazoo, MI: Cistercian Publications, is the classic study of Bernard's mystical theology, with a new introduction by Jean Leclercq which points to the enduring voice of his writings.

Leclercq, J. (1976) *Bernard of Clairvaux and the Cistercian Spirit*, trans. C. Lavoie, Kalamazoo, MI: Cistercian Publications, offers the best short introduction to Bernard's thought with an eye to its continued spiritual vitality.

Merton, T. (1982) *The Last of the Fathers: Saint Bernard of Clairvaux and the encyclical letter "Doctor Mellifluus,"* San Diego, New York, and London: Harcourt Brace Jovanovich, provides a fair-handed historical assessment of his contribution with a passionate attentiveness to the spiritual depth of his writings; also includes Pope Pius XII's encyclical issued on the eighth centenary of Bernard's death (1953).

9

MECHTHILD OF MAGDEBURG (c.1210–c.1282)

The Flowing Light of the Godhead

ULRIKE WIETHAUS

> You want me to continue to write, but I cannot. Bliss, glory, brightness, intimate love, truth: these so overwhelm me that I have become dumb, unable to say more of what I know.
>
> (Mechthild, *The Flowing Light of the Godhead* VI.41)

Despite this declaration of defeat, the Beguine Mechthild of Magdeburg is one of the most engaging female mystical writers of the late Middle Ages. After more than seven hundred years, her writings, an often stunningly beautiful and always bold compendium of spiritual teachings, remain provocative and uncompromising. Some of her contemporaries would have agreed with this assessment, albeit critically. Mechthild notes that she is rejected by some like "filthy ooze" and writes that "I was warned against writing this book. People said: If one did not watch out, It could be burned" (II.26). Medieval Christians thought it difficult to access biblical knowledge and searched for trustworthy contemporary revelations to provide spiritual maps for the present and future. To the distress of some of her peers, Mechthild was certain that her writings were just that: a continuous stream—a *flowing light*—of divine revelations to supplement and extend the biblical canon into the present moment. No wonder then that the scribes who copy her book were promised extraordinary rewards in heaven. According to divine decree, the written product of their labors is to be transcribed onto their clothes in heaven, so that "all these words shall appear written on their outermost garments, forever visible in my kingdom/ In heavenly shining gold above all their adornments" (II.26).

The worldview that provided the framework for Mechthild's spiritual authority and authorial excellence is difficult to imagine today. She lived in a world in which people routinely expected miracles to happen, in which the dead communicated with the living, and where devils and angels were ubiquitous. Fasting and ascetic practices such as self-flagellation were believed to be essential spiritual tools. Alternative scenarios of reality could not be experienced through video games and films, but there was abundant time and meditative space available to experience one's own soul as a mirror of divine reality. Oral rather than electronic communication flourished through publicly shared and appreciated poetry, songs, debates, sermons, and storytelling. Nonetheless, conditions conducive to a mystical way of life had to compete with human nature, then as much as now. Mechthild knew this well: "Although God's tenderness and intimacy are in themselves eternal and noble, they are unfortunately so foreign in this world that all who truly grasp them are not at all able to describe them" (VI.20). Highly regarded by Beguines, Dominicans, and Cistercian nuns, Mechthild dared to speak of it and write of it, fashioning her own unmistakable style and mystical teachings.

AUTHOR AND AUDIENCE

Fortunately for contemporary readers, most information about this fearless spiritual teacher can be extracted from her own writings, with a few additional details furnished by her contemporaries. Raised and educated in the life-world of medieval German nobility, Mechthild wrote that she was much beloved by her relatives and friends. Family and relatives remained a frame of reference for her and her community throughout her life. She prayed for the souls of her mother and father, and comforted her brother Balduin, a sub-prior in the Dominican order. She advised her students not to burden themselves with too much concern for their families, yet to help those relatives who also wished to lead a spiritual life. Visits by relatives who had not taken religious vows could severely tempt her students' resolve for a spiritual life in voluntary poverty. In Mechthild's view, "when a person in religious life sees his relatives and dearest friends fashionably dressed and decked out, he indeed needs to be armed with the Holy Spirit so that he not entertain the thought: you could have had such a life" (VII.27). Mechthild wrote that she had committed a severe sin in her early childhood, for which she did extensive penance. She received her first ecstasy, or divine greeting, at the age of twelve. From this point on, Mechthild began a daily regime of ascetical practices and, unwilling or unable to continue her life in the midst of her family, she left for the city of Magdeburg to join a small community of Beguines, its size perhaps not exceeding eight members.

The Beguines found spiritual support and theological instruction through the relatively new order of Dominican friars, but their autonomy irked Magdeburg's ecclesiastical administration. In 1260 or 1261, the Beguines' right to self-governance was revoked by church authorities. Their ties to the Dominican order severely curtailed, the women's community was put under the authority of the secular clergy. Many of Mechthild's complaints about spiritual hypocrisy and corruption might reflect these events, as when she writes:

> Now the time has come when some people, who have the appearance of being religious, torment the bodies of God's children and martyr their spirits. For he wants them to resemble his beloved Son who was tormented in body and soul.
>
> (I.25)

While living in Magdeburg, Mechthild seems to have risen to the position of *magistra* to teach younger women and to offer advice to a larger circle outside of her community. Like other Beguines, she provided extensive spiritual services to the city community, in particular through her prayers for souls in purgatory and by visiting new graves to "greet both body and soul" (IV.22).

As was common for older women of the nobility, but in her case perhaps also precipitated by the hostile clerical reception of her works, Mechthild eventually retired to a community of Cistercian nuns in nearby Helfta, where she continued to teach and write until ill health led to her death twelve years later. Her family might have financed her sojourn at Helfta, or she might have used her own funds, since Beguines were allowed private income and ownership.

SYNOPSIS

The first readers to attempt a synopsis of Mechthild's works were the medieval Dominican scholars who collated and later translated the German version into Latin. They adapted chapter headings for quick reference, reorganized sections around specific topics, and prepared a short index of theological themes by following the structure of a theological handbook (the so-called *summa*). They also excised controversial sections deemed too erotic or critical of the clergy.

Heinrich of Halle offered guidance in how to read her book in a more spiritual manner. Approached with "pious intent," he asserted, Mechthild's writings will provide "solace and spiritual grace" (Prologue). He asked readers to study it with the same attitude as reading the Bible: piously, trusting, eager to understand its deeper meaning. Evoking the dimensions of biblical meaning as understood by medieval Christians, Heinrich defined Mechthild's focus as historical and mystical: historical in that her work assists in ordering contemporary life and recalls biblical events of the past; mystical in that it offers prophecies about the life to come, both individually (pertaining to the fate of souls in purgatory), and collectively (pertaining to the end of days).

Mechthild herself, however, moves beyond Heinrich's somewhat generic guidance. Formed by decades of ascetical practice and the mental discipline of daily prayers, she knows her writing to be a living extension of the Divine. Her writing pulls strands from the core of her mystical experiences and hard-won metaphysical system into the ebb and flow of daily events. Always unpredictable, like life itself, her writing is active participation rather than reflective distance.

The Flowing Light as an extension of Mechthild's visions and ecstasies

Mechthild began to work on *The Flowing Light of the Godhead* when her credentials as an ascetic and visionary were well established. Heinrich of Halle names the year 1250 as the beginning of her literary career. Not unlike notable other medieval writers (e.g., Hadewijch,

Hildegard of Bingen, or Peter Abelard), Mechthild excelled at composing spiritual poetry and songs, some of which might have been performed with musical accompaniment. Young noble women were expected to entertain with song and musical instruments, and it is therefore likely that Mechthild was trained from a young age in the art of composing rhymes and melodies.

Composed in a northern German dialect, her writings were intended to circulate in her community as an extension of her orally delivered teachings. Her poems as much as her prose texts are works of pastoral care, mystical pedagogy, and theological instruction. In the physical sense, her book was an edited compilation of initially unbound sheets of vellum (paper become common in Germany only at the beginning of the fourteenth century), written and sent out as circumstance demanded and divine inspiration commanded. In a lively example of the place of her writings in the teacher–student relationship, Mechthild opens one of her dispatches with the following words:

> I said in one passage in this book that the Godhead is my Father by nature. You do not understand this and say: "Everything that God has done with us is completely a matter of grace and not of nature." You are right, but I am right, too. Consider this analogy . . .
>
> (VI.31)

No individual section exceeds a few pages in length. A likely scenario of dissemination is that the original was sent to groups or individuals for contemplative reading, discussion, and prayer. Mechthild may have kept a copy of her writings, which could have been prepared by a fellow Beguine or by her confessor Heinrich of Halle. Collecting these works over the span of more than fifteen years and possibly in collaboration with Mechthild, Heinrich eventually organized the loose sheets into a book. Once Mechthild moved to Helfta, the nuns there continued this patient process of collation and thus contributed to what became the final and seventh book of *The Flowing Light*. If the total number of sections in *The Flowing Light* is compared with the reported number of years of her literary productivity, Mechthild's literary activity averages to about one chapter or section per month. Although she likely wrote in intervals of uneven length, this equation demonstrates that her literary activities actually represented only a fraction of her religious life. As she notes at some point, "I have set down many a long description with few words" (VII.1). Visions of the afterlife of individual souls, perhaps requested by mourning relatives, visions of the future of the Dominican order, and divinely inspired explanations of theological questions, monastic dilemmas, and ascetic practices suggest that she provided much-needed community education and counseling. Her advice on liturgical matters includes step-by-step instructions for conducting mass and the reading of hours in a monastic setting.

Mechthild insisted that reading her works was ineffective without divine participation; she thus closed one of her chapters with the words, "Dear friend of God, I have written for you this path of love. May God infuse it into your heart! Amen" (I.44).

Metaphysical core: the soul's exile and return

The Flowing Light weaves together three distinctly medieval codes and communities: first, the language and culture of the land-owning nobility in their castles; second, the semi-autonomous urban subculture of the Beguines with its emphasis on asceticism, poverty, and assistance for souls in the afterlife and at the moment of death; and third, interwoven with the others yet more university-trained, the itinerant network of Dominican friars whose code, shared through sermons and worship with the Beguine communities and the nobility, was biblical, liturgical, and theological. All three communities were shaped by a dynamic urban medieval milieu and rattled by a contradiction of voices and strong personalities.

In a brilliant fusion of personal experiences and theological knowledge as transmitted by the Dominicans, Mechthild popularized complex Neoplatonic teachings and possibly kabbalistic teachings on the Shekhinah (Hebrew for the feminine "Divine Presence"). Her conceptual vehicle was the value system of courtly love fused with bridal imagery from the Hebrew and Christian scriptures. Mechthild makes several references to the well-established Jewish community in Magdeburg, and it is entirely possible that she knew and reflected about Jewish mystical teachings of the feminine aspect of God in exile, a concept that resembles her own teachings about the soul. Key biblical resources for the construction of Mechthild's bridal mysticism include prophetic literature (Is 49 and 62), apocalyptic themes (Ez 16:6–15; Rev 19:7–11; 21:2), and allegories (Mt 25:1–13; Mk 2:18–22).

Mechthild's metaphysical system articulates a story of distance and closeness, of descent from heaven and ascent to heaven, of abandonment and return. The cosmic drama of creation, fall, and apocalypse takes place on the plane of eternity and simultaneously in earthly time and the individual human soul. Medieval people assumed that a visionary like Mechthild could perceive and elucidate the invisible, supernatural connections between all three dimensions and move freely across the borders between the material and spiritual realms. Scholarly studies of *The Flowing Light of the Godhead* have tended to emphasize Mechthild's teachings on the individual soul, imagined as bride of Christ, and often overlooked the underlying communal and cosmological dimensions of her teachings. Mechthild understands individual existence primarily as an extension of communal and cosmological patterns. In their trajectory from birth to death to afterlife, individual lives repeatedly encounter the same existential choices as a community. A community in turn embodies in time and space the apocalyptic fate of all of humankind, and indeed the earth. For Mechthild, cosmology, Christology, and anthropology fold into one comprehensive worldview. All is undergirded by a deep sense of divine goodness, or the practice of love (*Minne*).

With exquisite elegance and depth of thought, books III and IV contain Mechthild's core teachings in narrative form. Her story begins in the dimension of eternity, that is, outside of history. Here, the Trinity exists without beginning or end. History begins with the creation of angels, who serve as dukes and servants of the heavenly court. Out of desire, the Trinity creates a perfect bride for itself. The bride is fashioned of two elements: the human soul, made from divine essence, and a pre-lapsarian perfect human body. Because of her essential sameness with divine essence, God vows never to turn away from the soul, yet provides her with free will and thus the choice to turn away from him. The human soul is noble. The potent medieval metaphor of nobility underscores that soul and God are of the same substance. Thus, the soul is quite literally "Goddess" of all non-human created beings, including angels, and destined always to be the appropriate bride of the Divine.

Poisoned by having eaten the forbidden fruit in paradise, the body loses its own primal perfection, yet the soul retains her capacity for divine perfection. The soul, now imprisoned in an impure body, "cried out in great darkness for her Lover" (III.9). What is true on an individual level is true on the collective and cosmological level: all earthly time after the expulsion from paradise is a time of exile, filled with suffering and evil. Yet there is respite: during ecstasies, the well-prepared soul-bride may briefly visit the heavenly court. Leaving behind the post-lapsarian body as in a sleep, the soul-bride tastes the bliss that the future will bring.

Since God, unlike his bride, has not impaired his ability to love, the divine Bridegroom is forced to follow his soul-bride into exile by taking on a human body. In a *processio* reminiscent of Neoplatonic levels of being, Christ descends from heaven to ransom his bride from the prison of her sins. His mission is to reunite with his exiled bride to bring her back to the heavenly court. In preparation for the courtly reunion, Christ redeems the exiled soul in the way that medieval hostages were ransomed when captured: by paying the highest possible price. Following the custom of marriage preparations among the nobility, the liberated bride now needs to prepare herself for her return. She must embrace and practice "holy virtues and true innocence" (IV.14). In Mechthild's terminology, "spiritual" people or "friends of God" are those who strive for such preparation. Properly prepared and reunited with her bridegroom, the soul bride fulfills her destiny and becomes a noble wife. As a lady (*Frouwe*), she rules at the heavenly court with her divine spouse.

In light of this cosmic drama of loss and redemption, Mechthild's insistence on the centrality of virtues and the joy of ecstasies becomes clear. Book I is filled with erotic poetry, seducing the reader into the world of bridal mysticism. The remaining six books apply the core narrative to the ebb and flow of events in her community. Whereas the first book contains most of her love poetry, later books are weighed more heavily toward themes such as purgatory, prophecies, advice for monastics, and explanations of biblical texts.

INFLUENCE

Mechthild's influence seems more prominent today than it was in the past. The Catholic diocese of Magdeburg sponsored a "Mechthild Year" that ended on September 13, 2008. To commemorate the eight hundredth anniversary of her birth, more than fifty lectures, workshops, art exhibits, and even specially baked "Mechthild cakes" explored and celebrated her spiritual legacy. But it is nearly impossible to reconstruct her impact on her fellow Beguines and the Helfta nuns, although she is fondly remembered by Gertrud the Great, who seems to have known her well. German Dominicans kept her teachings and writings alive for the next two hundred years, yet not without editing and censorship. The original manuscript edited by Heinrich of Halle is lost; the official Dominican version, translated into Latin, dates from around 1285. The earliest uncensored text is a translation into another German dialect by a group of scribes, completed in 1345, which was circulated among Dominican sisters in the vicinity of Basel. The German Dominicans Dietrich of Apolda, Heinrich of Nördlingen, and Meister Eckhart appear to have been strongly influenced by Mechthild's writings.

Contemporary scholars lose sight of *The Flowing Light of the Godhead* in the early sixteenth century. In 1861, the only complete German manuscript now extant was rediscovered in the monastic Einsiedeln library in Switzerland. This find allowed the identification of fragments in a few other religious manuscripts. In the twentieth century, *The Flowing Light of the Godhead* became the domain of German literary studies until the feminist spirituality movement of the eighties and nineties rediscovered Mechthild of Magdeburg as a spiritual teacher and foremother. Gertrud von Le Fort, a German contemporary author, has fictionalized Mechthild's work in her novel, *Die Abberufung der Jungfrau von Barby* (*The Call of the Virgin of Barby*, 1960).

To encourage a rediscovery of her teachings, the cathedral of Magdeburg displays special stained glass windows; excerpts of *The Flowing Light of the Godhead* have become an integral element of women's spirituality publications in the United States and Western Europe. The rebuilt monastery at Helfta proudly evokes Mechthild's years at Helfta, and for the last twenty-five years or so, her teachings have occasioned a steady stream of scholarly studies.

READING THE TEXT TODAY

Mechthild links her narrative to a wide range of biblical and theological themes, reapplying its message in an astonishing variation of scenarios and settings. She vividly evokes the lifeways of medieval nobility: arranged marriages, the pursuit of courtly love, tournaments, war. Steeped in the logic of keeping hostages and ransoming captives, Mechthild herself releases souls from purgatory through prayer, tears and sighs, and penance. Like a feudal lord, God is bound to her soul through a mutual oath of allegiance and obliged to recognize the ransom she offers.

The medieval core

Mechthild's teachings on the human soul may strike a reader today as inaccessible due to its use of aristocratic concepts, the emphasis on asceticism and chastity, or even the notion of divine eros. Feminists might find the soul's trajectory from bride to wife stifling, and Christians who search for a viable spiritual path might despair about their inability to experience ecstasies and visions. Western Christianity has perhaps lost a sense of the presence of the supernatural and otherworldly that constituted Mechthild's life-world. Although not completely disavowed, apocalyptic thought has become marginal. The soul has almost disappeared into a definition of human self that is determined by its biological make-up. To complete a litany of woes, the administrative and clerical structures of the church, so despised by Mechthild, have won out over the mystical strands of Christianity, or so it seems.

Mechthild's combination of visionary self-confidence and theological sophistication thus testifies to a Christian spirituality that seems anachronistic. Nonetheless, a patient engagement with her writings can accomplish today what it meant to accomplish during her lifetime: providing for a deeper reading of Biblical texts, and inviting reflection and practice to rediscover the meaning of time and history, of soul and community. The key to her writings lies in understanding her refusal to compromise with the ecclesiastical powers of her day, as well as her good luck to be raised in a culture still on good terms with ascetic practices and ecstasies and still receptive to female spiritual teachers. Her writings reflect medieval Christianity's ability to boldly reinvent itself, giving birth to the mendicant orders such as the Dominicans and to lay religious movements such as the Beguines. Her authority as a female teacher derived from her aristocratic upbringing, her disciplined spiritual practice, her determination to live a life of integrity in community, and finally, her extraordinary literary talents.

Mechthild's instructions

Reading Mechthild today might best be accomplished, however, by following her own instructions for the use of *The Flowing Light of the Godhead*. Contemporary authors wish to reach as wide an audience as possible. Not so Mechthild. Her book is intended only for those women and men who have committed themselves to a life of the spirit—in her terminology, the "friends of God" or "spiritual people." Unlike the mass-produced and readily discarded books used today, Mechthild understood *The Flowing Light of the Godhead* to be a powerful, living, and literally breathing entity an audience would connect with through the act of reading or listening to it being read. She described its power metaphorically: the book's white sheets of paper represent the humanity of God; its written words, a manifestation of divine essence, flow continuously from God into the soul; speaking the words while reading them—using one's breath and sound—manifests the Holy Spirit and unlocks divine truth. To fully understand its message, one must read it nine times, much as medieval monastic practice demanded repetition as a tool for spiritual growth—be it of prayers, chants, confession, acts of penance, or ascetic practices.

The Flowing Light of the Godhead demands as a first step that spiritual seekers enter Mechthild's archetypal narrative of soul exile and retrieval, of souls captured and ransomed. Reading Mechthild, can a Christian community recreate space and time for something akin to the human soul, an ineffable divine/human essence that transcends death and the iniquities of any social order? Can contemporary human beings see once more with the eyes of the soul? And if contemporary Christians were to acknowledge a collectively experienced soul loss, how then could they go about the work of ransoming?

The Flowing Light of the Godhead provides a measure of the distance Western Christianity has traveled from a mystical, ascetically oriented spirituality of exuberance and boldness to a measured, cautious, bureaucracy-heavy Christianity. It can also teach the limits of academic study. In Mechthild's words, "what good are lofty words without works of mercy?" (VI.30). Her writings are the product of a period of intense religious uncertainty and divisiveness. She knew full well that her teachings could be submerged by secular concerns and loyalties.

Return of the medieval?

Mechthild wrote with future generations in mind, and thus she might not be astonished that the Beguine movement is making a comeback in Germany. These twenty-first century Beguines have formed a national association. Its website posts a contemporary definition of a Beguine, which offers yet another invitation to contemplate Mechthild's legacy. The definition states with a dose of humor: "A Beguine is an outspoken, exemplary, vibrant, courageous, curious, free, talented, fair-minded, resilient, spontaneous woman, free of corruption and perfume." Mechthild likely would have agreed.

TRANSLATION

Mechthild of Magdeburg (1998) *The Flowing Light of the Godhead*, trans. F. Tobin, Mahwah, NJ: Paulist Press.

FURTHER READING

Grundmann, H. (1995) *Religious Movements in the Middle Ages*, Notre Dame: Indiana University Press, is a reprint of a classic study of the new orders and the contributions of women, first published in Germany in 1932.

Hollywood, A. (1995) *The Soul as Virgin Wife: Mechthild of Magdeburg, Marguerite Porete and Meister Eckhart*, Notre Dame, IN: University of Notre Dame Press, offers a comparative study of mystical feminine imagery for the soul.

Keller, H.E. (2000) *My Secret is Mine: studies on religion and eros in the German middle ages*, Leuven, Belgium: Peeters, is a helpful overview of the development and decline of bridal mysticism in Germany.

Newman, B. (1995) *From Virile Woman to WomanChrist*, Philadelphia: University of Philadelphia Press, is an astute analysis of courtly love mysticism.

Poor, S.S. (2004) *Mechthild of Magdeburg and Her Book*, Philadelphia: University of Philadelphia, is an important analysis of the textual transmission of *The Flowing Light of the Godhead*.

Tobin, F. (1995) *Mechthild of Magdeburg: a medieval mystic in modern eyes*, Columbia, SC: Camden House, is an indispensable review of Mechthild scholarship.

Wiethaus, U. (1996) *Ecstatic Transformation: transpersonal psychology and the work of Mechthild of Magdeburg*, Syracuse, NY: Syracuse University Press, offers a study of ecstasies and visions in *The Flowing Light of the Godhead*.

10

BONAVENTURE
(c.1217/21–1274)
The Soul's Journey into God

ELIZABETH A. DREYER

In Cantos XI and XII of Dante's *Paradiso*, the Dominican Thomas Aquinas sings the praises of the Franciscans, and the Franciscan Bonaventure lauds the Dominicans. Dante places Thomas and Bonaventure in the Heaven of the Sun, a dazzling fiery world of light, dance, and song, reflecting the beauty and wisdom of God. Bonaventure's historical existence was quite different, marked by conflict and challenge.

At the second Council of Lyons (1274), Bonaventure was instrumental in temporarily healing the rift between the Eastern Orthodox and Western branches of Christendom over whether the Holy Spirit proceeded from the Father alone or from both the Father and the Son (*filioque*). At the University of Paris, he addressed the anger of the secular masters who bitterly opposed Franciscan poverty and challenged the right of mendicants to teach. The Dominican and Franciscan friars had become popular instructors, infringing on the income and prestige of secular clergy. Bonaventure also saw the new dialectical approach to theology as a threat to the more traditional "pious" scriptural, monastic methods of study. Within the Franciscan Order, Bonaventure was faced with a growing divide between the Spirituals who fought to maintain strict adherence to the Rule laid down by Francis, and those who wanted to modify the practice of poverty to include ownership of property and books. Bonaventure struggled to find a middle way that was true to Francis's founding vision, yet open to the adaptation required of a growing Order with new ministerial demands.

It is likely that the experience of so much discord motivated Bonaventure to imagine an alternative vision of unity and peace reminiscent of the ideal of Francis. He created a remarkable theological and spiritual synthesis that linked a metaphysics centered in Christ and the Trinity; the divine, the human, and the cosmos; intellect and love; the academic and the pastoral. The *Itinerarium mentis in Deum* (*The Soul's Journey into God*) is a striking example of this synthesis. Bonaventure wanted to show how the mystery of Francis's spirituality of creation and cross applied to all, especially those called to study. To express the fullness of God more adequately, Bonaventure juxtaposes opposing tendencies—a method Ewert Cousins calls the "coincidence of opposites"—light/darkness; alpha/omega; center/circumference. Christ is fully human and fully divine; God is awesome Creator of the universe and humble, self-emptying man on the cross; humans are made in the image of God and sinners; Franciscans are called to simplicity and also a profound appreciation for beauty. Bonaventure's was truly a "both–and" vision of reality.

AUTHOR AND AUDIENCE

Unfortunately, not much is known about Bonaventure's early life. Medieval people did not keep detailed records, and when they did, the data often did not survive. Bonaventure was born John Fidanza in Bagnoregio, Italy, near Viterbo, to Giovanni di Fidanza and Maria Ritella between *c.*1217 and 1221. It is uncertain when or why he changed his name to Bonaventure. Francis was an inspiration from his earliest days. Bonaventure studied at the local Franciscan friary, and in his life of Francis (*Legenda minor*), he notes that as a child he was cured of a grave illness through his mother's intercession to St. Francis (d.1226).

In 1235, Bonaventure went to the University of Paris, joining the Franciscan Order either in 1238 or in 1243 when he became Master of Arts. His professors included two eminent Franciscan scholars, Alexander of Hales and Odo Rigaldus. He received his license to teach in 1248 and was ordained c.1250. Both he and Thomas Aquinas were awarded the degree of Doctor of Theology in October 1257.

Bonaventure was a prolific author. Influenced by Augustine, Pseudo-Dionysius, Richard and Hugo of St. Victor, and Bernard of Clairvaux, Bonaventure wrote philosophical treatises, biblical commentaries, theological texts, and spiritual, pastoral works. His writings fill ten volumes in the Quarrachi edition, *Opera omnia*.

But the course of his life changed dramatically in February 1257, when, at forty, Bonaventure was elected Master General of the Franciscans. The Franciscan Order then comprised thirty provinces, 1,100 convents with nearly 25,000 members. Bonaventure wrote the *Itinerarium* in 1259 as a spiritual guidebook for all the brothers, but especially for teachers and students. The text argues compellingly that academics who desire a deeper life with God can indeed follow Francis to the heights of mystical contemplation. The way to God included not only creation, the human person, and ministry to the poor, but also knowledge. Speculation was legitimate as a medium of union with God. Thus, the method and content of the *Itinerarium* are highly intellectual, but also passionate and poetic. It is helpful to have a guide to light the way through this dense but rewarding work.

In 1273 Bonaventure was made Cardinal-Archbishop of Albano. He played an active role in the first four general sessions of the Second Council of Lyons (1274). In May, the Franciscans also held a General Chapter at Lyons. Jerome of Ascoli, later Nicholas IV, succeeded Bonaventure as General of the Order. Bonaventure was taken ill and died on July 15, 1274 at the age of fifty-seven. Pope Sixtus IV canonized him in 1482, and Pope Sixtus V declared him a Doctor of the Church in 1588.

Persons who knew Bonaventure described him as a gentle, humble man with a kindly visage. He is known as the Seraphic Doctor, a title that points to his warmth, loving wisdom, and angelic, mystical qualities. Evidence of his humility includes a tale that when Gregory X's envoys brought Bonaventure his red hat as Cardinal-Archbishop of York, they found him washing dishes. He asked them to hang the hat on a tree outside until he had finished. Oddly, there is no official modern biography of Bonaventure, a lack that may have pleased this self-effacing friar. The depth and passion of his love for God and his desire for the holiness of others are visible in his writings, as is his debt to St. Francis of Assisi, the Poverello, whose vision Bonaventure worked to further in a mode quite different from what Francis might have envisioned.

SYNOPSIS

The *Itinerarium mentis in Deum* has long been known as a jewel among Christian spiritual classics. The text is notable for its unusual wedding of profound metaphysical and mystical ideas. On the one hand, it reverberates with allusions to key philosophical ideas of the thirteenth century, such as how humans know God and whether the world is eternal. On the other hand, the text describes a spiritual path that runs from Francis's love affair with God, through creation, to mystical death with Christ on the cross. In response to challenges to the Franciscan way, Bonaventure integrates it with the Great Tradition, placing the cross at the culmination of the journey. The cross links the divine and the human, leading the faithful to a life of compassion and love.

The title: *Itinerarium mentis in Deum*

Translations of the Latin title vary. *Itinerarium* means journey or way. On one level, Bonaventure describes this journey in ordered steps. Medieval thinkers were fascinated with the idea of hierarchy, an idea given powerful expression in the writings of Pseudo-Dionysius in the fifth century. While people today are likely to associate the term with church officials, medieval thinkers understood hierarchy as the order and harmony of the universe—humans being in right relationship with themselves, the universe, and God. Readers should not be misled into thinking that Bonaventure recommends a strict series of stages. The *Itinerarium* is not a detailed account of personal spiritual experience, but a map or template for the path to union with God.

The metaphor of the journey to describe the spiritual life is well established in many religious traditions. Taking a trip, going on a pilgrimage, moving through life from beginning to end are familiar activities. Humans instinctually ask: Where did I come from? Why am I here? Where am I going? It is a capacious metaphor that lends itself to diverse interpretations. Believers across the globe address these questions in the context of their specific geography, time, and circumstances. The *Itinerarium* is a powerful Franciscan expression of the journey metaphor from the world of the thirteenth century.

The term *mentis* is translated "soul" or "mind"—terms that are problematic for twenty-first century readers who associate "soul" with disembodied spirit, and "mind" with the brain. In a medieval context, the term *mens* points to a broader meaning. The term might be translated as "person," encompassing physical, psychological, emotional, intellectual, and spiritual dimensions. The prepositional phrase *in Deum* is usually translated as "to God." But Bonaventure's deep conviction that humanity and all of creation participate in the divine life, suggests rather "into God"—a phrase that presages the powerful divine/human intimacy expressed in the final chapter.

The *Itinerarium* is composed of a prologue and seven chapters. The first six chapters are set up in pairs that mirror a pattern of the Christian life. The journey is begun "out" in the world of creation, moves "in" to interiority, and then "up" to God. Chapter seven transcends all elements of the journey, beckoning the pilgrim beyond human reason to mystical union with Christ on the cross. Bonaventure turns to an architectural image to describe the journey from the outer atrium to the intimacy of the inner court of the human being where God dwells, and thence up to God (3.1).

Beginning the journey in the spirit of Francis of Assisi

The prologue sets the scene with an invocation to the Father, the Son, Mary, and Francis. The Spirit is absent at this juncture, but will appear later at crucial moments. Considering the conflicts Bonaventure faced, it is not hard to understand his emphatic plea for peace, a mark of the mystical transport and the goal of the journey. The inspiration for the *Itinerarium* came to Bonaventure at La Verna in the mountains above Arezzo, where Francis had his encounter with the Crucified (1224). Bonaventure wanted to "drink in" the spirit of Francis in contemplation as he struggled to lead the Franciscan community.

The image of the six-winged Seraphim who hover above the Lord becomes the touchstone for the central six chapters of the *Itinerarium*. Two wings cover the face; two cover the feet; two fly, as the angels chant, "Holy, holy, holy is the Lord of hosts; the whole earth is full of his glory" (Is 6: 1–3). Thus the scene is set for a journey that brings together the divine/human, heaven/earth, intellect/affect—a union made possible by the divine/human Christ. Fervor must accompany reading; devotion supplements speculation; admiration completes investigation; exultation overflows from observation; piety fuels industry; love infuses knowledge; humility serves understanding; divine grace illuminates study (prologue, 4).

God in the world

Chapters one and two can be viewed through the image of a mirror. The ordered beauty of the universe mirrors the Trinity. Medieval texts abound in endless rounds of triads: there are three ways of seeing, three forms of reality, three types of humans, etc. Because the world was created by God who sent the Son to take on flesh, it is a microcosm, filled with vestiges, shadows, echoes of the divine first Principle and Exemplar of all reality. Although sin obstructs human destiny, prayer (the entryway of the journey), provides the light and grace to find humanity's true end. Under Neoplatonic and Augustinian influences, Bonaventure begins the journey in the material, temporal sphere. The complexity of nature, the multiplicity of species, and the immensity of the universe mirror the divine.

How do people come to know all this created beauty? Bonaventure's epistemology is a mix of Aristotle's idea that knowledge is generated via the five senses, and Augustine's theory that a divine light shines on the mind making human knowledge possible. Exposure to the exquisite proportion of created reality produces pleasure. Its beauty, sweetness, and wholeness (2.8) lead humanity to the uncreated perfection and fount—the Eternal Art. Since the world reveals the being of God, humans are without excuse when they refuse to notice created things and to know, bless, and love God in them (2.12).

God within

Chapters three and four move from creation to the inner workings of the human person (interiority). With Augustine as his primary guide, and grounded in the conviction that human beings are made in the image and likeness of God (*imago Dei*), Bonaventure finds traces of the Trinity in the operations of memory, intellect, and will (Gen 1: 26). He treats these operations from the perspective of nature/philosophy and then of grace/scripture. These chapters underline the splendor of the human person fully alive in God, and the incredible intimacy between the divine and the human.

Bonaventure is well aware that life is full of cares, woes, and sins that distract people from the contemplative appreciation of themselves as made in God's image. The daily round of a fast-paced world can block awareness of the invitation to divine intimacy. But through Christ, who is the ladder and the door (Jn 10:9), humans can bridge the gap through repentance and sacrifice. It is through the theological virtues of faith, hope, and love that humans are purified, enlightened, and made whole (4.3). Once the image of God in humanity is re-formed, the floodgates of divine love open. Bonaventure turns to the poetic, erotic mood of the Song of Songs to describe this new life in which the spiritual senses of hearing, sight, taste, touch, and smell are aroused. Through these two steps, the mind becomes the house of God inhabited by divine wisdom (4.8). Humans become daughter, spouse, friend of God; member, sister, co-heir of Christ; temple of the Holy Spirit whose grace is poured forth into human hearts (Rom 5:5).

God's Being and Goodness

In chapters five and six, the focus moves from "in" to "up." After con-sidering creation and human interiority, Bonaventure invites the reader to dwell on the invisible and eternal things of God: first on God's unity through the attribute of being; then on the individual Persons through the attribute of goodness. What is it like to contem-plate the divine brightness? Bonaventure describes it as superluminous darkness. Since human eyes are accustomed to the opacity of material things, they cannot absorb the divine brightness which appears as darkness (5.4).

In a philosophical excursus, Bonaventure methodically argues to the nature of God's Being and Goodness, and the certitude of know-ledge of God's existence (via Anselm's ontological argument). God is eternal, simple, actual, perfect, one—that than which nothing greater can be thought. He describes the utter fullness of God through opposites: God is first and last; eternal and most present; most simple and greatest; most actual and most changeless; most perfect and most immense; supremely one and pervading all things (5.7). Thus, con-templation of the divine being arouses awe and admiration.

Under the rubric of the Good, Bonaventure describes a dynamic God filled to overflowing with goodness. The very nature of the divine goodness means that it cannot be hoarded or self-contained. It flows outward within the Trinity in the processions of the divine persons and is extended beyond the Trinity in the divine mission—

the free creation of the world. God is not only one but three—a mystery worthy of wonder and admiration (6.3), as are the divine and human natures joined in the one person, Christ. But as he approaches the heights of the divine mystery, Bonaventure never abandons the earth or humanity. Christ is the ineffable Savior who brings together that which by logic should remain apart—divinity and humanity; spirit and matter.

The dénouement

The *Itinerarium* ends on a soaring mystical note. The soul dies a mystical death with Christ on the cross in the presence of the entire Trinity. After the labors of contemplating God in and through creatures, humanity, and divine attributes, the soul soars into ecstasy, passing over (Pasch, Passover) beyond itself into God. It is a moment of rejoicing and peace, modeled by Francis at La Verna. The cares of the world and the efforts of the intellect are left behind—a leap made possible only through the Holy Spirit. One of the most beautiful passages in all of Christian spiritual literature, this chapter rewards frequent, slow reading to allow its affirming and exhilarating message to be absorbed. This experience of white flame is enkindled by Christ in his most burning Passion. The cross stands at the center as cares, desires, and imaginings are silenced. "My grace is sufficient for you (Jn 13:1, 14; 2 Cor 12:9); "it is enough for us" (7.6).

INFLUENCE

It is unfortunate that the *Itinerarium* is not as well known as other Christian spiritual classics. In spite of its complex nature as a philosophical, theological, and mystical work, the *Itinerarium* has always appealed to different types of people: academics, church leaders, ordinary seekers. It became a foundational document for Franciscan spirituality, functioning much like the *Spiritual Exercises* among Jesuits. But like all classics, its influence reaches out to all Christians.

The manuscript tradition suggests that the *Itinerarium*'s influence grew with time. Of the 138 extant manuscripts, only five are from the thirteenth century. There are forty from the fourteenth century and ninety-one from the fifteenth. Interpretations of the text reflect the various historical contexts in which it was used. In the early modern period, when arid speculation threatened to distance theology from the affections, preaching, and spirituality, the *Itinerarium* helped restore mystical, poetic, and experiential dimensions. Chapter seven was seen as a particularly effective corrective to over-confidence in reason, providing a stellar example of that *docta ignorantia* ("learned ignorance") associated with Nicholas of Cusa (1401–64). In the nineteenth and twentieth centuries, the text was mined primarily for its philosophical content because of the preoccupations of the time and a desire to give Bonaventure due recognition as a philosopher alongside Thomas Aquinas.

READING THE TEXT TODAY

The world in which the *Itinerarium* was written is long gone. The contemporary approaches to metaphysics, epistemology, anthropology, and scripture are radically different. People no longer speak of the world as a mirror of the Trinity, creating endless triads to make the point. In many ways, the *Itinerarium* is an encounter with difference, challenging readers to use imagination and intellectual energy to cross over into another world. On the other hand, Bonaventure's articulation of a spirituality of heart and head continues to draw those who hunger and thirst to know and be moved by God's love; those who treasure creation and want to care for it; those drawn to a holistic vision of reality; those willing to risk the kind of ecstatic, mystical death to which Bonaventure beckons. How specifically does the *Itinerarium* speak to people now?

God and the world belong together

To begin, Bonaventure refused to uncouple the world from God. His grasp of the incarnation is a standout in the Christian tradition. He took the Christ-centered vision of Francis and shaped it into a compelling, creation-centered theological spirituality. He eschews the path of flight from the world in favor of openness to a theology of beauty. His synthesis of Christology, Trinitarian thought, and creation theology calls people to a loving, contemplative gaze at the world. To learn about the world is to learn about God. The world is the divine footprint; God is available to everyone at every level of the created order. Bonaventure's work offers a compelling argument against dualism by feeding human efforts to understand the world as sacred, to seek the wisdom of right relationship with creation, and to become ecologically responsible for a world that participates in the very life of God.

Christology

Within this cosmic vision, Bonaventure's Christology speaks to the contemporary experience of Christ as friend and brother. Instead of the regal, glorious Infant of Prague, Bonaventure offers the Christ of the crèche and the cross. Most important for readers today is Bonaventure's conviction that the human Jesus provides the most profound insight into both God and the world. Christ is the center of the cosmos and the heart of history. And in this same Jesus, Christians meet the humble, condescending Trinity. This Jesus teaches the way of renunciation, conversion, and compassion for the poor and suffering of the world—images confronted daily in the media now. The cross has never been more important than in this consumerist, affluent, technological, yet starving, bleeding world. The way to mystical heights is *through* history, *through* humanity, *in and through* the God-man Jesus on the cross who dwells in the loving creativity of the Father and the transforming power of the Holy Spirit.

The *Itinerarium* exudes confidence in the human ability to know, love, and be united with God—all the while conscious of human limitation and sin. The way is not solitary, a point often missed in an age of radical individualism. The medieval context of community life and ministry was so taken for granted that it seems invisible—a lacuna that readers must fill. Bonaventure's convictions about human possibility were not deadened by the strife and corruption around him. Realistic about suffering and conflict, he nonetheless allowed the power of the Spirit to prevail, leading others to peace and intimacy with the divine. In the midst of twenty-first century suffering from human evil and natural disasters, Christians are called to engage the cross and mirror divine peace, coherence, and integration within themselves and the world. The *Itinerarium* beckons Christians to lives of committed, compassionate action and profound sacramental contemplation. Bonaventure provokes and inspires Christians to follow the mystical path of contemplative wonder, allowing grace to nurture and enhance their ability both to taste the love of God in the silent darkness beyond knowing, and to use their talent and creativity for the sake of the world.

Heart and mind together

Finally, Bonaventure charts a course which honors the cooperation of the affections and the intellect. To the extent that people embrace a narrowly radical empiricism, or succumb to irrational emotions, they forfeit the wisdom that is the fruit of loving knowledge and intelligent loving. Bonaventure challenges readers to go beyond a narrow empiricism to taste and relish all types of knowledge. But the very nature of the *Itinerarium* places intellectual work at the forefront of the spiritual journey and invites Christians to bring rigorous intellectual inquiry and the experience of faith into conversation. Bonaventure honors the incredibly rich and complex intellectual capacity of humanity as a sacred vehicle to encounter God. But intellectual work is a pale shadow of itself when it functions without love.

In the end, says Bonaventure, those who seek God must transcend the things of the mind which, as a means to the goal, are incapable of carrying them into the mystical death with Christ on the cross. The Dominican-trained poet Dante echoes Bonaventure's way of integration and wholeness. In the final Canto of the *Paradiso*, Bernard of Clairvaux, the mystical doctor of the affections, becomes Dante's guide as he comes face to face with the Trinity. The intellectual metaphor of vision is retained, but it is a vision transformed by love.

> *What then I saw is more than tongue can say.*
> *Our human speech is dark before the vision.*
> *The ravished memory swoons and falls away*
>
> *As one who sees in dreams and wakes to find*
> *the emotional impression of his vision*
> *still powerful while its parts fade from his mind—*
>
> *just such am I, having lost nearly all*
> *the vision itself, while in my heart I feel*
> *the sweetness of it yet distill and fall*

* * * * * * * * * * * * * *

Oh grace abounding that had made me fit
    to fix my eyes on the eternal light
until my vision was consumed in It!

I saw within Its depth how It conceives
all things in a single volume bound by Love,
of which the universe is the scattered leaves;

* * * * * * * * * * * * * *

Here my powers rest from their high fantasy,
but already I could feel my being turned—
instinct and intellect balanced equally

as in a wheel whose motion nothing jars—
by the Love that moves the sun and other stars.
            (Dante, *Paradiso* XXXIII, trans. John Ciardi*)

TRANSLATIONS

Bonaventure (2002) *Itinerarium mentis in Deum*, trans. Z. Hayes, with introduction and commentary by P. Boehner, St. Bonaventure, NY: Franciscan Institute Publications.

Bonaventure (1993) *The Journey of the Mind to God*, trans. S.F. Brown, Indianapolis/Cambridge: Hackett Publishing Company.

Bonaventure (1978) *The Soul's Journey into God, the Tree of Life, the Life of St. Francis*, trans. E. Cousins, Mahwah, NJ: Paulist Press.

FURTHER READING

Cusato, M. and F.E. Coughlin, eds. (1997) *That Others May Know and Love: essays in honor of Zachary Hayes*, St. Bonaventure, NY: The Franciscan Institute, is a collection of essays on Bonaventure and the wider Franciscan movement, its philosophy, theology, reform, and contemporary relevance.

---

* *The Divine Comedy* by Dante Alighieri, translated by John Ciardi. Copyright 1954, 1957, 1959, 1960, 1961, 1965, 1967, 1970 by the Ciardi Family Publishing Trust. Used by permission of W.W. Norton & Company, Inc.

Delio, I. (2001) *Simply Bonaventure: an introduction to his life, thought, and writings*, Hyde Park, NY: New City Press, is a fine place to begin to learn about St. Bonaventure and his thirteenth-century context.

——(2005) *The Humility of God: a Franciscan perspective*, Cincinnati, OH: St. Anthony Messenger Press, is an informative, thematic approach to the concept of God in the Franciscan tradition that focuses on Bonaventure and other early Franciscan figures.

Hayes, Z. (1981) *The Hidden Center: spirituality and speculative Christology in St. Bonaventure*, New York: Paulist Press, is a classic study on the place and role of Christ in Bonaventure's theology.

——(1999) *Bonaventure: mystical writings*, Crossroad Spiritual Legacy Series, NY: Crossroad, adopts the structure of the *Soul's Journey into God* to illustrate Bonaventure's gift for weaving together intellectual and affective threads into a tapestry of theological wisdom.

11

MARGUERITE PORETE
(d.1310)

The Mirror of Simple Souls

MARIA LICHTMANN

Burned at the stake a full century before Joan of Arc, Marguerite Porete makes a challenging subject for contemporary appropriation. Some time in the late thirteenth century, Marguerite wrote a mystical treatise with the deceptively simple title, *Le mirour des simples âmes*, "The Mirror of Simple Souls." But the text was not linked to its author until the twentieth century. Marguerite's refusal to recant her seemingly heretical doctrines got her the dubious distinction of being the first person burned as a relapsed heretic by the Paris Inquisition in 1310. Despite her distance from us in time, there is much to recommend her as a peculiarly postmodern saint. At the time Marguerite was executed, the institutional church was enjoying its heyday of scholasticism. Yet, Marguerite called it the "Little Church" because it failed to embody the simplicity and surrender of those lovers totally dedicated to God in the truly "Great Church." The courage and integrity she showed in her willingness to face her condemnation for eighteen months without a word of self-defense correspond to the defiant break her mystical treatise makes with those (male) inquisitors who represented the institutional church. Her life was of a piece with her work, a mirror of *The Mirror*.

In perhaps another respect, she appeals to the postmodern age. She most likely belonged to what can be considered an early women's movement of semi-religious women called "Beguines." She speaks to a sisterhood that lived outside monastery walls, among ordinary people, some of whom practiced an extraordinary street mysticism. Her treatise abounds in female metaphors, even for God, whom she addresses as Lady Love. Marguerite was unapologetic about being a woman in an exclusively male preserve.

Cautions are to be exercised in reading Marguerite's mystical treatise, as the three theologians who approved it advised. In the history of Christian spiritual classics it is customary to speak of a spiritual journey, but in Marguerite's text we encounter a wild rollercoaster ride of ascent to the heights followed by a plunging to the depths. Marguerite's mysticism can seem stark and unsentimental. It speaks a language of annihilation, a self-naughting that may feel alienating to contemporary sensibilities. It may even seem Buddhist in its outright rejection of knowing, and feeling, and willing.

AUTHOR AND AUDIENCE

Her life

Only in the year 1946, with Romana Guarnieri's announcement in L'Osservatore Romano, was The Mirror of Simple Souls reconnected to its author. Guarnieri based her finding on articles taken from the inquisition process and found in the text of Marguerite's writings. Little is known about Marguerite except through the documents of the Inquisition archived at Paris and what is found in the text. Her book is addressed to both "actives and contemplatives," and to the "lost souls"—those too involved in the active life to find God—and "sad souls" who long for God but do not know the way to God.

Her book

Marguerite's book had been publicly burned in her hometown by the local bishop, Guy of Colmieu, sometime between 1296 and 1306. At that point, Marguerite sought the counsel of three theologians and obtained their approval. Because she continued to promote her work, and despite the theologians' qualified approbations, Marguerite was charged with being a relapsed heretic and commanded to appear before the papal general inquisitor of France, William of Paris, in late 1309.

Her inquisition and death

This inquisitor, William of Paris, was also the confessor to King Philip the Fair, a fact that played a large role in bringing Marguerite to her tragic end. Philip the Fair had been persecuting the Knights Templar, a crusading order whose wealth he coveted, which put him out of favor with the papacy. He chose to re-establish his loyalty to the pope by bringing charges of heresy against the first suspected heretic to come his way. While the Dominican inquisitor was engaged in prosecuting the Knights Templar, Marguerite remained in prison for a year and a half. During the inquisition by twenty-one theologians, who read only a list of fifteen articles extracted from her treatise, Marguerite remained silent, and was condemned to death on May 31, 1310. The next day, she became the first heretic burned to death in the Paris inquisition. Those who witnessed her execution were, according to the chronicler, moved to tears at her "nobility and devotion" in the face of death.

The Beguines

The inquisition document calls Marguerite a "Beguine." Beguines were a semi-lay, semi-religious movement, mostly of women, who took no regular vows but sought to live the Gospel outside monastery walls—some in private homes, some in communal arrangements —partly in response to the growing corruption of the clergy. They supported themselves through spinning, weaving, and caring for the sick. Marguerite may have been a solitary Beguine or come from a Beguinage community in northern France. Because of lack of canonical approval, Beguines increasingly stirred suspicion by their lay preaching in vernacular languages. In 1274, at the Council of Lyons, Beguines were accused of reading and interpreting the Scriptures on street corners. That was what Marguerite's treatise states as its explicit mission, to teach and nurture "The Little Church"! There could hardly have been any purpose more irritating to these learned men of the academy and hierarchy. In addition, Marguerite apparently had no clerical patron to speak for her, thus increasing her marginality and vulnerability. Sadly, Marguerite's lack of support extended even to the Beguines, as she confesses in a telling piece of poetry:

Beguines say I err, priests, clerics and Preachers,
Augustinians, Carmelites, and the Friars Minor,
Because I wrote about the being of the one purified
    by Love.

(p. 122)

SYNOPSIS

Marguerite's apophatic mysticism

What was it in her mystical doctrine that Marguerite was willing
to go to her death to defend? Marguerite's mysticism has much in
common with the apophatic mysticism of the fifth-century Syrian
monk, Pseudo-Dionysius. This theologian-monk, mistakenly thought
to be a follower of St. Paul, said that God was beyond anything we
can know, beyond being itself. When Marguerite appropriates this
lofty teaching, she uses familiar literary devices of her day: themes
of courtly love involving a king's daughter who, when she hears of
King Alexander, takes up the mirror—the gift of her Lover, which is
her book and a reflection of his love. At the end of the Prologue, Love
itself speaks, and an allegorical dialogue primarily among Love, the
Soul, and Reason ensues.

Besides the Dionysian mystical tradition, her treatise draws on the
Beguine tradition of God as Love, a cosmic principle of Goodness
overflowing all boundaries. The response to this Love is a gradual
simplification or "annihilation," what we might call "egolessness,"
based in "knowing nothing" and "willing nothing." What shows up
in Marguerite's mirror is the utterly transparent soul, simplified and
brought to nothing. In a move of radical self-negation, she allows
herself to be transformed in the service not of anything penultimate,
even the virtues, but of the ultimate Love itself. Marguerite's consistent gaze upon and consequent identity with this Source, often
called the Trinity, where she was before she was created, is the distinguishing mark of her treatise. Willing-Nothing becomes in
Marguerite a positive act whose ultimate effect is transformation into
the nothingness and all of God.

Marguerite's text is, with the possible exception of the writings
of Meister Eckhart, the most forcefully apophatic in the history of

Christian theology. That is, it is full of a negative theology that negates what can be spoken about God in order to leave the way open for deeper affirmations, which in this text become God's (actually Love's) "speech." To know God for Marguerite is to go by way of knowing nothing, willing nothing, and ultimately becoming nothing in order to "know" the nothingness of God. Even to will the will of God speaks of a too conventional piety for Marguerite. When Marguerite prescribes leaving behind the virtues, it sounds antinomian (lawless), but for her it is leaving behind self-will. How well Marguerite discovered what Thérèse of Lisieux was to say seven centuries later: "the weaker one is without desires or virtues, the more suited one is for the workings of this consuming and transforming Love." No socially constructed set of virtues could replace the self called into being by God. Paradoxically, the naughting of self-will becomes the deep inner freedom to become love.

The dialogue of reason and love

The work is divided into about 140 "chapters," most of which are less than a page long. The treatise acts like a spiritual handbook as Love explores with the Soul the early stages of seven states of being. In the dialogue between Reason and Love, Reason breaks in repeatedly to object, "For God's sake, Love, what does this mean, what you have said?" Love has to explain to Reason that it is no longer the Soul's will which wills, even to will the will of God, but only the will of God that wills in her. Such paradoxes and annihilations of intellectual understanding baffle the rational mind until finally Reason expires and leaves the dialogue to Love and the Soul. Reason and the Virtues—rationalism and moralism—are moved by the fear of hell and Judgment Day, but Love has freed the Soul from fear. The annihilated soul is the liberated soul. As self-will disappears, the Soul begins to experience equanimity with regard to shame and honor, poverty and wealth, love and hate, even hell and paradise!

> Whoever would ask such free Souls, sure and peaceful, if they would want to be in purgatory, they would say no; or if they would want to be certain of their salvation in this life, they would say no; or if they would want to be in paradise, they would say no. But then with what would they will it? They no longer possess any will,

and if they would desire anything, they would separate themselves from Love.

(p. 86)

Although such statements must have shocked Marguerite's inquisitors, we can find them in the writings of other mystics and even of the saints.

The opposition within the text had prophetic consequences for Marguerite's fate. In her treatise's allegorical dialogue between Reason and Love, and therefore between the Little Church and the Great Church, she anticipates the failure of communication between these theological universes that she will fatally undergo in her inquisition.

Marguerite's way of seven stages

In chapter 118, Marguerite lays out the itinerary of the seven stages of her mystical journey. The Soul begins with the Holy Church's commandments (the two great commandments of love of God and neighbor), a point of departure that should give the lie to those who call this work antinomian. In the second state, Love invites God's special lovers to the evangelical counsels exemplified by Christ. In the third stage, the Soul does the works of perfection, but becomes attached to them in a spasm of activist zeal. Realizing her attachment, she abstains from these works which keep the will alive. This "pulverizing" of the self is in order to "enlarge the place where Love will want to be" (p. 118). The soul then passes into the fourth state's embrace of union, marked by meditation and its delights. These consolations make her proud and deceive her into thinking it is the highest gift God can give here below. Marguerite exploits the language of the courtly love poets, and Beguine love-mysticism, in order to subvert it. The soul passes beyond this state, thereby offering a subtle critique of its affective mysticism. In the fifth state, delivered from her own will, she stands in the Divine Light, seeing "what God is, that God IS" from whom all things are and she is not.

By God's expanding light, she is shown that she must place her will in the place from which it came, in God. Such a gift transforms her into Love itself. Now the soul has become nothing and yet everything, finding herself in an abyss so great that there is no beginning or measure or end. At this lowest depth, viewing her own wretchedness, she sees the true Sun of highest goodness, which draws her into Divine Goodness as mistress. Her fall is perfect, for it humbles the once prideful spirit blinded by feelings of love at the heights of contemplation of the fourth state. But there is still duality in this state, and so the soul goes into the sixth state where she sees neither God nor herself, but God sees God in her. At this point, the soul is free and pure and clear but not yet glorified; for that will come only when the soul leaves the body in the seventh state.

Was Marguerite a heretic?

The inquisition documents contain only two articles that were presented to the twenty-one theologians assembled at Paris:

1. That the annihilated soul takes leave of the virtues nor is any longer in their service, because it does not have them to its use, but the virtues obey the soul.
2. That such a soul does not care for the consolations of God nor for God's gifts, nor ought it to care nor can it, because all its intention is toward God, and thus its intention toward God would be impeded.

The anonymous chronicler writing for the king adds another article:

3. That the annihilated soul in love gives to nature all that it desires without remorse of conscience.

Juxtaposed to this last supposed antinomian statement in the text are the words: "but such nature is so well ordained by transformation of unity of Love, to which the will of this Soul is conjoined, that nature asks nothing which is forbidden" (p. 9). In the minds of the inquisitors the main objections to Marguerite's book were its heretical rejection of the system of mediation offered by the institutional church and its antinomianism. That the soul would "take leave of the virtues" sounded heretical to these theologians, who, as Marguerite's book predicted, would have used the language of reason. But in her total schema, aiming only at achieving certain virtues would have seemed a theology of works superseded by her more holistic way of Love, the "mistress of the virtues." In light of the actual text, it appears that Marguerite was in part judged heretical because of her insubordination in the face of the church she considered "lesser." In the year immediately following Marguerite's death, the Council of Vienne in a papal bull titled *Ad nostrum* condemned eight "Errors of Beghards [the men] and Beguines about the state of perfection," several of which sound remarkably like the articles taken from Marguerite's work.

INFLUENCE

One person who not only understood Marguerite but almost certainly was influenced by her was Meister Eckhart. Eckhart, who shared the house of Dominican preachers with Marguerite's inquisitor general, William, just two years after her death, would have had access to her text there. It is now generally agreed that Eckhart's Sermon 52, on poverty of spirit, shows dependence on Marguerite's text. In Eckhart's sermon, he describes a truly poor person who wants nothing, knows nothing, and has nothing. The person who wants nothing has no attachment to penances or other external exercises, a frequent theme throughout Eckhart's work as in Marguerite's. Like Marguerite, Eckhart goes beyond the well-intentioned project of willing to do the will of God, to being "as free of his own created will as he was when he did not exist." Both Marguerite and Eckhart point daringly to a return to the Source or Ground of Being where they once were; in her words, "For God is and she is not. Then she is stripped naked of all things, for now she is without being, there where she had being before she might be" (p. 135). Such a person knows nothing, for that very knowledge introduces the duality of subject and object, as well as the reduction of the object to the knowing subject. Eckhart's poverty of spirit entails an even greater degree of poverty, in which a person has nothing, not even a place for God. Before, he had said that a person should become a place for God, but now, he reverses himself, under what many believe is Marguerite's influence, and declares that God should be his own place.

If Marguerite's influence on this late sermon of Eckhart's is profound, the influence of Marguerite's condemned book was amazingly widespread even in her lifetime. Disengaged from its author, Marguerite's book lived on in anonymous editions, finding its way into orthodox centers such as Benedictine monasteries and the convent of the Magdalenes at Orléans. An early translation was made into Middle English by a Carthusian with the initials "M.N." who added his glosses to passages he thought particularly controversial. It even passed for the work of the Dutch mystic Jan Ruysbroeck, for a time. Margaret, Queen of Navarre (1492–1539), sister of the king of France, was deeply influenced by the text and wrote poems proclaiming that "the soul that calls on you/ By this your name [Far-Near], for my choice, better speaks / Than all the teachers who have labored long/ In study." The manuscript continued to be copied and translated from its original Old French into Latin, Italian, and Middle English, even into the twentieth century, without attribution to its condemned author, until in 1965 Romana Guarnieri published the text now tied to the process of inquisition against Marguerite Porete.

READING THE TEXT TODAY

Marguerite's text continues to pose as many difficulties today as it did when first presented to the ecclesiastical authorities and theologians of her day. But since the text has been reconnected to its author only in the last fifty years, modern scholarship has shown intense interest in it, opening it to new interpretations and appreciations. Yet, the text is transgressive, crossing the boundaries of what it was safe to say about the church in her day, and what language is capable of saying about God. In assessing its importance for contemporary readers, it may be best to begin with the caveat of Godfrey of Fountains who advised that not many should see it, for "they might leave their own work and follow this teaching . . . for it is made of a spirit so strong and so knowing that there are but few such or none at all." Marguerite's text offers the added difficulty of being fairly unsystematic, circling round its subject again and again. Although the dialogue form keeps it lively and engaging, its very opacity and esoteric nature may put modern readers off.

The text today

Yet, despite these warnings, this age may be better attuned to hear the message of the book than when uncompromising theological orthodoxy institutionalized in the Inquisition ruled the day. Marguerite's downright rejection of reason as the dominant force of the person and the institutional church, and her supplanting of it by an ontology of love, constitutes a powerful corrective in this time as well as hers. Her preaching of a radical divestment not only of possessions but of the possessiveness that grasps after them, speaks to the need of a non-consumerist ethic for the twenty-first century. Marguerite's way of radical simplicity, of a soul so transparent that it mirrors only God, is a way of letting God be God in all God's wondrous capacity.

Marguerite's mystical dialectic of being and nothingness may at first seem austere. But for those looking East to find authentic mystical experience, her voice points to an experience of nonduality, an identity of self and Other, that is nearly unique in the West. Hers is not a God who has been objectified, externalized, and pushed to the outskirts as a "God-of-the-gaps" until faith in such a God finally collapses. Marguerite teaches the bedrock basics of the spiritual life. In Christian theological terms, her seven stages encompass the paschal mystery played out in the interior life of the soul. Marguerite's annihilation and transformation into Love may be compared with Thérèse of Lisieux's offering of herself as a holocaust to God's infinite love and mercy. Her path of annihilation opens onto the presence and affirmation of God everywhere in the world. From the fall into the nothingness of God issues a way into the world that is free of self-preoccupation and willfulness.

The Mirror of Simple Souls may have arrived at a time in the history of spirituality when people who are post-Reformation, post-Enlightenment, and post-Vatican II are more ready to hear it. Marguerite's rejection of external systems of mediation—penances, fasting, even the sacraments—can be viewed more sympathetically today than it was by her accusers. The confrontation between reason and love that she dramatized goes on in many arenas in the twenty-first century, as in the sometimes contentious relationship between science and religion. Given the emphasis on the priesthood of all believers in the documents of Vatican II, Marguerite's lay, women-centered, vernacular mysticism can be met with far more interest and respect, even if the voices of women as teachers and nurturers of the institutional church are still somewhat suspect.

Her "woman's way"

The postmodern age is far more receptive to a spirituality unencumbered with excessive affectivity and self-inflicted bodily suffering. Marguerite eschews aspects of embodied spirituality usually associated with medieval women; there are no tears of compunction, no sexual metaphors for the ecstatic relation to God, no bodily suffering as means of identification with the humanity of Christ. Her apophatic mysticism does not at first resemble the physicality of devotion to the eucharistic and ascetic piety of many women mystics. Transubstantiation takes place not in the sacrament of the altar but in inner reality, in being "brought to nothing" so that Love can take its place. Unlike several women who went before her, most notably Hildegard of Bingen, Marguerite's spirituality is not dependent on a visionary impulse, making it more accessible to a postmodern age skeptical about visions. Marguerite deconstructs anything that could stand between herself and God—from the arid theology of the Schools, to the moralizing of the sermonizers, to even the Beguines' love-mysticism. Her mysticism is almost Zen-like in its objection to all kinds of "means." And yet she spoke as a woman to women and peopled her text with an endless array of female characters.

Contemplation in action

Even within her limited circumstances, as an uncredentialed woman denied access to university education or theological training and living on the margins, Marguerite made her mystical way available to others. As a Beguine, her availability to her own age, straddling secular and sacred worlds, carries over more readily to contemporary lifestyles than a cloistered spirituality. The impossible desire she had to teach the overly rationalist church about love, her "apostolate," could be realized today through her text. Marguerite's simple souls turn the world upside down, making up the church of God's true lovers whose task it is to teach and nurture the "little church." Her message for "actives and contemplatives" can reach both the activists in this hyperactive age so in need of the contemplative moment and the contemplative seekers—those she called "sad souls"—in need of encouragement on the path.

As one who found herself outside the bounds of the establishment, Marguerite in her sympathies and antipathies may find an echo in the twenty-first century among those outsiders to the ecclesial establishment who call themselves "spiritual but not religious." Marguerite gives voice to those marginalized and excluded from the centers of power whether by reason of their gender or sexual orientation or other form of alienation. Marguerite's own life, her courageous silence before her inquisitors, and her refusal to recant her teaching of love, may be the clearest mirror of a simple soul.

TRANSLATIONS

Porete, Marguerite (1993) *The Mirror of Simple Souls,* trans. E.L. Babinsky, New York: Paulist Press, with an introduction that sets Marguerite's work in the context of the Beguines in France, explores events leading to her trial, and discusses the nature of the soul and its transformation and union with its source in the Trinity.

Porette, Margaret (1999) *The Mirror of Simple Souls.* trans. E. Colledge, J.C. Marler, and J. Grant, Notre Dame, IN: University of Notre Dame Press.

FURTHER READING

McGinn, B. (ed.) (1994) *Meister Eckhart and the Beguine Mystics: Hadewijch of Brabant, Mechthild of Magdeburg, and Marguerite Porete,* New York: Continuum, contains excellent essays on Eckhart's relationship to the Beguines in the context of a developing vernacular theology.

Murk-Jansen, S. (1998) *Brides in the Desert: the spirituality of the Beguines,* Maryknoll, NY: Orbis, treats the origins and development of the Beguine movement and key images in Beguine spirituality.

Robinson, J.M. (2001) *Nobility and Annihilation in Marguerite Porete's Mirror of Simple Souls.* Albany: State University of New York, addresses themes such as the Trinitarian origins of the soul and the spiritual nobility of souls called to union with God.

12

GREGORY PALAMAS
(1296–1359)

Triads in Defense of the Holy Hesychasts

JOHN A. McGUCKIN

St. Gregory Palamas is a Byzantine paradox. Writing as a monk who spent much of his life withdrawn in solitude and rustic contemplation, his theological works are redolent with gracious light and divine illumination. Yet he was also one of the figures of the early fourteenth century around whom an endless stream of controversy flowed, like a river in torrent. His life focused on hesychasm (quiet retirement for prayer), but his career in court and palace involved him in all manner of intrigue, and even in civil war. Rival claimants to the throne used him as a theological symbol for and against their claims. Patriarchs of Constantinople heaped honors upon him but also condemned his teachings and had him thrown into prison. His life of ups and downs reads like a historical romance. He remains a figure of the Eastern Christian tradition who exquisitely bridges theology and spirituality, refusing to allow them to go their separate ways to the detriment of each. He is regarded by the Eastern Orthodox today as someone who combines fidelity to the tradition with the resilience necessary to apply that ancient tradition in vigorous new directions (as a "sign of contradiction" to the spirit of the age if necessary), but always with an open and generous spirit of engagement with his contemporary society.

AUTHOR AND AUDIENCE

St. Gregory Palamas was born into a high aristocratic family in Constantinople in 1296. He studied in a curriculum shaped heavily by Aristotelian principles and governed by the formal disciplines of rhetoric, physics, and logic. But as a young adult Gregory turned his back on political life and took the habit of a monk, much impressed by the presence in Constantinople of monks from the great monastic colony of Mount Athos. He studied the spiritual theologians at the capital under the guidance of Theoleptos the Metropolitan of Philadelphia, and shortly afterwards, in 1316, decided to go to live on Athos himself.

Here the young Gregory studied for three more years under the spiritual master Nikodemos while he himself lived the cenobitic (or community-based) monastic life at Vatopedi monastery. After that he spent three years at the Great Lavra monastery. In 1322, when Gregory was twenty-six years of age, he adopted a stricter monastic lifestyle of solitude, asceticism, and mystical prayer—the lifestyle of a "hesychast." In 1325 this existence was disrupted, however, by the increasing pirate raids on Athos that were harrying the smaller monasteries, and so Palamas left to study for a short time at Thessaloniki.

In 1326 Palamas was ordained a priest and withdrew for a while to a hermitage at Berrhoea, where he followed the classical hesychastic way of life: five days dedicated to silence and interior prayer, and the weekends given over to liturgical celebration in the company of a monastic community. Five years later he returned to Mount Athos and continued the solitary life, though he also assumed priestly duties at the Great Lavra. There in 1334 he wrote a *Life of St. Peter the Athonite* in which he argued that Athos had originally been a series of small hermitages, only later built up into larger foundations by St. Athanasios the Athonite. What posed at first glance like a hagiography contained a political message about who had the right to represent the essence of Athonite monasticism: coenobites whose spirituality was built around a regular cycle of church offices and manual labor, or hesychasts given over more to solitude and interior prayer?

It was at this time that an Italo-Byzantine monk called Barlaam of Calabria crossed Gregory's path. Barlaam was chief among a small set of Byzantine theologian-philosophers bent on developing Eastern

Christian thought in a certain pro-Western direction. Barlaam was a devoted student of philosophical method and a court theologian serving as ecumenical liaison officer for Emperor Andronikos III and Patriarch John Kalekas. He was not uncritical of the West, having written several treatises criticizing papal governance theory and Latin doctrine known as the Filioque, which declared that the Holy Spirit proceeds from the Son as well as the Father .

Barlaam argued that since God was unknown and unknowable in his essence, no theological term could ever properly describe him. All experience was derived from sensory material media (here he showed a heavy reliance on Aristotle) and so the human experience of God must by definition be material, and therefore "not God." Humans ought not to despair of having a useful understanding of God, but they should know that such a thing would be built up cumulatively on the basis of an expanding intellectual culture. In the end, all experience and knowledge of God will be merely symbolic and tentative. In the case of ecumenical debate between East and West, the precise words for or against the Filioque were perhaps not so important, since all theological utterances were deficient anyway. Nevertheless, Barlaam concluded, in such cases one ought to rely on patristic precedent and scriptural authorities, so the Latins ought not to insist on the Filioque. Even though this was being packaged as a form of theological ecumenism, Gregory Palamas saw through it immediately for what it implied on the wider front.

Gregory's first controversial work against Barlaam was *Apodeictic Treatises on the Procession of the Holy Spirit*. In his embarrassment at having his semi-official ecumenism attacked, Barlaam decided to turn his guns on the monks with heavy sarcastic force. He caricatured his Athonite opponents as ignorant rustics who wanted to hide their intellectual smallness under a cloak of obscurantist appeals to mysticism. The monks prayed with a fervent interiority, saying that they could even on occasions "see" the divine light with their bodily eyes. This was nonsense, Barlaam argued, since if they saw a light at all it had to be a material one, and therefore not God. So he derided the hesychastic movement as a group of *omphalopsychoi* ("psychic navel-gazers"). When the Athonites formally asked Gregory to defend their honor and their cause, he entered the controversy with new force.

Palamas's theological argument on behalf of what would later come to be called "Hesychasm" or "Palamism" was more than simply a rebuttal of Barlaam's insult to the monks. Convinced that the whole coherence of Christian truth was at stake, he insisted that it is possible for a disciple to be graced with an authentic experience of God, not merely a symbolic or deficient experience. In the same way as the Incarnate Lord was not a defective example of one of the persons of the Holy Trinity, so too the vision of the divine light that the saints enjoyed in deepest levels of prayer was nothing less than a real and authentic communication with the divine presence. Admittedly, Palamas said, God as he is in and to himself, his interior Being, is so transcendent that the divine essence (*ousia*) is unapproachable, incommunicable, and unknowable. But this does not mean that God is absent. God's infinity also means that he is infinitely approachable. All human beings are fashioned in such a way that the structure of their ontology is patterned after God's very image. This level and action of God's presence is the immanence of his divine energies (*energeia*) in the cosmos. These energies are fully and authentically divine, so they are properly called the "uncreated energies" of God. Through them humans have direct experience of God himself in his salvific and creative outreach—not according to his essence, assuredly, but an experience of God himself nonetheless. In the deepest levels of their atomic structure, wherein they are composed in being by God's energy, humans are thus made divine sacraments: mysteries and miracles of grace, never simply "material" things.

Using St. Gregory of Nyssa, Palamas argued that even in his infinite transcendence God makes souls capable of an infinite longing for God, a reaching out to him (*epektasis*) that can never be fulfilled in this life but will go on in the next, almost like the falling of a created soul endlessly into the everlasting abyss of God's love. This endless *epektasis* should not be taken as a radical separation of the finite creature from an infinite God but rather as the deepest communion of intimacy, for the endless fall into God is the only real experience possible of communion in infinite being. This immortal salvation in the light of God's eternity happens even here on earth, and will continue from age to age.

After his *Apodeictic Treatises*, Palamas wrote what would become his major and most famous work: *Triads in Defense of the Holy Hesychasts*. Then in 1340 he organized the Athonite monks to issue a public manifesto of spiritual theology (the *Hagioritic Tome*) and had it signed by the Athonite leaders. The war of theologies was then in full swing and had to be addressed at the capital. Emperor Andronikos III and Patriarch John Kalekas summoned a local synod at Constantinople in June 1341 where Barlaam was made to climb down and Palamas was recognized as an authentic spokesperson for Orthodox theology. Barlaam left Byzantium for residence in Italy, where the erstwhile opponent of Latin thought swallowed enough of his objections to be appointed bishop by the pope in the year following.

Before the council of 1341 could be officially ratified by the Emperor, however, Andronikos III died, and a civil war broke out in Byzantium. In its course Patriarch John encouraged Gregory Akyndinos (someone censured along with Barlaam in the council of 1341) to renew the attack on Gregory Palamas's orthodoxy. For many years to come scholastic thinkers (of whom there were many in fourteenth century Byzantium) would look upon Palamas's victory as a defeat of scientific rationalism by the monastic party, and were far from happy with it.

In 1342 Palamas was arrested at Constantinople on a charge of political treason and held in prison. In 1344 he was condemned as a false theologian and deposed by the patriarch's synodical court. Eventually, however, early in 1347, Palamas was released and honored by the new emperor and his circle. Gregory's close friends and disciples Isidore, Kallistos, and Philotheos became the next three patriarchs of the capital in succession. The last of these would posthumously canonize Gregory and compose his life, as well as the liturgical offices to commemorate his memory in the church.

In May 1347 Gregory was appointed as archbishop of Thessaloniki, although the city was still held by resistance forces from the civil war and it was three years before he could take up residence there. After 1352 Gregory's health began to fail, and most of his writings touch upon the theme of mortality. While on a sea journey to Tenedos in 1354 he was captured by pirates, spending a year in captivity in Asia Minor. On November 14, 1359 he died and was celebrated almost immediately at Constantinople, Athos, and Thessaloniki as a saint. His disciple Philotheos, then patriarch of Constantinople, canonized him in 1368. His feast was also celebrated on the Second Sunday of Great Lent as a reminder that his doctrine was not simply that of an individual, but that of the whole Eastern Church.

SYNOPSIS

The *Triads in Defense of the Holy Hesychasts* (1337–41) was given this name by Philotheos because it comprises a series of three sets of three treatises on the central arguments of St. Gregory's theology. In this work, which is very much dependent on the two great patristic theologians of antiquity, St. Gregory the Theologian and St. Maximus the Confessor, Palamas states all his major ideas.

Apophatic theology

These discourses are a work which celebrates what has come to be known as apophatic theology: an approach to the experience of the divine that lays its stress on what cannot be known about God, rather than on what can be affirmed by the application of reason and experience. Apophaticism literally means a "turning away from speech" and implies that experience of the divine in quiet stillness (hesychasm) is far more revelatory than deductive logic. In Gregory's hands in the *Triads*, however, apophaticism is expounded in a more positive light than it had traditionally been approached.

The foundations for his doctrine lay in St. Gregory of Nazianzus's and St. Gregory of Nyssa's attack on the Eunomian heresy in the fourth century, when in the face of a strict rationalist type of deductive theology, they had emphasized that God in his own being is utterly transcendent and unknowable. In Palamas's argument with Barlaam, this had been used against him in the argument that if all theology was discourse about the unknowable God it was, at best, simply symbolic exchange about a reality humans could not immediately experience or comprehend. However, in defending the principle of the nearness of God, and the direct immediacy of experience of him, Gregory did not abandon the apophatic method but rather applied it more paradoxically, answering Barlaam's syllogistic way of "reasoning around" the idea of transcendence with this stunning insight: "God is not only above all knowing, He is, of course, above all unknowing too" (1.3.4).

In other words, the argument that, as transcendent, God is un-experienceable in reality, fails to take into account his divine immanence as Lord of creation. The glory of the Creator is that he is unapproachable in his own being but reaches out to humanity in his creative and revelatory energies of love. To that extent he is accessible in his transcendence (for humans understand the majesty of God and his unapproachability by their real experience of him) and also transcendent in his accessibility (for even in his incarnation he remains the God of wonders and mysteries, far more inaccessible in the humility of his passion than any Hellenist ever thought the high god of the Platonists would be in his majesty).

Essence and energies

In the *Triads*, Gregory affirms strongly that God is unapproachable in his essence but experienced in his energies. There is a real distinction between the essence and the energies, but they are not radically separated. The being of God is divine essence (*ousia*), but so too the energies of God's outreach to the world (the force of creation and creative sustenance of all being, the force of grace that deifies and saves humankind and reveals the Godhead to the disciple) are all divine forces too. They are the "uncreated energies" of God. Humans do not need to worry so much about how to find those energies since the energies find them. The saving divine presence renders persons into transfigured beings who pass from being mere mortal flesh into the mystery of Christ's deification of the human race through the incarnation. As divine energies they are not just external operations of God, but the Presence itself in its active salvific role.

The *Triads*, therefore, refute a chief implication that Gregory deduced from Barlaam's argument. For Palamas insists that experience of the divine energies is the direct experience of God in the soul, not a merely symbolic experience (1.115.4). When Barlaam laughed at the possibility of a claim that anyone praying (saint or sinner) could ever "see" God, or "feel" God in their bodily condition, Gregory said that this was the entire point of prayer: to meet God in the here and now of flesh, the meeting ground which God himself had appointed for humanity in his decision to become incarnate. To this extent all of Palamas's theological thought was built up out of the Christ-mysticism of the Ecumenical Councils. He was well aware of this from the beginning and knew his system was fundamentally a sophisticated re-statement of ancient patristic conciliarism (1.193.4–18).

Transfiguration on Mount Thabor

In the third of the *Triads*, Gregory turns to express this doctrine in what would become for him a determinative image: that of the disciples being illuminated with unearthly radiance when they witnessed the effulgence of divine glory on Mount Thabor (Mk 9:2–8). The radiance emitted from Christ was the divine glory in itself. Yet it streamed in visible form, from Christ's material, yet divinized, body. The disciples saw with their eyes the divine energy which cannot be seen with human eyes alone, because their eyes were also illumined with divine grace to receive the revelation that began in the flesh and ended in the very heart of God himself. What this means for Gregory is not simply a wonderful reflection on the Incarnation of God (though it is this of course) but more so a whole program of theology in which he insists that to separate out concepts such as "natural" and "graced" in the manner of much of Western theology from the time of Augustine onwards, was a mistaken approach, one which scholasticism compounded in its relentless categorization of theological thought. All the world is suffused with the divine presence: all is graced. There is nothing in it, least of all the radiant sacrament of God which is the human being, that can be called "merely natural."

INFLUENCE

St. Gregory Palamas always had a "school." First of all it was the circle of high political laymen and clergy gathered around him in the court of John Kantakouzenos. As they rose to prominence under John, they were able to occupy the highest offices of the church and ensure that Gregory's theology (which was seen as the common theology of the monastic heritage) would hold very strong sway over Eastern Christianity. At times of crisis, when the Eastern Church felt hemmed in from the East by the political domination of Islam, and from the West by the more subtle intellectual pressure of the Latin Church (eventually both Catholic and Protestant), Orthodox theologians remembered Gregory Palamas.

In the fourteenth century the theologian Nicholas Cabasilas applied hesychast principles to the liturgy of the church and helped effect a change away from the civic context of ceremonial worship favored in confident imperial times, toward a liturgical appreciation that was mystical and highly charged with eschatological symbolism, more fitting for the long centuries of oppression when the church was increasingly carried on the backs of monastics and hermits.

In the seventeenth century when the weakened Byzantine Church was under the yoke of the Turks and influenced by strong Latinizing movements, leading churchmen turned once again to the example and the texts of St. Gregory. One such example is the reaction that occurred after the Protestantizing efforts of Patriarch Cyril Lukaris and the Latinizing trends emanating from the school of Kiev. Patriarch Dositheos of Jerusalem in 1693 sent the works of Palamas to Moscow to be translated into Russian for the guidance of the Orthodox. This encouraged a great hesychastic movement in the Slavic churches which endures to this day. It produced magnificent artists who were hesychastic, such as Theophan the Greek and St. Andrei Rublev, and a whole school of Russian saints such as St. Sergey of Radonezh, St. Seraphim of Sarov, and the Optina hermits, to name only a few.

In the eighteenth century in Greece, St. Nicodemus of Athos published the great collection of hesychastic texts called the *Philokalia*, which contained important spiritual works of Gregory. St. Paisy Velichovsky in Romania and the Russian bishop Theophan the Recluse energetically spread this Philokalic tradition around the Orthodox world, using it to effect a great spiritual renovation that has lasted into modern times. Father John Meyendorff has argued that Palamas's influence is responsible for turning the Orthodox church strongly toward mystical awareness of the person—a factor that would work to its advantage in having to face more than six hundred years of subjugation under Islam, or murderous communists who killed Orthodox spiritual leaders, closed or burned schools, and suppressed normal intellectual life and culture in Eastern Christianity.

READING THE TEXT TODAY

Theology as ascetic exercise

For Palamas, humanity is not simply a mortal creature struggling like a worm in the dirt of a vast and overwhelming cosmos; the human person is a mortal creature in transit to immortality, a creature in the process of ongoing deification in Christ. Prayer is thus the most powerful medium of theological reflection, the source of intuition of the Spirit's charisms and the ever-active presence of God within. A scholastic or intellectualist theology divorced from mystical experience, therefore, is not worth the paper it is printed on. All who represent authentic theological teaching in the church are expected first and foremost to live out their teachings and to embody doctrine in a praxis that is illumined by Christian discipleship. Palamite theology is, above all, an ascetic exercise.

Palamas is not arguing that the saintly theologian ought to be dim obscurantist or reject secular learning. He is objecting to the emerging preponderance of scholastic theory (which he thought to be especially witnessed in Thomism) that theology ought to afford philosophy a high value in determining true thought about God, since philosophy was the handmaid of theology. Palamas saw Greek philosophy as a wandering and frequently erroneous guide, imbued with paganism and humanistic self-referentialism. It needed to be baptized in Christ before it could illuminate anything at all about the life of God. His resistance to Barlaam is not a fight of mysticism against rationality, but a more precise fight among the learned as to the proper role of "natural theology." For Palamas, there is no such thing as "natural theology" in distinction from "revealed theology." All of cosmic being is a sacramental revelation, and all is full of the potentiality of the revelation of the divine presence that holds it in being.

Hesychasm and the Jesus Prayer

At the popular level, the subtlety of his literary works yielded to the image of Palamas as a great defender of the hesychastic tradition of the use of bodily methods of quiet interior meditation, especially using the repeated invocation of the Jesus Prayer ("Lord Jesus Christ, Son of God, have mercy on me") to still the inner mind into receptivity of the divine name and presence within it. Hesychasm came and existed before Palamas, and would remain long after him. What St. Gregory really contributed was not so much a new system of Orthodox theology as a putting-together of all the patristic elements to make a radical and extensive defense of monastic ascetical and mystical practices. This would have a long and important after-life.

Holding theology and spirituality together

One of the unforeseen results of Palamas's work was the tendency to fix in Orthodox thought a kind of "oppositionism" to Western patterns of theology: designating the latter as "scholastic" and "rational," sometimes without really considering the matter fully. Some Orthodox today tend to cling to aspects of Palamas's theology taken out of context and use it as an identifying marker of "True Orthodoxy" in opposition to the West, and all things Western. Insofar as Palamism was, and remains, true Orthodoxy, it is surely better to follow St. Gregory's own wiser counsel by seeking to engage the intellectual issues at a deep and intelligent level. His insistence that theology could not be divorced from spirituality is a call for seriousness in the spiritual life, just as much as it is a call to accountability in the theological academy.

Authentic theology teaches how to live

People who live today, in an age when intellectual religious pundits offer so many different Gospels, might learn from Gregory Palamas that the truly wise and holy Christian disciple is one who draws upon the deep tradition of the fathers and martyrs to take pearls of doctrines that prove themselves in their practical application. The really authentic Christian theology is that which teaches men and women how to live: how to live freely, how to live joyfully, and above all how to live in the spirit of Christ who transfigures and sanctifies all that he touches by admitting a fragile humanity into the wondrously luminous presence of the living God who deifies his chosen. This is what St. Gregory stands for above all else. In this, his life and work remains a bright witness to the church.

TRANSLATION

Gregory Palamas (1973), *The Triads*, trans. N. Gendle, New York: Paulist Press.

FURTHER READING

McGuckin, J.A. (2001) *Standing in God's Holy Fire: the spiritual tradition of Byzantium,* Maryknoll, NY: Orbis, reviews Orthodox spirituality, providing material about the mystical thought of Palamas's patristic sources and monastic predecessors, as well as a general introduction to hesychasm.

Mantzarides, G.I. (1984) *Deification of Man: St. Gregory Palamas and the Orthodox tradition,* trans. L. Sherrard, Crestwood, NY: St. Vladimir's Seminary Press, offers a ground-breaking study with special reference to the notion of deification by grace.

Meyendorff, J. (1974) *Byzantine Theology: historical trends and doctrinal themes,* 2nd edn, New York: Fordham University Press, gives a review of the whole range of Orthodox thought, placing Palamas in the light of what went before and came after in Orthodox theology.

—— (1998) *St. Gregory Palamas and Orthodox Spirituality,* Crestwood, NY: St. Vladimir's Seminary Press, provides a study of Gregory Palamas in reference to the spiritual life by one of his most learned students in the twentieth century.

13

JULIAN OF NORWICH
(c.1342–c.1416)

Showings

ELISABETH KOENIG

In May of 1373, Julian was so ill that she and the people with her believed she was on the verge of death. Suddenly, Julian saw a vision at once "living and vivid and hideous and fearful and sweet and lovely": the face of Jesus on the cross began to bleed from under the crown of thorns. Given, as she says, "space and time" to contemplate this one image, Julian marveled as it gave rise to fifteen more "showings," or revelations, about God's love. These showings vividly impressed Julian with God's intimate presence to her, and their gentle power made her feel both loved and whole within herself and fundamentally at one with God and her fellow Christians. Years later she would write, "The love of God creates in us such a unity that when it is truly seen, no man [sic] can separate himself from another." Julian had understood that spiritual and social realities are not opposed to one another; at the profoundest level of spiritual integration, "we are all one in love."

Julian expresses surprise that after feeling death invade her body, she not only didn't die, but felt fully alive and well. Next, a spiritual event perhaps even more startling happened: Julian's habitual heavy experiences of judgment, shame, and blame miraculously were lifted, and a lifelong perplexity about how God could love human beings who are bent on thwarting his creative purposes began to be resolved. Julian saw clearly that the life of prayer and doctrines about God don't primarily concern truths that will be revealed in the hereafter. Rather, both theology and contemplation can lead to an experience of God in this life that is existentially real, even somatically felt.

In the twenty years after her visions and near-death experience, Julian faithfully worked on a book whose goal was to do more than merely tell people about this possibility. She seems to have wanted, not only to explicate the theological meaning of her visionary experience, but to do everything in her power actually to recreate it for her readers so that they, too, "might all see and know the same as I saw." The extraordinary popularity of her book in the late twentieth and early twenty-first centuries suggests that, for many readers, Julian succeeded. Although her writing is often challenging and difficult, it engagingly shows forth Julian's compassion and humility, her theological acumen and creative interpretation of scripture, and her profound spiritual psychology. Moreover, the book expresses each of these through a brilliant use of rhetoric, a painterly eye, and a measured sense of drama. The effect can lead to a re-patterning of consciousness, so that habits of thought that were obsessive, sinful, or unwell, become reshaped to conform to the gospel message that God has the most loving intentions for human beings, regardless of what they have done or their current state.

AUTHOR AND AUDIENCE

Julian's authorial voice is warm, self-aware, and welcoming of her readers. It is paradoxical, then, that this woman essentially has vanished from history, divulging only a few spare facts about herself in her book. Thus readers tend to make Julian into the kind of person they want and need, and scholars contend in fierce but necessarily speculative debates about who she was, when she wrote her short and long texts, whether she was "unlettered" as she claims to be or had achieved a high level of her erudition, and whether she was an anchoress before or only after her visions. Was Julian a nun, a mother, a feminist, a scholastic or monastic or vernacular theologian (she was the first woman to write in Middle English), an advocate of creation theology, or a universalist? Was she upper class, or an early proponent of democracy against feudalism? Was she a theologian interested in Christian doctrine, or a mystic who transcended all times and cultures? Passages from her book can be used to argue for and against most of these possibilities, but they don't necessarily clarify her true identity. Like a good spiritual director or psychotherapist, Julian abstains from speech about herself. Not even her baptismal name is known: she took on "Julian" almost certainly after she became an anchoress at St. Julian's Church in Norwich.

Two scribes of the fifteenth and seventeenth centuries wrote that Julian was a "recluse" and an "anchorite," and a recluse named Julian is mentioned in four wills of the period, although it is not proven in each case that Julian of Norwich was the intended beneficiary. Anchorites and anchoresses were people deemed by their bishop to have the vocation of being "immured" or locked for life into a cell, often affixed to a church. They spent their days in prayer and meditation, earned money with a little sewing, and offered spiritual counsel. Julian apparently had an excellent reputation. Margery Kempe, who dictated a book about her own spiritual adventures, came all the way from Bishop's Lynn (today's King's Lynn) to seek Julian's guidance. The Book of Margery Kempe gives the only contemporary acknowledgment of Julian's existence.

Julian states clearly that she writes out of a pastoral concern for her "fellow Christians," "lovers of God," and "those who will be saved." Some scholars speculate that Julian was part of a circle of laywomen and nuns who read devotional texts together and that she may have written for these women. Everyone around her would have been suffering the effects of the Black Plague which swept through Norwich three times during Julian's lifetime. Moreover, the Hundred Years War between England and France dragged on and on. Due in part to these and similar disruptive influences, the fourteenth and early fifteenth centuries knew a constant struggle over authority. At one time during the Great Schism of the church, there actually were three men claiming to be pope; peasants revolted against nobility they deemed unjust; and individuals such as Julian strived to find their own authoritative voices, while leaders in church, academe, society, and government sought to maintain the familiar hierarchical structures.

SYNOPSIS

Julian wrote a short text, apparently relatively soon after her visionary experience, and a long text some fifteen to twenty or even more years later. The differences between the two texts are considerable, and scholars have used historical-critical methods in their attempts to date precisely when they were written and to discuss the relationship between them. The most striking disparity is that the Long Text develops two pieces of related material that were not included in the Short Text because, as Julian says, she didn't yet understand them: the parable of a lord and his servant, and Julian's theology of God as mother. This synopsis will focus on the Long Text; however, the Short Text is a valuable work also worthy of attention.

The Long Text follows the natural divisions of the sixteen revelations, whose numbers are given as titles (e.g., "Second Revelation"), while chapters are numbered consecutively throughout the book. The initial chapter describes very briefly each of Julian's revelations. The first "revelation of love" is about Jesus Christ's "precious crowning of thorns," and here Julian indicates that somehow her visionary experience gave rise to theological meaning. She says that "in this [revelation] was *contained and specified* the blessed Trinity, with the Incarnation and the union between God and man's soul . . . in which all the revelations which follow are founded and connected." Much later, in her parable of the lord and his servant, Julian gives another hint about how this particular vision spelled out its spiritual meaning: "in this marvellous [sic] example I have teaching within me, as it were the beginning of an ABC, whereby I may have some understanding of our Lord's meaning." These two statements indicate that Julian's book is, in some sense, the result of interpreting the visions she saw in 1373. In addition, these remarks begin to instruct the reader about the nature of contemplative practice. Although Julian has many interests, and her constructive theological expertise has been the subject of much discussion in recent years, her book is arguably an extended training in the effects of long-term prayer.

Prayer

"Prayer unites the soul to God," Julian says in the fourteenth revelation. This showing develops Julian's teaching on prayer, its discussion opening out to her parable of the lord and his servant and the theology of the motherhood of God. These not only articulate

Julian's innovative theology, but also describe metaphorically what prayer is like through the vicissitudes of life. Both the parable, which Julian calls an "example," and the "God as mother" theology contain Julian's evolved understanding of God's love, and their meaning shines through everything she writes before and after them in the Long Text.

In an early discussion of prayer in chapter 6, Julian suggests that prayer involves learning "wisely to adhere to the goodness of God," and this she calls the highest form of prayer. Julian teaches that God's goodness meets human beings in places where they least likely would be looking for it. In an astonishing passage, she describes how God is present even to the process of bowel elimination! It is by means of contemplative prayer that souls learn to adhere to God, to be united to him, and God himself "will teach a soul how it should bear itself when it contemplates him." The parable of the lord and his servant and the theology of the motherhood of God are examples of this teaching. These deepened Julian's understanding of what can happen between a soul and God through many years of contemplative praying, and they both merit close reading and extended reflection.

The parable was given to Julian in a moment of great distress and perplexity. In order to keep on seeking God despite her failings, she had to know how God could love sinners who clearly were blame-worthy, especially when the church taught that they were destined for hell. Julian had cried out to Lord Jesus, "[H]ow shall I be comforted, who will tell me and teach me what I need to know, if I cannot at this time see it in you?" The answer came in the form of the parable: a lord sits in state and sends out his servant to do his will. The eager servant rushes out, loving to accomplish his lord's desire. But right away, he falls into a ditch and is greatly injured there. He can't get up or help himself at all. But the cause of his greatest grief is that he can't turn his face to look on his loving lord, who is very close to him. Later, Julian will be fascinated by the lord's "demeanour" [sic] and his "loving regard." He gazed constantly and lovingly on his servant with an expression of compassion mingled with pity, joy mingled with bliss, and this "merciful regard of his lovely countenance filled all the earth, and went down with Adam into hell, and by this continuing pity Adam was kept from endless death." (In the parable, the image of the servant conflates, as in a dream, meanings associated with Adam, Christ, and all humankind.)

Many years of contemplating the parable resulted in healing and integration for Julian. Moreover, her interpretative spelling out of its instruction led, in passages following not long after the parable, to her theology of God as mother. Both the servant as Christ and the mother as Christ do "the greatest labour and the hardest work there is" which is equivalent to the reformation and restoration of the human being following sin. Like the Lord with his loving face in the parable, the mother's response to sin is mercy and love.

Sin and evil

Because Julian so insistently emphasized God's love, she has sometimes been accused of not taking sin seriously enough. However, a close reading of her actual response to sin and evil reveals that, for her, they are horrible and, indeed, most grave. In a sleeping vision, Julian experiences the devil set at her throat, with his ugly, red face ("like a newly baked tile"), close to hers. She awakes more dead than alive.

Julian calls sin "the sharpest scourge" that can afflict a soul; "there is no more cruel hell than sin." It "belabours, breaks, and purges" the human being and makes one think that one is "not fit for anything but . . . to sink into hell." However, her visions taught Julian to look on sin from the perspective of God's all-embracing love. From this position, sin is *nothing*: "[sin] has no kind of substance, no share in being, nor can it be recognized except by the pain caused by it." This notwithstanding, Julian continues to mourn and sorrow over sin and wishes that God had prevented it before it happened. But Jesus tells her, "Sin is necessary, but all will be well, and all will be well, and every kind of thing will be well." Julian remains perplexed, and she is never given a rational solution to her problem. Instead, her visions, especially the parable and the "God as mother" theology, *show* her how God's judgments are different from human judgments. Sin is vile and very serious, but God "doesn't want us to withdraw our love from ourselves or our fellow Christians, anymore than he withdraws his love from us on account of sin." God looks on fallen people with the love Julian sees in the lord's face as he gazes at his servant, and with the love of the mother who tends her child even when she stumbles or is covered with mud.

Atonement

Julian's theological interest leads her to develop her "God as mother" theology in terms of the three persons of the Trinity, and throughout the book, especially in the parable, she reflects on the mystery of the incarnation. However, Julian was "taught that [she] should contemplate the glorious atonement," and this certainly is her greatest theological concern. The atoning is more pleasing and more honorable, "without comparison, than ever Adam's sin was harmful."

Julian's Middle English uses the word "one-ing" to convey her understanding of atonement. It means a profound joining together of that which sin has broken apart. Her discussion of it is rich and complex and has dimensions that clearly are objective and theological. But atonement is also personal and spiritual: Jesus works through his passion to unite human persons' "sensuality" with their "substance," meaning that everything in them that resists God is joined to everything in them that never departed from God. These long and highly nuanced discussions in Julian's book are valuable because they describe accurately and convincingly a process of integration that takes place over the course of a lifetime when a person spends extended periods in contemplative prayer.

INFLUENCE

So much medieval material has been lost that it is difficult to know whether or not Julian's book found a broad audience during her lifetime and the centuries after. Margery Kempe is the only contemporary who mentions her, but she says nothing about Julian's writing. Not until the seventeenth century, when a Carthusian copied part of it for members of his order, is there evidence that people read Julian's book. The ones who did read it appear primarily to have been monastics, not the laypeople Julian seems to have intended. Two exiled English Benedictine convents in France knew the work, and they apparently provided the copy text which became the basis of Serenus Cressy's printed edition of 1670. This edition prompted the bishop of Worcester, Edward Stillingfleet, who worried that Roman Catholicism would destroy the Reformation's achievements in England, to attack both the publisher and the work. He called it "the Blasphemous and senseless tittle tattle" of a "*Hysterical* Gossip." No Protestants read

Julian's book until the second half of the nineteenth century, although some Transcendentalists, including Henry David Thoreau, seem to have done so.

Three modernizations of the work appeared in the nineteenth century, but it wasn't until the early years of the twentieth century, when people became intensely interested in what they came to call "spirituality," that Julian's book reached a popular audience. Grace Warrack modernized one of the medieval texts, bringing Evelyn Underhill's attention to Julian, who appears in chapter 4 of Underhill's *Mysticism* as a "simple and deeply human English-woman." Underhill's friend Charles Williams believed Julian's work was second in importance only to Dante. In his effort to depict redemption, Williams ends his first novel, *War in Heaven*, with Julian's "All shall be well." C.S. Lewis read Julian, but seems not to have been attracted by her writing. T.S. Eliot, the High Church Anglican, saw Julian as important both as a representative of English tradition and someone with a transcendent vision. His poem "Little Gidding," the last of the *Four Quartets*, uses Julian's words "And all shall be well and / All manner of thing shall be well" to speak of a future redemption of time when "the fire and the rose are one." Julian appears in three novels: H.F.M. Prescott's *The Man on a Donkey* (1952), which is about the dissolution of the monasteries at the time of the English Reformation; Annie Dillard's *Holy the Firm* (1977), about the seven-year-old Julie Norwich whose face is burnt off in a plane crash; and Iris Murdoch's *Nuns and Soldiers* (1980), which tells the story of a nun who leaves London for the New World. In 1987, the American poet Denise Levertov published a sequence, "The Showings of Lady Julian of Norwich 1342–1416."

Today, Julian's work is immensely popular. Her cell in Norwich, which was destroyed in the seventeenth century, rebuilt, then bombed in 1943, and rebuilt again in 1953, has become a shrine that attracts many pilgrims from all over the world. "Julian groups" in England and the American Order of Julian of Norwich meet regularly to read Julian's works.

READING THE TEXT TODAY

Some folk speculate that the reason Julian's book wasn't popular in her own time is because it is so complex and difficult, and this problem remains today. Although people continue to read *Showings* for devotional purposes, no one who remains content with its affective dimensions alone will benefit fully from its offering. Julian's book is a work of constructive theology as well as an instruction in contemplative prayer. Its contributions to today's conversations about the theology of salvation (soteriology) and theology of the church (ecclesiology) have only begun to be plumbed. However, for some readers there will be resistances to overcome and problems to be worked through before they can benefit from Julian's richness.

For example, Julian's emphasis on affective and moral union with God still creates anxiety for those who suspect that all human speech about experience of God is contaminated by sin and the will to power. In addition, Julian's vision of Jesus's passion, especially with its all-pervasive flow of blood, can be off-putting to people who don't assent to her belief that genuine knowledge of God can come through an affective response to God's salvific work through Christ on the cross. Julian shared this belief with her contemporaries, who were reacting against scholasticism's excessive rationalism with a newfound joy in feeling and the rich contributions it can make to the spiritual life. But this is not good news for people today who may have suffered from overly sentimental, and manipulative, forms of piety.

Julian's theology of salvation

However, Julian's spirit is far closer to that of the Protestant Reformers than may be apparent on first reading of her book. Readers have expressed astonishment when they realized that Julian draws on the same texts from the Gospels, Paul, and Augustine that Calvin and Luther did, and for much the same reasons. Her goal is to remind the church of the gospel message that human beings are both sinners and saved at the same time. This simultaneity of sin and redemption is precisely the teaching, conveyed through imagery, of the parable of the lord and his servant, as it is the theme of her interpretive theological explorations.

Moreover, Julian's focus on Christ's passion deserves respect as the means by which she is working through a theology of salvation. Unlike some of her contemporaries (Richard Rolle, for instance), who were fascinated by the morbid details of Jesus's crucifixion and meditated on them in order to deepen remorse for sin, Julian, the artist-theologian, does something different. She uses the imagery of Christ's flowing blood to make God's love visible to people who already believed, as the church had taught them, that they were fallen and destined for hell. In Julian's literary and theological use of it, the blood is an image of the incarnation. She sees Christ's blood as identical to that in human bodies: "it is our own nature," she says, and, as such, it signals how intimately interior is God's love to human beings. But the blood also has an external trajectory, symbolizing the objective power of God's salvific act: plenteous "as the waters of the earth," Christ's blood descends down to hell where it "breaks its bonds, and delivered all that were there," then forcefully mounts up to heaven.

These passages only hint at the power and efficacy of Julian's ultimate theology of salvation. As the argument in *Showings* intensifies, it offers today's seekers a way out of the crisis of credibility that confounds contemporary discussions of soteriology. If people no longer accept accounts such as Anselm's satisfaction theory of Christ's death as the means by which God's honor is repaired after the damage done to it by human sin, they may find that Julian's description of the saving effect of Jesus's face provides them with an alternative that is at once wise, theologically and spiritually profound, and psychologically true.

When Julian represents Jesus's face and her beholding of it, she constructs an understanding of salvation that faithfully adheres to scripture and theological tradition and, at the same time, generates a fresh and innovative approach to soteriology. Julian's theology is conjoined with the persistent practice of contemplation that she advocates. In numerous places in *Showings*, before, during, and after the parable, what Julian sees when she contemplates is the Lord's face. And this sight compellingly mirrors back to her a felt experience of substantial personal identity that compensates for the annihilating blame and judgment of human beings. This is no illusion, but intensely real. It restored Julian to an integrity which she evidences in every sentence of her beautifully crafted book. Her early desire to offer readers the experience of being beloved of God so realistically that they "might all see and know the same as I saw" is fully met in Julian's descriptions of the Lord's face and its theological expansion.

The whole creation together in love

In Julian's view, salvation is never a matter of personal spirituality alone. Rather, individuals who are restored to wholeness find a greater depth of relation with all of creation, especially humankind. When Julian sees herself finally "bound to [God] in love as if everything which he has done he had done for me," she immediately moves to the understanding that "the love of God creates in us such a unity that when it is truly seen, no man [sic] can separate himself from another." This has far-reaching implications for ecclesiology because it essentially means that every Christian is the church in microcosm, and their union with God actually constitutes the church as ever-present reality. Nowhere is this more beautifully expressed than in Julian's culminating vision. After a night of struggle with the devil at her throat, she says, "our good Lord opened my spiritual eye, and showed me my soul in the midst of my heart." But this is no solipsistic image; more gloriously: "I saw the soul as wide as if it were an endless citadel, and also as if it were a blessed kingdom, and from the state which I saw in it, I understood that it is a fine city" (p. 313). Julian, the solitary, saw that her soul is preeminently social, and from such a vision of love, there was no turning back.

TRANSLATIONS

Julian of Norwich, *Showings* (1978) trans. E. Colledge and J. Walsh, Mahwah, NJ: Paulist Press.

FURTHER READING

Abbott, C. (1999) *Julian of Norwich: autobiography and theology*, Cambridge: D.S. Brewer, shows how Julian derives her authority from her experience.

Aers, D., and Staley, L. (1996) *The Powers of the Holy: religion, politics, and gender in late medieval English culture*, University Park: The Pennsylvania State University Press, contains literary and historical essays about the crisis of authority in fourteenth-century England.

Baker, D.N. (1994) *Julian of Norwich's "Showings": from vision to book*, Princeton: Princeton University Press, considers Julian's thought in the context of medieval theology.

Jantzen, G.M. (1987) *Julian of Norwich: mystic and theologian*, Mahwah, NJ: Paulist Press, shows how Julian's concerns are relevant today.

Nuth, J.M. (1991) *Wisdom's Daughter: the theology of Julian of Norwich*, New York: Crossroad, argues that Julian is best understood as a theologian.

Watson, N., and Jenkins, J. (eds) (2006) *The Writings of Julian of Norwich: a vision showed to a devout woman and a revelation of love*, University Park: Pennsylvania State University Press, is a Middle English edition of the texts which contains an important introduction and many explanatory notes.

14

ANONYMOUS
(fourteenth century)
The Cloud of Unknowing

STEVEN CHASE

One of the most appealing lines in *The Cloud of Unknowing* is this provocative phrase: "Indeed, a soul is wherever it loves" (60). And yet, the book's opening words have an ominous tinge:

> To you, whoever you are, who may have this book in your possession . . . I lay this charge on you . . . You are not to read it to others, or to copy it; nor are you to allow it so to be read in private or in public or copied . . . except by someone or to someone who, as far as you know, has resolved . . . with steadfast determination truly and sincerely to be a perfect follower of Christ.
>
> (*The Cloud of Unknowing*, Prologue)

Imagine someone in the mid 1970s finding this book in the labyrinthine, windowless caverns beneath Grand Central Station in New York City. It is August, always hot in Manhattan, and hotter here below the city's sticky asphalt streets. The air is stale, almost nauseous, thick with sweat and anxiety, dull and dingy in the twenty-four-hour light. Swarms of rush-hour commuters pick their way through the crowds. Down one corridor is a small book shop. Few notice it, fewer stop; those who do pause only to pick up a newspaper, hardly breaking stride. In a dark corner hides the single copy of *The Cloud of Unknowing*. The dust jacket indicates it was written anonymously six hundred years ago and contains instruction on the art and practice of Christian contemplation. A random turn of its pages finds, "it is love alone that can reach God in this life, and not knowing" (8), and "with devout, pleasing, impulsive love strive to pierce that darkness. You are to smite upon that thick cloud of unknowing with a sharp dart of longing love" (6).

In the sweltering bustle of obsessive schedules and departures and connections, this poor little book is so out of place. Or is it? Under the influence of Pseudo-Dionysius (c.500), Richard of St. Victor (d.1173), and major theologians such as Augustine, Gregory the Great, and Thomas Aquinas, the anonymous fourteenth-century author produced a masterwork of mystical insight and contemplative wisdom. Today, the *Cloud* author's teachings, striking images, and practical, common sense have inspired a renewal in Christian contemplative practice.

The warning given by the *Cloud* author that the text's contents were not for everyone was no doubt a responsible bit of advice in the fourteenth century. Today, however, the warning will strike most readers as an invitation into something deeper, something soulful and holy. For "a soul is where it loves," even in the depths of Grand Central station where, as the Cloud author assures us, "the path to God is measured not by yards but by desires" (40).

AUTHOR AND AUDIENCE

After years of scholarly argument, the identity of the author of *The Cloud of Unknowing* remains unknown, shrouded not only in the wars, unrest, plagues, and schisms of the fourteenth century, but in the author's own obvious wish to remain anonymous. Based on evidence internal to the *Cloud* and the author's other writings, the consensus is that the writer was probably a Carthusian priest and recluse living in the East Midlands of England. The author writes in the vernacular, with a vigorous and intelligent Middle English. A classical rhetorical and grammatical style indicates a fluent control of Latin as well. The date of composition is as uncertain as the *Cloud*'s authorship; current scholarship suggests it was written between 1362 and 1390. It is unlikely the author was a woman. Though women were writing texts on spiritual direction, contemplation, and the spiritual life, women of the period were for the most part denied education in

Latin and were nearly universally excluded from the kind of theological training evident in *The Cloud of Unknowing*. Most importantly, words at the end of the treatise are in the form of a liturgical blessing as would have been given only by a priest.

The most prominent influences on the *Cloud* are Pseudo-Dionysius's *Mystical Theology* and commentaries on it by various writers, especially the thirteenth-century Victorine Thomas Gallus (*c.*1200–46). Nearly as influential is another Victorine from the twelfth century, the contemplative mystic and exegete Richard of St. Victor. Six additional works attributed to the *Cloud* author supplement themes present in the *Cloud*, including discernment, spiritual guidance, mystical theology, and contemplation leading to union with God. Like the *Cloud*, the additional works are characterized by common-sense practical advice on discernment of spirits, exhortations to virtue, and spiritual practice.

The Cloud of Unknowing is written in the form of a letter of instruction on the arts of contemplation to a novice from an older monk or spiritual father. Three of the author's additional writings are addressed to the same "spiritual friend" and it is clear that the writer had been working as a spiritual director with this particular monk throughout the period of the writings. In using the genre of a letter of spiritual guidance addressed to a single individual, the *Cloud* author was perpetuating a tradition that assumed the writings would be passed from hand to hand and read in private or in ecclesial settings. The warning to the reader implies that the book would indeed be passed on, while later in the book the author explicitly addresses "young men and young women who are beginners in the school of devotion" (45).

SYNOPSIS

The Cloud of Unknowing is a pedagogical text intended to teach the spiritual practice of contemplative prayer. The author's teaching is grounded in the Christian tradition known as *via negativa* or apophatic spirituality. This "negative theology" avers that, just as a clay pot can never know the mind of the potter, humanity as a part of creation can never know the mind of God, the Creator. Human senses, imagination, and reason can know some things about God, but even with the aid of scripture, full knowledge of God is beyond human capacity; God is mystery. But the *Cloud* author does not stop there. Instead he turns to the equally well established tradition known as the *via positiva* or cataphatic spirituality. Also known as affective spirituality, in this tradition full "comprehension" or union with God is possible, not through the mind or senses, but through the medium of love. In making use of both traditions, the *Cloud* author creates a masterful spiritual synthesis: to human reason God remains a mystery, but through the medium of love, God is accessible. The author's teaching on contemplation thus involves two techniques: the first, relying on apophatic spirituality, is a practice that empties the self of all thoughts or intellectual reflections that would interfere with a purely loving relationship with God, putting these under a "cloud of forgetting"; the second, relying on cataphatic spirituality, is a practice by which human love enters the "cloud of unknowing" wherein God truly "resides" as Love.

A single sacred word

The beauty of the *Cloud* author's synthesis is that both techniques are united in a single, simple word. The author suggests words of a single syllable, such as "love" or "God." During prayer, the word is introduced slowly and internally as a symbol of the contemplative's intention to consent to God's presence and action within. In the apophatic phase, whenever the contemplative becomes aware of a thought or reflection, he or she simply returns to the word, gently covering the thought and placing it under a "cloud of forgetting." Thus emptied of all thoughts, the contemplative is free to engage the connective, cataphatic phase of the prayer symbolized by the "cloud of unknowing." In this phase, the sacred word becomes a symbol of love itself. It is an "arrow of love" sprung from the loving soul straight to the Love that is God. In the "cloud of unknowing" all is divine presence: the soul in love rests in Love.

The cloud of forgetting

Though the techniques of contemplative prayer are simple on the surface, the author is concerned that the reader understand the many practical nuances encountered in contemplation. In a style that is organic rather than systematic, he describes all manner of "creatures" (or thoughts) that disturb the contemplative's focus on love. These include thought and reflection as well as any memories, images, distractions, illusions, sins, intentions, psychological insights, or dreams. Even holy thoughts are to be placed under the cloud of forgetting: "I make no exceptions . . . in this practice it is of little or no profit to think of the kindness or the worthiness of God, or of our Lady or the saints or angels in heaven, or even of the joys of heaven" (5). He admits and welcomes appropriate times and places for such meditations, but this contemplation is not that time or place.

The dark cloud of unknowing

Different angles of vision and perspective are also important for the *Cloud* author's finely shaded teaching on the component of love in contemplative prayer. This component "consists entirely," he says, "in this darkness and in the cloud of unknowing, with a loving impulse and a dark gazing into the simple being of God himself alone" (8). As an experienced spiritual guide, the author circles around the contemplative "goal" of Love with patience and imagination. It is "a devout, pleasing, impulse of love strive[ing] to pierce that darkness above you," he writes. "You are to smite upon that thick cloud of unknowing with a sharp dart of longing love" (6, 12). Elsewhere he offers a variety of images suggestive of human love contemplatively seeking the love of God: use "a humble impulse of love . . . have him as your aim" (3); continue with "a simple reaching into the cloud" (3); employ "a sudden impulse flying up to God" (4, 6, 26); lovingly "pierce the cloud of unknowing" (7); imitate the Lord by "lifting your love to Christ" (9); proceed by "dark gazing into the simple being of God himself alone" (8); imagine a "blind impulse of love secretly beating on the cloud of unknowing" (9); and remember that "short prayer pierces heaven" (38).

"Ten thousand opportunities"

Through the grace of contemplation, one single word purges the soul of reflective thought and focuses loving consent to a fine, sharp point capable of piercing the mystery of divine love. This single word is a sacred symbol of a desire for God that can be redirected effortlessly in less than a moment: "It is an exercise that does not take a long time before it can be truly done, as some men seem to think," the *Cloud* author writes, "for it is the shortest possible of all exercises that men can imagine. It is neither longer nor shorter than an atom" (4). Thomas Keating, a leading teacher of contemplative prayer based on the teaching of the *Cloud*, was once approached by a woman after a period of contemplative prayer. "It didn't work," she lamented, "my mind was racing with ten thousand thoughts." Keating answered without hesitation: "ten thousand opportunities to return to God!" Ten thousand opportunities to return to God, but as the *Cloud* author is aware, also ten thousand opportunities for temptation and distraction. The contemplative practice is simple—no more effortful than an atom is long—but it comes with an imperative:

> Fasten this word to your heart, so that whatever happens it will never go away. This word is to be your shield and your spear, whether you are riding in peace or war. With this word you are to beat upon this cloud and this darkness above you. With this word you are to strike down every kind of thought under the cloud of forgetting.
>
> (*The Cloud of Unknowing*, 7)

The practice of contemplation

After laying out the basics of the prayer in the first seven chapters, the author addresses issues that are likely to arise during the practice of contemplation: 1) the variety of thoughts that may emerge and how to place them each under a cloud of forgetting; 2) the impact of sin and virtue; 3) the relation of the active and contemplative lives; 4) the nature of love itself; 5) the essential role of grace; 6) suggestions for perseverance and discipline; 7) how contemplation fits into the broader tradition of *lectio divina*; 8) discretion or discernment necessary as the prayer deepens over time; 9) self-awareness as the means to avoid a variety of illusions that can occur during the prayer; 10) the essential balance of a healthy mind, healthy body, and healthy spirit; 11) the acquisition of stillness and centering acquired over time; 12) ecstatic (instantaneous and short-term) and habitual (lingering, long-term) aspects of contemplation; and 13) signs for testing whether or not one is called by God to this kind of contemplation. The organic way in which the author places all of these teachings within the *Cloud* leads many commentators to fault the author for constant digression and lack of thematic development. It would be much more accurate to say that, whether consciously or unconsciously, the author's style reflects the patterns and structure of the contemplative prayer he teaches. Read straight through, as the *Cloud* author suggests the book should be, the attentive reader actually catches a glimpse of the patterns he or she will encounter as contemplation is practiced over time.

Charity and humility

Ever practical, the *Cloud* author teaches not only a method of contemplation, but a way of life; contemplation influences a life of virtue, and virtue shapes contemplation. Two virtues in particular have transformative implications for the life of contemplation: charity and humility. If the sacred word becomes ineffective, the *Cloud* author advises: "Try to look over their shoulders, as it were, as though you were looking for something else: that something else is God, surrounded on all sides by the cloud of unknowing" (32). That "something else," from the human perspective, is charity, and "this desire, charity, always wins easement" (32). Humility is itself the very grace of contemplation. Humility "merits to have God himself coming down in his power . . . to take you up, to cherish you and to dry your spiritual eyes" (32). As the *Cloud* author writes in a beautiful image that summarizes the work of charity and humility: "[t]ry to be the wood and let it [both the practice and grace] be the carpenter, the house, and the husbandman dwelling within the house" (33). Ten thousand distractions are ten thousand opportunities to return to this house of God's dwelling.

INFLUENCE

With few exceptions, *The Cloud of Unknowing* remained an obscure bit of contemplative wisdom from the time of its writing until the last century. Already by the time of its sequel, *The Book of Privy Counsel*, the *Cloud* had become the object of severe criticism and controversy. With apophatic and mystical theology fading out of style, with the Wycliffe controversy marginalizing all but the most orthodox writings, and later with Humanism, the Renaissance, the Protestant Reformation, and the Enlightenment all casting doubt on the authorial authenticity of the Dionysian writings, the *Cloud* went "underground." Only in the twentieth century did it emerge as a primary resource for those seeking ancient Christian sources for contemporary Christian longings.

One exception to the *Cloud's* long obscurity was a short chapter-by-chapter commentary by Fr Augustine Baker (1575–1641), a Benedictine monk who undertook the practice outlined by the *Cloud's* author. Other than the odd copy found in personal libraries, real interest in *The Cloud of Unknowing* did not resurface until the work of Evelyn Underhill (1875–1941), who appreciated it as a Christian mystical text. The Trappist monk and writer Thomas Merton (1915–68) assimilated the *Cloud* both as a mystical text and as an important resource for the practice of contemplation. His fellow Trappists credit Merton for seminal conversations leading to the "centering prayer" movement, whose essential points are derived from *The Cloud of Unknowing*.

Other twentieth-century writers such as the novelist Aldous Huxley (1894–1963) and the psychologist Ira Progoff (1921–98) showed interest in the *Cloud* as a mystical text. It has also figured in recent debates about Christian mysticism. William Johnston, who wrote a full-length study of the *Cloud*, critiques both Huxley and Progoff for what Johnston sees as a misreading of the *Cloud* author's teaching as "transcending" Christian doctrine through mystical experience. In a similar manner, Denys Turner's book *The Darkness of God* makes use of the *Cloud* to critique the modern fascination with "mystical experience."

With its similarity to some forms of Eastern meditation practices, the *Cloud* is also proving itself to be an accommodating partner in interreligious dialogue and practice. But the book's greatest influence by far has been its impact on the practice of Christian contemplative prayer. Were he alive today, the *Cloud* author would be surprised (and understandably cautious) about the extent of that impact, but he would be gratified that it is being put to the practical use for which it was intended.

READING THE TEXT TODAY

The Cloud of Unknowing can be read as a historical/theological text, as a mystical treatise, and as a manual of spiritual guidance for a particular form of Christian practice, that of contemplative prayer. As an historical/theological text, it is of interest for its reception and use of several writers in the apophatic tradition. Written in the vernacular in Chaucer's century, it is roughly contemporaneous with other mystics such as Richard Rolle, Walter Hilton, Julian of Norwich, Meister Eckhart, John Tauler, Henry Suso, John Ruysboeck, and Catherine of Siena. It is remarkable that a writing dedicated to contemplative peace could be produced during a century of frequent war, social unrest, and popular revolt, plagues, the church's "captivity at Avignon" (1305–78), and the commencement of the Great Schism (1378).

Regarding the work as a mystical text, the reader must be cautious. The *Cloud* author nowhere indicates he is producing a "mystical treatise" as we think of it today. In fact, reading the *Cloud* as a text describing and proscribing "mystical experience" misses the primary focus of the author's teaching and intent. In the final chapter of the book, which is devoted to discerning whether one is called to this contemplative practice, the very first "test" is that the reader not rely simply on some "congenial feeling" as a reason for reading the book (75).

A practical guide for Christian contemplation

Though the world of the *Cloud* author is vastly different from the world of today, the most relevant reading of this spiritual text is precisely the reading the author intended, which is to use it as a guide for practicing a particular form of Christian contemplation. By the mid 1970s, the world was ready to read this spiritual text in just this way. Influenced by fellow Trappist Thomas Merton, a group of monks led by Frs Basil Pennington, Thomas Keating, and William Menninger developed a contemplative practice based in all its essentials on *The Cloud of Unknowing*. Known as "centering prayer," it is today taught and practiced worldwide. The image of the "center" is intended to evoke less imaginative reflection than the image of the "cloud"; "center" is almost an imageless image. But however it is named, the "centering prayer" movement is a good example of how a "classic" spiritual text of any age may be read as a guide to Christian formation and spiritual practice.

One of the recurrent tensions in spiritual texts as well as in spiritual practice is the tension between what is prescribed as technique and what is experienced as consolation. When the *Cloud* is read as a mystical text, consolation is often emphasized over technique. But the *Cloud* itself focuses on contemplative technique and the desire to persevere in contemplative prayer. Very little is said of consolation, the experience of the prayer itself, or of its stated goal to become "oned," in union with God. Besides the obvious fact that the *Cloud* author does not believe anything *can* be said of this union, very little is said of the experience itself because, according to the author, technique can do no more than cultivate open receptivity to grace. Beyond human receptivity, God alone shapes the contours and content of contemplation. And so the *Cloud* author advises the contemplative: "During this time be blind. . . . It is enough for you to feel moved in love by something. . . . If this is the way of it, then trust steadfastly that it is God alone who moves your will and your desire: he alone, entirely of himself" (34). It is not technique, it is not experience, it is not good fortune that moves human desire and will; for the *Cloud* author, God alone moves and forms the human mind and heart by way of love.

Even the image of the "center" stands in the way of this blind trust in "God alone . . . mov[ing] your will and your desire." A physical "center" implies spatial relationship, which in turn requires thoughtful reflection. In a series of chapters devoted to the illusion of prepositions ("in," "up," etc., and this would include "to the center" as well), the author displays his remarkable, even humorous, power of vivid expression (51, 52, 57–60), and an unceasing desire for a keen, clear, and trusting relationship with God that is stripped of all illusion. Writing of those who do indeed believe God is literally "up," he says:

They look up to the stars as though they would reach above the moon, and cock their ears as though they could hear angels sing out of heaven . . . dew, which they think might be angel's food, which appears to come out of the air and falls softly and sweetly into their mouths. And so it is their habit to sit with their mouths open as though they were catching flies.

(*The Cloud of Unknowing*, 57)

Heaven also is neither down nor up, behind, in front or at the center: "whoever has a true desire to be in heaven, then in that moment he is in heaven spiritually" (60). And most tantalizing of all: "a soul is wherever it loves" (60).

Keeping body and soul together

The text's practical focus calls for a healthful, holistic integration between body and soul at every level of living, loving, and contemplation. "This work," the author says, "demands a great tranquility and a clean bill of health as well in body as in soul" (41). Read in this way, the text serves as a spiritual director as well: "often patience in sickness pleases God much more than any satisfying devotion that you might have whilst you are in good health" (42). Most refreshing of all is the author's insistence that the soul and body together participate in divine connection at the highest levels in this life: "God forbid that I should separate what God has joined together, the body and the spirit; for it is God's will to be served both in body and soul, and to give man his reward, in bliss, in both body and in soul" (48).

From metaphysics into mystery

The Cloud of Unknowing is a compassionate letter from a spiritual master to a novice seeking practical advice on both the active and contemplative components of the Christian life. Behind the teaching is a sophisticated, integrated metaphysical system, at the core of which is the awareness that the system can only be accessed through contemplative practice and that, finally, the system itself is really only an illusion. What is not an illusion is love. *The Cloud of Unknowing* is written from the perspective of an illuminated consciousness of God. Its simple, practical, yet subtle teaching guides the contemplative reader into desire, longing, love, and mystery as God. Where the soul finds mystery it finds itself. This does not mean *The Cloud of Unknowing* is anti-intellectual or irrational; its contemplative way of knowing is the way of practice, stillness, connection, and relationship wherein the sacred mystery reveals that the soul *is* because the soul *loves*.

TRANSLATION

Anonymous (1981) *The Cloud of Unknowing*, ed. J. Walsh, Mahwah, NJ: Paulist Press.

FURTHER READING

Bourgeault, C. (2004) *Centering Prayer and Inner Awakening*, Cambridge, MA: Cowley Publications, places centering prayer based on the *Cloud* within the classic Christian contemplative tradition.

Johnston, W. (1975) *The Mysticism of the "Cloud of Unknowing": a modern interpretation*, St. Meinrad, IN: Abbey Press, is the best source on the *Cloud* as mystical text, by a major interpreter of Eastern and Western mysticism, with foreword by Thomas Merton.

Keating, T. (2000) *Open Heart, Open Mind: the contemplative dimension of the gospel*, New York: Continuum, is a comprehensive introduction to "centering prayer" based on teaching from *The Cloud of Unknowing*, by a founder of Contemplative Outreach Ltd, which has a website at http://www.centeringprayer.com/

Turner, D. (1995) *The Darkness of God: negativity in Christian mysticism*, Cambridge: Cambridge University Press, is an excellent source placing the *Cloud* as mystical text within the broader Christian apophatic tradition.

15

CATHERINE OF SIENA
(1347–80)
Dialogue

DARLEEN PRYDS

Catherine of Siena was by all accounts a great talker, at least in the final years of her life. She was feisty and passionate, stubborn and willful, completely devoted to the love of God—and she let many people know it. It was this devotion that fueled her acts of piety, her political interventions, her forms of preaching, and her writing. Appreciating Catherine's passionate personality and knowing her gift of oral persuasion make it understandable how the *Dialogue* became immediately popular among her contemporaries. Recognizing the depth of prayer and breadth of learning that went into the work's composition makes it understandable why the *Dialogue* remains a classic in the tradition of Christian spirituality.

Written in Italian between 1377 and 1378, just before Catherine died at the age of thirty-three in 1380, the *Dialogue* stands as a capstone work in which she put into writing the summation of spiritual and theological themes she had written about in letters and spoken about with her followers. Although she was declared a "Doctor of the Church" in 1970 (along with Teresa of Avila), Catherine herself was not educated in any formal way. Instead, she is said to have achieved the ability to read miraculously during a period of self-imposed isolation. And while she authored many letters (of which nearly 400 are extant) and the *Dialogue*, she composed by way of dictation rather than by writing the text herself. Especially in her *Dialogue*, this oral speaking style is evident.

As a lay woman who achieved prominence as a political adviser, albeit as something of a gadfly, Catherine takes an unusual position in the history of Christian spirituality. She was widely recognized as a holy woman by her contemporaries because of her mysticism; in turn, it was her reputation as a mystic that propelled her into an active advisory career during which she impressed her will and opinions on prominent leaders of her day. Popes, queens, senators, and archbishops all endured her exuberantly expressive epistles. Some of them followed her advice; others disagreed with her and pursued their own opinions. But none of them could fail to notice the mystic from Siena; neither could the local faithful who turned to Catherine for inspiration and spiritual advice.

While Catherine's career as a political adviser is best documented in her letters, it is the *Dialogue* that gives glimpses into her more private career as a spiritual director and local religious leader. Normally, this kind of spiritual guidance offered by lay women goes completely undocumented in historical sources. As a result, the tradition of women functioning as spiritual teachers has frequently been overlooked and forgotten. Catherine, however, had access to resources through her contacts with Dominican friars that gave her the opportunity to dictate spiritual thoughts and images and then blend them together into a book. While her actual conversations of advice and teaching were never recorded, the *Dialogue* reflects those sessions of spiritual direction in tone, style, and content. The *Dialogue* remains for us then a rare masterpiece of the private teachings of a lay woman.

AUTHOR AND AUDIENCE

We know about Catherine's life primarily from the *Vita*, or *Life*, written by her confessor and spiritual director, Raymond of Capua, who was a prominent and influential member of the Dominican Order. As with so many people with holy reputations, Catherine's biographical details are shrouded in a hagiographical veil. Hagiography, of course, differs from biography in its central purpose, which is to promote its subject's reputation for sanctity. Therefore, hagiography often reflects more about contemporary expectations of holiness than it does about verifiable facts concerning the subject's life. To that end, one can surmise that details of Catherine's *Vita* may have been exaggerated to meet the author's agenda, but, in general, paint the picture of a woman whose faith journey started when she was young.

Raymond depicted Catherine as exhibiting an unusual capacity for spiritual seriousness and dedication from an early age. As the twenty-fourth of twenty-five children, Catherine's spiritual yearnings made her different from the rest of the children early on and may very well have been influenced by her family situation. Vowing to remain a virgin by the age of seven, Catherine would later, as an increasingly determined adolescent, make sure her parents failed in their attempts to broker a marriage deal by shaving off her hair in an effort to make herself unappealing to any prospective groom. After the kind of arguments and testing of wills that adolescents are known to have with their parents, Catherine persevered in her desire and vocation to live as a celibate woman, consecrated to God. While she did not enter a monastic community, she was, after some amount of trial, accepted into a group of lay women who were associated with the Dominican Order. Known as the *Mantellate*, this group had developed as a pious outlet for widows and older women. When Catherine accepted the group's habit as a young adult of eighteen years old, she immediately made a striking addition to the group.

Catherine's affiliation with the *Mantellate*, in fact, made a striking impact on her. Immediately, her spiritual life intensified and she insisted on a period of self-imposed solitude. Leaving her room in her parents' home only to attend mass, Catherine lived for three years in silence and near absolute solitude. This period of near isolation lasted somewhere between three and seven years, and probably dated roughly between 1362 and 1370. During this time she is said to have miraculously achieved the ability to read. Regardless of the veracity of such a legend, this period certainly played a significant role in her spiritual formation. With its silence, solitude, reading, and prayer, this period in Catherine's life acted as an incubator for her adult life as a mystic. Catherine's self-imposed quasi-monastic existence allowed her to cultivate in private an intense and rich spiritual awareness that is rare.

Raymond expressed the epitome of this period as a mystical marriage between Catherine and Christ. For Raymond, and presumably for Catherine, this image of marriage reflected the intensity, seriousness, and sacramentality of her union with Christ. Upon this mystical marriage, Catherine's spirituality suddenly transitioned into active and dramatic expression. She began giving great attention to public acts of charity, such as feeding the poor and caring for plague victims. She became a spiritual director to many people, including her confessor Raymond of Capua, who helped spread her reputation so that growing numbers of followers listened to her teachings. This growing fame and broad influence helps account for Catherine's political activism, which she asserted through letter-writing. Such a role was rare for a woman of the fourteenth century, but Catherine addressed letters to popes and monarchs, urging them with passionate rhetoric to look after the best interests of the church, which to her mind centered on the return of the papacy to Rome. Even more unusual than a woman taking up a political role was the fact that these leaders, including popes Gregory XI and Urban VI, listened to her counsel, at least eventually, as Catherine proved to be a persistent advocate for her causes. But Catherine has also become notorious for her extreme asceticism in the last third of her life. Eventually reaching the point where she would consume only the consecrated host and herbal teas or broths, Catherine's ascetical eating habits led to a state of inedia or the inability to eat. Labeled by some scholars as anorexia, her extreme fasting has led others to see Catherine as endeavoring to experience as fully as possible the passion and sufferings of Christ. This latter interpretation is supported with other evidence of extreme devotional behavior, such as Catherine's experience of the stigmata (albeit allegedly invisibly).

SYNOPSIS

Any attempt to summarize and digest the *Dialogue* is necessarily going to change the tone, structure, and sense of internal coherence of the piece, since Catherine wrote it in a way that reflects an extended conversation developing over days and weeks rather than a spiritual treatise with linear structure. Themes reappear and new pieces are added. The work is repetitive and does not follow a clear development of argument or, at times, a theme. In that regard it offers a refreshingly organic structure that reflects many lay people's understanding of spiritual truths.

The *Dialogue* rests on the same premise that the ancient oracle at Delphi had taught: "Know thyself." Self-knowledge is the cornerstone of Catherine's spirituality in this text, since the self reflects God in this world. From knowing one's self, one then desires and seeks God.

When one comes to know God, in a state of confidence through this self-knowledge, one can seek reform of the corruption first within the church, and then within the world at large. These radiating circles of spiritual awareness and desire are found throughout the *Dialogue* and provide the backbone for many spiritual themes and theological threads in the text.

The prologue sets up the premise for the entire work, while also establishing the tone. In it a restless soul (that is, Catherine herself) desires God. Having prepared through prayer and a growing self-knowledge, the soul seeks knowledge of God, and then seeks a more perfect union with God through truth and love. Four prayers of petition end the first section of the prologue, initiating the dialogue that will continue between the soul and God throughout the text. The soul first seeks a petition for herself; second, for the reform of the Holy Church; third, for the entire world, with special concern for those who rebel against the Holy Church; and finally, for any "special cases" that arise. While general in their wording, these four petitions provide the reader with an outline of the parameters (and priorities) of the soul. First and foremost the soul is seeking from God, through petitions, an on-going conversation with God. Through this conversation she reveals her primary concern with her own salvation and spiritual union with God. She is then concerned about the church's reform. The world at large is of concern as it intersects with the church. Finally, she expects that she will occasionally encounter unanticipated situations that need particular attention.

In the first section on the way of perfection, Catherine explores the preparation of the soul to unite with God, who is Infinite Good:

> Here is the way, if you would come to perfect knowledge and enjoyment of me, eternal Life: Never leave the knowledge of yourself. Then, put down as you are in the valley of humility you will know me in yourself, and from this knowledge, you will draw all that you need. No virtue can have life in it except from charity, and charity is nursed and mothered in humility. You will find humility

in the knowledge of yourself when you see that even your own existence comes not from yourself but from me, for I loved you before you came into being.

(p. 29)

While suffering is used to punish the soul, no amount of earthly suffering could possibly elicit sufficient satisfaction for the sins humans commit. Therefore suffering is to be considered a punishment, often, rather than satisfaction for sin. Catherine proposes that true atonement for sins comes first in self-knowledge and love of God. With constant and honest knowledge of the self, the soul in humility can find God through the self, and extract from this knowledge all it needs.

The soul then puts into action all the truths that it apprehends through relationships with neighbors. All scandal, cruelty, and hatred emerge from the selfishness which, Catherine states, has affected the state of the Holy Church and all of Christianity. Self-serving actions only cause rifts in the social body. Instead of these kinds of selfishness, God wants people to be interdependent, ministering with one another, thereby distributing the graces and gifts that each person has freely received from God. Bound together ultimately by the love of God, people are to serve one another through love of neighbor.

After listing virtues that God has given to humanity, Catherine writes in the voice of God:

I have distributed [all virtues and graces] in such a way that no one has all of them. Thus have I given you reason—necessity in fact—to practice mutual charity. For I could well have supplied each of you with all your needs, both spiritual and material. But I wanted to make you dependent on one another so that each of you would be my minister, dispensing the graces and gifts you have received from me. So whether you will it or not, you cannot escape the exercise of charity! Yet, unless you do it for love of me, it is worth nothing to you in the realm of grace. So you see, I have made you my ministers, setting you in different positions and in different ranks to exercise the virtue of charity. For there are many rooms in my house. All I want is love. In loving me you will realize love for your neighbors, and if you love your neighbors you have kept the law.

(pp. 37–8)

Catherine then introduces the theme of the "Bridge," which is the central image for the text. Since humans are incapable of offering sufficient satisfaction to God for their sin, God offered his son Jesus as the Bridge which is the necessary avenue between God and humanity. Those who choose to avoid journeying along the Bridge will be forced into the raging waters below and drown. But by choosing the spiritual journey that takes one across the Bridge, the soul may experience a union with God that is imperfect in this life but made perfect upon the completion of this life.

The bridge is described as having characteristics of both the human person of Jesus and a physical bridge. Sharing in human flesh, Jesus is a bridge with three steps to correspond to three spiritual stages in which humans can approach God: the first, the feet, represents affections by which humans first are attracted to God. The second, the heart, represents love, by which humans cultivate the goodness of God. And the third, the mouth, represents peace which comes from knowing God. Catherine expands on this image of the bridge, elaborating the physical details of the structure that represent spiritual challenges. For example, the bridge which is this spiritual journey to God has walls to protect the traveler from the elements, just as faith helps shield the faithful soul from experiencing the full blows of suffering.

In her discussion of the Bridge, and throughout the text, Catherine, like all good preachers, punctuates her discussion with concrete images and graphic language that make her meaning memorable. For example, as she explains how the Bridge came into being as a result of divine justice and the need for atonement for sin, she writes that God sent his only Son, the Word, by whom the pus of Adam's sin was drained, leaving only the scar that represents the human inclination to sin. Never one to shy away from the harsh truth or graphic details, Catherine turns to physical images that could affect the reader viscerally, in order to evoke the same kind of visceral responses she is known to have experienced in her own faith journey.

In keeping with this graphic description, it is clear that for Catherine, the journey of the soul is not a casual one. The soul is responsible for cultivating virtues—first from knowing one's self, then from knowing God—and then warding off the vices of pride, selfishness, impatience, and lack of discernment. Each of these vices stems from an inappropriate concentration on the self. But the virtuous attention to the self brings the soul closer to God through acts of love. The vices create a soul that experiences the full effects of suffering, but virtues protect the soul. The life of the soul prepares it for that moment of death at which the will is no longer free. Should the soul die in a state of loving charity, the soul will be bound by the chains of love; but should the soul die in deadly sin, the soul will be bound in the chains of hatred. Thus the journey across the Bridge has eternal significance.

To travel across the Bridge requires one final component: desire. While human desire can distract the soul from its intention to cross the bridge, one must deeply desire or, as Catherine writes, one must truly "thirst," otherwise the traveler will weary or be distracted by pleasure and will fail to persevere. The role of desire is deeply seated in Catherine's *Dialogue*, for Catherine herself, as a deeply sensual and passionate seeker, experienced the yearning of spiritual thirst, and yet also saw desire's potential to derail a spiritual quest. By focusing one's desire on knowing God, the soul is able to endure the suffering that necessarily affects all humans. The soul whose desires stray from the Divine, however, is conversely distracted from God and wallows in misery caused by suffering. Thus desire, appropriately directed, keeps the soul on the straight path of the Bridge to God.

Having established the groundwork of her *Dialogue*, Catherine then explores the subjects of personal discernment, true and false emotions by way of a discussion of tears, the nature of truth, the sacramentality of the church, Divine Providence, and holy obedience— all as integral components of the implications of the journey across the bridge, that is, an individual's faith journey.

The *Dialogue* concludes with a statement made in the words of God as a summary of how he answered the restless soul's questions and his final words of support and direction, followed by her prayers of thanksgiving for his love and his sacrifice of his Son.

INFLUENCE

The *Dialogue*'s fame spread immediately among Catherine's followers because of their dedication to her and interest in her words. Her followers included those local faithful who remain anonymous but are known to have turned to Catherine for spiritual advice. Their ability to read her text would have been hit or miss, but considering how spiritual communities functioned in late medieval Europe, with a community needing just one literate reader for a text to influence a wider group, one can imagine that the themes and ideas in the *Dialogue* would have circulated vigorously among her followers. Given the potential role for preachers, especially the Dominicans who supported Catherine, in disseminating ideas, the immediate spread of Catherine's influence was clearly not monopolized by the literate population and not based solely on the publication of the *Dialogue*. Her fame among a broad sector of the Italian population led Pope Pius XII to name her co-patron saint of Italy with Francis of Assisi.

Upon the creation of the printing press, the *Dialogue* was among the first books printed in Italy and farther afield in England, Germany, and Spain. Interest in the text inspired its translation, so that one can find new editions and new translations of the *Dialogue* in every century since her death. Since the text was originally written as one long continuous "conversation" or literally as a dialogue, editors very quickly helped the readers by dividing the text into chapters. By the sixteenth century, as the readership broadened, the text was further divided into larger sections that were called "tracts" or "treatises." While the divisions and subsections facilitate the modern reader's understanding of the meaning, they alter the original fluid and organic composition. Nevertheless, enough of this original flow of the text must still be evident, as the translator of the most recent English edition felt obliged to apologize to the reader for the cumbersome and obtuse writing style that remains an inherent challenge in reading the text.

READING THE TEXT TODAY

When reading the *Dialogue*, one senses implicitly the restlessness of the author. The restless soul of the text reflects Catherine's own impatience and even agitation, which is reflected in the repetitive and redundant themes. A modern reader accustomed to reading cogently argued books and essays may easily tire from the meandering nature of this classic text unless the reader remembers that the organizing principle for the work is that of a dialogue. Like all conversations that span months (remember the *Dialogue* was written over the course of two years), themes repeat and develop slightly differently at each reprisal. For centuries respective editors of the text have tried to reframe the work in linear fashion, dividing it into sections with subtitles to make it palatable to their own contemporary readers. But the original integrity of the work rests on the organic organizational principle of a conversation, with all the inherent redundancies, incomplete thoughts, and meandering digressions. When accepted as an appropriately composed text on its own terms and in its own format, the work stands out in the history of Christian spirituality as an important and rare piece of evidence of lay theology in general, and more specifically, of a lay woman's approach to theology and to spirituality.

With this in mind, modern readers will facilitate their own apprehension of the text if they read the work aloud, if possible, so that they actually experience the text in the style in which it is written, as a conversation. In addition, the book is best read in short passages. Reading the text by sampling passages, just as if one might pass by a group of friends (or strangers) engaged in a conversation and stop to linger for awhile, allows one to focus on respective threads without the distractions of repetitions. When the conversation shifts and becomes less engaging, the person moves on.

While the *Dialogue* lacks the feisty passion of Catherine's letters, especially her later letters, it nevertheless reveals how theological and spiritual ideas that were disputed by the intellectual elite in sophisticated debates at the universities could be digested by a lay woman, most likely through hearing sermons and through her own spiritual direction. In turn the work illustrates how these ideas are presented in a genre that takes the form of a conversation that would have been readily understood by contemporaries.

When reading the text, it is important to remember the personal preparation Catherine undertook in order to write it. The three-year period of solitude and silence starting when she was about eighteen was truly a period of intense spiritual and intellectual formation for Catherine. One can only speculate about what Catherine experienced through prayer, meditation, and study during this period. Nobody knows exactly what she was reading, but one can assume she was reading spiritual texts. Because of the allusions to scriptural themes and images in the *Dialogue*, it is likely she also read and absorbed scripture.

The themes that may resonate most strongly for the modern reader have to do with Catherine's concern with self-knowledge as the basis of the spiritual journey. Self-reflection cultivates true humility for the seeking soul when it comes to realize the infinite goodness of its Creator. Seeing vestiges of God's goodness in his creation, the soul can recognize her own gifts and then, in a sense of holy responsibility, bring those gifts forward to help the surrounding community, including the church. Far from mapping out a spiritual path on which a person cultivates the persona of a shrinking violet or a reclusive contemplative, Catherine in the *Dialogue* has issued a call to lay people to embrace their respective vocations and put them to good use. Of particular note is Catherine's insistence on calling out the corruption and exploitation within the church. While the particular forms of abuse of power she witnessed were often political in nature, there is a sense in the power of her writing that she is aware of the potential for wide-ranging abuse within ecclesiastical institutions and finds each individual soul responsible for reforming Mother Church. The *Dialogue*, then, presents a model of prayer-based activism which stems from a person's inner confidence about one's vocation and God-given talents.

TRANSLATION

Catherine of Siena (1980) *The Dialogue*, trans. S. Noffke, New York: Paulist Press.

FURTHER READING

Dreyer, E.A. (1999) *A Retreat with Catherine of Siena: living the truth in love*, Cincinnati: St. Anthony Messenger Press, offers a spiritual application of Catherine's texts and experiences.

Hilkert, M.C. (2001) *Speaking with Authority: Catherine of Siena and the voices of women today*, New York and Mahwah, NJ: Paulist Press, argues that Catherine of Siena provides a role model for women's religious leadership today.

Kearns, C. (1980) *The Life of Catherine of Siena by Raymond of Capua*, Wilmington, DE: M. Glazier, is a highly readable translation of the classic piece of hagiography about Catherine and a good companion volume to reading the *Dialogue*.

Luongo, F.T. (2006) *The Saintly Politics of Catherine of Siena*, Ithaca, NY: Cornell University Press, analyzes the political drive that stemmed from Catherine's mysticism.

McDermott, T.K. (2008) *Catherine of Siena: spiritual development in her life and teaching*, New York: Paulist Press, offers a new systematic discussion of Catherine's mystical thought.

Noffke, S. (1988-2007) *The Letters of Catherine of Siena*, Tempe: Arizona Center for Medieval and Renaissance Studies, reveals the passionate fruits of her mysticism and gives a vivid glimpse into Catherine's feisty personality in the last decade of her life.

16

MARTIN LUTHER
(1483–1546)
The Freedom of a Christian

TIMOTHY J. WENGERT

Around 1518 Martin Luther, already embroiled in a struggle that
would lead to the Reformation, permanently changed the spelling of
his name. Until then, consonant with family usage, he was Martin
Luder. That is the way he had inscribed his name into the matricu-
lation book at the University of Erfurt when he began his studies
there in 1501 and the way he signed his name in his earliest publications. Then, starting in December 1516 through the beginning of
1519, Martin Luder, following the example of many humanist scholars
of his day (including his colleague, Philip Melan-chthon [from
Schwartzerdt, black earth]), signed his name in Greek: *eleutherius*,
the free one, before settling for a shortened form of the same word:
Luther. In 1532, when asked about the meaning of his name, he
averred that "Martin" was derived from Mars, the god of war, and
Luther from *eleutherius legis* ("free from the law").

It was no accident that in 1520, at the height of his struggle with
the Roman church over salvation (by faith alone or by works), Luther
wrote a tract entitled *The Freedom of a Christian*. It set the program
for evangelical Christians (as Lutherans are still called in Europe),
revealing (as Luther believed) a Pauline theology of freedom from the
terror of the law and freedom in the comfort of God's forgiveness in
Christ. What Paul wrote in Galatians 5:1 ("For freedom Christ has
set us free"), Luther turned into a catchphrase for his theology,

transforming his name to indicate the life-changing effect. Luther's lectures on Galatians in 1516 employed the Greek text and argued that Paul was speaking here about freedom from works of law. In the published commentary of 1519 Luther contrasted the believer, whom Christ frees from sin and the law and makes a servant of righteousness, with those who trust their own works and the power of their own wills and thus are free from righteousness and instead slaves of sin and the law.

Romans 1:17 ("For in [the gospel] the righteousness of God is revealed through faith for faith") may have triggered Martin Luther's "breakthrough" to a new understanding of how people stand before God, but Luther also had other favorite texts from scripture that shaped his theology. On the one hand, he used Romans 10:17 ("So faith comes from what is heard, and what is heard comes through the word of Christ") to insist that faith is not a human decision but rather happens when people hear the good news of Christ and, through the power of the Holy Spirit alone, trust it to be true for them. On the other, Luther also often referred to Colossians 2:23, where Paul rails against (to use Luther's rendering in his translation of the New Testament) "self-chosen spirituality" (*selb erwelte Geistligkeit*). Thus, for Luther, freedom arises from Christ's word and eliminates self-chosen piety and works in favor of good works divinely made for the believer: trust in God, love of neighbor.

AUTHOR AND AUDIENCE

Martin Luther was born on November 10, 1483 in Eisleben, son of Hans, a miner (later, mine owner), and Margaretha. Luther attended school in Mansfeld, Magdeburg, and Eisenach before entering the University of Erfurt, where he received his bachelor and master of arts degrees by 1505. On the way back from his parents' home to Erfurt, where he was to begin studying law, Luther was caught in a thunderstorm and vowed to become a monk. He entered the observant Augustinian monastery in Erfurt, was ordained in 1507, and studied theology in Erfurt and Wittenberg. In 1512 he replaced his patron and confessor, Johann von Staupitz (the head of the Augustinians in German-speaking lands), as professor of Bible, lecturing on the Psalms, Romans, Galatians, and Hebrews before returning to the Psalms in 1519. He also oversaw several Augustinian monasteries and in 1514 began preaching at the city church.

Reacting to John Tetzel's preaching of indulgences, on October 31, 1517 Luther (apparently) posted on the Castle Church door Ninety-Five Theses for debate, which were quickly published and translated into German. They caused a sensation, not only for their theological innovation but also for their implied attack against papal authority. Luther quickly became embroiled in other controversies, first over indulgences and papal authority but then over the number of sacraments (1520) and the approach to biblical authority and monastic vows (1521). Excommunicated in 1520 by Pope Leo X and condemned as an outlaw of the Holy Roman Empire in 1521, Luther was placed in protective custody at the Wartburg Castle by Elector Frederick, before returning to Wittenberg in 1522. He later opposed Erasmus of Rotterdam on the enslavement of the human will (1525) and Ulrich Zwingli on the presence of Christ in the Lord's Supper (1525–9). In 1529 he produced two popular catechisms for general use and in 1536 published his theological "last will and testament," the Smalcald Articles. He married an escaped nun, Katharina von Bora, in 1525. Of their six children, four survived to adulthood. He died in Eisleben on February 18, 1546.

In 1520, Luther produced four foundational tracts: an appeal for princes to aid church reform, an attack that narrowed the sacraments from seven to two, an essay on good works, and Latin and German editions of *The Freedom of a Christian*, prefaced with a direct appeal to Pope Leo X. In the summer of 1520, after the pope had promulgated his bull(etin) of excommunication, the papal legate to the German lands, Karl von Miltitz, enlisted von Staupitz to urge Luther to moderation. Under the influence of one of Elector Frederick's most trusted counselors, Georg Spalatin, Luther agreed to write directly to the Pope and to write a more general, polemic-free tract on Christian freedom to elucidate his theology. Although published separately in German, they form a unity, demonstrating Luther's concrete relation to the papacy and the underpinnings of his theology.

SYNOPSIS

Luther's *Freedom of a Christian* began as a 1519 Palm Sunday sermon on Philippians 2:5–11, published as *On the Two-Fold Righteousness*.

When read in the light of the attached letter to Pope Leo X, Luther's proposal, that a believer is simultaneously a free lord and an obedient servant, becomes concrete in addressing the pope as obedient subject and free witness to Christ's authority. Luther used many rhetorical techniques to win readers to his side. Luther intended not simply to present readers with a tract *about* Christian freedom but to free his readers by "preaching Christ" and destroying their "self-chosen spirituality."

The inner person is free lord

Before introducing the theme of the tract, Luther defines faith not as a human work or decision (a "virtue") but as a relation (an "experience") of trust in God, effected by God. This definition elucidates this tract's proposal for Christian freedom, which Luther presents as a paradox.

> I shall set down the following two propositions concerning the freedom and the bondage of the spirit: A Christian is a perfectly free lord of all, subject to none. A Christian is a perfectly dutiful servant of all, subject to all. These two theses seem to contradict each other. If, however, they should be found to fit together, they would serve our purpose beautifully.
>
> (*Freedom of a Christian*, p. 344)

Luther unpacks the first half of this paradoxical statement by providing readers with three basic definitions. First, he defines the human being in terms of soul and body, not in philosophical but in theological terms: the "body" means the outer person and its old, carnal nature; the "soul" is the inner, new creature of faith. Human works, even works thought of as "spiritual" (such as meditation), have nothing to do with this inner, new person. Second, Luther discusses the one thing needful for the freedom of the New Creature: the Word of God, defined not as words in the Bible but as the good news of God reconciling the world in Christ. New persons receive the Word not by doing works but by faith, that is, by trusting God's promise as true *for* them. The heart of sin is unbelief—not trusting the God who forgives sin. Luther's third definition describes how faith is born in the believer through the Word. Here Luther introduces another crucial distinction between law and gospel ("commands and promises"). Commands simply reveal human sin and cause despair. Into this predicament steps the gospel.

> The second part of Scripture comes to our aid, namely, the promises of God . . . saying, 'If you wish to fulfill the law and not covet, as the law demands, come, believe in Christ in whom grace, righteousness, peace, liberty, and all things are promised you' . . . Thus, the promises of God give what the commandments of God demand and fulfill what the law prescribes so that all things may be God's alone. . . . He alone commands; he alone fulfills.
>
> (*Freedom of a Christian,* pp. 348–9)

Upon this foundation, Luther lists the powers of faith for the inner person. Faith unites the person with God's Word; it causes the inner person to justify God's judgment against him or her; and it effects an exchange between the believer and Christ, the bridegroom. This traditional Christian metaphor, based upon a distinction in Roman law, teaches how in a marriage the property of one spouse becomes the possession of the other and vice versa.

> By the wedding ring of faith [Christ] shares in the sins, death, and pains of hell which are his bride's. As a matter of fact, he makes them his own and acts as if they were his own and as if he himself had sinned; he suffered, died, and descended into hell that he might overcome them all. . . . Thus the believing soul by means of the pledge of its faith is free in Christ, its bridegroom . . . and is endowed with the eternal righteousness, life, and salvation of Christ its bridegroom.
>
> (*Freedom of a Christian,* p. 352)

From these three powers arise certain fruits. First, faith alone fulfills the first commandment ("You shall have no other gods") and all others. Second, the marriage of faith excludes all works. Finally, through faith in this bridegroom, believers become priests and kings, in a spiritual sense: their power is perfected in weakness (2 Cor 12:9); as priests they pray for others and teach God's mercy. Because the Reformation was a reform of preaching, Luther comments on the preaching office. It does not simply provide historical facts about Jesus or harp on human works said to earn God's favor. Luther relates preaching directly to trusting Christ: "Rather ought Christ to be preached to the end that faith in him may be established that he may not only be Christ, but be Christ for you and me" (p. 357).

The outer person is servant of all

Luther now turns to the second half of the paradox. Good works do not arise out of the law and *having* to fulfill its demands, but out of the freedom of faith. To be sure, Luther insists that Christian freedom is not license. Instead, it means freely controlling the flesh (the outer person) and serving the neighbor.

First, freed by faith alone, the believer is at the same time at war with the flesh. Here Luther uses Paul's description of the battle in Romans 7 to describe the believer's double life as *simul iustus et peccator* (at the same time righteous and sinner), daily "crucifying the flesh with its passions and desires" (Gal 5:24). Such works do not justify a person before God but are the fruit of justifying faith. Luther provides three analogies relating faith and works. First, like Adam and Eve in the garden, believers do works to please God and to avoid idleness. Second, a bishop works in his office not to deserve or earn the office but precisely because he already is declared bishop. Thus, "Good works do not make a good [person], but a good [person] does good works; evil works do not make a wicked [person], but a wicked [person] does evil works" (p. 361). Luther attacks Aristotle's notion that doing virtuous things makes a person virtuous and insists that good trees (made good by God's grace alone) bear good fruit. Third, a good or bad builder builds a good or bad house and not the other way around. Faith's fruits appear to be the same as the works of unbelievers but spring forth freely from trust in God, not the self.

Second, the believer is free to love and serve the neighbor. One is free to live for the other not the self, precisely because works do not determine one's relation to God. This is to have the mind of Christ (Phil 2:7). Christ is, in Augustinian terms, first *sacramentum* (sheer gift "for us"), before being *exemplum* (example) for the justified.

Although the Christian is thus free from all works, he [or she] ought in this liberty to empty himself [or herself], take upon himself [or herself] the form of a servant, be made in the likeness of [human beings], be found in human form, and to serve, help, and in every way deal with his [or her] neighbor as he [or she] sees the God through Christ has dealt and still deals with him [or her].

(*Freedom of a Christian*, p. 366)

Thus, the Christian is a "Christ" to the neighbor, doing to the neighbor exactly what Christ has done for him or her. This is the "joyous exchange," part two, where the Christian, who by faith alone is king and priest and receives all that belongs to Christ, now exchanges all of those benefits with the undeserving neighbor.

Hence, as our heavenly Father has in Christ freely come to our aid, we also ought freely to help our neighbor through our body and its works, and each one should become as it were a Christ to the other that we may be Christs to one another and Christ may be the same in all.

(*Freedom of a Christian*, pp. 367–8)

Luther concludes with examples from scripture of such behavior, but he also identifies himself as one who criticized papal pronouncements but still followed medieval rules in Christian freedom for the sake of the weak. He summarizes the tract this way.

We conclude, therefore, that [Christians live] not in [themselves], but in Christ and in [their] neighbor. Otherwise [they are] not Christian[s]. [They] live in Christ through faith, in [their] neighbor through love. By faith [they are] caught up beyond [themselves] into God. By love [they descend] beneath [themselves] into [their] neighbor.

(*Freedom of a Christian*, p. 371)

This concludes the German version. In the Latin, Luther adds a post-script, discussing how one distinguishes the weak (for whose sake one follows ceremonies) from stubborn tyrants whom one must resist. One must freely confront "unyielding, stubborn ceremonialists," while always protecting "the weak-minded" who do not understand justification by faith and might confuse Christian freedom with license and trust elimination of ceremonies rather than Christ. Christians

cannot do without ceremonies, but they must never confuse ceremonies with meriting forgiveness of sins or earning God's blessing.
Unlike other reformers and reform movements, Luther insists that
the real problem is not the ceremonies but trust in them.

INFLUENCE

A 2007 scholarly analysis of *The Freedom of a Christian* by Reinhold
Rieger notes the widespread influence of this tract. First and foremost,
Martin Luther's colleague at the University of Wittenberg, Philip
Melanchthon, included Luther's basic insights and a direct reference
to the tract in what was to become the first and most influential
handbook of Protestant theology, the *Loci communes theologici* of
1521. In that form, it influenced many of the most important theologians of the age, including John Calvin, who made no direct reference
to Luther's tract. Other sixteenth-century figures, especially Lutheran
theologians of the second generation, also show familiarity with the
tract and its arguments, including Abdias Praetorius (1524–73), a
theologian from the electorate of Brandenburg, who was involved
in controversies with other Lutherans over the law and the necessity
of good works. In 1563, at the height of these controversies, the tract
itself was republished in Magdeburg. It heavily influenced the
language of the Formula of Concord (1576) in its article on good
works.

Of course, Luther's early opponents wasted no time in attacking
this tract. They included Kaspar Schatzgeyer, Jodocus Clichtoveus,
Jacob Hoogstraeten, Thomas de Vio (Cajetan) and (later) Girolamo
Seripando, who in 1560 wrote a refutation entitled *On Christian
Righteousness and Freedom*. Seripando, who also published a
commentary on Galatians against Luther, objected strenuously to the
simultaneity of freedom and servitude in the Christian life as a
misreading of Paul's comments in Galatians 5:13f. and Romans 8:28.
He also complained that Luther did not properly understand the
difference between the soul and the body, confusing philosophical and
theological concepts.

Since *The Freedom of a Christian* has consistently found a place
in the publication of Luther's works since the sixteenth century, it
has always been available to and used by Lutheran theologians
throughout the centuries. Biographers of the late-nineteenth and

twentieth centuries have invariably pointed to the pioneering nature
of this work and its popularity. Between 1520 and 1526, the tract was
published seventeen times in German and eight times in Latin, with
an English translation appearing in 1579. In English-speaking realms,
its popularity peaked with several printings of the English translation
in the last hundred years. Reflections on the tract by two influential
German theologians, Eberhard Jüngel and Helmut Thielicke, have also
been translated into English. Today, Roman Catholic and Protestant
thinkers alike recognize this tract as one of Luther's finest.

READING THE TEXT TODAY

The Freedom of a Christian approached Christian life and faith so
as to call into question notions of spiritual advancement in Luther's
day, and it challenges common approaches to "spirituality" today. No
human works of any kind can reach God. Faith, defined in such a way
as to eliminate works, is an alternative to all "self-chosen spirituality."
It grounds Christian life and piety not in an inner "spiritual" journey
but in being sent out into the world, so that one may better speak of
Luther's "carnality" rather than "spirituality."

Not by *any* works

Contemplation and meditation are two monastic "buzz words" for
spirituality. Yet Luther includes these, too, in defining works of the
outer, old creature, even while admitting that they are "works" of
the soul. Luther takes dead aim at much of what passed (and passes)
for Christian spirituality. He is suspicious of any method or exercise
designed to move the person into a closer relation to God, precisely
because it focuses on human activity as a precondition for reaching
true spiritual satisfaction.

For Luther, the problem always comes down to whether one's
relation to God is conditional (in some way dependent on something
human beings do) or unconditional (completely dependent upon God's
grace and mercy in Christ). Thus, when Christians define prayer,
ascent to God, or even faith itself as things that they must achieve—
even with God's help—then all is lost and what looks spiritual is
instead delusion and the Old Creature's addiction to itself. Luther

defines humanity's sinful condition as being curved in upon itself (*incurvatus in se*). In contrast, the Christian life is totally dependent upon God's mercy. This assertion, coming from the good news of God's grace, does not simply inform human beings of something, so that they must work to become as passive as possible. Instead, God's mercy works on the Old Creature as law, killing its spiritual schemes, and as gospel, raising up the New Creature of faith, who trusts God alone. Thus, the Holy Spirit works chiefly in using God's Word to make believers out of unbelievers, not in aiding human beings to do spiritual works.

Living by faith alone

In *The Freedom of a Christian*, faith is not a work human beings do for God or with God's help but precisely what God works in them through hearing the Word. Luther insists that the inner person can do without everything except the Word of God and that "faith alone is the saving and efficacious use of" that Word. This assures an externality to Luther's vision of the Christian life, since by "Word" he means the actual, aural (or sacramental) event of hearing God's judgment (law) and grace (gospel).

But what is such faith? It is not a human decision earning God's favor, nor is it merely historical knowledge of salvation—as if knowing the right answer or the appropriate Bible passage could save. Instead, Luther ties faith to experiencing God's Word, that is, the proclamation of God's mercy. Thus, faith is not a decision; it is trust created by God's faithfulness. This undermines much of modern Christian piety, which emphasizes God's grace as long as it does not hinder the human will's ability to choose God. For Luther, when human beings exercise their own powers, they sin, trusting themselves rather than God.

Faith's origin in God's merciful Word explains Luther's vivid metaphors (marriage, priesthood, and kingship) to depict the life of faith. They grow out of the experience of faith in God's declaration of the human sinner as righteous. The bride in the marital metaphor common in many strains of Christian mysticism has nothing but sin as her own, and the bridegroom nothing but righteousness and mercy. Faith effects a joyous exchange not based upon certain ontological presuppositions about the nature of God and human beings but rather (more literally) upon the actual relationship of marriage defined by Roman law. Indeed, figuring out an ontological basis for union with Christ simply indicates the Old Creature's penchant for avoiding death and controlling God. Faith ends speculation and rests in God's Word.

Living in the world

Later in his career, Martin Luther described biblical reading using a monastic schema, beginning with prayer (*oratio*), because the Word is so foreign to the Old Creature's reason, and moving to meditation (*meditatio*), a careful examination of the text to discover the Holy Spirit's intentions. Then, instead of moving to the expected *illuminatio* or *contemplatio*, Luther asserted that such prayerful reading results in attack (*tentatio*). Luther makes the same move in *The Freedom of a Christian*, where he does not send believers into themselves to find God or to get in touch with the divine, but instead drives them outside of themselves to struggle against the flesh and to serve the neighbor.

Thus, everyday life that serves the neighbor *is* the Christian life. This conviction eliminates, in Luther's eyes, every "self-chosen spirituality" and puts human beings in their place: trusting God and loving the neighbor. This is the aspect of Luther's thought that has been least appreciated. For Luther, a "spiritual" experience will not happen tucked away in some far-off retreat center away from the humdrum of life but in actual encounters with Christ the Bridegroom in the Christian assembly that send one out into the world to be Christ to the neighbor. This "self-emptying"—a direct result of Christ's self-emptying—fills every action of the believer with spiritual consequence, precisely because of its "unspiritual" nature in the eyes of the world. Indeed, faith and unfaith, not virtue and vice, make good and evil works.

This freedom to serve completely changes the venue for good works. There are no special Christian works, recognizable on the outside as Christian. The works of everyday life look the same, whether performed by a believer or unbeliever. Faith alone determines everything. Having been joined with Christ by faith and participated in all that is Christ's, one becomes a Christ to the neighbor, exchanging the neighbor's sin and weakness for one's God-given, Christian righteousness. The very paradoxical nature of the life of faith alone makes it far more "carnal" than "spiritual"—bound to an external Word of promise, experienced as faith's relation with Christ, and freed to serve actual neighbors in down-to-earth ways.

TRANSLATIONS

From the Latin:

Martin Luther (1971) *The Freedom of a Christian*, trans. W.A. Lambert and H.J. Grimm, in *Luther's Works* [American Edition], vol. 31: *Career of the Reformer I*, Philadelphia: Fortress Press, pp. 327–77. [This translation, cited above, is also available in Martin Luther (2005) *Martin Luther's Theological Writings*, ed. Timothy Lull, 2nd edn, Minneapolis: Fortress Press, 2005, and in Martin Luther (1970), *Three Treatises*, Philadelphia: Fortress Press.]

Martin Luther (2008) *The Freedom of a Christian*, trans. and ed. M.D. Tranvik, Minneapolis: Fortress Press.

From the German:

Martin Luther (2007) *The Freedom of a Christian*, trans. P.D.W. Krey and P.D.S. Krey, in *Luther's Spirituality*, New York: Paulist Press, pp. 69–90.

FURTHER READING

Arand, C.P. and Kolb, R. (2008) *The Genius of Luther's Theology: a Wittenberg way of thinking for the contemporary church*, Grand Rapids: Baker Publishing House, is a fresh look at Luther's theology and its importance for today.

Jüngel, E. (1988) *The Freedom of a Christian: Luther's significance for contemporary theology*, trans. R.A. Harrisville, Minneapolis: Augsburg Publishing House, is the only in-depth study of *The Freedom of a Christian* available in English, written by one of Germany's premier systematic theologians.

Lazareth, W. (2001) *Christians in Society: Luther, the Bible and social ethics*, Minneapolis: Fortress Press, is an engaging look at the relation between Luther's approach to the Bible and his ethics.

Lohse, B. (1999) *Martin Luther's Theology: its historical and systematic development*, trans. R.A. Harrisville, Minneapolis: Fortress Press, is a classic analysis of Luther's theology.

Wengert, T.J. (ed.) (2009) *The Pastoral Luther: essays on Martin Luther's practical theology*, Grand Rapids, MI: Eerdmans Publishing House, is a collection of essays that examine the practical aspects of Luther's theology and their impact on parish life.

17

IGNATIUS OF LOYOLA (1491–1556)

The Spiritual Exercises

ELIZABETH LIEBERT

"The Preparatory Prayer is to ask God our Lord for the grace that all my intentions, actions, and operations may be ordered purely to the service and praise of His Divine Majesty" (46). So retreatants are to begin each time of prayer in the pattern of Ignatius of Loyola's *Spiritual Exercises*. This little book, in the unpromising literary form of directions, sets out a pattern for a retreat leader (the "director") to help another (the "retreatant") to make a retreat of thirty days. Since Vatican Council II, it has funded a veritable renewal of the ministry of spiritual direction and retreats. These directions have been published more than 4,000 times for an estimated 4.5 million copies and have transcended their author's own setting at the dawn of the Reformation, eventually reaching other Christian churches and affecting both religious and secular groups outside Christianity.

How can such a little book have such an impact? Perhaps it is because the aim of the book is to point beyond itself. It puts the individual directly in touch with God; indeed, the heart of the retreat dynamic is the exchange between the director and the retreatant around the retreatant's personal experience of God. As Ignatius says, "For, what fills and satisfies the soul consists, not in knowing much, but in our understanding the realities profoundly, and in savoring them interiorly" (2). The *Spiritual Exercises* also takes adaptation seriously, making flexibility the heart of the principles guiding the director. Its spirituality addresses whole persons in their various contexts and encourages personal responsibility for their own spiritual growth. "Making the Exercises" is costly, not only in time but, more importantly, in commitment. Prayer is to spill over into daily life and daily life is to feed prayer, with contemplation and action as two faces of the same reality.

AUTHOR AND AUDIENCE

Ignatius of Loyola (Íñigo), born in 1491 to Basque parents of minor nobility in what today would be northern Spain, was the youngest of thirteen children. As a youth, he was sent by his brother to apprentice under the chief treasurer of Castile and later sought employment with his relative, Antonio Manrique de Lara, recently appointed Duke of Navarra. He had a reputation for wildness during the years of his young adulthood, tasting the excesses of court living at the end of the age of chivalry.

Ignatius himself supplies details for the next seventeen years, revealing the connection between his own experiences of God and the directions he wrote for the one giving the retreat. He wanted others to be able to help many people by means of the things he had learned through personal experience.

A misfortune launched Ignatius on his spiritual journey. In a skirmish between warring factions at Pamplona, Ignatius suffered a cannon-shot to his legs, shattering the right one. Carried home to Loyola to recuperate, he faced not only a long convalescence but also the reality that his days as a courtier were unceremoniously terminated. As he began to feel better, he asked for books to read. The household had only two, a translation of *The Life of Christ* by the Carthusian author Ludolph of Saxony and the *Lives of the Saints* (*The Golden Legend*) translated by Jacopo Verasse. This type of reading was not at all what Ignatius had in mind, accustomed as he was to romances like *Ámadis of Gaul*! In his enforced confinement, however, he picked them up and read them over and over. He eventually began to notice his own reaction to what he was reading, especially the succession of his thoughts and feelings. As he says, "he began to marvel at the difference and to reflect upon it, realizing from experience that some thoughts left him sad and others joyful. Little by little he came to recognize the difference between the spirits that were stirring." The essence of what are later called the "Rules for Discernment of Spirits" is already present, needing only to be refined and written down.

As Ignatius regained his health, he determined to exchange his worldly life for the life of a pilgrim. At his first stop, Monserrat, he put down his sword, exchanged his courtly clothes for pilgrim garb, and began to make his way toward his ultimate destination, Jerusalem. He paused at Manresa, a small town on the banks of the Cardoner River, and what was to have been a short stay turned into ten months of intense spiritual growth and formation. This period saw him fall into and recover from a serious case of scruples (extreme and repeated self-doubt about the state of one's soul), gain some common sense and balance about self-care, place himself under spiritual direction, receive extraordinary spiritual revelations, and hone his rudimentary preaching and pastoral skills. By 1524, the skeleton of the *Spiritual Exercises* was in place. For the next twenty-four years, Ignatius pondered his growing experience with the *Exercises* and revised his manuscript. The final text was approved by Pope Paul III in 1548 and issued in an official Latin edition. Ignatius himself continued to use a Spanish text, and this autograph edition, with his marginal notes and minor corrections, still exists.

These years were momentous ones for Ignatius. He studied, filling in gaps in his education; he preached within the boundaries set for him by the Inquisition, before which he appeared several times; and eventually he took up studies in Paris. Here, he gathered around him the nucleus of what became the Society of Jesus (Jesuits), fellow students at the University of Paris. The final nineteen years of Ignatius's life were spent in Rome, managing the issues of the rapidly growing Society, writing its *Constitutions*, and maintaining a voluminous correspondence. Some of his close companions prevailed upon him to write personal reminiscences of his early life, and he finally consented. The resulting text, completed only months before his death, is usually call the *Autobiography*, though it is more a rhetorical text for the instruction of young Jesuits. He died in 1556.

SYNOPSIS

The Spiritual Exercises is a manual, a book of instructions for the one giving a retreat. It is not, then, a book to be picked up and read for edification. Indeed, simply reading through the book may have the opposite effect! But when its directions are imparted by a sensitive director able to adapt the suggested exercises to the needs and experiences of the person making the retreat, and when the retreatant comes to them with openness, generosity, and commitment, they can offer a life-transformative process culminating in a new level of apostolic zeal and effectiveness.

Ignatius understood the term "spiritual exercises" to include "every method of examination of conscience, meditation, contemplation, vocal or mental prayer" (1). Likewise, he had a variety of people in mind for the *Spiritual Exercises* and suggested that they can be made in many ways. For people who need basic Christian formation, he proposes simple exercises designed as much for catechesis as for spiritual formation (18). For those who desire and can benefit from learning to find an appropriate way to pray, he offers a palette of prayer forms, from which he trusts each person can find a way of prayer that is a "pleasing experience" (238–60, 24–44, 46–9, 62–4, 101, as well as numerous bits of advice scattered throughout). For those facing an important decision, he suggests several ways to come to a decision in prayer (169–89). For one who serves in public ministry, he offers reflections on thinking in harmony with the Church (by which he meant the Roman Catholic Church of his time) (352–70). For those living a busy, committed life, Ignatius designs a way to follow the retreat a little at a time while living at home and continuing one's ordinary activities (19). But for those with sufficient generosity and time, he proposes a model of retreating from ordinary life for a period of approximately thirty days, and, with the assistance of a spiritual director, moving through a structured sequence of prayer experiences (20). This latter model structures the text.

The *Spiritual Exercises* begins with a series of notes for the director. The first twenty-two paragraphs reveal the heart of the *process* of the *Spiritual Exercises*. As Ignatius's discusses who should—or can—make the *Exercises*, he sets out the principle for adapting everything that follows. The *Spiritual Exercises* can profit any person of good will and sufficient generosity. Directors, however, must assess the context, abilities, and generosity of each retreatant, and adapt every part of the retreat to each individual's needs, circumstances, and abilities. Ignatius insists on giving retreatants as much as they are willing to receive or as much as their circumstances will allow, no more, no less. Retreatants bring openness, generosity, a willingness to wrestle with any "disordered affections" that are uncovered, and a commitment to talk over what is happening as a result of doing this or that exercise. Directors, for their part, must bring to their role self-knowledge, knowledge of the *Exercises*, and a particular kind of asceticism in which they remain "like the pointer of a scale in equilibrium, to allow the Creator to deal immediately with the creature and the creature with its Creator and Lord" (15). Finally, in a note he calls the "Presupposition," Ignatius sets out a radical principle guiding the conversation between the director and the retreatant: each is to be more eager to put a good interpretation on the other's words than to condemn them and to try every possible means to correct any misunderstanding (22). These principles of adaptation, conversation, and pastoral presence transcend their location in the *Spiritual Exercises* and form powerful guidelines for pastoral practice in general.

The hinge between the process of the retreat and its content contains a rather dry paragraph often named "Principle and Foundation" (23). Here, Ignatius introduces the radical spiritual freedom called "indifference," which both facilitates and characterizes the fruit of the retreat. Nothing is more basic to the working of the retreat than attaining this spiritual freedom, and retreatants are to desire, pray for, and choose this spiritual freedom as God offers it. Ignatius knew, however, that spiritual freedom grows gradually, and so all subsequent exercises begin with a renewal of the prayer for spiritual freedom.

The first "Week": knowing oneself as a redeemed sinner

The retreat *content* falls into periods of uneven length called "Weeks." Each Week is characterized by a deep kind of transformation and prepares for the subsequent one. In the first Week, the crucial grace is to understand oneself as a redeemed sinner. To help internalize this realization, retreatants first learn a process for self-reflection called Examen (24–44), which, when practiced regularly, teaches them to search for God's presence and work not only in the retreat, but also in everyday life. They then learn a prayer form called "meditation," or turning over with one's mind various mysteries of faith with the goal of personally appropriating them (46–54). Although the meditations in the *Spiritual Exercises* deal with abstractions such as sin, one's personal sinfulness, and hell, Ignatius's goal is that they become personally meaningful to each retreatant according to the grace that God offers. Those who know deeply not only that they are sinners but also that they are personally redeemed are in the best position from which to begin the journey as a disciple of Christ our Lord.

The second "Week": invitation to discipleship

The second Week continues that journey of intimacy, focusing attention on the person and work of Christ. New tools are necessary, and they appear at the appropriate points. First, retreatants learn a method of prayer ("contemplation") for entering imaginatively into the mysteries of Christ's life. Each contemplation begins with three introductory points: setting the context, composing the setting through imagination, and asking for the particular grace desired, and it closes with personal conversation or "colloquy" with Christ, the Father, or Mary. The retreatants proceed by means of such contemplations through important moments in the life of Christ. Once this form of prayer is mastered, it can be used outside the retreat, and for this purpose, Ignatius includes numerous suggestions for such "second Week" prayer (261–312). Strategically sprinkled among the contemplations are meditations on the experience of being called by an earthly king and by our eternal King (91–100), the challenge to follow the flag of Christ rather than the flag of the "enemy of human nature" (137–48), the difference in the responses of three groups of persons to burdonsome money (150–7), and three degrees of humility (165–8). These "Ignatian meditations" invite retreatants to ever deeper discipleship. Immediately following the last of these meditations, Ignatius places exercises for making decisions; at this point, retreatants formulate their life-defining decisions about the context of their discipleship (169–89). Significantly, Ignatius sets this decision making squarely within the continuing contemplations on the life of Christ, with whom the retreatant's relationship is growing ever deeper and more personal. The second week's grace, then, is a growing knowledge of how Christ is calling each retreatant personally and concretely.

The third "Week": participating in Christ's passion

The major teachings are complete, but the retreat journey still has much ahead. In the third Week, retreatants accompany Christ through his death, testing the depth of discipleship in the process. The third Week grace is to participate intimately and personally in Christ's sorrow and anguish, experiencing deep grief "because of the great suffering Christ endured for me" (203).

The fourth "Week": finding God in all things

By the time the fourth Week opens, Ignatius's directions almost disappear. Retreatants know well the pattern of personal engagement with Christ, but now it is the risen and glorified Christ with whom they engage. The final exercise—to deeply experience the love of God expressed in the Creator's continual "labor" in all things so that retreatants can meet God anywhere (230–7)—both names the grace of the fourth Week and impels retreatants back to ordinary life as changed persons who see God in all things.

Rules for discernment

Ever the methodical teacher, Ignatius closes the *Spiritual Exercises* with more process directions for the director. The most significant are points for discerning the motions that retreatants experience along the way. These "Rules for Discernment of Spirits" are divided into two sets, the first dealing with the more blatant strategies that the "enemy of human nature" uses to derail the retreatant's spiritual progress, and the second dealing with the more subtle temptations "under the appearance of good" that are more likely to deceive the more experienced disciple. Ignatius clearly means for these Rules also to be used outside of the context of the *Spiritual Exercises*, and they constitute a significant contribution to the discernment tradition.

INFLUENCE

Ignatius was not an innovator; everything that appears on the *Spiritual Exercises* can be found already within the history of

Christian spirituality. But the way Ignatius put these fragments together did create a new synthesis. The *Spiritual Exercises* reorders the traditional practice of *lectio divina* (spiritual reading) from reading, meditating, praying, and contemplating to reading, meditating, imaginative contemplating, and praying, a new order that subtly orients the prayer toward life in the world. The Examen looks for God's presence and human response in the midst of daily life, and decisions made in the context of the *Spiritual Exercises* are ordered by whatever offers service to God our Lord. The final contemplation on the love of God for every aspect of creation invites retreatants to live out God's love for all things. The resulting synthesis is an active, everyday, practical spirituality, oriented to mission in the world.

All members of the Society of Jesus, past and present, are formed spiritually within the matrix of the *Spiritual Exercises*. The *Constitutions* of the Society of Jesus, also written by Ignatius, weave the personal spirituality of the *Exercises* into a corporate spirituality Together these two documents create a template for an entirely new kind of religious order. This active, apostolic religious life changed the face of Christianity in the West by creating an enormous network of ministries geared to the needs of varied times and places. For the first time, religious men were trained alongside laity in "secular" occupations. Jesuit astronomers and mathematicians, for example, deeply impressed the sixteenth-century Chinese, who quickly employed what they learned from their European counterparts in perfecting their calendar. The Jesuits themselves soon recognized the potential for multiplying their effect through schools, establishing the first worldwide coordinated system of education in which Jesuits and other young men were trained together, all suffused within the *Spiritual Exercises*.

The principle of adaptation at the heart of the *Exercises* also spawned significant experiments in inculturating the gospel message in very different settings. Mateo Ricci in China, Roberto de Nobili in India, and the Reductions in Paraguay each adapted their approach in response to local conditions and stresses. For example, Jesuits in sixteenth-century Mexico and Peru believed in the innate equality of the native people and began the unprecedented innovation of educating the sons of the native Indians alongside the sons of the Europeans. In New France in the seventeenth century, under very different social-political conditions, Jesuits began seriously to learn how the local native persons actually interpreted their world, their language, values, and religion. They began to develop an intentional strategy: "go in through their door, in order to lead them out through ours," thereby employing positively what Ignatius described as the evil one's strategy (cf. 332)! Though each experiment was eventually snuffed out by political and ecclesial authorities, the *possibility* of inculturation remained, to spring up again in the post-Vatican II world.

The *Spiritual Exercises* also influenced the development of the modern spiritual direction and retreat movements. In response to Vatican II, the Jesuits began to re-examine their foundational documents and practices, including the *Spiritual Exercises*. In returning to Ignatius's practice of working individually with each retreatant, they quickly recognized the need to train many more persons, Jesuit and non-Jesuit alike, to direct the *Spiritual Exercises*. These training programs offered both the skills and a hospitable context in which the contemporary practice of spiritual direction could emerge. As these programs matured, they have further honed the understanding and practice of individual and communal discernment.

READING THE TEXT TODAY

Accessibility

The *Spiritual Exercises* presents a number of challenges to the contemporary reader. The text is not intended to be read but prayed, ideally under the guidance of a skilled director, and relatively few persons can organize their lives to make the full *Spiritual Exercises* in this manner. Fortunately, the form of the *Exercises* for the person engaged in ordinary life is increasingly accessible. Several experiments in offering the *Spiritual Exercises* via internet also exist, with varying results.

Reinterpretation and adaptation

Some images that would have been non-controversial in Ignatius's time are off-putting today and necessitate, at minimum, careful reinterpretation. Many stumble over Ignatius's militaristic images, his perspective that one's body is "filled with corruption and foulness" (58), his dualistic view of good and evil that includes regular references to the enemy of human nature, and the famous "What I see as white,

I will believe to be black if the hierarchical Church thus determines it" (365). In the context of their time, such images nourished a company of Jesuits who significantly changed the face not only of post-Reformation Europe but also of the newly colonized lands of India, New Spain, Brazil, and New France through an unprecedented fusion of education, exploration, trade, and evangelization. But not only has colonialism as a political-economic strategy unraveled, so too has the underlying theological and philosophical synthesis upon which it was based. Likewise, the post-Tridentine Roman Catholicism that both formed and was formed by Jesuits immersed in the *Spiritual Exercises* has given way to a pluralism that extends throughout the church and deep into the ranks of the Society of Jesus itself. If the *Spiritual Exercises* depended for its efficacy upon its author's worldview, it could be seen as an impediment to important spiritual issues of today, such as empowering formerly colonized peoples, reclaiming the body and the created world as sources of divine revelation, and forging cooperation across religious bodies.

Embedded at the heart of the *Spiritual Exercises* is a simple principle that allows their reinterpretation in radically changed contexts: the *Exercises* are to be adapted to the needs and desires and graces of the one making them (18). In the hands of a skilled director, the *Exercises* can become, as necessary, a school of prayer, a school of discernment, and a seedbed for discipleship and mission. Recent biblical scholarship can replace Ignatius's rather limited biblical understanding without compromising his insights about biblical prayer. Contemporary psychological understandings can fill out Ignatius's grasp of the way temptation lures people into settling for less than they are called to and his keen understanding of how desire functions to pull humanity deeper into relationship with God. New and personal images can arise out of each retreatant's experience of prayer. A spacious and generous application of this principle of adaptation, then, can accommodate a variety of theologies and ecclesiologies.

A holistic spirituality

Many people associate the *Spiritual Exercises* with highly rational and structured prayer. This criticism turns out to be more about an adaptation of the *Exercises* for a particular post-Tridentine cultural situation, and not about the *Exercises* themselves. In their original form, the various exercises are decidedly incarnational, meant to appeal to the whole person, body, imagination, affections and will, as well as intellect. Examples abound. Retreatants are invited to arrange all the details of their day, including their bodily postures, in such a way that they are more disposed to prayer. They are to find an appropriate balance in their eating (210–17). They are to pay attention to their desires, and attend to them as they pray. In choosing styles of prayer, persons are invited to pray not only on the Ten Commandments, but also on the five senses of the body (247–8). In the *Spiritual Exercises*, contemplation is understood not as letting go of all images, but as entering through imagination into the heart of the mystery of Christ. Indeed, Ignatius's ultimate goal for prayer is that each one would find a form that is pleasing, effective, and satisfying (238).

A spirituality open to all, for all

Another criticism of the *Spiritual Exercises* is that they are overly individualistic and inherently elitist. Only relatively well-off persons have the time and means to make an extended retreat, and exercises that invite one to be unattached to wealth, money, or power (149–57) imply that the retreatant actually has such a choice. A focus on each individual's relationship with God can too easily stop short of forging a spirituality that addresses issues of justice and the needs of others. The early contexts into which the *Spiritual Exercises* were introduced and practiced lend weight to these charges. For reasons of prudence, Ignatius very soon began to draw boundaries around the contexts in which the *Spiritual Exercises* were offered to women, with the result that over time fewer women were exposed to the *Exercises*, and those who were belonged increasingly to the upper class. Ignatius associated with movers and shakers as a means of furthering the mission of the Society, and Jesuit spiritual directors regularly showed up in royal courts. The humanist curriculum of Jesuit colleges tended to attract the children of the upper class more frequently than those of the lower classes. But today, arguably more non-Jesuits than Jesuits are prepared to direct the *Spiritual Exercises*, more women than men have actually made them in some form, their intrinsically lay nature has been reclaimed, and increasing numbers of Protestants seek them out. A deepening understanding of the corporate dimension of discernment has encouraged lively new responses to situations of structural injustice. As any dynamic spiritual text must, the *Spiritual Exercises* has transcended its origins and now belongs to the living spiritual heritage of the whole church.

TRANSLATIONS

Ignatius of Loyola (1991) *The Spiritual Exercises,* trans. G. Ganss in *Ignatius of Loyola: the* Spiritual Exercises *and selected works*, ed. G. Ganss, New York and Mahwah, NJ: Paulist Press.

Fleming, David (1996) *Draw Me into Your Friendship: the Spiritual Exercises: a literal translation and a contemporary reading*, St. Louis: Institute of Jesuit Sources.

FURTHER READING

Dyckman, K., Garvin, M., and Liebert, E. (2001) *The Spiritual Exercises Reclaimed: uncovering liberating possibilities for women,* New York and Mahwah, NJ: Paulist Press, adapts the imagery and dynamic of the *Spiritual Exercises* to sensibilities and needs of contemporary women.

Ivens, Michael (1998) *Understanding the Spiritual Exercises,* Herfordshire, England: Gracewing and Surrey: Inigo Enterprises, provides an accessible yet scholarly commentary on the *Spiritual Exercises*.

Lonsdale, David (1990) *Eyes to See, Ears to Hear: an introduction to Ignatian spirituality*, London: Longman & Todd and Maryknoll, NY: Orbis Books, places the *Spiritual Exercises* within the larger context of Ignatius's thought world.

Melloni, Javier (2000) *The Exercises of St. Ignatius of Loyola in the Western Tradition,* Herefordshire, England: Gracewing and Surrey, England: Inigo Interprises, sets the *Spiritual Exercises* within the history of Christian spirituality.

Modras, Ronald (2004) *Ignatian Humanism: A dynamic spirituality for the 21st century*, Chicago: Loyola Press, describes the Renaissance humanism that provided the cultural setting for the *Spiritual Exercises* and illustrates how its spirituality fared in other cultural contexts.

18

TERESA OF AVILA
(1515–82)
The Interior Castle

MARY FROHLICH

When she started writing *The Interior Castle* in June of 1577, Teresa
said the book would be "about prayer." But five months later, just
one week after completing it, she wrote that "It treats only of what
[God] is." What Teresa had unveiled as she worked her way through
this text was that the journey of prayer is long, demanding, and
complex, but it is also as simple as the brilliant light of God that
eternally pours itself forth at the center of the human soul. The image
that organizes her exposition is that of the human person as "a castle
made entirely out of diamond or of very clear crystal" (I:1,1), created
to be the glorious dwelling place of God. Comparing God to both light
and living water, she writes: "It should be kept in mind here that the
fount, the shining sun that is in the center of the soul, does not lose
its beauty and splendor; it is always present in the soul, and nothing
can take away its loveliness" (I:2,3). Even though a person may ignore
or obscure the light, God's outpoured love remains the fundamental
reality of his or her being.

Repeatedly, Teresa emphasizes that in this wonderful castle there
are "many dwelling places" (cf. Jn 14:2). In her words, "I say that you
should think not in terms of just a few rooms but in terms of a million;
for souls, all with good intentions, enter here in many ways" (I:2,12).

The Spanish word *morada* that is translated as "dwelling places"
traditionally was rendered as "mansions," but in fact *morada*

refers to a "home" or "abode," not to a large, luxurious building. Each of the seven sections of *The Interior Castle* has a plural title, that is, "The First Dwelling Places," "The Second Dwelling Places," and so on. Teresa is best understood not as presenting a lockstep path through seven clearly defined rooms, but rather a wandering journey that, on its way to the center, frequently criss-crosses and doubles back to discover new aspects of each set of dwelling places. Movement through the castle finds a radical unity in God, but immense potential diversity in the ways that different people actually make the journey.

AUTHOR AND AUDIENCE

Teresa de Ahumada y Cepeda was born in Avila, Spain, in 1515. Her father's family was among the Jews who had been forcibly converted to Christianity in 1492. Since Jewish blood was considered "impure" and prevented one from participating in many economic and cultural benefits, it was extremely important for the family to hide this heritage. Being a member of a marginalized group and having to deal daily with oppressive cultural codes of honor and status sharpened Teresa's consciousness of justice issues and underlies her forceful lifelong critique of such codes.

Teresa had nine brothers and two sisters. All the siblings who were close to her in age were boys. She grew up playing with her brothers, often exercising leadership among them, and was doted on by her father. Yet she quickly discovered the many male privileges from which a patriarchal culture firmly excluded her. Her mother, constantly pregnant and sickly, died when Teresa was twelve. When she was about thirteen her eldest sister married, but the marriage turned out to be an abusive one. Later on her younger sister also had a difficult marriage. As a young teenager Teresa read the novels of chivalry (the "Harlequin romances" of her day) and flirted dangerously with boys, but she had very mixed feelings about marriage. Meanwhile, nearly all her brothers participated in the conquest of the Americas as soldiers, adventurers, and fortune hunters.

At age twenty Teresa entered the Carmelite Monastery of the Incarnation in Avila. Throughout her life she imaged religious life as a spiritual form of being a "soldier and adventurer" for God. Yet her first nineteen years as a religious were a constant struggle with lukewarmness. She loved to chat—and flirt—in the parlor, and at one point even gave up prayer altogether. She was thirty-nine years old when a profound experience in front of a statue of the wounded Christ turned her around. An intense mystical relationship with Christ developed rapidly. She began to desire a milieu in which she could live her deepest ideal of the religious life to the full. In 1562, at age forty-seven, she founded St. Joseph's Monastery in Avila, the first of seventeen monasteries of the Discalced Carmelite reform that she spearheaded. Her vision was of small, fully enclosed, poor communities that lived the Carmelite contemplative life in its most radical form.

In 1562 Teresa wrote her *Life*, and four years later *The Way of Perfection*. In 1573 she began her *Foundations*, which she continued to work on until her death nine years later. In 1577, at the age of sixty-two, Teresa wrote her most mature text, *The Interior Castle*. All of Teresa's writings were prepared primarily for her sisters in the monasteries she founded, but she also had to be sensitive to the fact that they would be intensively examined by the Spanish Inquisition, which was very active at the time. As a woman with leadership skills, the child of Jewish converts, and a mystic, Teresa was in three categories that were regarded with suspicion. Her writings combine a mood of spontaneity and conversation with considerable sophistication in employing rhetorical devices to make her points—some of them quite challenging to the reigning ideology—without getting in trouble.

The Interior Castle was written well after Teresa received the culminating mystical grace of "spiritual marriage" in 1572. The circumstances of its writing were inauspicious: her other writings were being examined by the Inquisition, she was facing accusations of scandal and disobedience, and she had been firmly ordered to stop her work of reform. Despite the press of numerous troublesome business negotiations, she wrote the chapters up to V:2 in about five weeks, took a break of three and a half months, and then completed the rest in four more weeks.

SYNOPSIS

The "First Dwelling Places"

After first presenting her image of the many-roomed castle, Teresa considers how one may enter into the castle. Sadly, some people remain forever in the "outer courtyard" of the castle, not aware or not caring about the treasures that lie within. Such people are like the paralyzed, who cannot use the powers they were born with.

The door to the castle is "prayer and reflection," practiced with attention. Those who enter these First Dwelling Places are people who at least occasionally pause in the midst of their occupations and entrust themselves to God. Yet they are very vulnerable, for when they try to enter the castle a great many "vermin," "wild animals," and "reptiles" slip in with them and try to prevent them from enjoying what they find. They are in great danger of falling into mortal sin, which is like tar or a black cloth placed over the crystal so that the sun shining within it has no effect.

Even in these first beginnings, Teresa is at pains to note that what is most important is "what the Lord does in a soul" (I:2,7). By awakening to God's presence within, one grows in self-knowledge and humility, which are more important than anything else for one's spiritual growth.

The "Second Dwelling Places"

What primarily distinguishes the Second Dwelling Places from the First is that

> These persons are able to hear the Lord when He calls . . . through words spoken by other good people, or through sermons, or through what is read in good books, or through the many things that are heard and by which God calls, or through illnesses and trials, or also through a truth that He teaches during the brief moments we spend in prayer.
>
> (II:1,2–3)

The person tries to respond, but "the attacks made by the devils in a thousand ways afflict the soul more in these rooms than in the previous ones" (II:1,3). In order to continue forward, one must vigorously take up traditional spiritual practices such as using one's reason to combat temptation, seeking good companions, consulting people with experience, conforming to God's will, accepting the cross, and getting up after falling.

The "Third Dwelling Places"

These are the dwelling places of those with "well ordered lives." They avoid sin, do penance, practice charity, and frequent the sacraments. Yet in prayer, these people often experience dryness and distraction. This upsets them very much, because in their opinion they are leading very good lives. Teresa is hard on the people of the Third Dwelling Places. They are on the verge of a turning point in the journey, and they are in great danger of turning back instead of plunging forward. They have achieved everything that can be accomplished by human effort, and now the first inklings of a crisis—this time experienced not as the uproar of the devils, but as the boredom of dryness—are upon them. Some give up the whole enterprise and return to the First Dwelling Places. Others begin to think that they have already achieved the pinnacle of the spiritual life and are ready to teach others.

Either response, says Teresa, is fundamentally a lack of humility. "With humility present, this stage is a most excellent one. If humility is lacking, we will remain here our whole life—and with a thousand afflictions and miseries" (III:2,9). The most important practices at this stage are humility in the face of lack of consolation in prayer, promptness in obedience, and avoidance of a judgmental attitude toward others' faults—for "it is very characteristic of persons with such well-ordered lives to be shocked by everything" (III:2,13).

The "Fourth Dwelling Places"

"Supernatural experiences begin here," says Teresa (IV:1,1). For the first time, the soul directly hears the Lord's own voice:

> Like a good shepherd, with a whistle so gentle that even they themselves almost fail to hear it, He makes them recognize His voice. . . . It wasn't through the ears, because nothing is heard. But one noticeably senses a gentle drawing inward.
>
> (IV:3,2–3)

This "prayer of recollection" is the first way that an entirely new kind of spiritual experience begins to manifest itself.

In the beginning of these experiences one must still practice active meditation, because passive recollection is not so frequent. But with time the experiences intensify to become those Teresa calls "spiritual delight" (as distinct from the "consolation" that comes at least partly from our natural responses). Then "one should leave the intellect go and surrender oneself into the arms of love, for His Majesty will teach the soul what it must do at that point" (IV:3,8). Determination to do God's will, humility, detachment, love, gratitude: these are the practices appropriate to this stage.

The "Fifth Dwelling Places"

"Union" is the word Teresa uses to distinguish the Fifth Dwelling Places. The soul, like a worm that enters a cocoon to be transformed into a butterfly, sleeps in Christ in deep unknowing. Teresa adds:

> In loving, if it does love, it doesn't understand how or what it is it loves or what it would want. In sum, it is like one who in every respect has died to the world so as to live more completely in God.
> (V:1,4)

The sign that enables one to know that this is a true experience of union is the certitude that remains afterward. "God so places Himself in the interior of the soul that when it returns to itself it can in no way doubt that it was in God and God was in it" (V:1,9).

At this point Teresa begins to introduce the metaphor of betrothal and marriage. The union she has just described is like the first meeting between two who are going to be betrothed. (The custom of the time was that a period of formal meetings preceded the period of betrothal, which preceded the marriage.) Teresa is careful to point out that even if God does not give one the favor of this "delightful union" she or he need not feel dejected, for the essence of union consists simply in total surrender of one's will to God. Surrender of will makes the soul soft, like wax prepared to receive the impression of God's seal; it goes forth from the experience of union as God's own, ready to receive "what His Son had in this life" (V:2,13). For the first time, the soul's love of neighbor is such that it suffers pain in "the intimate depths of [its] being" when it sees the great suffering of other persons and of God due to the many evils in the world (V:2,11). The real test of this prayer is that the love of neighbor does not end with the end of prayer time, but carries over into practical action.

The "Sixth Dwelling Places"

Over one-third of *The Interior Castle* deals with these dwelling places. Teresa carefully describes and distinguishes locutions, imaginative and intellectual visions, raptures, suspensions, flights of the spirit, and many other experiences given only to mystically gifted souls. But she stresses that it is very dangerous to desire such experiences, for "greater glory is not merited by receiving a large number of these favors; rather, on the contrary the recipients of these favors are obliged to serve more since they received more." She affirms, "The safest way is to want only what God wants" (VI:9,16).

In the Sixth Dwelling Places God comes "as quick as a falling comet," wounding the soul "in the most exquisite way" (VI:2,2). This paradoxical joining of the most intense peace and delight with the most intense pain is a sign that this is not from the devil, for the devil can only give either disturbing pain or a false delight. Another sign that it is from God is that its fruit is the desire to suffer for God and to withdraw from earthly satisfactions.

The spiritual betrothal takes place when God "gives the soul raptures that draw it out of its senses" (VI:4,2). "God carries off for Himself the entire soul, and, as to someone who is His own and His Spouse, He begins showing it some little part of the kingdom that it has gained by being espoused to Him" (VI:4,9). A sign that these are true raptures, not caused by some constitutional weakness, is that one gains immeasurable understanding from them. One may not be able to explain what one has understood—in fact, unless God wishes it, it will be impossible—but it is "inscribed in the very interior part of the soul and never forgotten" (VI:4,6).

Despite the advanced state of this soul, it is at this juncture that Teresa goes into great detail about the necessity of never abandoning the humanity of Christ. Even though the work of the intellect in prayer has long since been superseded by the work of the loving will, there will be need at times to "blow on the fire" by representing gospel scenes with the intellect. Only in the seventh mansion, when one walks always with Christ, is that need rarely experienced.

In the passage to the Seventh Dwelling Places, the soul experiences a pain infinitely more intense than any yet mentioned. The soul feels absolutely distant from God; "it is like a person hanging, who cannot support himself on any earthly thing; nor can it ascend to heaven" (VI:11,5).

The "Seventh Dwelling Places"

At last the Lord brings the soul into his own dwelling place, calling it to its very center and giving it an intimate intellectual vision of the Trinity. This "spiritual marriage" is as different from any previous favor as the difference "between two who are betrothed and two who can no longer be separated" (VII:2,2). While all other experiences of union come and go, this one stands fast. The soul is "almost always in quiet" (VII:3,10). Not only is it no longer bothered very frequently by distractions, dryness, or the devil's antics, it also rarely experiences raptures anymore.

Yet, "the calm these souls have interiorly is for the sake of their having much less calm exteriorly and much less desire to have exterior calm" (VII:4,10). They experience a "deep interior joy" in persecution, and even have a "particular love" for their persecutors (VII:3,4–5). The whole purpose of this spiritual marriage, says Teresa, is that we might imitate Christ in "good works, good works" (VII:4,4–6).

INFLUENCE

Even during her lifetime, Teresa's teachings were controversial. Some theologians wanted to identify her with a problematic spiritual movement of the time, the *Alumbrados* or "enlightened ones." They asserted that she, like other members of this movement, chased after mystical experiences by practicing extreme passivity in prayer, and even encouraged others in lax attitudes toward moral life. They regarded with suspicion her claims of special knowledge based on experiences of God, since a good Christian should simply affirm official doctrine. Even more fundamentally, her authority to teach at all was rejected on the grounds that God does not give this authority to women.

These criticisms continued and even intensified after her death. Most of the theologians who examined her works, however, found them sufficiently orthodox. Teresa's writings were officially published in 1588, and from then on their popularity swelled. When a French translation appeared in 1601, Teresa's insights quickly became foundational for the burgeoning movement of French spirituality as well. By 1622 when Teresa was canonized, her teachings were already being regarded as normative for Catholic teaching on the mystical life. This is still the case today, especially for the schema of the seven sets of Dwelling Places that Teresa presents in *The Interior Castle*.

READING THE TEXT TODAY

Readers today can profitably approach this text in at least three ways. One can read it to get to know Teresa as a brilliant woman who, under difficult circumstances, wrote her way to both a resolution of her own identity issues and a resounding place in history. Or, one can read it to discover the theological vision that emerged as she mulled over both tradition and experience in the midst of an era of profound change. Finally, one can read it to sit at the feet of Teresa the spiritual master.

Teresa the writer

Teresa was sixty-two when she wrote *The Interior Castle*. In an era when life expectancy at birth was probably about forty, this was quite elderly. One way to understand the psychological context of the book is as part of Teresa's ongoing "life review" process. Life review is a natural psychological process that increases from midlife onward. It is a search for how to tell one's life story in a way that makes sense and integrates the painful, fragmented aspects as well as the successes. The fact that Teresa was under great stress at the time of writing *The Interior Castle* no doubt intensified the process. Another challenge was that she was instructed not to write in the first person (as she had done in her *Life* fifteen years earlier), but instead to present the story in more generalized terms. Teresa met the challenge by making her own both the traditional schema of seven spiritual stages and the trope of architecture as a model of the spiritual world. Both of these had been widely employed by others before her, but never with such freshness, verve, and depth as this. Teresa's genius as a writer emerges as she weaves her personal experience together with insights and images from a wide range of traditional sources.

Teresa's conversational tone and scintillating use of images quickly draw the reader into her world. She holds her organizing image of the crystal castle loosely as she repeatedly tests out fresh ways to express the inexpressible. For example, in just two paragraphs of the Fourth Dwelling Places she deploys imagery of the expanding heart, foolish shepherds, a spring swelling the interior being, a brazier giving off sweet-smelling perfumes, the purest gold of divine wisdom, and the absorbed faculties (IV:2,5–6). Despite the profusion of disparate images, there is no doubt in the reader's mind that Teresa is describing an experience that is deeply integrating and transforming.

The most significant shift of imagery in the text occurs in the Fifth Dwelling Places when Teresa begins to work with the analogy of betrothal and marriage. Earlier on, the predominant relational image was that of the divine King and his servants and vassals. She even goes so far as to refer to the human beings with whom God communes as "foul-smelling worms" (I:1,3). In the Fifth Dwelling Places, just as the "worm" enters the cocoon to become a "butterfly," the relational imagery changes to that of the Spouse and his beloved. Both on psychological and spiritual levels, this shift signals the relational healing that propelled Teresa into the new roles of foundress, teacher, and spiritual guide.

Teresa the theologian

The larger context of Teresa's personal challenges was that she lived at a time when both church and culture were going through a change of eras. This makes her theology of particular interest today, at the cusp of another change of eras. In her case, the Protestant Reformation was challenging the Roman Church, unleashing both creativity and defensiveness. Culturally it was Spain's Golden Era of wealth and triumph, but on a broader scale the profound changes associated with the dawn of what is called "the modern era" were already beginning to brew. As a woman, Teresa did not receive the classical education accorded to aspiring clerics and theologians. While a handicap in some ways, her lack of formation in traditional patterns of thought left her freer to respond to the newness of what was emerging. It was daring for her to use as her primary theological sources both personal experience and the images that she collected from a variety of sources, including scripture, other kinds of texts, and her culture. Most innovative, however, was the clarity of her narrative theological anthropology of the dynamic mutual indwelling of persons and God. By shifting the theological center to the interior of the human person, Teresa provided a fresh yet deeply orthodox theology for the emerging "modern" era in which emphasis would shift from a static and objective cosmology to the dynamism of human subjectivity.

As a theology born in an era of deep change, Teresa's method and model continue to be remarkably apropos for current needs. This has been affirmed by the Roman Catholic Church which named her a Doctor of the Church in 1978, as well as by the many theologians and others who employ her as a theological source. In the present time of ecosystemic crisis, a key issue is moving beyond anthropocentrism to a theology that affirms God's redemption at work in all creation. While on first glance Teresa's "interior castle" may appear anthropocentric, a closer look reveals that the real center for her is Christ who is both divine and human. Thus, it is not primarily the human person who is at the center, but God creating and redeeming the human person in intimate union with God's own being. It is a comparatively small step to add that God is the intimate center not only of human persons, but of the entire created web of life. While Teresa herself does not directly take this step, she makes a powerful contribution by affirming that reverent contemplative intimacy is the key to human participation in Christ's redemption of the whole web of life.

Teresa the spiritual master

More than anything else, Teresa is a companion and guide to living the spiritual life. With great wisdom, she points out the most prudent paths, describes the experiences and obstacles one may expect to encounter along the way, and teaches the nuances of the practice of discernment. She models the humor, confidence, and self-effacement of one who knows that what God is doing for her is infinitely more important than anything she can do for herself. Even as she spins out her magnificent story of the crystal castle with its million rooms and seven kinds of dwelling places, she constantly reminds her readers that finally we need only know one thing: the love of God poured out within us for the sake of our neighbor and our world.

TRANSLATIONS

Teresa of Avila (1988) *The Interior Castle*, trans. K. Kavanaugh and O. Rodriguez, Mahwah, NJ: Paulist Press, is the best translation available.

Teresa of Avila (2007) *Interior Castle*, trans. E.A. Peers, Mineola, NY: Dover Publications.

FURTHER READING

Ahlgren, G.T. (2005) *Entering Teresa of Avila's Interior Castle: a reader's companion*, New York: Paulist Press, guides the reader through the text with a special emphasis on Teresa as theologian.

Medwick, C. (2000) *Teresa of Avila: the progress of a soul*, New York: Alfred A. Knopf, is one of the better recent biographies of Teresa.

Muto, S. (2008) *Where Lovers Meet: inside The Interior Castle*, Washington, DC: Institute of Carmelite Studies, makes Teresa's teachings accessible and connects them to psychological insights.

Seelaus, V. (2005) *Distractions in Prayer: blessing or curse? St. Teresa of Avila's teachings in "The Interior Castle,"* Staten Island, NY: St. Paul's, offers a wise spiritual director's perspective on Teresa as teacher of prayer.

Williams, R. (1991) *Teresa of Avila*, New York: Continuum International, provides an accessible introduction to Teresa's historical and cultural context, writings, and spiritual doctrine.

19

JOHN OF THE CROSS (1542–91)

The Dark Night

DAVID B. PERRIN

Any discussion of "the dark night" of John of the Cross must begin with a definition of this term. First, in 1578 or 1579, John wrote an eight-stanza poem called "The Dark Night." ("The Dark Night," with quotation marks and without italics, will be used consistently here to refer to the *poem* exclusively.) A few years later, he wrote two commentaries on this poem. The first commentary, written over the period 1581–5, he titled *The Ascent of Mount Carmel* [*The Ascent*]. The second, written over the period 1584–5, he titled *The Dark Night*.

To confuse things even further, John refers to a particular moment in the spiritual journey outlined in his two commentaries as "the dark night of the soul." This latter expression has caught the popular imagination in today's world and is often used without any knowledge of its origins. For example, when another person is struggling with something major, someone might say, "Oh, that person is really going through a dark night." In this case the expression is used improperly to refer to all kinds of dire situations, or to intense soul-searching after some calamity in life.

This was not what John had in mind when he penned the phrase "the dark night." It does not describe some passing psychological state, but a profound state of being-in-love: of being so intimately united with God—a God who can be neither understood nor fully known—

that the individual is plunged into the darkness of this unknown. Life no longer makes sense except as a kind of prison in this glorious state of the loving embrace of a mysterious God.

AUTHOR AND AUDIENCE

John of the Cross (1542–91) was born Juan de Yepes y Alvarez in Fontiveros, Spain. After he entered the Carmelite order, he took the name John of the Cross. John lived during the dawn of the modern age in Europe, a time of unparalleled importance for Spain on the world scene. The political and material prosperity of the country had been guaranteed by the marriage of Ferdinand of Aragon and Isabella of Castile in 1469, which united the whole of Spain. With the "discovery" and conquest of the New World in 1492, new and immeasurable riches came flowing into Spain's many ports. However, many Spaniards remained untouched by this newfound wealth, and dire poverty was widespread.

As a child, John felt poverty's effects first hand. Due to his father's death at an early age, and his mother's inability to support their three children, John was placed in an orphanage. His childhood experiences of the need to care for and share with others remained with him throughout his life. At the age of twenty-one he joined the Carmelites, beginning his lifelong journey as a monk.

In their religious life, the people of sixteenth-century Spain lived in various and sometimes diverse settings. Numerous religious communities had sprung up, including the monasteries of the contemplative orders, such as the Cistercians and Carthusians. Popular and frequent public devotions were made to Mary, the Mother of God. Late medieval devotions included the centrality of the passion of Christ and the cult of the saints. The Spanish Inquisition, established in 1478, was still very active during John's life. This fierce institution had sweeping and, at times, harsh powers in everything concerning matters of faith. Anyone who showed signs of extreme religious fervor or departed from accepted patterns of orthodox teachings was in danger of being denounced to the Inquisition.

During his lifetime, John assumed several positions of leadership. He was rector of two Carmelite colleges; assisted Teresa of Avila (1515–82) in the reform of the Carmelites, which became known as the Discalced Carmelites ("discalced" means shoeless; Carmelites, who had a strict vow of poverty, went without shoes); was prior of several Carmelite residences; and even served as Vicar-Provincial, a major church office, of the Carmelite group in the south of Spain. It was in this climate of ferment in political, ecclesial, and social circles that John wrote "The Dark Night" and its two commentaries, *The Ascent* and *The Dark Night*.

Who were the earliest readers of these works? John served as spiritual director to many Carmelite nuns and friars, and to a group known as *beatas*. The *beatas* were devout laywomen who practiced rigorous piety while living within the confines of their own homes. These were among the earliest individuals to benefit from John's sublime writings. He used his writings to instruct these groups in their spiritual pilgrimage.

The Ascent and *The Dark Night*, which describe the first parts of the spiritual pilgrimage, tend to emphasize a harsh kind of asceticism or self-discipline of the body. But his literary works do not end there. Although they are little read, even today, two other major works by John speak of the latter parts of the journey, the more advanced parts: *The Spiritual Canticle* and *The Living Flame of Love*. The *Canticle* and the *Flame* are commentaries based on other poems by John with the same titles.

Despite the positive evaluation of the world reflected in *The Living Flame of Love* and *The Spiritual Canticle*, John is still best known for his seemingly pessimistic attitude toward the world, as reflected in the commentaries *The Ascent* and *The Dark Night*. To get a balanced appreciation of what is contained in "The Dark Night" as revealed in *The Ascent* and *The Dark Night*, it is helpful to read John's works (which are contained in a single book) in their entirety. The scholar writing for an academic audience or the pilgrim who seeks to be nourished at the well of John's deep wisdom would benefit from this approach to "The Dark Night."

SYNOPSIS

The Ascent and *The Dark Night* are two parts of a single work: the "dark night" is the summit of "Mount Carmel." Mount Carmel is a metaphor John of the Cross uses for the lofty state of perfection, culminating in union with God. John admonishes all to aspire to this state—especially the Carmelite nuns and friars under his care.

The combined commentaries of *The Ascent* and *The Dark Night* present a remarkable Christian spiritual itinerary from the point at which an individual first seeks God to the point where he or she experiences union with God.

Both *The Ascent* and *The Dark Night* are divided into books, chapters, and paragraphs for easy reference. There are three books in *The Ascent* and two books in *The Dark Night*. These divisions are a simple way to bring a range of thoughts into a coherent and progressive reflection as John moves along the description of the purification process and the maturation of the human being. The commentaries are also filled with many excursions, where John explores a number of topics related to his main line of thinking. He eventually finds his way back to the main topic and continues again until he decides to make another excursion. The reader should not be tempted to skip these excursions—in the end, they provide a rich context that brings depth and perspective on the main points being interpreted from the poem.

The method John uses to produce the commentaries on the poem is to treat each stanza individually—he ponders each word, phrase, or line, and thoughtfully explains its meaning. He looks on each in one way, then another. He weaves into his reflections numerous scriptural quotes to ensure that his insights and teachings are solid. It is remarkable that John could explore the same poem twice and end up with two distinct but complementary presentations on the spiritual journey from the beginning to the fullness of union with God.

Active and passive nights

In order to reach union with God, the individual must pass through a series of nights, or purifications. The necessary purifications are accomplished in two ways: actively, by the efforts of the individual assisted by the grace of God; and passively, by the action of God exclusively. For example, active efforts that may assist someone to be transformed may include deciding to set aside more time for prayer, or being more disciplined about helping others. The active journey is the main focus of the commentary in *The Ascent of Mount Carmel*. The passive journey is the main focus of the commentary in *The Dark Night*. The passive nature of the transformation process refers to God's abiding presence in the soul that wells up, for example, in the transformation of people's attitudes despite themselves (for example, through God's grace, people can become more patient, despite their own inability to be so).

During the journey through both the active and the passive nights, John describes a further division of each: a night of sense and a night of spirit. This division again conforms to moments of purification or transformation. As a result, the following sequence describes the spiritual itinerary seminally portrayed in John's "The Dark Night":

Active Night of Senses
Passive Night of Senses } *The Ascent of Mount Carmel*

Active Night of Spirit
Passive Night of Spirit } *The Dark Night*

It is the Passive Night of Spirit that is commonly known as the *dark night of the soul.* This defining moment of human/spiritual development will be briefly described below. For now, it is important to understand why John uses the metaphor of the "night" to describe the journey of union with God.

The metaphor of "night"

The metaphor of the night, John says, reflects the darkness that the human soul experiences in the beginning, in the middle, and at the end of the journey to union with God. God is so mysterious that, throughout the journey, the darkness, or the distance of God, exists— even though the experience of God wells up from within the depths of the human heart. This is the paradox of John's *dark night*: the human capacity to know and experience God is like living in the darkness of a cloud, yet, at the same time, the human capacity to know and experience God is apparent in intimate experiences of love, joy, and reconciliation with people all around.

In the beginning, the individual sets out on the journey in faith, not quite knowing what lies ahead. This is the darkness of the night of which John speaks. In faith, John encourages the pilgrim to leave the enslaving attachments to the material things of this world that would hold a person back from being attached to God. The darkness of faith accompanies each and every decision to detach not only from enslaving attachments to things, but also to detach from enslaving attitudes, beliefs, and feelings. Slowly but surely, through the subtle and mysterious mix of the pilgrim's own actions and God's grace, the pilgrim encounters the fullness of union with God—the goal of the journey in "The Dark Night."

Of course, union with God is also experienced all along the way. God, John insists, is never far from the pilgrim, but until the pilgrim is purified through the journey, he or she does not know this. Eventually, however, with due persistence, the pilgrim ascends the mount and begins to experience ever more intensely God's presence in the world and in his or her own life. Because the *dark night of the soul* is the phrase John uses most often to describe this intimate presence of God, it deserves a little more in-depth attention.

The dark night of the soul

The *dark night of the soul* refers to the most intense experience of the purification process. Due to the closeness of God perceived at this point, John says that the pilgrim "feels so unclean and wretched that it seems God is against him and he is against God" (*DN* Bk. II, Ch. 5, 5). So intense is this experience that the individual appears completely lost.

This experience is the culmination of what may have been years of persistent commitment to growing in the ways of God. What is happening here is a constitutive and fundamental reorientation of the personality structure. In the *dark night of the soul*, the individual can no longer sustain, in any way, comfortable illusions about who he or she is before others or before God: one stands naked before God and before oneself in this phase of the journey. John calls this a dark night since the natural light of one's own capacity to know and make sense of things no longer functions in any familiar way, and the light of God has not yet been revealed in its fullness. The *dark night of the soul* is therefore not a passing psychological state that one will get over. It is a theological and spiritual category that describes the state of existence that opens up the radical awareness of one's absolute and utter dependence on God.

As the Christian continues in his or her journey, the loving presence of God in life grows in intensity. This awareness, of course, is of no consolation during the *dark night of the soul*. What does stand out, however, is that in the public forum, those experiencing the *dark night of the soul* will scarcely be seen to be doing so at all. What will be seen abundantly are generous acts of charity, spontaneous acts of forgiveness and reconciliation, and extreme moral integrity. The person will be perceived as joy-filled and will exude intense happiness as well as depth of character. An acute awareness of the profound love of God is embodied in the day-to-day life of pilgrims in this phase of the ascent of the mount, which precedes the fullness and culminating phase of the spiritual journey—full union with God.

Union with God

Union with God represents the completion of the transformation as one's life conforms to God's in every possible way. At this point the individual has been drawn fully into participation in the Divine nature, so that his or her life displays all the loving attributes of God in this world. Inordinate affections, desires, or impulses all but cease to exist, and thus almost completely eliminate the individual's drive toward unwanted actions or harmful decisions. In this state of union, the individual knows that the human vocation rests in God's vision for the world: to grow in a self-liberating love that moves the individual to give his or her life over for others.

INFLUENCE

John of the Cross is one of the most notable Christian thinkers, and is recognized as such especially by those interested in asceticism and mysticism. Because "The Dark Night" and its commentaries have inspired many writers and practitioners, John has formed spiritually and intellectually countless numbers of Christian pilgrims over the centuries. In addition, John's work has inspired artists of all kinds, including poets, painters, songwriters, and playwrights.

Thomas Merton, the famous American Trappist monk, was inspired by John's *The Dark Night* to publish *Ascent to Truth* (1951). Jacques Maritain (1882–1973), the French scientist and philosopher, was preoccupied with the cultivation of the interior life as exhibited by John. This is evident in his open letter published in *Vie Spirituelle* (1923) titled "On the call to mystical life and to contemplation."

However, John's writings have not only interested writers strictly focused on Christian ascetical and mystical life. He has also inspired those who had less interest in the theological focus of his writings and more interest in his deep wisdom on psychological growth and spiritual/human transformation. This is evidenced in the work of the Canadian psychologist R.M. Bucke (*Cosmic Consciousness: a study in the evolution of the human mind*, 1900), who, in turn, inspired the American psychologist and philosopher William James (*The Varieties of Religious Experience*, Gifford Lectures 1901–2). Furthermore, John has been read with great interest not only by Christians, but by those of other faiths, such as Jews, Muslims, and Buddhists. For example, William Johnston's *The Still Point: Reflections on Zen and Christian Mysticism* (1970) reflects Buddhist interest in John's writings.

But John's influence has had its negative aspects as well. In view of the lofty ideals of complete surrender to God sought at the peak of Mount Carmel, many readers have interpreted *The Ascent* and *Dark Night* as espousing a flight from the world in order to reach Mount Carmel's summit of holiness in another world called heaven. In short, for some people, the descriptions of the journey that emphasize bodily mortification or punishment and material deprivation took on too great an importance. The true goal of the journey was lost, to the point that the world was seen as a horrible place to be.

John did urge a check on inordinate sensual and material attachments, as noted above, but in the earliest readings of the commentaries on "The Dark Night," these attachments were often seen as being ends in themselves, rather than means to an end. So popular was this approach to reading *The Ascent* and *The Dark Night* that the loving descriptions of the journey detailed in *The Spiritual Canticle* and *The Living Flame of Love* were almost completely ignored, even up to today. Doom and gloom seemed to be far more attractive to readers than the hope-filled expressions of God's love described in the *Canticle* and the *Flame*.

It was only in the latter half of the twentieth century, when John's writings were read as an integral whole, that a more balanced appreciation of "The Dark Night" and its commentaries became evident. It is important, therefore, when reading the commentaries on "The Dark Night," to read them in the context of John's entire work. It would be helpful to read *The Spiritual Canticle* and *The Living Flame of Love* first to grasp John's full range of thinking in "The Dark Night."

READING THE TEXT TODAY

Two key principles must be kept constantly before the reader when reading "The Dark Night" and its two commentaries, *The Ascent* and *The Dark Night*.

First, John uses poetry *and* prose to convey his experience of God and the transformation of an individual so he or she reaches the full potential of his or her humanity. Second, John firmly believes that God's grace does not destroy human nature but works through it to lead the individual to full union with God. Keeping these two principles in mind will help the reader avoid slipping into a negative evaluation of human nature and of the world, as is easily done, especially when reading *The Ascent* and *The Dark Night* for the first time. Behind these two principles stand a number of topics that will further assist the contemporary reader in appreciating John's rich and original approach to graced living that is seminally reflected in "The Dark Night."

One night, many expressions

Although John speaks of sequential active and passive nights, he astutely holds that there is really only one night. It is characterized by distinct moments as God invites the individual deeper and deeper into relationship. The night of "The Dark Night" is not linear but, consistent with human nature, is more cyclical in nature. Human beings grow and mature in a non-linear fashion, sometimes taking two steps ahead only to find themselves several steps back later on due to one thing or another. John teaches that a deep commitment to patience and trust is required for the journey into the dark night.

For example, even though an individual may reach the highest level of development possible in this life after having passed through the *dark night of the soul*, John admits that love can always grow deeper. Movement from one stage of development to the next is simply a way of characterizing the human journey. "The Dark Night" and its commentaries aim to point to a model of how people grow in life with God, with as many unique variations as there are people.

A description of what it means to be human

John does not offer a program or a set of instructions that, once followed, will ensure success in spiritual/human development. Clear recipes for "success" seem to be popular today, but this is not what John has in mind. What he does offer is a description of the fundamental realities of life and what it means to be a faith-filled human being. On the one hand, he describes the tragedy of broken promises, the reality of inescapable human weakness, and the pain of being alone due to narcissistic behavior. On the other hand, he narrates the infinite joy of finding authentic love, of experiencing the divine presence in nature, and of discovering the pleasures of sensual human love.

A careful reading of "The Dark Night" and its commentaries uncovers a wealth of insight into what it means to be fully human and fully alive in Divine love—that is, living a life of religious faith. The primary characteristic of religious faith in the dark night is informed by being-in-relationship, not knowledge gained from text or doctrine. Text and doctrine are dislodged in the dark night to make way for a new way of knowing the world of human relationships.

John does not dwell on the morbid circumstances of life. He is not so much the doctor of the *dark* as he is a champion for the *light* of life, which is God. John is convinced that individuals grow fully into their human potential only when they are centered on God and come to know the world through the eyes of God. The dark night functions on the level of love, both in its fullest expression as well as in an intense awareness of one's lack in this area.

God invites and transforms

What John describes in "The Dark Night" and its commentaries is the profound experience of human freedom achieved through a reordering of human affections and relationships. Individuals, says John, rather than remaining attached to sinful or debilitating affections and relationships, are constantly being invited by God through the events of life to consider another way of knowing and being in the world. In the dark night, God's light shines on people's false knowledge of themselves. The distorted and enslaving conditions that cause them to be plunged into the darkness of the illusions they hold about life are illuminated. However, God does not stop there. The dark night is not an end in itself, nor is it a once-and-for-all experience. Rather, it is an ongoing journey of transformation, purification, and growth.

Through God's constant invitation to love freely, the individual is slowly transformed, gaining insight into another way of living that frees the individual from all that is enslaving. As a person grows in freedom and self-knowledge, far from being detached from this world, he or she grows ever more deeply into being involved with life through acts of charity, forgiveness, and self-giving love. But this journey of transformation is mysterious. The pilgrim is plunged ever more deeply into the mystery of faith. John says that each person is called to be holy—that is, to participate in the redemption and transformation of the world as his or her unique circumstances of life allow.

John's conception of the active and passive nights safeguards the free gift of God's grace to humans, but also leaves an active role for the individual to play in the spiritual journey. Human freedom and God's gracious action in human life are carefully balanced in "The Dark Night" and its commentaries. The pilgrim of the dark night grows in humility, which allows him or her to see all things in a radical new way; to appreciate other people in a new light; and to reverence the world as a work of God.

What John offers the contemporary reader is the value of boundaries and limits. For John, having less can mean having more— less of what is destructive and leads to despair, and more of what makes people truly happy. John's reflection is especially significant in a consumerist society where unbridled attachments result in the endless consumption of goods of all kinds, to the point where even people become objects to be used, abused, and discarded. What John offers today is a way to a meaningful, productive, and engaged life.

TRANSLATION

The Collected Works of St. John of the Cross, trans. Kieran Kavanaugh and Otilio Rodriguez, Revisions and Introductions by Kieran Kavanaugh, rev. edn, Washington, D.C.: Institute of Carmelite Studies Publications, 1991.

FURTHER READING

Bourne, P. (1992) *St. John of the Cross and the Dark Night*, Long Beach, CA: Wenzel Press, is a classical and systematic analysis of both *The Ascent* and *The Dark Night* commentaries.

Howells, E. (2002) *John of the Cross and Teresa of Avila: mystical knowing and selfhood*, New York: Crossroad, is a comparative theological analysis of the mystical journey as outlined by these two great contemporaries and reformers.

Perrin, D.B. (1997) *For Love of the World: the old and new self of John of the Cross*, Bethesda, MD: International Scholars Press, portrays the transformation of the memory, will, and intellect, that results in the new self that resides on Mount Carmel.

Ruiz, F. (2000) *God Speaks in the Night: the life, times, and teaching of St. John of the Cross*, trans. Kieran Kavanaugh, Washington, D.C.: Institute of Carmelite Studies Publications, portrays John's Spain, his life, and writings in abundant colored pictures and descriptive prose.

Welch, J. (1990) *When Gods Die: an introduction to John of the Cross*, New York: Paulist Press, is an excellent introduction to all aspects of John's work, including the theological, psychological, and sociological.

20

FRANCIS DE SALES
(1567–1622)

Introduction to the Devout Life

WENDY M. WRIGHT

When the beloved Roman Catholic bishop Francis de Sales died prematurely in Lyon, France at the close of the year 1622, word spread like wildfire among the many people he had touched over his very public lifetime. De Sales had been accompanying the court of his native country of Savoy as it toured through France, and crowds gathered to mourn his passing. When his body was brought back to the town of Annecy where he had resided as the exiled Catholic bishop of Geneva, a public cult soon grew up. Flowers and votive offerings piled up at his tomb and streams of pilgrims visited the site. Soon his fellow countrymen mounted a campaign to have their favorite son declared a saint, despite the fact that recent reforms in the official Catholic process forbade canonizing anyone until three-quarters of a century after their death.

Among the many reasons for de Sales's popularity was his small book entitled *Introduction to the Devout Life*, which caught the imagination of his day and, as its many subsequent editions suggest, has continued to encourage generations of Christians in the walk of faith. Engaging in style, it was written for the ordinary person: the housewife, the grocer, the local government official. Devotees piled flowers and candles upon his gravesite not simply because he was a renowned preacher and spiritual guide or because they venerated him as a supernatural miracle-worker or admired in him an austere, otherworldly holiness. They felt that he had spoken the truths of their own hearts and allowed them to cultivate the presence of God in lives that were far from the austerity of the monastery or the isolation of the desert wilderness. Francis de Sales had helped them to see how their deepest desire—to love God and to love as God loves—was possible amidst the busyness and burdens of ordinary life.

AUTHOR AND AUDIENCE

Louise de Chastel was typical of the many people Francis de Sales inspired and with whom he corresponded. The young wife of Claude de Chaumont, Seigneur de Charmoisy, had sought counsel from her bishop about how to pursue a serious life of Christian devotion in the midst of the luxury and distractions of courtly life. For centuries it had been commonly assumed that those with a serious call to love and serve God would find a place primarily in monasteries, vowed religious life, or the priesthood. But times had changed. During the previous century the Protestant reformations that swept Europe had challenged the idea that there were set-apart forms of life for the serious Christian. There had been movements of laypersons committed to devout Christian practice long before the Reformation. But now, in Catholic Savoy and France at the dawn of the seventeenth century, the idea of lay devotion caught fire. Ecclesial reforms of all sorts brought a revitalized spiritual energy. Spirituality was in vogue in upper class salons and among the bourgeoisie. Treatises on the spiritual life were being newly translated or composed, and spiritual guides were sought out.

The young de Sales was born in 1567 into this reenergized Catholic culture. His aristocratic Savoyard parents prepared their eldest son Francis to take his place as a societal leader. Inspired by the Christian humanist vision taught by his Jesuit schoolmasters in Paris, de Sales early on developed his own synthesis of the spiritual life. He believed that God desired devout persons in all walks of life to act as leaven in the rising loaf of Catholic Christendom. Later, his most ardent ministry would be to those, like Mme de Charmoisy, not recognized as the traditional ecclesial or spiritual elite.

Introduced to the rhapsodic language of the Song of Songs by a Benedictine scholar in Paris, the young student began to conceptualize the relationship between God and humankind as a compelling love story. At the center of his poetic vision was the image of a world of intertwined divine and human hearts. The Trinitarian God could metaphorically be said to possess a dynamic, relational, and life-giving Heart that is the source and end of all Love. Creation itself is the result of the intrinsic dynamic of Love flowing out in self-gift and drawing back into union with itself all that it has created. Human beings too have hearts—dynamic cores involving the intellect, reason, affect, and will—that are made in the divine image and designed to beat in rhythm with the Heart of God. Although at root human hearts tend toward union with God and the good, sin has wounded them so that their movement is, as it were, arrhythmic. What is needed is a heart to bridge the human and divine realms, a fully human heart that is also divine.

Thus at the center of Francis de Sales's vision was the Jesus who enjoined all to come and learn from him for he was gentle and humble of heart (Mt 11:29–30). These particular qualities of Jesus's heart were not seen by the Savoyard as accidental, for he felt that the reign of God was to be realized not in the attitudes so characteristic of the "world"—power over others, self-assertion, or the acquisition of status, wealth, or honor—but through the practice of the little, relational virtues such as gentleness and humility. Christian discipleship consisted in the long-term transformation of the heart, indeed, an exchange of hearts, so that one could "live Jesus," and say with Saint Paul that "I no longer live but Christ lives in me" (Gal 2:20).

This profound transformation into and through Love, Francis believed, occurs in both vertical and horizontal directions: through prayerful communion with God and in the context of human communication. Hearts that are claimed for the gentle, humble heart of the Crucified One inspire and draw other hearts to them, causing them to conform to the movement of divine Love. Heart speaks to heart. All forms of communication thus are avenues through which Love might flow. Preaching, teaching, correspondence, and spiritual guidance can draw others to the divine source; these are among the arts of "winning hearts" so dear to the Savoyard. All human relationships, especially friendship, community, and marriage and family life, are potentially avenues through which one's heart is transformed to be what it was created to be. This vision of a world of intertwined divine and human hearts won by and for Love undergirds the distinctive school of spirituality of which Francis de Sales would later be known as founder—the Salesian tradition.

When the nineteen-year-old de Sales left Paris for the University of Padua to pursue an advanced degree, his family expected him to study law in preparation for assuming his duties as family heir. Instead, the young man undertook advanced studies in theology and eventually convinced his parents to honor his desire to enter the priesthood. Soon he became an assistant to the (exiled) bishop of Geneva, was sent as a missionary into Protestant territories and, upon the bishop's death, assumed the episcopal rank. As reforming shepherd of his flock, Francis labored for the remainder of his fifty-five years in the fields of his diocese, the seat of which (Annecy) was in Savoy, as Geneva was at the time an exclusively Protestant city. He preached, taught, offered spiritual guidance, reformed existing orders, established an innovative women's religious community (the Visitation of Holy Mary) with widowed Baroness Jane de Chantal, and took up his pen. His voluminous correspondence, his theoretical *Treatise on the Love of God*, and the popular *Introduction to the Devout Life* today witness to his unflagging pastoral care.

When Bishop de Sales wrote his series of advisory letters to Louise de Chastel, he was engaged in winning her heart for the love and service of God precisely as a young wife and mother, in other words, in the "state of life" in which she found herself. These letters later became the basis of the book that de Sales composed for the many lay women and men who felt drawn to deepen their spiritual lives, indeed to live more fully their Catholic identity. In it the reader is addressed as "Philothea" (Latin feminine for "Lover of God").

SYNOPSIS

The *Introduction to the Devout Life* sets out a five-part formative program designed to "lead the soul from its first desire for the devout life" toward an internalization of life practices that help one fully realize love of God and neighbor. "Devotion" is described as love that is enabled by divine grace to do the good carefully, frequently, and promptly. The devout life is imaged, in one of the metaphors so typical of the Savoyard's writing, as Jacob's ladder. This ladder has two sides, prayer and the sacraments, by which the devout person ascends toward and receives the grace of God, and a set of rungs by which one advances from virtue to virtue, either by supporting the neighbor or by prayerful union with God. Although de Sales insists that all Christians are called to pursue such an intentional life, the practices he recommends are to be adapted to the particular reader, taking into account her or his life responsibilities, temperament, strength, and ability. Further, a spiritual guide should be engaged in order to progress surely in the process of establishing the devout life.

Preparing the soul

Following these preliminary remarks, part one offers a set of meditations for the process of "purgation." In de Sales's era, the ancient threefold movement of the Christian spiritual life—purgation, illumination, and union—was assumed to be the pattern by which the human person grows into conformity with God in Christ. Thus the *Introduction* begins by making space for the divine in the heart and mind of the initiate. The good desires that lead "Philothea" to desire a devout life are likened to flowers in a garden. But for flowers to flourish, the garden's vines must be pruned and weeds pulled out. Thus sinful tendencies—those actions and attachments that turn people in on themselves and away from God—must be acknowledged and confessed. A series of ordered reflections directs the reader to consider the goodness of creation, the true end for which humanity is created, God's goodness, and the human tendency to turn away from God. Each meditation is fashioned so that the reader personalizes them, becoming conscious of the blessings she has received and the ways in which she has failed to respond in gratitude. Always, the interior dimension of the devout life is stressed. It is not enough to refrain from openly hating or slandering someone; nurturing hate or slander in the heart is also to be avoided. Likewise, while de Sales has no intrinsic objection to the sports, parties, or fine clothing required for someone in Mme de Charmoisy's situation, he counsels that inordinate attachment to such goods is a hindrance to the cultivation of a devout life. The first section closes with meditations on death, judgment, hell, and paradise which put the personalized reflections in a cosmic context. The meditations end with a prayerful act of "election": the intentional choice of the path of devotion.

Planting the seeds

The second part presents "Philothea" with practices that encourage
a deepening love of God and neighbor, which the bishop considers
the two arms of love. He first suggests several modes of prayer that
can cultivate a sense of the presence of God: consideration of the life
and passion of Christ, vocal prayers such as the *Our Father* and
the *Hail Mary*, the rosary, a short formula for methodical meditation,
a morning exercise, an evening exercise, "spiritual retreat" (frequent
retiring to the heart in the manner of birds returning to their nests),
and daily spontaneous prayers. These private prayers are to be nurtured in the context of the wider life of the church, so the Savoyard
goes on to recommend weekly attendance at Mass (stressing frequent communion which was not common at the time), participation
in the daily liturgical offices, and the practice of sacramental confession. In addition, he commends veneration of the saints, the private
reading of spiritual books (including Augustine's *Confessions*,
Teresa of Avila's writings, and the lives of the saints), and the practice of discernment (under the heading "How we should receive
inspirations").

Cultivating the garden

In the theological tradition the bishop inherited, the spiritual and
moral life were conceived of as inseparable. Part three of the *Introduction to the Devout Life* thus is concerned with the practice of the
virtues. Echoing Saint Paul, de Sales presents charity or love as the
greatest of the virtues, the one toward which the entire Christian life
orients but, using a charming (if entomologically inaccurate) rhetorical
figure, he suggests that just as the king of the bees never flies into the
fields without a host of his subjects, so charity can never enter a heart
without a train of other "little" virtues, such as gentleness, patience,
and humility. These little virtues, all of which are relational, can be
practiced in any state in life, especially in the lives of his primary
readers whose lives mirror that of Mme de Charmoisy. Humility
receives special treatment: its deepening levels are explored and
its true, as opposed to false, exercise is clarified. The asceticism
Francis de Sales teaches his devout pupil is a profoundly interior one.
He recommends modesty in dress, temperance in consumption,

consideration in speech, integrity, generosity with material goods, and restraint in actions, but in contrast to much preceding spiritual literature, the Salesian spirit does not emphasize extreme penance or bodily mortification. It asks instead a hidden, interior asceticism that allows the devout person to move gracefully through the ordinary cares and social interactions of life while inviting the gentle, humble Jesus to inhabit the heart.

Particularly interesting in this third part dealing with the virtues is the inclusion of the topics Friendship and Marriage. Francis feels that while persons in monastic community may not have the need for particular friendships, true friendship is a necessity for those living "in the world." De Sales contrasts the walk of those who travel on level ground and do not have to lend each other a hand with those whose path is rugged and slippery and thus must hold each other's hands to move safely. As one of the most luminous theorists of spiritual friendship in the Christian tradition, de Sales distinguishes false friendships of all sorts: those that are frivolous, flirtatious, or based solely on self-advancement or sensual pleasure are to be avoided. But true, spiritual friendship the Savoyard considers a unique, mutual, and communicative form of love which can lead the friends to a deeper experience of divine love. Heart speaks to heart. Francis de Sales's advice for married persons is also quite progressive for his time. While he assumes, as do his Catholic contemporaries, that one of the important fruits of marriage is childbirth and child rearing, he does not feel that this is the only fruit of marital love. Instead, a true union of hearts is foremost in his mind. The maintenance of such a union is, he counsels, encouraged by mutual affection and tender regard. Marriage should have as its center the sort of love that characterizes true friendship.

Weeding and pruning

The last two sections of the *Introduction* concern themselves with sustaining the devout life. They confirm Salesian spirituality's reputation for being inspired common sense. Much of part four treats questions that "Philothea" might ask after she had been practicing the presence of God and cultivating virtue for some time: How does one deal with the tendency to grow tepid in spiritual practice? What if one gives in to vanity, jealousy, envy, or undue anxiety? How might one handle painful criticism? What if one is tempted to pursue a questionable relationship? What harm does it do to harbor desires for forbidden pleasures? How does one confront spiritual dryness? Is devotion really about having good feelings all the time? These questions the bishop confronts with his customary forthrightness and common sense, encouraging his reader in the very real, often banal, struggle to gradually become conformed to a new life. The gentleness with which he addresses those he guides is evident; harshness toward one's self or others is not conducive to the cultivation of love. But sustaining this gentleness is a firm resolve and a clear-sighted view of the possible problems that a person might encounter over time.

The fruitful life

As a positive counter to the fourth part, which focuses on what to avoid, part five offers "Philothea" a series of encouraging meditations designed to periodically renew and confirm the choice of an intentional devout life. Francis again draws upon classic forms of meditation to help the reader be mindful of the wider context of the personal practice of devotion. A yearly resolution, periodic self-examination as to how one is with God, neighbor, and one's self, and guided reflections on the expansiveness of divine love and the examples of the saints confirm the person attempting to "live Jesus" in the midst of the busyness and burdens of an ordinary life.

INFLUENCE

From the time that the *Introduction to the Devout Life* was published in its definitive edition in 1619, it captured the imagination of the public. Although intended for Catholic readers, even in de Sales's day it was widely read in Protestant circles. To cross the confessional divide, some versions excised references that were deemed too tradition-specific, such as the suggestions for hearing Mass. By the end of the nineteenth century over four hundred editions of the work had appeared. The *Introduction to the Devout Life* was the backbone of what has become known as the "Salesian Pentecost" of the nineteenth century. Throughout Europe, in a Catholic Church struggling against the forces of modernization, political revolution, secularization, and industrialization, Salesian spirituality was revived.

The *Introduction* was not the only factor in the revival (de Sales's theological vision enunciated in the *Treatise on the Love of God* appealed to the era that embraced Romanticism, and he was seen as a defender of the Roman faith), but it was a significant one. Several new religious communities were founded on Salesian principles, including the Salesians of Don Bosco, the Daughters of Mary Help of Christians, the Congregation of the Missionaries of Saint Francis de Sales, and the Oblates and the Oblate Sisters of Saint Francis de Sales, all of which carried the spirituality into their varied ministries.

In the nineteenth and twentieth centuries the Visitation of Holy Mary, which Bishop de Sales and Jane de Chantal had founded themselves, sponsored convent schools in Europe and North America where young women were nurtured in the commonsense spirituality of the *Introduction*. Some of these schools continue to operate today. In addition, a vigorous network of pious lay associations grew up— one, the Daughters of Saint Francis de Sales, with ecclesial canonical status—that promoted the spiritual vision outlined in the Savoyard's most popular work. Up until the mid-twentieth century and the varied literature for laity issuing from the Second Vatican Council, the *Introduction* remained a staple of Catholic literature. It continues in print today both in classic translation and in adapted and updated versions designed to be accessible to the contemporary reader.

READING THE TEXT TODAY

The Catholicism of the early modern period was marked by intense spiritual energy as well as the rigid confessionalization that was the legacy of the European reformations and the ensuing wars of religion. By the time de Sales arrived at maturity, the lines between Catholics and Protestants were sharply drawn, but some of the terrible violence of the confessional wars had begun to wane. Recent scholarship has identified Bishop de Sales as a key figure in the emergence of a new piety. The fiercely ascetic and penitential spirit of previous decades was replaced by a gentler, more optimistic one emphasizing a compassionate impulse to serve the poor and uncatechized. A new stress on civility and manners emerged, along with the impulse to order both the ecclesial and social body. The late medieval European spiritual world, basically an oral one, was giving way to a society in which literacy was dominant. Christians began to adopt a more spiritualized understanding of faith and to value inward prayer and moral convictions more than externalized means of communicating with God. Salesian spirituality, with its emphasis on a transformed heart and the practice of the gracious little virtues, is exemplary of this trend. As today's Catholic Church has its genesis in the early modern era, the vision that Francis de Sales presents should not seem utterly unfamiliar to present-day readers.

A church of the past

At the same time, there are some obviously anachronistic elements of Philothea's guidebook. For example, the recommendation about private meditation or the recitation of a rosary while attending the Eucharist alludes to a Catholic world before Vatican II's instruction for conscious participation in the vernacular liturgy. More subtly, the *Introduction*'s meditations on classic themes such as death, hell, and judgment may put today's readers off, accustomed as they are to equating spirituality with feelings of affirmation, serenity, and wholeness. The methodical and programmatic nature of some of the *Introduction*'s prayers may chafe against the grain of modern sensibilities as well. While to those advanced in the life of prayer the bishop would recommend following the unique promptings of the Spirit and perhaps practicing a less discursive, formulaic prayer, he never suggested giving up mental prayer altogether. He considered the scriptural and theological content of meditation to be essential and formative.

Rhetoric from the past

Similarly, the ornate language of the original, even in a good translation, may daunt some who delve into the *Introduction* for the first time. De Sales was a brilliant rhetorician and preacher who knew the power of a story, image, or metaphor to arrest the attention and drive home a point. For Philothea he chose images that would be appealing and familiar. Thus the practice of gathering a spiritual bouquet at the end of a prayer time so that she could enjoy its scent all day mirrored the habit Mme de Charmoisy and her friends had of carrying about actual floral nosegays. Similarly, de Sales's odd botanical or zoological allusions come from the literature or popular science of the time; for example, he illustrates the instruction to engrave the name of Jesus on one's heart so that all one's actions will then bear that name by reference to an almond which, if engraved with a name and planted, will produce a tree bearing almonds with the same marking. The image worked better, perhaps, in the seventeenth century, but the point holds up well in the twenty-first.

Still a classic text

For all of its cultural otherness, the *Introduction to the Devout Life* nevertheless offers itself today as a classic spiritual text. The "universal call to holiness" enunciated at Vatican II, which has been credited with initiating a spiritual renaissance for the laity that has swept through the Christian churches, was in fact anticipated by Francis de Sales by four hundred years. Likewise, the positive valuation of marriage and friendship as contexts for spiritual development, now assumed in most religious circles, was a favorite theme of the *Introduction*'s author. More strikingly perhaps, the early modern Savoyard wrestles with questions that contemporary readers of all denominations wrestle with. How do I find God in the midst of the busyness and burdens of family life and work? Can I develop a deep, genuine life of prayer without living like a hermit? Can I really be a faithful disciple in my own ordinary, undramatic way? What does it take to order my priorities and get what really matters to the center of attention? How do I sustain my relationship with God over the long haul? What part do my friends or my children and spouse play in my walk of faith? Who am I in relation to the God who made me? What is asked of me—not some generic Christian, but me?

TRANSLATION

Francis de Sales (1972) *Introduction to the Devout Life*, trans. J.K. Ryan, New York: Doubleday Image Books.

FURTHER READING

Coster, D. (2000) *Francis de Sales*, Noorden: Bert Post, is a fresh, engaging portrait of the saint, translated from the Dutch.

Ravier, A. (1988) *Francis de Sales: sage and saint*, trans. J.D. Bowler, San Francisco: Ignatius Press, is a reliable biography by a noted interpreter.

Stopp, E. (1997) *A Man to Heal Differences: essays and talks on St. Francis de Sales*, Philadelphia: Saint Joseph University Press, highlights the insights of the late, renowned scholar of Francis de Sales.

Wright, W.M. (2004) *Heart Speaks to Heart: the Salesian tradition*, Maryknoll, NY: Orbis Books, chronicles the tradition that emanates from the founder until the present.

21

GEORGE HERBERT
(1593–1633)

The Country Parson

PHILIP SHELDRAKE

In his 1670 life of George Herbert, Izaak Walton prefaces his description of Herbert's life and ministry as Rector of Bemerton in a dramatic
and spiritually heroic fashion:

> [I] bespeak the reader to prepare for an almost incredible story of
> the short remainder of his holy life; a life so full of charity,
> humility and all Christian virtues, that it deserves the eloquence
> of St. Chrysostom to commend and declare it.
>
> (Isaak Walton, *The Life of Mr. George Herbert*)

Walton then describes how George Herbert, immediately after
induction as Rector of Bemerton, was discovered by a friend lying
prostrate in prayer before the altar in the church. Walton goes on to
say that in the course of this experience Herbert conceived of certain
rules of priestly life and made a vow to keep them. According to
Walton, Herbert wrote down the rules and it was these that appeared
posthumously as *The Country Parson*. For Walton, George Herbert
was above all a model of sanctity and so his *Life* sets out to reinforce
this viewpoint. While this perspective has some validity, George
Herbert, Anglican priest and poet, was a person of many parts. It is
this complexity, combined with tensions in his personality and a deep
inner spiritual struggle, that make his writings rich and memorable

as works of Christian spirituality. On the one hand, Herbert has achieved classic status as one of the greatest English poets. On the other hand, he was also a major figure in the emergence of a distinctive spiritual tradition in the Church of England during the first half of the seventeenth century and is usually identified with the group of theological and spiritual writers known as the Caroline Divines.

While George Herbert is most widely and popularly known for his poetry, notably his major collection entitled *The Temple*, equally important is his lesser-known treatise on the priestly life entitled by Herbert as *The Country Parson, His Character, and Rule of Holy Life* but additionally in some published editions called *A Priest to the Temple*. The focus of the treatise is Herbert's understanding of the theory and practice of pastoral care. However, this pastoral concern is linked all the way through the treatise to a framework for the support and development of the spiritual life of a priest. Without such attention to spirituality, pastoral care would be superficial and empty activity. Equally, the spiritual lives of those with whom the priest works is the focus of Herbert's more complete vision of pastoral care. In this sense Herbert does not make a rigid distinction between the themes of pastoral theology and what people nowadays think of as "spirituality." It is also worth remembering that in the minds of many commentators even Herbert's poetic collection *The Temple*, while having a more obviously personal and spiritual flavor, is also carefully constructed with a didactic and pastoral purpose.

AUTHOR AND AUDIENCE

George Herbert was born in 1593 into the English aristocratic and powerful Pembroke family. He had an illustrious academic career as a pupil at Westminster School followed by Trinity College, University of Cambridge, where he became a Fellow in 1614. Initially, Herbert seemed destined for a public career. He became Public Orator of the University in 1620 and then a Member of Parliament in 1624. Although Herbert apparently began divinity studies as early as 1616, he was only ordained deacon by special dispensation at the end of the 1624 Parliament. There was then a further long pause before ordination as a priest in Salisbury Cathedral in September 1630, after he had already been inducted as Rector of Bemerton just outside

Salisbury. Unlike many aristocratic clergy, Herbert chose to live with his wife and family alongside the church. His role as parish priest lasted less than three years, for he died on March 1, 1633.

The various delays between his divinity studies, ordination as deacon, and ordination as priest suggest that Herbert struggled with the contrary attractions of a public career and vocation to the priesthood. There were probably external factors associated with unfavorable political shifts during the 1624 Parliament. However, Herbert's writings, notably his poetry, show signs of inner spiritual struggle— not least a recurring sense of unworthiness in the face of God's love.

All of George Herbert's writings were published posthumously. His poetic collection *The Temple: Sacred Poems and Private Ejaculations* appeared in 1633, the year of his death. His second major work, *The Country Parson*, was first published in 1652. There were a number of other minor published works in English and, in addition to the published works, a number of extant letters (including some within Walton's *Life*), Herbert's will, and one of his orations given at Cambridge.

The church context of the first part of the seventeenth century was a period of tension between mainstream loyalists like Herbert who supported the liturgy, order, and formularies of the Church of England established under Queen Elizabeth I and those labeled Puritans who believed that Reformation principles had been compromised by retention of a threefold hierarchy of bishops, priests, and deacons as well as a formal liturgy in the Book of Common Prayer.

The precise purpose of Herbert's treatise *The Country Parson* is ambiguous. According to Isaak Walton, it derived from Herbert's own need for a rule of life. The 1632 preface partly supports this when it states that "I have resolved to set down the form and character of a true pastor, that I may have a mark to aim at." However, the didactic purpose of the text is underlined by the concluding sentence: "The Lord prosper the intention to myself and others, who may not despise my poor labours, but add to those points to which I have observed, until the book grow to a complete pastoral." Those "others" would most likely be fellow priests or those considering this calling. In the end, the treatise is not simply a practical manual but clearly has a rhetorical purpose not only to *instruct* but to inspire the reader to a deepening sense of call and to a more profound response.

SYNOPSIS

The Country Parson consists of a preface, thirty-seven chapters on personal and pastoral themes (for example, "The Parson's Life"; "The Parson Preaching"; "The Parson's Dexterity in Applying of Remedies") and two prayers before and after sermons.

Didactic model

Herbert's model of pastoral care is didactic through example as well as word. Some people find the style too definitive, but it is important to read the treatise alongside *The Temple* poems where the painful realities of inward spiritual struggle haunt the pages. It is clear that Herbert was a devoted servant of God's Word and this reflected the Reformation sensibilities of his Church. At the heart of the parson's knowledge and ministry are the scriptures—the primary means of divine communication and moral transformation. Herbert believed in the power of expository preaching. "The Country Parson preacheth constantly: the pulpit is his joy and his throne" (ch. 7, "The Parson Preaching"). Knowledge of scripture was central. "The chief and top of his knowledge consists in the book of books, the storehouse and magazine of life and comfort, the holy Scriptures" (ch. 4, "The Parson's Knowledge"). Yet also "there he sucks and lives." For Herbert there is a sacramental quality as the Word of God is present behind the written words. Consequently, the priest is to approach scripture in a spirit of prayer rather than only intellectually. "The second means [of understanding] is prayer, which if it be necessary even in temporal things, how much more in things of another world, where the well is deep, and we have nothing of ourselves to draw with?" (ch. 4).

Apart from preaching, Herbert commended the importance of other forms of teaching such as catechizing, which is "a work of singular and admirable benefit to the Church of God" (ch. 5, "The Parson's Accessory Knowledge"). This "admirable benefit" consists of three things: infusing knowledge of salvation in everyone, building up this knowledge spiritually, and through this knowledge inspiring reformation of life (ch. 21, "The Parson Catechizing").

Pastoral care and the church

George Herbert's approach to pastoral care is ecclesial. While the parson is "the deputy of Christ" (ch. 1, "Of a Pastor"), the priest is also the representative of the church. An important dimension of the priest's teaching is preparation for public worship and sacraments. So, the parson "applies himself with catechisings and lively exhortations" in preparation for Communion Sundays" (ch. 22, "The Parson in Sacraments"). Yet, preaching has its limits, for its purpose is to lead to prayer. "Resort to sermons, but to prayers most: / Praying's the end of preaching" (*The Temple*, "The Church Porch," lines 409–10).

Herbert's parson was more than a weaver of words. In the Church of England, the priest's teaching role was expressed above all in leading public prayer. The spirituality of the Book of Common Prayer promotes the Daily Offices and Holy Communion as the main school of the Lord's service. The liturgy was the foundation of the life of a parish as both human and religious community. For this reason, Herbert's parson was to give special attention to the dignity of public worship (ch. 6, "The Parson Praying") and to the church building and its furnishings (ch. 13, "The Parson's Church").

A holy life

Herbert's emphasis on holiness underlines that priesthood is not merely a job but a way of life involving every context, including the management of household and family (ch. 10, "The Parson in his House").

Herbert recommended that the priest be fed by study. "The Country Parson hath read the fathers also, and the schoolmen and the later writers, or a good proportion of all" (ch. 5). Yet without holiness, nothing counts. So "The country parson's library is a holy life" rather than only books (ch. 33, "The Parson's Library"). The notion that ministry relates to a holy life also applies to preaching. Its effectiveness is enhanced, "First, by choosing texts of devotion . . . moving and ravishing texts, whereof the Scriptures are full. Secondly, by dipping and seasoning all our words and sentences in our hearts, before they come into our mouths" (ch. 7). The priest's "eloquence" consists in communicating a sense of transformative engagement with God and God's Word.

Herbert stresses that the parson is to nurture each person's specific vocation (ch. 32, "The Parson's Surveys"). Equally, the priest is not to despise the holiness of the lowliest people. "He holds the rule, that nothing is little in God's service. . . . Wherefore neither disdaineth he to enter into the poorest cottage. . . . For both God is there also, and those for whom God died" (ch. 14, "The Parson in Circuit"). Yet alongside a common Christian calling, Herbert retained a "high" view of ordained ministry. Interestingly, while he allows that for practical reasons a priest may marry, yet "The country parson considering that virginity is a higher state than matrimony, and that the ministry requires the best and highest things, is rather unmarried than married" (ch. 9, "The Parson's State of Life").

For Herbert, there is a special intimacy between God and those who preside at Holy Communion. "Especially at Communion times he is in a great confusion, as being not only to receive God, but to break and administer him" (ch. 22). The tension between an awesome calling and human frailty is clear. Although in the poem "The Priesthood" ordained ministry is described as a "Blest Order, which in power dost so excel," the priest can only respond with a sense of unworthiness. In the poem "Aaron," playing on the image of the priest vesting before services, the "poor priest" is naturally dressed in profaneness. Yet if the priest puts on Christ, "in him I am well drest."

Priest as spiritual guide

Herbert's parson is also a spiritual guide. The priest has "digested all the points of consolation" (ch. 15, "The Parson Comforting") and seeks to alleviate scruples, not least concerning distractions in prayer (ch. 31, "The Parson in Liberty"). In attending to the spiritual state of parishioners, the priest should respond according to need. Thus Herbert advises vigilance with those who seem untroubled and support for those in temptation (ch. 34, "The Parson's Dexterity in Applying of Remedies"). He follows the Prayer Book and echoes the advice of other Caroline Divines in recommending "particular confession" ("this ancient and pious ordinance") for people who are afflicted (ch. 15). Spiritual guidance more widely is ordinary rather than extra-ordinary. A thread of what might be called spiritual conversation runs through *The Country Parson* whether in church, while entertaining guests in the parsonage (ch. 8, "The Parson on Sundays") or visiting people's homes (ch. 14). This ministry of spiritual guidance through "good discourses" is also shared with the priest's family and servants, "so that as in the house of those who are skilled in music all are musicians, so in the house of a preacher, all are preachers" (ch. 10).

The art of complete care

Herbert's model of ministry and care is broadly based. Apart from spiritual comfort, Herbert is interested in physical healing. This may reflect both his own history of poor health and his contact with country traditions of herbal remedies. Chapter 23 ("The Parson's Completeness") suggests that healing is a crucial part of the priest's parochial role. The parson should ensure the provision of basic medical care; earlier, in chapter 10, healing skills are among the qualities to be sought in a wife. If neither the parson nor the parson's wife has medical skills, Herbert suggests keeping a physician in the household or developing a relationship with a nearby physician. Herbert argues that herbal medicine is not a difficult skill, recommends certain books and the development of herb gardens, and gives examples of herbs and their uses. However, a link between physical and spiritual well-being is maintained. "In curing of any the parson and his family use to premise prayers, for this is to cure like a parson, and this raiseth the action from the shop to the church."

More broadly, Herbert's parson seeks to be involved in every aspect of parish life. To the modern reader this "total care" may seem oppressive, but in the context of the times is better understood as holistic. "The Country Parson desires to be all to his parish, and not only a pastor, but a lawyer also, and a physician" (ch. 23). "Lawyer" refers to an ability to offer legal advice and arbitration in disputes. For such complete care, local knowledge is the bedrock, and so visiting around the parish is a critical task for every weekday afternoon (ch. 14).

Herbert's parson is to address specific needs rather than generalities and is to adopt practices and ways of speaking that are appropriate to the people concerned. So, stories and sayings may be more effective than abstract ideas (for example, ch. 7). Because the parson deals with country people, it is important to be familiar with the everyday tasks of agriculture. In all this, the parson is to emphasize the reality of divine providence to counteract any lingering fatalism about events, weather, or the natural order of things (ch. 30, "The Parson's Consideration of Providence"). He must respect ancient customs in the village, including ones with devotional origins such as processions or the blessing of lights (ch. 35, "The Parson's Condescending").

INFLUENCE

In some ways, George Herbert's longer-term influence is difficult to assess with precision. Over the last twenty years there has been a considerable revival in scholarly writings on Herbert, but these have been primarily literary, theological, or contextual rather than either pastoral studies or spirituality.

There has also been a scholarly debate about whether Herbert should be thought of as more Protestant or Catholic in his sympathies. The emphasis, for example, on the centrality of scripture and preaching seems to favor the former, but some medieval allusions as well as Herbert's sacramental and Eucharistic emphasis seem to favor the latter. Indeed, in the nineteenth century Herbert was known by representatives of the Oxford Movement, and the poet Gerard Manley Hopkins, originally a High Church Anglican and subsequently a Catholic convert, saw Herbert as a spiritual forebear. However, this debate is certain to be inconclusive precisely because it is polarized. In his own context, it is more accurate to see Herbert as a mainstream Anglican in the classic Elizabethan "middle way" (though the word "Anglican" was not used in the seventeenth century). Herbert's treatise was the first attempt in the English Church to offer a practical, pastoral manual. Although he was no Puritan, Herbert's reputation for holiness left a favorable impression on people such as Richard Baxter who considered that this was "a man who speaks to God like one that really believeth a God."

Herbert has a long-standing literary reputation as a great seventeenth-century English poet. The spiritual impact of the poetry is also well attested. Several poems have become well-known hymns with ecumenical popularity. The profundity of the poetry inspired the English composer Ralph Vaughan Williams who set some to music as the *Five Mystical Songs*. Herbert's poems also appear in the appendix to the English version of the Roman Catholic Divine Office. Simone Weil, a religiously unconventional figure, was introduced to the poetry just before World War II while spending Easter at the

French Benedictine Abbey of Solesmes. While meditating on one poem, "Love III" ("Love bade me welcome"), Weil seems to have had a deep mystical experience of Christ.

Unlike the poetry which has an established place in the English literary canon, the specific influence of the text *The Country Parson* is less easy to assess. The Puritan Richard Baxter's *The Reformed Pastor* appeared in 1656, a mere four years after *The Country Parson*, and was probably influenced by it. The treatise was reprinted in 1671 and again in 1675 around the time of Isaak Walton's *Life*, so it seems likely that the work continued to have some impact on the English Church in the later Stuart period. However, overall, most modern studies of George Herbert concentrate on his poetry and have little to say specifically about *The Country Parson*. Despite this, Herbert's treatise has become one of the historical classic texts used in courses on pastoral theology and Christian spirituality in England.

READING THE TEXT TODAY

Herbert's understanding of pastoral care and the priestly life is conditioned by his historical, theological, and social context. Modern readers of *The Country Parson* are often struck by the social and religious assumptions that distance the text from their own times. Herbert, while recommending a simple life for priests and warning them against too close an association with local landowners, came from an aristocratic background and his portrait of the priest is still somewhat patrician and paternalistic. Equally, the established church remained hierarchical in its understanding of priesthood.

Limitations of the text

Herbert's country parson operates within fixed social and ecclesial models. Indeed, *The Country Parson* promotes a tightly ordered spirituality. The orderly life of a priest, the right ordering of liturgy and church buildings, the good order of the parishioners, the maintenance of proper order in society and the State are perhaps rather quaint reflections of Herbert's notion of divine order and harmony. Yet they also portray a spirituality that is deeply institutional.

Herbert's parson exists in an ambiguous relationship with his parish. On the one hand, the priest is to mix freely with parishioners, to eat with them or to have them eat in the parsonage. The priest is to view unfeigned friendliness as a pastoral tool. Yet the boundaries remain. The priest has an exclusive role in leading worship, dispensing sacraments, and in key aspects of pastoral care. The pastoral model is not a collaborative one except in a limited way in relation to the parson's own family. The priest is an autonomous person of power whose household has servants, financial means, and, above all, knowledge. Their role in relationship to parishioners is quasi-parental—even the parson's children and servants are dispensers of charity and spiritual wisdom to others rather than receivers.

Rereading the text

Contemporary readers are therefore faced with the question of whether this "classic," while obviously not above criticism, is still "useable" outside its original context. On the one hand, they can only approach the text from the perspective of their own horizons of meaning and value. On the other hand, they would fail to respect the integrity of the text if they merely picked what immediately resonated with their own assumptions while ignoring the structure or context of the text as a whole. In fact there needs to be a two-way conversation between the contemporary readers and the text so that the wisdom of the text is able to challenge them in its strangeness, yet they are also free to question the text critically. The result is a rereading of the text where readers today may find meanings that were unavailable to a previous generation of readers.

It is also important to place *The Country Parson* alongside *The Temple* poems to obtain a balanced understanding of Herbert's approach both to spirituality and to pastoral care. On its own, *The Country Parson* hardly suggests that the parson shares the same spiritual world as everyone else. Its approach is more austere and didactic than the poetry. The emotional reticence of the text serves to emphasize a certain detachment in pastoral ministry. The honest self-exposure and spiritual depth of the poems (which also have a didactic and pastoral purpose) rights the balance by suggesting that struggle and personal transformation also lie at the heart of Herbert's view of ministry.

As already suggested, the poetry itself was also a means of communicating certain spiritual and pastoral values. As a means of teaching, the poetry does not have as its primary aim the communication of information about faith, or of instruction for a moral life. Compared to the language of *The Country Parson*, the language of the poetry has an evocative quality that more readily touches the emotions. It also has the capacity to unlock the imagination. Poetry is more readily able to speak to the mysterious, ambiguous, and complex nature of religious faith and practice. The pastoral value of the poetry when set alongside *The Country Parson* is that together they may touch the modern reader in a more intimate way than the treatise on its own.

Key values and contemporary use

It is now possible to suggest underlying features of George Herbert's model of the pastoral life that continue to offer valuable material for contemporary reflection, if not precisely for literal imitation. First, pastoral care is not merely an activity but a way of life. What is offered to others is drawn from experience, spiritual as well as practical, and from values that are lived out by a Christian minister. Second, pastoral care demands a difficult but vital balance between detachment and passionate engagement. Third, a truly pastoral life is not merely a pale reflection of social work. It touches the human and spiritual depths and is inextricably linked to spirituality, prayer, and worship. Fourth, pastoral care is associated with what is today called "adult religious education" and "spiritual formation." For example, Herbert spends a great deal of time writing about the communication of adequate knowledge to parishioners, both in terms of doctrine and of spiritual discernment. Yet, the poetry especially also suggests that there is a form of spiritual "knowledge" to be found in aesthetic appreciation and the love of beauty that goes beyond the purely rational. Fifth, the pastoral life does not merely concern the care of individuals in isolation but also the nurturing of a community of faith, worship, and charity. Finally, the pastoral life touches upon all aspects of human existence rather than simply the obviously religious elements.

In the end, *The Country Parson* attempts to outline a way of life and a set of relationships rather than a series of abstract spiritual theories or a list of practical pastoral strategies. Consequently, the image of pastoral care that emerges from the text is flexible because it is inherently adapted to times, people, and circumstances.

EDITION

George Herbert (1995) *The Complete English Works,* ed. A.P. Slater, London: David Campbell Publishers.

George Herbert (1981) *The Country Parson; The Temple,* ed. J.N. Hall, New York: Paulist Press, is another edition of Herbert's two major works but with a substantial and useful introduction.

FURTHER READING

Cooley, R.W. (2004) *Full of All Knowledge: George Herbert's "Country Parson" and early modern social discourse,* Toronto: University of Toronto Press, is one of few studies of *The Country Parson*— primarily social history rather than theology.

Hodgkin, C. (1993) *Authority, Church and Society in George Herbert,* Columbia: University of Missouri Press, has a useful chapter on *The Country Parson* entitled "Doctrine and Life: Herbert's protestant priesthood."

Sheldrake, P. (ed.) (2009) *A George Herbert Reader,* London: SCM-Canterbury Press, is an edition of extracts from Herbert's writings organized in thematic sections with substantial introductions.

Veith, G. (1985) *Reformation Spirituality: the religion of George Herbert,* Toronto: Associated University Presses, is a detailed study of Herbert's writings from a Protestant theological standpoint.

22

MADAME JEANNE GUYON
(1648–1717)
A Short and Very Easy
Method of Prayer

BO KAREN LEE

Few Christian authors have been as widely misunderstood and condemned, yet simultaneously celebrated and revered, as Madame Jeanne Guyon. Commentators such as Ronald Knox, in his well-known book *Enthusiasm*, reckoned her a madwoman, while John Wesley, Kierkegaard, and Schopenhauer deeply admired her wisdom. Today, Guyon's influence on the American churches can still be traced through the Holiness movement, as well as prayer conferences of various stripes that focus on her work. Her books continue to be reprinted by a wide variety of publishers in multiple languages. Yet her writings provoke opposition in other corners. While some observers laud her piety, others deride what they consider to be "mindless mysticism."

During her lifetime, Guyon was the pivot of even greater controversy. Her teachings were adopted by the famous churchman François Fénelon, and with his support she rose to prominence in the courts of Madame de Maintenon (the second wife of King Louis XIV), serving as her spiritual counselor. Nonetheless, her "unconventional" teachings on the interior life, first expressed in 1685 in her *Moyen court et très facile pour l'oraison* (*A Short and Very Easy Method of Prayer*) won her some powerful enemies. After bitter interrogations in 1694, King Louis XIV consigned her to a dungeon in Vincennes in

1695, and then to the infamous Bastille for several years, followed by house arrest until her death in 1717.

Though condemned by the Catholic church, Guyon gained a loyal following of Protestants, some of whom surrounded her at her death-bed. Her writings continued to be received beyond the boundaries of France into Europe, the Americas, and even Asia. Admittedly, Guyon's language can be erratic and extreme, often difficult to swallow. Yet, her writings convey a persuasive power. Her emphasis on self-abandonment, or complete surrender to the hands of God, appeals to many, even as her corollary teachings on sacrifice, suffering, and submission provoke conflicting responses.

As Guyon explained in her *Short and Very Easy Method of Prayer*, the "chief end of humanity" was to "enjoy God" both "in this life" and forever. This enjoyment, however, came at a steep price. If the highest call of life was to find one's pleasure in the greatest good, she argued that one consequently had to forsake "lesser" pleasures. Inferior joys were a mere façade—a barrier to the purest pleasure available only in God. In order to attain the greatest good, purgation of lesser loves was required. This purgation required a complete aban-donment also of the self—of one's desires, will, and attachments. According to Guyon, wholehearted surrender to the will of God enabled the soul to "make room," so to speak, for the divine presence, and this she deemed "true prayer." Even when expressed in perplexing language, Guyon's ultimate goal was to create radical hospitality within the soul for the fullness of God.

AUTHOR AND AUDIENCE

Madame Jeanne Guyon (1648–1717) was born in Montargis, France, into a pious Catholic family. Her parents took little care for her education, shuttling her around from convent to convent as the young girl contended with frequent illness and a frail constitution. At the age of sixteen, she married a wealthy neighbor, Jacques Guyon, twenty-two years her senior. Rather unhappily wed (as described in her *Autobiography*), she developed a habit of "interior prayer" during this time, which would later deepen under the guidance of her confessor, Father François La Combe.

When the death of her husband in 1676 freed Guyon from the constraints of marriage at the age of twenty-eight, she felt called to spread her teachings on the interior life. She left home within a few years and advanced further in her life of prayer, as she traveled throughout Geneva, Turin, and Grenoble to guide others in the spiritual life, often in small gatherings. These gatherings inspired her to write for her friends, with *The Spiritual Torrents* appearing in 1682 and her *Short and Very Easy Method of Prayer* a few years later. Her confessor, Father La Combe, also encouraged her to begin writing her *Vie* (*Autobiography*) which would be completed in 1709. Guyon also set about the task of writing biblical commentaries to further elucidate her ideas, most notably her *Commentary on the Song of Songs* in 1688. In poor health, Guyon returned to Paris in 1686. There she gained the avid support of François Fénelon and served in the court of Madame de Maintenon.

Guyon's works were not intended for wide circulation, but her *Short and Very Easy Method of Prayer* went to press in 1685. Reaching beyond her friends, this book came under official scrutiny shortly after the Quietist controversy erupted in Rome. (Quietism advocated perfect stillness and passivity in the Christian life.) Chief among the book's opponents was the indomitable Bishop Jacques-Benigne Bossuet. Religious authorities were on the alert against "novelty" during this period, and Guyon became a prime target because her writings sounded dangerously similar to the Quietist teachings of Miguel de Molinos, condemned by Pope Innocent XI in 1687. King Louis XIV had also revoked the Edict of Nantes, thereby limiting religious freedom. Her *Short and Easy Method of Prayer* was thus placed on the *Index of Prohibited Books* in 1688, and her books were burned throughout various cities in France.

A prolific writer and serious student of the Scriptures—a great rarity in her day, especially for an uneducated Catholic woman—Guyon produced over twenty biblical commentaries and fifteen treatises, as well as a three-volume work, *Justifications*, that provides a 1,200-page theological defense of her orthodoxy. When her work came officially to trial in 1694, Bishop Bossuet won the day in seeing her teachings overthrown, and the majority of Catholic authorities disowned her. Though imprisoned and later confined to house arrest, Guyon did not stop writing. As Archbishop of Cambrai, Fénelon continued to promote her teachings (even if in disguised form). The Dutch Protestant Pierre Poiret preserved and published her works, and her thought was well received in the Netherlands, Germany,

Switzerland, England, and China. Her influence on John Wesley and the American Methodist movement, as well as the early Quakers, has also been acknowledged.

SYNOPSIS

According to Guyon, all people are invited to experience the "depths of Jesus Christ" not only in the life to come, but here and now. She thus invites her readers to learn the way of interior prayer, which she considers the path to the deepest enjoyment of God. Guyon calls this a "short and very easy method of prayer" but concedes that not all are willing to enter this path. Indeed, though this "method" becomes "method-less" in its final stages, the route seems anything but simple.

In this work of twenty-four chapters, Guyon addresses various themes in moving "from the shallows to the depths." She advises her reader on "first steps" and ensuing periods of dryness, exhorts her audience to go deeper through the key of "abandonment" and "inward turning," and then moves through the experience of silence and stillness to union with Christ. At its heart, the secret to Guyon's method is the attitude of abandonment or full surrender, which she also calls "annihilation" of the soul. In order to understand her language, however, context must first be given.

Enjoying God in prayer

> The end of our creation, indeed, is to enjoy God, even in this life; but, alas! how few there are who are concerned for this!
>
> *A Short and Very Easy Method of Prayer*,
> trans. Brook (ch. 20, p. 65)

According to Guyon, prayer is an essential means by which to enjoy the presence of God. In *A Short and Very Easy Method of Prayer*, she guides her reader through three kinds of prayer, from "beginning" stages to "more advanced." Through each of them, the savoring of God's presence is central (even during times when God seems absent).

In the first level of prayer, Guyon encourages her reader to "meditate" on small portions of Scripture—to chew, taste, savor, swallow, and digest. Through "praying the Scriptures" one is led to "behold the Lord" or "wait in God's presence" (ch. 2, p. 7; this and all subsequent citations from the translation published by SeedSowers). Guyon writes that Scripture ought to lead the individual to a deep *enjoyment* of God, rather than mere understanding. Thus, one prays in this manner with the heart (that is, with loving attention), not simply with the mind (ch. 2, pp. 10–12). As one grows in this prayer, one is then called to move "inward," where God dwells, and to experience the "prayer of simplicity" or "stillness" (ch. 3, p. 19). This silence is not inactivity, but rather results from overflow: it is a "rich, abundant" silence. In other words, there is so much that can be said, that one remains silent in the enjoyment of God (ch. 12, p. 61).

The third and final kind of prayer, however, plunges the individual into the depths of Jesus Christ. It moves from "times" set apart for prayer, to a life of prayer. Prayer then suffuses the entire day (ch. 6, p. 31). According to Guyon, a "fresh attitude" is needed for this transition, which she calls *abandonment*. The surrender of the self is the key to the "inner court," to "fathomless depths" (ch. 6, p. 33). Through surrender, one extricates oneself from attachments to self, one's desires, and the world, and is released into the immensity of God's good will (ch. 6, pp. 34–5). One "loses" oneself in this release, only to find oneself secure in God's providential care.

This decisive act of resignation may look like reckless abandon, but Guyon calls it the "highest action of the will" (ch. 11, pp. 56–7). It is a decision to cease self-effort and to rely completely upon God's leading. In order to be sensitive to God, however, one must "be still" (ch. 12, p. 61). In this place of sheer passivity (which is nonetheless an active choice), one is then "swallowed up" in God's activity, work, and power, and enjoys God more completely. In Guyon's language, one is "poured" into God's vastness, and is "overcome" and "filled" by God, in loving mutual exchange. At the same time, one is no longer attached to the pleasures of "enjoying God," but learns to love God "purely," even through seasons of dryness, darkness, and trial.

Self-abandonment: the key to union

Although surrender is the key to deeper intimacy with God, it comes at a cost. In abandoning one's will, one also renounces self-interest, desires, and hopes. Furthermore, abandonment entails forgetfulness of oneself as one "sinks" into "nothingness" before God's vast embrace. Guyon writes that the self is "dissolved" and "destroyed"; by this she means that its own operations come to a halt (ch. 20, pp. 89–90). The individual no longer strives but rests completely in God, led by God's actions. This is what Guyon calls "true prayer," when one is utterly consumed like a burnt offering before God (ch. 20, pp. 87–90). Nothing of the "self" remains. Yet she goes on to explain: "There is a principle of nature here. The Lord never allows a void or an emptiness in nature to remain. He comes to the place of nothingness—and emptiness—and instantly fills it with Himself" (ch. 20, p. 91).

In this attitude of abandonment, one lets go even of routine petitionary prayers or self-examination and confession of sins. The individual invites God to pray through her, rather than exerting self-effort to pray in a certain way. God then searches the heart, exposes secret sin, and allows the individual to be purified by God's convicting fire (ch. 15, pp. 73–8). This then prepares the soul for union with God, as "like is joined to like." Again, this requires stillness before God, and the cessation of frenetic, multiple activities. Intercessory prayer comes about in the same way: the individual is led by God into various prayers by listening attentively for God's lead (ch. 17, p. 82). The individual's own desires and petitions are secondary to God's will, indeed, "lost" in God. But Guyon adds, "If God is your mover, you will move much farther in a short time than all your repeated self-effort could ever do" (ch. 22, p. 115).

Despite its benefits, self-abandonment is no simple matter. It means trusting God even when circumstances are unfavorable. According to Guyon, trusting the sovereignty of God through experiences of suffering is difficult, but necessary, in order to be lost most fully in God's loving embrace. One gives up one's rights, but then finds oneself enveloped in God's vastness. Guyon writes, "But is not annihilation a bitter thing? Oh! If only you knew the virtue and the blessing which the soul receives from having passed into this experience" (ch. 20, p. 91). This is the mystery of surrender: one dies to self, only to "bear fruit" in unexpected ways. "Unless a grain of wheat falls into the earth and dies, it remains just a single grain; but if it dies, it bears much fruit" (Jn 12:24).

As Guyon explains:

> Your Lord once declared that He alone has life. All other creatures have 'borrowed' life . . . He wishes to give you divine life, and He wishes you to live by that life instead of the life of your soul. At the same time, you should make room for denying your soul, that is, denying the activity of your own life. The only way you can make room for the life of God to dwell in you and to live in you is by losing your old Adam life and denying the activity of the self.
>
> (*A Short and Very Easy Method of Prayer*, ch. 21, p. 100)

Guyon calls her reader to approach greater depths in prayer by surrendering the will to God's beneficent designs. The soul then grows in its passive capacity, stops exerting self-effort, and learns to receive "God's inclinations." Working in the individual, God shapes, purifies, and leads the soul, making it "fit" for union with the divine. Through this practice of absolute trust and self-abandonment, delight in God's presence becomes a continual experience, no longer relegated to set times of prayer.

INFLUENCE

The impact of Guyon's thought on the early Methodists in England, as well as the American holiness movement, has been widely documented. In her praise, John Wesley wrote, "How few such instances do we find of exalted love to God, and our neighbor; of genuine humility; of invincible meekness and unbounded resignation." Figures such as Count Zinzendorf, the early Quakers, Hudson Taylor, and Watchman Nee also recommended her *Short and Very Easy Method of Prayer* to those in their flocks. Furthermore, Guyon's writings influenced important thinkers such as Søren Kierkegaard and Arthur Schopenhauer, particularly in their reflections on the perplexities of grave suffering.

Less well known, perhaps, is her current popularity among various movements in America, as well as in Europe and Asia. Her writings fill bookshelves in unexpected places (for instance, in the heartland of China today), and are frequently the main textbooks for conferences on prayer and spirituality. Her *Short and Very Easy Method of Prayer* has gone through multiple English translations and reprints with different publishers (two in the year 2007 alone) and many Christian readers continue to clamor for her work and ideas.

Despite her popularity, Guyon's notions remain problematic. Much of her language offends modern sensibilities—particularly her ideas of surrender in the experience of suffering, as well as self-annihilation—and so academics have largely neglected her work. Indeed, some of her ideas evoke discomfort, if not consternation. Guyon indefatigably held that in order to enjoy the intimate presence of the divine, the soul must "lay itself on the altar of sacrifice," undergo acute afflictions, and submit itself entirely to the "good pleasure" of God. She went so far as to claim in her *Autobiography* that the soul must allow itself "to be totally surmounted and destroyed by the operations of love," if it desires to enter into the fullness of the divine (pp. 81–2). This pervasive language of annihilation has caused some commentators to diagnose Guyon's thought as violent, and pathological.

Others, however, have found life and depth in her writings by placing her words in a larger context that softens the harshness of her language. They are challenged by her call to radical self-abandonment, making allowance for the fact that her writing style is flamboyant, often failing to make helpful distinctions—for instance, between the distorted, fallen self (that which must be "annihilated") and the dignified self that reflects the image of God. With these concessions, they find profound nourishment in her writings. Schopenhauer, for instance, praised Guyon for her teaching on the denial of the will and recommended her *Autobiography* to his readers, calling her a "great and beautiful soul."

Regardless of one's final estimation of Guyon's thought, it is undeniable that her writings have wielded significant influence upon a wide number of movements and thinkers in the past three centuries, and continue to inspire lived spirituality today.

READING THE TEXT TODAY

What, then, is one to make of Guyon's problematic claims, and her call to complete self-abandonment? Might one find salutary resources in her writings, despite their erratic, excessive nature? Guyon transgressed linguistic conventions, and she certainly wrote "outside the bounds" of the theology of her time. Yet, one might find a kernel of truth in her writings that appropriately challenges the contemporary church, particularly a church enticed by consumerism, convenience, and the comfort-seeking of its larger culture.

Admittedly, there are limits to the retrieval of any relic, regardless of appeal or influence, and Guyon's work seems opaque at times. One ought to be vigilant against applying her insights haphazardly, particularly in contexts of abuse and unjust suffering. Those who face tragic sorrow might not be aided by Guyon's theology, and may even be outraged. (Still, those undergoing extreme affliction might find comfort in her writings, as various testimonies reveal.)

Retrieval of difficult themes needs to be handled with sensitivity to one's unique situation. It may be that her message is more appropriate for those who have settled for a comfortable, danger-free Christianity. In any case, her call to surrender and her reminder of the costs of discipleship hearken back to the words of Christ himself: "Then he said to them all: 'If anyone would come after me, he must deny himself and take up his cross and follow me'" (Mt 16:24). Whether because of misuse or excessive application, this indispensable element of the Gospel is often forgotten. Yet it remains at the heart of the Christian message.

Happiness in God (and its shadow side)

Rather than advocate harmful self-denial, Guyon argued that the way of self-sacrifice is the path to the deepest enjoyment of the greatest good. When preoccupations with the self are removed (whether it be in attitude, a sense of self-importance, or even self-protectiveness), room is created for the divine good to fill and satisfy. This call to deny oneself for the sake of Another and to consider again the cost of discipleship just might result in a revitalization of Christian identity and faith.

Guyon's *Short and Very Easy Method of Prayer* vividly integrates this theology of surrender with a theology of desire and delight. Self-abandonment is, in the end, the door to a profoundly satisfied self. With the Gospel writers, Guyon claims that in "losing" one's life, one will "find" and enjoy life to the fullest. In other words, she invites her readers to create space for the divine to dwell, becoming radically hospitable to God's presence. From this perspective, self-abandonment is the offering of the self to God in love.

Though Guyon calls this a "very easy method," it does not always come easily. Letting go of self-interested egotism can be acutely painful; it might even come through the experience of hardship or failure. But once the individual lets go of personal anxieties, fears, and a sense of control, freedom and joy are found. Self-surrender and radical trust in God—as opposed to self-hatred or self-effacement—are thus ultimately life-giving.

Freedom in surrender

Guyon's invitation to lay down one's life for the will of God is a challenging one, and the extreme tone of her language often surprises the reader. Guyon is after a greater good, however. She encourages the Christian to rely solely upon divine strength and leading, rather than self-effort—this, in the end, releases greater power. Through her *Short and Very Easy Method of Prayer*, Guyon wants to see the young in faith make a transition from anxious striving to stillness and pure trust in God. With the prophet Isaiah, she proclaims, "In quietness and trust shall be your strength" (Is 30:15). Full surrender thus becomes a pathway to a confidence and strength that are beyond the limits of human capacity. But the fullness of God is received "in proportion to the soul's . . . great, noble, and extensive passive capacity" (ch. 24, p. 135).

It is then up to the individual to have one's "passive capacity" enlarged by the act of surrender. Again, this is no simple matter. Guyon argues that the act of total dependence (another way in which she describes surrender or self-abandonment) while apparently passive, is rather the "highest activity" (ch. 11, pp. 56–7, ch. 21, p. 97). And this decision to surrender leads to true freedom. As she describes it, one need simply "hold the rudder" and "spread one's sails" to catch the wind of God's Spirit (ch. 22, pp. 114–5). This is what self-abandonment means for Guyon, and this is what she calls truest prayer.

How then does this help the reader, practically? Other than her detailed suggestions on "praying the Scriptures" and her encouragement to develop a "listening" posture in stillness before God, what might this "short and very easy method of prayer" entail in actual life, especially at the "deeper" levels? Guyon would likely respond that if one has difficulty surrendering oneself to God's care, one's desires (for God) are not yet strong enough. In other words, self-surrender ought to be an oblation of love, a self-giving that is voluntary and delightful. It finds its source in a greater desire: the longing to become more intimate with the object of desire, namely God. Perhaps her recommendation at this point would be that the reader look to the beauty of God and see whether God is indeed the "highest good," worthy of trust and devotion. When one's spiritual vision is sharpened, then one's capacity to desire (and thus to surrender) is most likely to grow.

Guyon concludes that in pouring out its love, the self is not diminished, but rather enriched, enlarged, and strengthened. The yearning for God becomes the driving pulse behind a radical loss of self, as dying to self leaves more room for God to "possess" and "fill" the whole of self. Only then can the soul come to know and enjoy God in intimate union. For Guyon, self-surrendering oneself to God is the secret to a more profound joy, and she commends this path to all of her readers.

TRANSLATIONS

Jeanne Guyon (1975) *Experiencing the Depths of Jesus Christ*, Jacksonville, FL: SeedSowers Publishing, is the most accessible modern translation of Guyon's original French, though under this variant title; except where noted, it is the text cited throughout this chapter.

Jeanne Guyon (2007) *A Short and Easy Method of Prayer*, trans. T.D. Brook, New York: Cosimo Classics, is a reprint of a translation that originally appeared in 1867.

FURTHER READING

Bruneau, M.-F. (1998) *Women Mystics Confront the Modern World: Marie de l'Incarnation (1599–1672) and Madame Guyon (1648–1717)*, Albany, NY: SUNY Press, provides a helpful historical account of the political opposition that Guyon faced and the circumstances that surrounded the Quietest controversy.

James, N.C. (2007) *The Pure Love of Madame Guyon: the great conflict in King Louis XIV's court,* Lanham, MD: University Press of America, provides a brief overview of Guyon's historical context and explicates her theology of the Holy Spirit for a popular audience.

23

JONATHAN EDWARDS (1703–58)

A Treatise Concerning Religious Affections

TIMOTHY HESSEL-ROBINSON

Jonathan Edwards's sermon "Sinners in the Hands of an Angry God" is frequently anthologized in high school and college American literature texts as a masterful example of colonial revivalist oratory. An unfortunate effect of this anthologizing is that Edwards is known to most people only as the author of "Sinners." The context and full content of the sermon are usually lost, leaving only the title and its menacing implications to haunt the imaginations of those who encountered it once upon a time. While theologians and scholars have long appreciated the richness and complexity of Edwards's thought, the popular image of colonial North America's most original and sophisticated theologian has been reduced to the caricature of a hellfire-and-brimstone, tent-revival preacher.

This is unfortunate because Edwards was a prolific author and works such as *A Treatise Concerning Religious Affections* continue to reward adventurous readers with spiritual insight. In fact, *Religious Affections* is a highly significant contribution to the history of Christian literature on spiritual discernment. Edwards's purpose in the treatise is to identify "the nature of true religion" (p. 84). He states in the preface that nothing is of more pressing importance to humankind than to identify the signs of genuine religious experience and practice. Edwards's urgency about the nature of true religion seems relevant today, when terrorist acts are being carried out across the globe in the name of some religious tradition or other. Equally violent responses to such acts have also been justified on quasi-religious grounds. Charismatic figures claiming guidance from religious experiences have caused unspeakable damage to their followers. The world has been shocked by events such as the mass suicide and murders carried out by disciples of Jim Jones in Guyana, the sexually exploitative and abusive practices of Branch Davidian leader David Koresh whose life and the lives of many of his followers ended in an apocalyptic standoff with FBI agents in Texas, and the stunning suicides of the Heaven's Gate religious group orchestrated by Marshall Applewhite.

In *Religious Affections* Edwards warned of the "inexpressibly dreadful" consequences that result when "true and false religion" are not distinguished through discernment. Of course he was addressing situations completely unlike those just mentioned, having something entirely different in mind when referring to the "dreadful consequences" of false religion. Still, Edwards's warnings and his instructions resonate across the years. From the earliest Christian centuries sages have stressed the importance of testing the spirits to determine whether they are of God or not. In *Religious Affections,* Edwards adds his voice to the chorus of Christian wisdom on discernment, offering the contemporary reader far more than hellfire and brimstone.

AUTHOR AND AUDIENCE

Edwards is widely regarded as colonial North America's most significant theologian and philosopher, one of the great intellectuals of US history. He has been variously, if exuberantly, designated as an American Milton and as "America's Augustine." Edwards lived during the Enlightenment, when reason and science began to dominate theology. New forms of religious practice also developed in response to emerging political and social arrangements. Engaging the ideas of Locke, Newton, Descartes, and Hobbes, Edwards devoted his enormous intellectual energy to reconciling Calvinist piety with the great philosophical and scientific developments of his time.

Jonathan Edwards was born in East Windsor, Connecticut on October 5, 1703 to the Reverend Timothy Edwards and Esther Stoddard Edwards. His grandfather was the Reverend Solomon Stoddard, one of the most influential clergypersons of colonial New England.

Thirteen children were born to Esther and Timothy, Jonathan being the only boy. Well educated by his father, Jonathan matriculated at the newly established Collegiate School in 1716, eventually taking both a BA and an MA from the institution that would come to be known as Yale during Edwards's time there. After serving brief stints as pastor at a Presbyterian church in New York City and at the village church in Bolton, Connecticut, he returned to Yale as a tutor. Jonathan was ordained to the ministry in 1727 and became his grandfather's associate at the congregational church in Northampton, Massachusetts. Later that year he married Sarah Pierpont, to whom he was drawn because of her deep piety. (One of his later works would include an account of Sarah's ecstatic experience, commending her as a model of Christian spirituality.) They had eleven children together. When Solomon Stoddard died in 1729, Jonathan assumed the sole leadership of the congregation, remaining there until a theological dispute with the congregation forced him from his position in 1749. In 1751 he moved to Stockbridge, Massachusetts to take charge of an English congregation and a mission to the Mahican Indians. In 1758 he agreed to become president of the College of New Jersey (now Princeton). On March 22, 1758 he died only two months after moving to Princeton, having contracted a full-blown case of smallpox from an inoculation intended to protect him from the disease.

Edwards wrote *Religious Affections* in the wake of New England's eighteenth-century revivals known as "the Great Awakening." "Awakening" was a term referring to localized episodes of religious fervor that frequently visited the region. Edwards demonstrated a keen interest in the dynamics of religious experience, first coming to fame with his account of Northampton's awakening published in 1837 as *A Faithful Narrative of the Surprising Work of God.*

Religious Affections, which developed out of a series of sermons on the place of the affections in the Christian life, was part of the debate about religious enthusiasm raging during the mid-seventeenth century. Boston's Charles Chauncy was a leading spokesperson for a group known as "Old Lights," who viewed reason as the supreme faculty which should guide the will, regarding the enthusiasms of the revivals with suspicion and contempt. An eccentric itinerant revivalist named James Davenport personified the other extreme, acting out the worst excesses of revivalist enthusiasm and challenging the Old Lights at every turn. Edwards lamented that Davenport and other enthusiasts damaged the cause of "experimental" religion because their behavior seemed to confirm the rationalists' case about the dangerous excesses of revivals. Firmly defending the role of affections in the spiritual life, Edwards steered a middle course in the debate in order to make his case. He affirmed that enthusiasm had its place, but wedded the affections firmly to the faculty of reason, critiquing the excesses that so offended Chauncy. *Religious Affections* offered an extensive, sophisticated, and precise accounting of the role of affections in the religious life, proposing means to discern their authenticity.

SYNOPSIS

Edwards's goal in *Religious Affections* was twofold: to establish the central place of "holy affections" in the life of faith and to develop criteria for distinguishing genuine affections from false ones. After a brief preface the text is divided into three parts. In part one, Edwards defines religious affections and makes the case for their importance in the Christian life. Part two lists twelve signs that he considers unreliable for determining whether affections are genuine or not. Part three is the longest section of the work in which Edwards expounds upon twelve "distinguishing signs of truly gracious and holy affections."

Affections in the life of faith

Understanding that he must define exactly what "holy affections" are, Edwards addresses the question immediately: "the affections are no other, than the more vigorous and sensible exercises of the inclination and will of the soul" (p. 96). He identifies two separate but interrelated faculties of the soul: the "understanding" by which reason operates and a person is able to rationally judge a thing or an action, and the "inclination," which determines how the soul is either attracted to or repelled by that which it observes. The soul never observes "as an indifferent unaffected spectator, but either as liking or disliking, pleased or displeased, approving or rejecting" (p. 96). Edwards frequently insists that genuine faith is not simply a matter of rational assent to doctrine, but involves deep loving affection and a sense of joyful trust.

In distinguishing and describing the two faculties of the soul, Edwards introduces an aesthetic sense, the role of beauty and desire, into the exercise of reason. However, he does not separate desire and reason, "head" from "heart," affect from rationality. Understanding and inclination are two moments within the soul's operations. Affections like love, hatred, fear, gratitude, and hope belong to God-given human nature as the "spring" of human actions, motivating all human pursuits.

Edwards combs scripture for affirmation that "Holy desire, exercised in longings, hungering and thirstings after God and holiness" is central to Christian spirituality (p. 104). He expounds upon ten points where he finds biblical support for his proposition about the role of affections, citing many instances in scripture where holy persons are shown expressing joy, sorrow, gratitude, zeal, and love. For Edwards, love is chief among the affections and the "fountain of all other affections" (p. 106). Jesus himself "was a person who was remarkably of a tender and affectionate heart . . . He was the greatest instance of ardency, vigor and strength of love, to both God and man [sic], that ever was" (p. 111). Edwards also finds evidence for the role of affections in the "ordinances and duties," those means of public expression appointed by God in scripture (p. 114). Singing, for instance, "seems to be appointed wholly to excite and express religious affections," while the sacraments do not merely instruct, but as "sensible representations" are intended to move the emotions of believers as well (p. 115).

Edwards maintains a unity of the human person as he appeals to rationalists and enthusiasts alike. His careful distinction between affections and passions demonstrates this unity. Affections are superior to passions because the former are guided by the will in response to reasonable assessments of situations, whereas the latter frequently escape the will's control, causing the mind to be "less in its own command" (p. 98). Many critics did not understand what Edwards meant by affections, mistaking them for emotional exuberance. Edwards is careful to point out that the affections are not unreasoning emotive expressions; rather, the emotional response is kindled by the mind's understanding grasp of a thing's nature. On the other hand, understanding is not complete unless one truly experiences what one has reasonably grasped. Edwards often illustrates this principle with his famous honey metaphor. One may understand that honey is sweet, but until one tastes honey, one does not truly know what sweetness is.

The rationalists feared that passions had overtaken reason in the revivals. Acknowledging that there were abuses in revivalism, Edwards resisted the extremists on both sides and tried to show the critics that genuine affections do not dismiss reason. In part three he puts the matter thus: "Holy affections are not heat without light; but evermore arise from some information of the understanding, some spiritual instruction that the mind receives, some light or actual knowledge" (p. 266).

Unreliable signs

Part two is addressed directly to those who already accept affections as a key part of the Christian life and who, indeed, boast, "I am not one of those who have no religious affections: I am often greatly moved with the consideration of the great things of religion" (p. 127). Edwards's primary concern is to assist those who acknowledge the affections to rightly discern the genuine movements of the Spirit. In doing so, he addresses many of the objections made by Old Light critics who said that emotional excesses invalidated revivalism. By listing the negative signs, some of which he drew from behaviors exhibited among revival enthusiasts, Edwards establishes some points of agreement with the rationalists who saw in such actions evidence of false piety. Edwards's cataloging of negative signs is not merely pragmatic, however. While he truly believed that affections are central to the religious life, he also firmly believed that they must be tested, for affections can be deceptive, leading people to false assurances or toward ruinous ends. For this reason, criteria for discernment are essential.

The first unreliable sign—"'tis no sign one way or the other" is how Edwards states the matter—is "that religious affections are very great, or raised very high" (p. 127). At this point he responds directly to both the enthusiasts and their critics. On one hand, those who dismiss emotion out of hand should heed the examples of strong emotional response in scripture. The Psalms encourage spirited rejoicing in God's presence, while Paul expresses a range of intense emotions in his letters. Thus, "they do greatly err, who condemn persons as enthusiasts, merely because their affections are high"

(p. 130). On the other hand, strong emotions do not guarantee the presence of grace. Again, scripture bears witness to this, the definitive example being the crowds who shouted "Hosanna!" as Jesus entered Jerusalem, yet soon turned on him to call for his crucifixion.

The second unreliable sign involves bodily expressions. One should not assume that ecstatic or disturbing physical experiences certainly indicate either the presence or absence of grace. Once again emphasizing his integrated anthropology, Edwards instructs his readers that all affections have some physical manifestation; such is the unity of the human person that "the mind can have no lively or vigorous exercise, without some effect on the body" (p. 132). Intense physical manifestations certainly do not guarantee the Holy Spirit's presence, for human beings can become highly excited about "temporal things." However, Edwards insists that *reason* does not preclude such bodily effects: "I know of no reason, why a being affected with a view of God's glory should not cause a body to faint" (p. 132).

Edwards continues in this vein, listing unreliable signs and carefully considering each side of each coin. This exercise demonstrates his efforts to ground discernment in both reason and experience, constantly probing beneath surface appearances to get at the true source of an experience. It also exhibits a reluctance to be dogmatic about any particular manifestation and a willingness to consider the authenticity—or inauthenticity—of a phenomenon based on the concrete particularities of its occurrence (which is not to suggest Edwards could not be dogmatic when he believed himself certain of something).

Genuine signs

In part three Edwards expounds upon twelve genuine signs of "truly gracious and holy affections." The first sign is, perhaps, the most complex and the one most open to misunderstanding. Genuine affections result from direct supernatural or divine operations which he calls "a new inward perception or sensation" of the mind given to the spiritual person, and a "new spiritual sense" (p. 205). Edwards claims that this sense is "entirely above nature," something that humans cannot manufacture; it must be conferred by God. Edwards speaks to the complete transformation of the self which occurs through the Spirit's work of sanctification. He emphasizes that the new spiritual sense is not a new faculty, but a "new foundation laid in the nature of the soul" that enables the understanding and the will to act in accordance with the Spirit's leading (p. 206).

In places it seems that Edwards opposes grace to nature, indicating a radical discontinuity between natural and infused faculties. He admits that the limitations of language obscure his meaning, but he is so thorough and precise with language that the result, within the whole context of his thought, is a remarkably sophisticated religious psychology that maintains the same integrated sense of the human person previously mentioned. His exposition of the first sign begins with a reading of Paul's distinction between the "carnal" and the "spiritual" persons. Here Edwards does not succumb to a dualism of the physical and the spiritual. Rather, he accurately understands and explains that Paul's categories have to do with sanctification:

> Now it may be observed that the epithet 'spiritual,' in these . . . texts of the New Testament, is not used to signify any relation of persons or things to the spirit or soul of man [sic], as the spiritual part of man [sic], in opposition to the body, which is the material part. . . . But it is with relation to the Holy Ghost, or Spirit of God, that persons or things are termed spiritual.
>
> (Religious Affections, p. 198)

Edwards goes through the signs of genuine affections: humility, a Christ-like character, the increase in spiritual appetites rather than in complacency, and so on. The twelfth sign has to do with sanctification and the practice of discipleship: "gracious and holy affections have their exercise and fruit in Christian practice" (p. 383). For Edwards, practice plays a key role in the discernment of genuine religious affections. It is not accidental that he devotes more space to explaining the twelfth sign than to any other sign. Edwards's empirical proclivities surely influenced his emphasis on practice as providing an observable confirmation of the genuineness of religious experiences. According to Edwards, practice is not an infallible sign, for there can be external actions without inward experience, rendering those actions hollow. However, he considers practice, or the fruits of the spirit, the most reliable of signs: "there are not sure evidences of grace, but the acts of grace" (p. 453). The practice of virtue results from the transformation of the innermost self. "False discoveries and affections don't go deep enough," Edwards observed, "but gracious affections go to the very bottom of the heart, and take hold of the very inmost springs of life and activity" (p. 393). Again emphasizing a holistic anthropology, Edwards stresses that the body's holy practices depend upon the soul's inclinations: "spiritual practice . . . is the practice of a spirit and body jointly" (p. 450). Experience and practice are not two separate and opposed things. Rather, "holy practice is one kind or part of Christian experience; and both reason and Scripture represent it as the chief, and most important and distinguishing part of it" (p. 451).

INFLUENCE

Samuel Hopkins and Joseph Bellamy developed a theological system based on Edwards's work, which came to be known as "the New England Theology" or "the New Divinity." Hopkins and Jonathan Edwards, Jr., saw a few of Edwards's works into print. However, in 1778 Yale President Ezra Stiles famously opined that the future would ignore Edwards and his writings would be relegated to obscurity. Edwards's influence appeared to be waning.

Initially promoted by New Divinity adherents, a "Second Great Awakening" burgeoned in the nineteenth century. Leaders of the awakening frequently appealed to Edwards for theological justification in promoting their revivals, although historians now regard the first "Great Awakening" as an invention of Edwards's later followers promoting their brand of revivalism.

Charles Grandison Finney, one of American revivalism's seminal figures, appealed to *Religious Affections* as he defended his emotionally charged revival techniques against detractors. Various editions of *Religious Affections* also circulated widely during the nineteenth century. For example, the American Tract Society distributed more than 75,000 copies of an abridged and edited version during the height of the Second Awakening. Edwards's prose was considered too dense and repetitive for lay audiences, so editors freely carved away at the text to produce popular versions. John Wesley was among those who published abridged versions of *Religious Affections*. Wesley found much in Edwards that was useful for promoting his form of piety, but under his editorship Edwards's twelve gracious signs became eight, much of Edwards's Calvinism was excised, and the mystical and aesthetic dimensions of the work were de-emphasized.

More recent scholarship has led to another Edwardsean revival. Scholars recognize his contribution to the heritage of North American revivalism and have come to appreciate the penetrating analysis of religious experience in *Religious Affections*. Also, as aesthetics has found a new role within theology, Edwards's work has been seen as a rich resource for reflection.

READING THE TEXT TODAY

Religious Affections speaks to the importance of discerning genuine religious experience. Edwards offers criteria for doing so rooted in scripture, reason, observable evidence consistent with each of these, and careful attention to the particularities of experience. Widely regarded by scholars as a masterful analysis of religious experience, it has consequently inspired numerous interpretations. Two dimensions are particularly relevant today.

Humility

Religious Affections urges appropriate caution against certainty in determining the sources and validity of the religious experience of others. Since Edwards wrote his rules for discerning genuine religious experience for a particular segment of seventeenth-century Protestant Christianity in the northeastern region of North America's English colonies, his signs for determining "true religion" should not be universally applied to the experiences of, say, Buddhists or Muslims. Caution is in order when attempting to apply them universally to Christians across traditions, cultures, and eras. Edwards himself counseled his readers that the signs he enumerated are not to be used to render judgment about the ultimate state of another's soul. Edwards warns, "It was never God's design to give us any rules, by which we may certainly know, who of our fellow professors are his, and to make a full and clear separation between sheep and goats" (p. 193). Rather, God reserves such determinations as God's own prerogative: Edwards declares that he would be guilty of the very arrogance against which he has been warning should he suggest that the signs he has laid out be used in such a manner.

One cannot even use these signs to finally determine the state of one's own soul. In Edwards's time there was great anxiety among

Puritan believers especially about the state of one's soul and the assurance of one's salvation; thus Edwards's warning served to encourage vigilance and guard against complacency. If anything, the contemporary period displays the opposite of such anxieties. On the one hand, narrow assurances dominate the pronouncements of would-be religionists and theocrats across the globe, while on the other, laissez-faire attitudes assume that any religious path, practice, or belief is as valid as another. Instances abound of self-appointed prophets claiming God's sanction to carry out "executions" of those whose morality or doctrine is judged deficient. Edwards's caution to humility is germane in such a context, as is his urging of a deeper evaluation of one's own experiences. In a world where adherents of multiple religious beliefs and practices live in close proximity, and where religion and violence are so thoroughly enmeshed, these cautions are imperative.

Practice

Still, there must be criteria by which religious experiences can be evaluated. Thus, another dimension of *Religious Affections* relevant for contemporary spirituality is its emphasis on practice. In contemporary spirituality, practices are understood to be theologically rich gestures by which religious ideas, moral convictions, and a sense of personal and communal identity find expression. Action and meaning are mutually interpretive. Practice gives the interior, subjective aspects of religious experience form, moving them into a more objective, observable realm. Practice shifts the emphasis from isolated interiority to the enactment of one's lived experience. In a "spiritual but not religious" culture, experience is often sought for experience's sake without regard for the moral, ethical, and communal obligations that accompany religious traditions. This sort of spiritual solipsism is frequently and rightly criticized as being inconsistent with authentic Christian spirituality. Edwards confronted the same kind of shallow conceit with his emphasis on the disciplined practice of Christian virtue. Edwards was concerned that persons not mistake deep emotional experiences as in themselves signs of the Spirit's presence; he argues against the adequacy of purely subjective experience to establish the presence of grace. As the chief of the gracious affections is love, so the supreme authenticating sign of genuine affections is love for Christ demonstrated through the practice of Christ's virtues. This point invalidates those who would claim inspiration of the Spirit for actions that exploit or abuse others in some way.

In the end, Edwards's appeal to the beauty of holiness, the aesthetic excellence of the moral life, holds deep appeal in the modern world. When religious experience is genuine, it inspires persons to long for the beautiful life, to be so possessed by God's Spirit that all of one's affections—understanding and will—are guided by that Spirit and all of life is understood as holy. "That beauty which [persons] delight in, they desire to be adorned with," writes Edwards, and "those acts which [persons] delight in, they necessarily incline to do" (p. 394).

EDITIONS

Edwards, J. (1959) *Religious Affections*, New Haven, CT: Yale University Press, is the edition cited here.

Edwards, J. (1994) *The Religious Affections*, Carlisle, PA: The Banner of Truth Trust.

FURTHER READING

Conforti, J.A. (1995) *Jonathan Edwards, Religious Tradition, & American Culture*, Chapel Hill, NC and London: University of North Carolina Press, discusses Edwards's influence on American culture and religion in the nineteenth century.

Lee, S.H. (2005) *The Princeton Companion to Jonathan Edwards*, Princeton, NJ and Oxford: Princeton University Press, contains essays by leading Edwards scholars on various aspects of his life and thought.

Marsden, G. (2004) *Jonathan Edwards: a life*, New Haven, CT: Yale University Press, is the definitive recent biography of Edwards by an eminent historian of American Christianity.

McDermott, G. (2000) *Seeing God: Jonathan Edwards and spiritual discernment*, Vancouver, BC: Regent College Publishing, attempts to apply Edwards's work to contemporary spirituality for a popular audience.

24

SØREN KIERKEGAARD
(1813–55)

An Occasional Discourse
(Purity of Heart)

DAVID J. KANGAS

Søren Kierkegaard confided to his journal that his work would some-day be translated into many languages. This was no boast, just a somewhat sober recognition of what he could no longer deny: his own genius and productivity. Reflecting upon his work in mid-career, Kierkegaard wrote of the experience of terror over having too many ideas:

> Since I became an author I have never for a single day had the experience I hear others complain of, namely, a lack of thoughts or their failure to present themselves . . . But many a time I have had the terrifying experience . . . of the frightful agony of starving amidst abundance, of being overwhelmed with riches.

Writing became a physical need for Kierkegaard: "Only when I am writing do I feel fine. If I refrain from it for just a few days, I immediately get sick, overwhelmed, burdened, and my head gets heavy and weighed down." The ideas flowed so copiously to his pen that, he said, "I could sit down and continue to write for a day and a night, and again for a day and a night; for there was wealth sufficient for it." He could do this, but he dare not: "If I had done it, I should have been broken . . . in mortal danger." Though he had to write, he knew the ideas, heedless of his well-being, would run him into the ground.

So he was damned if he did and damned if he did not: he only felt good writing, but the writing would kill him. The most important thing was that he understood this tormenting double bind to be a sign of God's calling. All in all, an astonishing outpouring came from Kierkegaard's pen: between 1840 and 1855 he produced some fifty-six volumes in the modern edition, running to more than twenty thousand pages.

AUTHOR AND AUDIENCE

Kierkegaard, author of books with titles like *Fear and Trembling* and *Sickness unto Death*, confided to his journal that a later age would most likely come to regard him as a "dark, somber figure." Though this is a superficial judgment, there is no doubt that the background of his life was dark and somber. His father, working in destitute poverty as a shepherd in the Jutland heath of northern Denmark, cursed God for his fate. With this began his obsession over the idea he had committed the "unpardonable sin" of grieving the Holy Spirit. When he subsequently got rich as a hosier in Copenhagen he attributed his wealth not to God's blessing, but to God's ironical curse—as if God were saying, "let the damned continue unperturbed in his damnation."

Søren Aabye Kierkegaard was born the last of seven children, five of whom died before he reached the age of twenty-two. His mother, Anne Lund, had married Kierkegaard's father, Michael Pedersen Kierkegaard, only months after Michael's first wife had died. And only four months after their marriage, Anne Lund—who before the marriage had been a housekeeper for Michael and his first wife—gave birth to her first child. So there were plenty of secrets for the young Kierkegaard to inherit.

Kierkegaard also inherited a sizeable fortune from his father, allowing him to spend his time walking the streets of Copenhagen by day, talking with whomever he happened to meet, and writing by night (he wrote standing up). Although he completed a degree in theology at the University of Copenhagen in 1840, passed his ordination exams, and occasionally considered taking up a rural pastorate, he never held any job or official post of any kind. His life was writing.

Three events dominated Kierkegaard's public life. The first was his scandalous decision to break off his engagement to Regina Olsen in 1841. It remains altogether unclear why Kierkegaard broke off this relationship. Whatever the reason, this event dominated Kierkegaard's life. The breakup with Regina, he said, had made him a poet. The second event was his confrontation with the Danish tabloid newspaper *The Corsair* in 1846. Kierkegaard exposed the real editors behind the gossipy newspaper and was then subjected to merciless caricaturing. *The Corsair* printed cartoons ridiculing Kierkegaard's clothes, his curved back, and his style of writing. Kierkegaard became the laughingstock of Copenhagen. The principal effect of this upon him was to deprive him of his beloved walks through Copenhagen. The final event was his showdown with the state Lutheran church in 1854–5. In a periodical he started titled *The Instant*, which went through nine issues before he fell ill, he pummeled the established church for its mediocrity, particularly in contrast to "New Testament Christianity."

On October 2, 1855, Kierkegaard collapsed near his home. He was taken to Frederiks Hospital, where he died six weeks later.

SYNOPSIS

The text that the English-speaking world has come to know as *Purity of Heart* bears the actual Danish title *En Leiligheds-Tale*, or *An Occasional Discourse*. The original Danish reader would not have been able to purchase the text all by itself. Kierkegaard had written a number of books in 1846 and decided to bundle three "edifying" discourses under the common title *Upbuilding Discourses in Various Spirits* (1847).

An Occasional Discourse takes the occasion of confession as a departure point for meditating upon James 4:8: "Keep near to God, then he will keep near to you. Cleanse your hands, you sinners, and purify your hearts, you double-minded." Kierkegaard divided his text into three sections: 1) an introductory section setting forth "the good" as that which, in truth, is the *only* thing that can be willed with an undivided will; 2) a large section devoted to what it means *truly* to will the good, which includes a descriptive exposé of the manifold shapes of double-mindedness, as well as an account of the good will; and 3) an appeal to the reader's "self-activity" for the work of appropriating the text.

The good will

The single injunction of Kierkegaard's text is to will "the good" in truth. Only in willing the good, he says, does a person overcome the divided will and truly will one thing. So what, one might ask, is the good? How may the good be represented? Where is it to be found? And how indeed can one will something unless one knows exactly *what* it is one is supposed to will? These are intelligible questions. And yet the reader shall not hear a single word about *what the good is* in Kierkegaard's text. Why not? It may be that the desire to grasp, represent, and determine the good is incompatible with a good will; it may be that the desire to have the good as an *object* of our will or knowledge flows from an already divided will.

Generally speaking, when one speaks of "the will," one thinks of a power to effect some change, to attain to some condition, to produce something "in the world." One thinks of the will as an active power to shape an "external" reality. And so naturally, when one thinks of willing *the good*, one immediately thinks of striving after some object or striving to alter reality around some definite purpose, plan, principle, or goal. One indeed might think that to will the good is to will some ULTIMATE THING. If this were the case, however, "purity of heart" would be tantamount to single-minded, monomaniacal obsession. Only the fanatic would be pure in heart. However, Kierkegaard consistently denounces the monomaniacal will. The good is not identifiable with any definite object, purpose, plan, goal, or principle. The reader therefore has to be vigilant not to be misled by the expression "purity of heart is to will one thing," for the good is not a *thing* at all. It can never be approached as a thing.

Understanding *An Occasional Discourse* will be impossible as long as one imagines that there is *first* the good and *then* the will that wills it. If this were the case, then prior to any willing of the good it would be necessary first to fix the meaning of the good. This would take time; arguments would have to be marshaled; competing conceptions of the good would arise; doubts would creep in. The good would become something remote, puzzling, requiring a special talent to understand. For Kierkegaard, however, this cannot be the way toward the good.

Yet insofar as the good cannot be any definite object, purpose, plan, or principle, what can the good be, except the *will itself*? Purity of heart, the good will, in other words, is not the constancy of the will around some great purpose, but rather a will that has decided upon itself, upon its own existence, upon the fact that it is. Purity of heart is the *consent to be*. Kierkegaard says the good will is the "will to do everything for the good or to suffer everything for the good" (p. 78). What is basically at stake in "doing all" or "suffering all" for the good, however, is the decision to open oneself up to reality, with absolutely no conditions, through a radical consent to be. This requires faith; or rather, this *is* faith. Strange to say, it takes great faith really to come to terms with the utterly simple and self-evident fact that one is.

The guiding idea of *An Occasional Discourse* is this: only in the consent to be, in the whole-hearted and unqualified affirmation of one's being given, does the will become one with itself. That is why the good never does, and never can, receive any general definition in Kierkegaard's text: the good is to be found *only*, each time, in the unqualified decision, always unique, wherein the self—which already is—nevertheless consents to be.

Double-Mindedness

Underneath Kierkegaard's exposition of purity of heart is an enigmatic circumstance: although human beings obviously exist, existence is something that can be refused. Moreover—something even more enigmatic—human beings normally *do* refuse their existence: not in a total way, perhaps, but in a partial way. Such partial consent to be is the root of what Kierkegaard calls "double-mindedness."

The partial refusal of one's own existence arises in the confrontation with the inherent vulnerability of being. To be is to be exposed to suffering, meaninglessness, mortality. Even more: although humans do not normally experience their existence this way, at times the bare fact of being confronts them in all its indigestible enormity. To be is to be burdened with anxiety, melancholy, despair. It is to face the "absurd," that which is radically without reason. In face of such experience, a powerful drive to secure one's being takes root in the will. It drives human beings into *flight* from their own existence. This, to flee from one's own existence, is double-mindedness.

What is double-mindedness? Quite literally it means to be "of two minds" about a matter of concern, or not to have arrived at a decision. One can be of two minds, for example, over what the best course of action might be. Yet this is really a state of *uncertainty*, which is not the same as double-mindedness. Or one may simultaneously want antithetical things, or not know what one really wants. This would be a state of *irresoluteness*, which is much closer to double-mindedness, but still not identical to it. For Kierkegaard, double-mindedness, in the strict sense, is a mode of *self*-avoidance and *self*-deception. It is a condition of irresoluteness arising from an unwillingness to confront some truth concerning oneself—ultimately, the unwillingness to confront the full gravity of what it means to exist as a self totally unique and incomparable with any other. To confront that is to assume a responsibility for one's own existence which no one else can assume.

The ways for a self to avoid itself, never to come to a decision concerning itself, are innumerable. Kierkegaard nevertheless lays out four basic types of double-mindedness: 1) willing the good for the sake of a reward; 2) willing the good out of fear of punishment; 3) willing the good "egocentrically," that is, for the recognition one might receive; and 4) willing the good "to a certain degree," or partially. The first three forms relate to the situation in which the person still perceives the good as if it were something outside the will itself. They reflect a double-mindedness in action, or what it means to act double-mindedly. In such cases, what determines whether one is double-minded or not is *how* one wills, not *what* one wills. To will solely in order to achieve something *by means of* willing is to will double-mindedly. To act for some end beyond the act is to separate the good from the willing of the good. The good, however, is the willing of the good. This means that the good is not a what, but a way. Any conception of the good that sees it as a destination or end-point rather than a process will inevitably be double-minded. The good is the good will, nothing else.

The last form of double-mindedness—willing the good "to a certain degree"—is the root and origin of all forms of double-mindedness. Kierkegaard calls this the "double-mindedness of weakness." What is at stake here is the partial or qualified affirmation of one's being. This form of double-mindedness involves a continual evasion, an avoidance and flight from one's being. The will seeks to hide from itself the full gravity, the full responsibility, implied in having a will. The will wills to keep itself in the dark concerning itself. This form of double-mindedness pursues its strategy of avoidance by keeping *busy*, by willing many things. So long as one remains in the "thick of life," constantly under the press of time to accomplish things, one never has to come to any decision concerning what it means that one *is* at all.

Underneath the busyness of the busy person, Kierkegaard implies, is the self's refusal to assume the gravity of its unique existence. There is really only one fundamental work or vocation of the human being: to become "conscious of oneself as a single individual." Kierkegaard writes of this vocation:

> But this I do believe (and I am willing to listen to any objection, but I *will* not believe it), that at every person's birth there comes into existence an eternal vocation, for that person in particular. Faithfulness to oneself with respect to this is the highest thing a person can do.
>
> (*An Occasional Discourse*, p. 93; altered)

With the birth of each human being, each singular or irreplaceable human being, reality as a whole is altered: an "eternal vocation" comes into existence that did not exist before. Each person is a singular task to themselves—a task, therefore, that no one else can assume in their place. To become and to remain faithful to oneself, however, is not to remain faithful to some fixed idea one has formed; nor is it to *construct* a unique self in distinction from others; nor is it to make some unique contribution that no one else has made. None of these are the "one thing needful." The work of remaining faithful to oneself goes in the contrary direction: it is a work not of self-assertion, but of confession. One remains faithful to oneself, or truthful in one's being, only in confessing one's infidelity to self, one's double-mindedness. The "self" to which one must remain faithful is the self as given, exposed, vulnerable in its being. The vocation of the human being, then, the one needful work, is the work of assuming the essential vulnerability of the human condition. Faithfulness to self means dropping the quest for an invulnerable state of security against risk and loss, and assuming the riskiness inherent in the human condition.

INFLUENCE

Considering the extraordinary output from Kierkegaard's pen, it is impossible to isolate lines of influence from *An Occasional Discourse* alone. Kierkegaard, however, was an important influence upon many trends of modern European thought: existentialism (Heidegger, Sartre, De Beauvoir, Shestov, Buber), neo-orthodox theology (Barth, Bultmann, Heschel), Frankfurt School critical theory (Adorno), modern literature (Henrik Ibsen, Franz Kafka, Richard Wright, Walker Percy) and post-metaphysical or "deconstructive" thought (Derrida, Levinas).

The core of Kierkegaard's interest for twentieth-century thought no doubt lay in his literary experimentation; his critique of systematic thought in the name of the irreducibly "singular" context of human life; his attention to the philosophical value of affective states like anxiety, melancholy, and despair; and, above all, his theorizing of the "subject" (or self). On the latter, the weight Kierkegaard assigned to the self's experience of possibility, along with the necessity of the self's defining or "choosing" itself—always in relation to a past it must inherit and a future it cannot anticipate—has been immensely influential.

READING THE TEXT TODAY

The contemporary reader will face certain stumbling blocks in reading *An Occasional Discourse*. The greatest of these, no doubt, will be in confronting what looks like the text's rampant individualism. Not only is the text dedicated to "that single individual," but the impression of individualism gains momentum when Kierkegaard raises certain questions designed to capture the practical implications of his notion of purity of heart. He writes: "So the discourse now asks you: *Are you living in such a way that you are conscious of being a single individual?*" (p. 127). To become conscious of oneself as a single individual would thus seem to be the point. This seems rather abstract. In addition, the movement toward purity of heart would thereby seem to be all about defining oneself in distinction from a larger group or community. The person who is pure in heart, it would seem, must be an isolated ego, solipsistically withdrawn from common concerns of human beings, hostile to what Kierkegaard dismisses as "the crowd." Human beings, says Kierkegaard, "are immediately corrupted as soon as they unite and become many" (p. 96).

Contemporary sensibilities have seen the importance of collective action and tend to formulate the problem of the good will in terms of systemic issues of justice. Fixation upon the individual's becoming conscious of herself or himself as an individual can be suspected as an effort, implicit or not, to prevent the issue of justice from being raised in any systemic way. If the text is not to be dismissed as a token of a "bourgeois" spirituality—as some of Kierkegaard's Marxist critics suggest—what might it offer?

Busyness

An Occasional Discourse puts its finger on some essential traits of the modern socio-politico-economic environment: namely, its frenetic pace, its desire to limit exposure to risk, its dedication to efficiency, calculation, verification of results, profit. All of these are summed up in one word: the essential *busyness* of the modern world. For Kierkegaard the condition of being busy is a sure mark of double-mindedness: "Just as the echo lives in the forest, just as stillness lives in the desert, so double-mindedness lives in busyness (p. 67)." And who is not busy? To be busy is a basic mode of existence in the modern world.

The continued relevance of *An Occasional Discourse* perhaps lies in its exposé of busyness as a strategy of avoidance. What is at stake in busyness is finally the human relation to time—*how* people inhabit time. To stay busy—and if one experiences one's life as busy, Kierkegaard implies, it is because one has *decided* to be busy—is to defer any confrontation with what *An Occasional Discourse* calls an "eleventh hour" in human life. The busy person inhabits time primarily on the basis of the many things that still need doing; in light of these many things, there is never enough time. On the other hand, the busy person never contemplates time itself running out; he or she never imagines no longer having time. The experience of time itself expiring is the "eleventh hour." This is not only an experience of mortality, although that is certainly part of it, but also of necessity. The "eleventh hour" is the time of unavoidable things. There is something peculiar about things that are unavoidable: one does not schedule them into time; rather, they structure their own temporality, throwing plans out of whack. The eleventh hour is the time in which one is called upon to do something that cannot wait, something neither planned for nor anticipated. All life, Kierkegaard suggests, transpires in the eleventh hour, but for the busy person the eleventh hour is always a long way off.

Confession

Something else transpires in the eleventh hour: confession. Confession does not belong to any particular season of life, Kierkegaard says. It belongs rather to those moments in which human beings are seized by the sense of the lateness of the hour. Unavoidable things are good tutors in this regard: they teach human beings that time does not belong to them, but rather they belong to time. The time of human life is not its own time. The most potent mark of this is that, as Kierkegaard says, "there is something eternal in a human being." The eternity or immortality of the human being is not first and foremost a comfort in *An Occasional Discourse*. Quite the contrary: it indicates an absolute powerless of the human being over time, that the human being cannot bring its own time to an end, and so does not control time. Immortality expresses the human being's inability not to exist, a necessity that cannot be altered by any effort. The busy person is not in a position truly to come to terms with this fact; rather, busyness is precisely a method of avoiding coming to terms with it. Nevertheless, every human life has its eleventh hour that becomes the time for confession, that is, for becoming truthful to oneself about one's existence—namely, about the fact that one belongs to time in an absolute way.

The attitude of confession, then, brings about a transformation in the human relation to time. Paradoxically perhaps, it enables one to experience, maybe for the first time, the sufficiency of time. There is only *one* thing needful—to become truthful to oneself concerning oneself—and there is time sufficient for that simple thing. There are perhaps still many things to do, but all of them can be *left aside* if necessary; none of them are truly necessary. Thus there is a liberation to time, a renewed sense of the plenitude of time for the busy person. In fact, Kierkegaard says, the "good puts on the slowness of time" (p. 63) for the sake of human beings. There is an allowance for the fact that coming to see that one belongs to time is an awareness that itself takes time to achieve.

To live within this new sense of time is to "clothe oneself in the impoverished form of the *unprofitable* servant" (p. 68, altered). Labor that demands a return on its investment, that seeks to secure itself against risk, that aims at swiftness and efficiency, is no longer required. One is enabled to see that there is *sufficient time* for useless labor and unprofitable works.

Kierkegaard refers in this regard to the story of the widow's mite (Mk 12:41–4). With her pittance she contributes more to the treasury than any of the others because "all of them have contributed out of their abundance; but she out of her poverty has put in everything she had, all she had to live on" (Mk 12:44). Kierkegaard's addendum to this story, situating it in today's efficient mindset, is very telling: "Indeed, if it had been a public fund drive [like today], it would have been possible that the solicitor had both benevolently and superiorly said to the widow, 'No, mother, please keep the mite'" (p. 85). A generosity that gives out of its poverty might be seen as a useless waste, an untimely and unprofitable work, perhaps even as imprudent and irresponsible. All giving should be with an eye toward effective results that can be verified. Yet in this benevolent "No, mother, please keep the mite" Kierkegaard senses a lost connection to that which grants human life the experience of sufficient and plentiful time.

TRANSLATIONS

Søren Kierkegaard (2009) *An Occasional Discourse*, in *Upbuilding Discourses in Various Spirits*, trans. H.V. Hong and E.H. Hong, Princeton, NJ: Princeton University Press, 2009, is the translation cited here.

Søren Kierkegaard (1946) *Purity of Heart Is to Will One Thing*, trans. D.V. Steere, New York: Harper & Row, is a reprint of a 1938 translation.

FURTHER READING

Garff, J. (2005) *Søren Kierkegaard: a biography*, trans. B. Kirmmse, Princeton: Princeton University Press, is the most recent biography.

Mackey, L. (1971) *Kierkegaard: a kind of poet*, Philadelphia: Pennsylvania University Press, provides an overview of not only the "aesthetic" writings but also the "edifying" writings.

Pattison, G. (2002) *Kierkegaard's Upbuilding Discourses: philosophy, theology, literature*, London and New York: Routledge, is one of the few full-length studies of Kierkegaard's "edifying" writings.

Perkins, R (ed.) (2002) *International Kierkegaard Commentary: Upbuilding Discourses in Various Spirits*, Macon, GA: Mercer University Press, includes several essays on *An Occasional Discourse*.

25

ANONYMOUS
(mid-nineteenth century)
The Way of a Pilgrim

SUZETTE PHILLIPS

Life, it is said, is a journey—at once wondrous and mundane, alterna-
tively beatific and corrupt. What is the traveler's destination on life's
path, but Love Itself? What is the path's landscape but the internal
and external twists and turns, highs and lows of ongoing experiences?
And what is the journey but that of transformation—of becoming
fully alive, and all one is created to be?

Each person's life journey follows a unique path comprised of a
multitude of moments and experiences—each one a gift. It is the
traveler's continual task to receive the gifts and recognize the hand
of the Divine working through people, places, and events. Every
experience is potentially transformative—positively or negatively—
and, seen with the eyes of faith, calls the traveler to perceive, relate,
think, speak, and act in new ways.

The Way of a Pilgrim is a compilation of four tales, depicting a
journey of life, transformation, and faith embarked upon by a simple
pilgrim—a *strannik*. The stories comprising the tales revolve around
this poor, lame, Christian man's outward journey through nineteenth-
century Russia, Ukraine, and Siberia, and his journey into his own
heart and that of God. The many people he meets, the numerous
events that occur, his deepening experience of prayer, and his growing relationships—with God, creation, others, and himself—are the
essence of the stories. In and through his experiences of life and faith,

the *strannik* is transformed, becoming more virtuous, more Christ-like.

The core of *The Way of a Pilgrim* is the *strannik*'s single-minded desire to learn how to pray unceasingly—to be ever mindful of being in the presence of God. Having been inspired by St. Paul's injunction to "pray without ceasing" (1 Thes 5:17), he seeks and finds someone to teach him the ways of unceasing prayer. The *strannik* is eventually introduced by his *starets* (spiritual elder) to the Jesus Prayer (the repetition of the phrase "Lord Jesus Christ, Son of God, have mercy on me"), and then to a collection of writings of the Eastern Christian spiritual masters known as the *Philokalia*. God and his *starets*, together with the Bible, the Jesus Prayer, and the *Philokalia*, are his guides along the journey.

The Way of a Pilgrim is an easily-read guidebook to the spiritual journey. It also taps into the wellspring of Eastern Christianity by introducing the *Philokalia* (an authoritative anthology of writings on the prayer of the heart) and offering guidance in the practice of the Jesus Prayer. Touted as the most popular and best-known book on Eastern Christian spirituality available to an English-speaking readership, *The Way of a Pilgrim* has inspired people from every walk of life to embark upon a spiritual path and enter into a profound relationship with God.

AUTHOR AND AUDIENCE

The Way of a Pilgrim has long been considered an anonymous work written by an uneducated *strannik* living in mid-nineteenth-century Russia (1853–61). The tales were believed to recount his real-life experiences, which were initially transmitted orally and then later recorded by the monks of Mount Athos. New evidence, however, suggests that *The Way of a Pilgrim* was written as a theological and literary text by one or several educated churchmen—including Hegumen Tikhon, St. Theophan the Recluse, St. Amvrosii of Optino, Archimandrite Mikhail Kozlov, or Arsenii Troepolskii.

Recent historical critical analysis claims that the earliest version of the tales is the work of two monks. The first author is believed to be Archimandrite Mikhail Kozlov (1826–84). Kozlov had originally been an "Old Believer" who converted to official (canonical) Orthodoxy and spent much of his life as a missionary. The second author is thought to be Arsenii Troepolskii (1804–70), also a wanderer who traveled between monasteries. Evidence suggests that Troepolskii used and supplemented Kozlov's work. The *strannik*, therefore, may have been a real person after all, or rather two real people, Kozlov and Troepolskii.

The publication history of *The Way of a Pilgrim* is complex. An 1881 version published in Kazan is thought to be the first edition. Troepolskii's reworking of Kozlov's writings is believed to have been the basis for the text, while it is suspected that Troepolskii's writings in turn were edited and supplemented by Hegumen Paisii Fedorov, superior of Saint Michael the Archangel Monastery of Cheremis in Kazan. Several editions then quickly followed, with a fourth edition published in Moscow by 1884.

The earliest known redaction of the four tales is thought to be the Optino redaction, a translation of which is found in T.A. Smith's *The Pilgrim's Tale*. This redaction, originating no earlier than 1859, was derived from a lost text composed by Kozlov. It is distinct from the later Athos, Sergiev, and Abbreviated redactions. The Athos redaction, of which there are no known copies, is similar to the Optino redaction. It is assumed to have been used by Fedorov as the basis of the 1881 Kazan edition. The Sergiev redaction is preserved in two manuscripts, Sergiev and Panteleimon. An Abbreviated redaction was published by the Russian monastery of St. Panteleimon on Mount Athos in 1882. This redaction, derived either from the Athos or Sergiev redaction, was published independently of the 1881 edition.

St. Theophan the Recluse's 1883 edition is a further redaction of the text. In this version, the role of the spiritual father is heightened and the *Philokalia* emphasized. A new edition of Theophan's text was published by the monastery of Saint Michael the Archangel in 1884. It is this 1884 publication of *The Way of a Pilgrim* that was translated in 1930 into English by R.M. French and later received universal distribution in multiple languages. This spiritual classic has remained in print and enjoyed a growing readership. Four different English translations have since appeared.

SYNOPSIS

The Way of a Pilgrim consists of four tales recounting the *strannik*'s journey. These tales are a first-person account of a *strannik* journeying with only a Bible and a knapsack containing dry bread. He begins his journey grief-stricken, keenly aware of his own sinfulness, and fundamentally conscious that a relationship with God and the acquisition of faith are indispensable in his journey. After having sought these things first and practicing various spiritual practices, unceasing prayer and contemplation are eventually revealed to him.

Throughout the narrative, the *strannik* tells of his search for true prayer, relates his frustration with conventional teachings on prayer, and practices the Jesus Prayer. He further recounts his wanderings, depicting the many people and trials that he encounters along his journey. Ordinary circumstances come to be points of departure for prayer and theophanies for both him and others.

The first tale

The first tale, "*The Tale of a Pilgrim*, how he acquired the gift of interior unceasing prayer of the heart," begins with the *strannik*'s succinct self-portrayal. This is followed by an account of the impetus for his longing to acquire unceasing prayer. His efforts to find someone to explain unceasing prayer to him follow, including his encounters with numerous clergymen. The *strannik*, after speaking with or listening to a sermon delivered by each of them, studies scripture so as to verify their teachings. He is left, however, dissatisfied, perplexed, and without any understanding of how to pray unceasingly. He consequently decides to stop listening to sermons, and instead searches for an experienced and knowledgeable interlocutor to explain unceasing prayer to him.

At this juncture, the *strannik* meets a nobleman (whose words he cannot understand) and then the kindly superior of a monastery (who further confuses him). Finally an old man—a monk of the great habit—catches up with him while he is walking and explains the meaning of unceasing prayer. The *strannik*'s discussion with the monk leaves him utterly overjoyed. The remainder of the first tale recounts the *strannik*'s earnest efforts to learn unceasing prayer under the guidance of the monk (his *starets*), discussions with his *starets*, his introduction to the *Philokalia*, the death of his *starets*, and his departure on his journey.

The second tale

The second tale, "*The Pilgrim's Tale* on the occasion of his second meeting, 13 December 1859," begins with the *strannik* relating his intent to travel to Siberia to visit the relics of St. Innokentii of Irkutsk, while continually praying the Jesus Prayer as he wanders. He then recounts his numerous experiences during his travels, telling first of being robbed by two soldiers who stole his beloved *Philokalia* and Bible. To the *strannik's* sheer delight, these are eventually returned to him. As he reads more from these works, he comes to understand the hidden meaning of the Word of God, true prayer, and creation.

The *strannik* goes on to relate events that occur while residing in a mud hut in a forest. There, he spends time in silence, reads the Bible and the *Philokalia*, dreams of his late *starets*, receives instruction on how to read the *Philokalia*, and senses the fruits of prayer in his feelings, his spirit, and in revelations. In addition to experiencing overwhelming happiness, abundant love for Christ and creation, clear understanding, purity of thought, and warmth of heart, he is touched by the omnipresence of the Godhead and carried off into absolute ecstasy. This grounds him in faith, insight, and knowledge.

Sometime after departing from the hut, the *strannik* is attacked by a wolf, an incident which he later discusses with a teacher. The *strannik* next relates his time as a church warden. Accepting a priest's invitation to take up the post for the summer months, he oversees the building of a new structure, prays in the chapel, and engages in conversation with visitors. Gradually, many seek him out to hear him read from spiritual texts or to receive his wise words of advice. He teaches several of them the Jesus Prayer, including a peasant girl (his first spiritual daughter) whom he is later falsely accused of seducing. In and through this incident he comes to know how his suffering benefits those under his spiritual care.

On the commemoration of the Holy Annunciation of the most pure Mother of God, the *strannik* relates being desirous of receiving the Holy Mysteries. After traveling through miserable weather and arriving soaking wet at a nearby church, he participates in the liturgical services. The following day, he experiences ineffable spiritual joy, only later to learn that his legs are paralyzed. A peasant agrees to cure him of his ailment in exchange for the *strannik* teaching his son how to read.

A steward known to the peasant's son later seeks out the *strannik* and requests of him that he read the *Philokalia* to him and his wife. On one occasion, the steward's wife begins to choke on a fish bone that has lodged in her throat. The *strannik* cures her (having been directed to do so by his late *starets* in a dream). This results in the townsfolk seeking him out and viewing him as a sorcerer. He quietly departs. The second tale concludes with the *strannik*'s arrival in Irkutsk, his encounter with a merchant who offers to pay for his pilgrimage to Jerusalem, and his waiting to travel to Odessa.

The third tale

The presentation of the third tale, "*The Pilgrim's Tale* on the occasion of his third and farewell meeting, 20 December 1859," differs from Tales One, Two, and Four. The shortest of all the tales, it is an encounter between the *strannik* and his spiritual father in which he aims to bid his spiritual elder farewell and thank him for his Christian love. His spiritual father requests that he recount his upbringing and life prior to his pilgrimage. The *strannik* agrees and proceeds to tell of his childhood, adolescence, and early adulthood; his relationships with his grandparents, brother, and wife; and his experiences of prayer. He also relates the beginnings of his pilgrimage fourteen years earlier. At the close of the narrative, the *strannik* indicates that he is unsure whether the Lord will favor him to reach his destination of Jerusalem.

The fourth tale

The fourth tale, "*The Pilgrim's Tale* on the occasion of a fourth and unexpected meeting," is a further, unanticipated meeting between the *strannik* and his spiritual father. His departure having been postponed, the *strannik* continues to recount additional experiences from his journeys. This forms the contents of the fourth tale.

After relating the circumstances surrounding his delayed departure, the *strannik* shares his experiences of a pious family with whom he dined, conversed, prayed, read, and wept. He notes having been impressed by the family's holiness and selfless care of the poor. The *strannik* relates several profound occurrences while with the family that seemed to heal him, call him further into discipleship, enable him to discover his identification with Christ, deepen his prayer life, and challenge his judgments.

One evening at dinner with the pious family, the *strannik* meets a blind beggar with whom he speaks about the Jesus Prayer and the *Philokalia*. He eventually travels with the blind man, comes to assume for him the role of *starets*, and guides him in the ways of prayer of the heart. All that he teaches the blind man he verifies in both scripture and the *Philokalia* so as to be true to the tradition.

The *strannik* recounts several additional incidents. One situation occurs in a post office where he is tempted by lust. The woman by whom he is tempted later experiences a profound conversion of heart (which he learns when he encounters her years later in a convent). He also relates his discussions with both a sickly priest and an old woman who had learned the way of unceasing prayer in her youth. His final account is of his dialogue with a retired captain whose eight-year-old godson acquired the gift of unceasing prayer. The *strannik*'s departure for Jerusalem concludes the tales.

At the close of the tales, one is not told whether the *strannik* arrives at his final destination. The reader only knows that the nameless *strannik* (with a handsome face and expressive eyes) is thirty-three years of age, the full measure of the life of Christ. He is honest, pure of heart, prudent, takes delight in self-knowledge, is agile in exploring the terrain of his mind and heart, and holds salvation and the attainment of eternal life as his priorities. Spiritually, he has experienced prayer of the heart and the various states of the spiritual life including conceptless union with God. He is very familiar with the words and teachings of the Bible and *Philokalia*, and verifies all that he thinks and teaches with them. The *strannik* exhibits self-control and austerity, is affable with humility, and shows abundant love toward all. This suggests that he is approaching the destination of his spiritual journey (if not his physical one): kenotic Christ-likeness—the whole aim of his vocation as expressed in his initial self-description.

INFLUENCE

The Way of a Pilgrim, considered to be one of the most influential spiritual books of the last hundred years, has had far-reaching impact since its writing in the mid-nineteenth century. Though it appeared to be destined for a limited circle of people (Slavic Eastern Christians), it managed to capture the attention of a wide and mixed readership. In the North American context, its broad reception and popularity is seen as a puzzling spiritual phenomenon.

Historically, *The Way of a Pilgrim* had an influential role in the twentieth-century rediscovery of hesychasm (from the Greek word for "stillness"), which is the form of Eastern Christian spirituality practiced by the *strannik*. This rediscovery, which involved an unearthing of the writings of the Greek patristic tradition, has been one of the most significant events in the intellectual life of the modern Western world. The hesychast tradition depicted in the patristic writings gradually came to be seen as a living tradition permeating every aspect of the Church's inner life. Translation of *The Way of a Pilgrim* into Western European languages, [German (1925), French (1928), English (1930)] was instrumental in subtly, inspiringly, and accessibly revealing hesychasm as a living tradition to the wider public.

The hesychast tradition depicted in *The Way of a Pilgrim* came as a welcomed revelation to the Western world. It challenged divides that had developed between abstract theology and individualistic "mysticism," *gnōsis* and *eros*, and knowledge and method (all of which had undermined the contemplative tradition). It further brought into question the rationale for searching for guidance in non-Christian Eastern religions rather than Christianity itself. This spiritual classic portrayed hesychasm (and contemplation) as being accessible to contemporary persons from various walks of life. It offered practical direction regarding unceasing prayer, even amidst a fast-paced world. It further introduced readers to the "secret science" of the *Philokalia* and the ways of contemplation. All of this was well received in the West.

The influence of *The Way of a Pilgrim* further broadened as it found its way into the fabric of North American society. Over the years, it appeared on radio (1986), in retreats, plays, and novels, and over the internet. One of the biggest surges in *The Way of a Pilgrim's* popularity and influence came with the publication of J.D. Salinger's best-selling novel *Franny and Zooey* in 1961. (Franny Glass, one of the novel's principal characters, is obsessed with *The Way of a Pilgrim* as well as with the practice of the Jesus Prayer). Salinger's work popularized *The Way of a Pilgrim* and inspired people from various faith backgrounds to embark on spiritual quests. Today, multiple websites of a spiritual as well as a non-religious nature refer to it, and publications abound.

While *The Way of a Pilgrim* is not the ultimate summation of the Eastern Christian spiritual tradition, it certainly has had a significant influence on the modern Western world and holds a prominent place within Eastern Christian spirituality.

READING THE TEXT TODAY

While the message contained within the stories of *The Way of a Pilgrim* is applicable today, numerous elements of the tales may make identification with the text difficult. Of particular note are the time and culture in which this spiritual classic was penned, and the grossly different culture and societal milieu in which people currently live.

Nineteenth-century Russia as depicted in the tales of the *strannik* is quaint, romantic, and reasonably safe. Today, however, people (more cynical after experiences of war, oppression, and terrorism) might have a harder time imagining wandering about the countryside, being warmly received by strangers, and having the opportunity to pray unceasingly.

Living in an increasingly secular society, many people are unfamiliar with the spiritual life depicted in *The Way of a Pilgrim*. Knowledge of the Divine is becoming anomalous, as are virtues (rather than rights), contemplation, spiritual disciplines, and the recognition of evil. The *strannik*'s indifference to earthly things, his interest in salvation and unceasing prayer, and his efforts to temper the imagination might seem unrealistic. In this postmodern Western world, however, *The Way of a Pilgrim* offers an alternative for those seeking truth and existential answers in materialism, psychology, science, philosophy, and non-Christian Eastern traditions.

Readers from a scientifically minded, health-conscious, and utilitarian culture (desirous of instant gratification) may also struggle to identify with other aspects of the *strannik*'s world. First, he is not self-reliant. Second, his slow, painstaking quest contrasts sharply with people's need for immediate results. Third, his practice of prayer when dealing with physical and emotional ailments may seem odd (he does not find immediate relief in medication). Fourth, living on dry crusts of bread may seem unrealistic and unhealthy—especially amidst today's availability of food.

The image of a person endlessly traveling is one that people today both would and would not identify with. Most individuals in the West are accustomed to extensive travel—a reality necessitated by growing urban sprawl and an expanding global market. Walking great distances on foot, however (let alone through Siberia, Russia, Ukraine, and Jerusalem), is not something that many people would entertain for reasons of time, safety, and convenience. Nonetheless, society is incessantly on the move, and one's identity is increasingly subject to scrutiny—realities regularly faced by the *strannik*.

Despite the differences in worldview between that of the *strannik* and people today, something powerful remains in this spiritual classic. A significant number of people continue to want to know if it is possible to pray without ceasing and to live mindful of being in the presence of the Divine. Modern interest in meditation and yoga may be a carryover of this desire. People long to experience something similar to the freedom and fullness of life that the *strannik* comes to know.

Accessibility and ecumenical nature

The tales of the *strannik* are easily understood and speak to people from diverse walks of life and of various ages. For the lay Christian, it offers untold inspiration and hope. For the mystic, it presents a wise outline of hesychasm. For the non-Christian, it may encourage various altruistic practices or confirm alternate forms of meditation. For the non-religious, it may be a wonderful piece of Russian literature of the likes of Tolstoy and Dostoyevsky. *The Way of a Pilgrim* is an accessible and ecumenical text.

Identification with the *strannik*

The *strannik* is a typical lay Christian and humble brother-in-Christ. As a character, he represents the common person, someone who has experienced life and suffering and can be trusted. Most people can relate to growing up in a family, learning new things, studying, traveling, interacting with others, chatting, dining, and experiencing life. The simplicity of the tales enables the reader to believe that what is revealed to and in the *strannik* could be revealed to anyone. His life, therefore, becomes a mirror reflecting that within each person that longs to find truth and live a virtuous, Christ-like life.

Potential in each person

The Way of a Pilgrim reveals the potential within each person to become all that one is created to be. Though orphaned and disabled early in life, and having lost everything and everyone of importance to him, the *strannik*'s potential unfolds. He learns to read, reflects on scripture, and studies the *Philokalia*. As he progresses in the spiritual life, his capacity for and relationship with God grows. He becomes less judgmental, listens more attentively, and acts more virtuously. Gradually, his fidelity to the wisdom of the tradition likens him to the apostles and fathers of the Church. From his humble and pained beginnings, the *strannik* becomes a *starets* as well as a living icon of Christ. This offers the reader hope of achieving one's own potential in Christ.

The monastery in the marketplace

The Way of a Pilgrim brings the innermost life of the monastery and the deepest need of the human heart into the marketplace. In this way, both the spiritual wisdom of the tradition and the art of contemplation are made available to everyone. The example of the *strannik* invites the reader to live a contemplative life that fosters profound intimacy with and love of God, self, others, and creation; a heartfelt response to the movements of God; and an experience of the many stages of the contemplative life, leading to union with God even beyond the realm of concepts. Throughout the tales, the *strannik* (while emphasizing right understanding), insists on the import of the heart wherein he and God commune.

Cautions

Several noteworthy cautions are needed when reading *The Way of a Pilgrim*. First, attempts to merely imitate the *strannik* are not helpful, as each person's journey is unique. Second, just as the *strannik* relies on a spiritual guide when learning of the Jesus Prayer and the *Philokalia*, the reader is encouraged to do likewise. The key for understanding hesychasm is given through belonging in doctrine and worship to the Church which gave it birth. Even within the Church, however, the person needs to learn from one who has had personal experience of contemplation. Otherwise, obsessive experiences like that of Franny in *Franny and Zooey* are not improbable.

TRANSLATION

Pentkovsky, A. (ed.) (1999) *The Pilgrim's Tale*, trans. T.A. Smith, New York: Paulist Press.

FURTHER READING

Billy, D.J. (2000) *The Way of the Pilgrim: complete text and reader's guide*, Liguori, MO: Liguori Publications, is a useful guide to the reading, understanding, and application of the text today.

Brianchaninov, I. (2006) *On the Prayer of Jesus*, Boston: New Seeds Books, is the classic guide to the practice of unceasing prayer as found in *The Way of a Pilgrim*.

Pokrovsky, G. (trans.) (2001) *The Way of a Pilgrim: annotated and explained*, Woodstock, VT: SkyLight Paths Publishing, is an abridged version of the text with facing-page explanations of names, terms, and references.

Spidlík, T. (1986) *The Spirituality of the Christian East*, Kalamazoo, MI: Cistercian Publications, is a systematic handbook of Eastern Christian spirituality with an extensive bibliography.

26

THÉRÈSE OF LISIEUX
(1873–97)

Story of a Soul

JOANN WOLSKI CONN

Does *Story of a Soul* reveal spiritual genius like the musical genius of Mozart or merely youthful sentimentality? Is *Story of a Soul* pious musings unworthy of scholarly attention or spiritual literature worthy of serious exploration? Sensible people have held these different viewpoints. Why are there such conflicting responses to this memoir from Thérèse of Lisieux, a French Catholic woman who, by conventional standards, never did much, and died at twenty-four years of age in 1897?

Story of a Soul emerged from two small notebooks and a few sheets of loose paper. Here, at the request of Carmelite nuns close to her, Thérèse poured out the story of her developing relationship to God in the context of family and her small Carmelite community. After her death, these intimate reflections were assembled for publication.

From its first publication in 1898 *Story of a Soul* was a popular success. Yet until the critical edition in 1956, the public was unaware that the first version of the "story of her soul" was not completely authentic but contained manuscripts that had been changed by Thérèse's older sister. This editing process not only corrected punctuation but also deleted words and added material that reflected her sister's more conventional religious and cultural assumptions. It allowed the core of her spirituality to shine through, yet hid Thérèse in some significant ways.

Although the current edition is reliably Thérèse's own words, the nature of her text leaves it open to conflicting interpretations. Because Thérèse died so young, her message could be dismissed as youthful enthusiasm. Because her message is so basic to Christianity, that is, love and confidence in God's mercy, it could be overlooked as simply conventional piety. Because Thérèse's approach to spiritual life has become synonymous with the vocabulary of "spiritual childhood" (though she never used that phrase), her message could unwittingly reinforce childish, self-centered spirituality. Because her passionate and poetic language could be mistaken for sentimentality, it takes close reading of her texts to discern the authentic contours of her spirituality.

But her abandonment to God was the fruit of discerning self-awareness and mature spiritual struggle. Thus, *Story of a Soul* conveys an inviting and challenging vision of spiritual life for today. It anticipated, through Thérèse's "little way," what has more recently been described as "the universal call to holiness" and demonstrates a practical spiritual path that embodies the heart of the Christian gospel. Its focus on God's merciful love and humanity's capacity for inclusive love and intimacy with God in ordinary life has appealed to millions of people all over the world. Contemporary persons do not seek saintly patrons who intercede for divine favors so much as they seek wise companions who have explored spiritual issues by asking urgent questions rather than by giving pat answers. *Story of a Soul* offers urgent questions and challenging answers that can expand spiritual meaning and offer new experiential possibilities.

AUTHOR AND AUDIENCE

Born January 2, 1873, Thérèse Martin was the youngest of five surviving daughters born to devout parents. Steeped in a French Catholicism that reacted to the secularism and anticlericalism of the Revolution, they responded by creating a separate pious world within the family. All five Martin sisters became cloistered nuns, four entering the same Carmelite monastery in Lisieux. Thérèse entered Carmel at age fifteen, and six years later began guiding the newest members in their life of solitude in a community of contemplative prayer focused on the needs of the world. She wrote three brief autobiographical manuscripts that eventually became the book, *Story of a Soul.* Her other writings include 266 letters, sixty-one poems, twenty-one prayers, and eight short plays performed as pious entertainment for her community. She died from tuberculosis on September 30, 1897.

Each autobiographical manuscript had an original audience of one person. In January 1895, Thérèse's sister Pauline, at that time the prioress of their monastery, asked Thérèse to preserve their Martin family memories insofar as they shaped the story of Thérèse's soul. By January 1896 Therese had filled one notebook. The second manuscript consists of two letters written in September 1896 when another sister, Marie, begged Thérèse to explain her "little doctrine," her distinctive approach to the spiritual life. In 1897, aware that Thérèse was dying, Pauline arranged to have Thérèse continue writing the account of her spiritual journey, this time addressing it to the current prioress, Mother Marie de Gonzague. Originally intending to use the manuscripts for the customary monastic obituary, Pauline eventually persuaded Thérèse to agree to publication as a way of spreading her "mission," that is, her desire to draw ordinary persons into a "little way" of response to Divine Love. Too weak to make revisions herself, Thérèse asked Pauline to make necessary corrections or changes.

Whatever Thérèse had in mind regarding revision, after Thérèse's death Pauline deleted, added, rewrote, and divided Thérèse's three manuscripts into eleven chapters and composed a twelfth in which she presented some of her "last conversations" with Thérèse and described her death. Extracts of letters, some poems, and testimony regarding Thérèse's holiness were attached. This first edition bore the title, *Sister Thérèse of the Child Jesus and of the Holy Face, Carmelite Religious, 1873–1897: Story of a Soul, Written by herself, Letters – Poems.* The critical edition of 1956 became possible when scholars working in the Lisieux archives finally had access to the original autobiographical manuscripts and were able to use modern chemical methods to reach below erasures. From then on these texts were identified as Manuscripts A, B, and C.

The two versions of *Story of a Soul* reveal two sets of cultural and religious assumptions. Pauline's version assumed it was best to present her sister as a perfect saint and hide any suggestion of childhood faults or neuroses. The critical edition, in contrast, does not wish to obscure any of the saint's imperfections or spiritual struggle. On the contrary, in continuity with Thérèse's own convictions, it assumes that human weakness is fully compatible with holiness.

SYNOPSIS

Childhood and early years in Carmel: manuscript A

The first manuscript (now chapters I through VIII of *Story of a Soul*) narrates the story of Thérèse's life as one of singing "*The Mercies of the Lord*" (13, italics indicates emphasis in the original text). Thérèse begins by opening the gospels and reflecting on the calling of Jesus's disciples. This call leads her to contemplation of her life as the mystery of God's preference and loving mercy.

Thérèse measures her life in three phases: strength until her mother died when Thérèse was four years old, painful weakness for the next ten years until Christmas 1886, then renewed strength that continued into her monastic life. Recalling phase one through a combination of family letters and her own memories, Thérèse describes her affectionate family life as permeated by prayer and constant attention to being good. She acknowledges selfishness, stubbornness, and feelings of nervousness or anxiety when she could not immediately confess her faults to her parents. On the day of her mother's funeral Thérèse chose her sister Pauline as "Mama."

Pauline is central to the second, most painful period, in which Thérèse became timid, crying easily, and finding comfort only within family intimacy. Pauline received all her confidences and explained religious mysteries. Her sisters Marie and Céline also cared for her every need. Thérèse so loved and admired her father that she declared that if he were accidentally killed she wanted to die with him. Moving out of this family tranquility into the nearby Abbey school in 1881, Thérèse found each day a miserable experience compounded by the loss of Pauline, who entered the Lisieux Carmelite monastery in 1882. Thérèse felt called to the same "desert" of Carmel, convinced this call was not because of Pauline, but only for love of Jesus. In 1883 Thérèse became sick with headaches, constant crying, and delirium. Marie, whom Thérèse now called "Mama," cared for her until fifty days later when Thérèse turned to the statue of Jesus's mother Mary that was near her bed, and prayed for her help. When Thérèse perceived Mary smiling at her, pain was replaced by joy. However, against her better judgment, Thérèse allowed the Lisieux Carmelites to learn of this private experience. When they recast it into a kind of saintly apparition, Thérèse was so confused that she not only thought she must have lied about it but condemned herself for divulging the incident. Consequently, she looked upon herself with "a feeling of *profound horror*" (67). In 1885 she suffered scruples, meaning a preoccupation with having sinned or committed faults. This continued for eighteen months.

A Christmas 1886 transformation ushered in her third phase of life. Thérèse attributes her recovery of lost strength to the child Jesus. Wishing now to forget herself, she prayed for sinners and memorized most of the spiritual classic, *The Imitation of Christ*. She asserts, "I wanted *to love, to love Jesus with a passion* . . ." (102). Hoping to enter the Lisieux Carmel immediately, she was delayed until September 8, 1888. Though she was pampered at home, Carmelite life promoted deeper maturity. She both struggled with her imperfections and trusted her desire to find a path to holiness that could support her sense of herself as inadequate. Whereas some people offered themselves to Divine Justice in recompense for the evils in society, Thérèse prayed, "O my Jesus, . . . consume Your holocaust with the fire of Your Divine Love!" (181)

"I shall be love": manuscript B

The second manuscript (chapter IX) incorporates two letters. The second, dated September 13, 1896, introduces the one already written September 8, 1896 and addressed to Jesus in order to allow freer expression of what Thérèse had learned about the "science of love," of "*surrender* and *gratitude*" (187–88). Although dying of tuberculosis and enduring profound spiritual darkness for the previous five months, Thérèse speaks only briefly of the storm raging in her soul. After describing a dream which briefly restored a feeling of heavenly love, she writes with the energy of her forceful desires and questions. Her thoughts converge on her infinite desires regarding her vocation.

Thérèse asks Jesus why she cannot be satisfied with her calling as a Carmelite. Instead she feels many vocations: warrior, priest, apostle, doctor, martyr, missionary. What can be the answer to these follies? First Corinthians 12 and 13 showed her that love comprised all vocations; therefore, she concluded: "O Jesus, my Love . . . in the heart of the Church, my Mother, I shall be *Love*" (194).

Asking Jesus how she might prove her love, Thérèse's poetic imagination seizes upon activities commonly seen in religious processions: strewing flowers and singing. Her flowers are the smallest actions done through love, a love that can sing even in the midst of suffering. She is confident that these manifestations of loving abandonment to God can be made useful to the church.

How can such an imperfect person as herself aspire to the plenitude of love? Identifying herself as a weak little bird that nevertheless has the eyes and heart of an eagle, Thérèse surrenders to her inability to fly into the sun of the Trinity. Her "folly" of trusting that God will accept her totally—she says "as a victim"—is rooted in belief that it is God's generous love which reaches unto "folly." Finally, she asks, "Why do I desire to communicate your secrets of Love, O Jesus, for was it not You alone who taught them to me and can . . . reveal them to others? Yes . . . I beg You to do it" (200).

Final reflections: manuscript C

The third manuscript (chapters X, XI) recalls desiring to be a saint yet feeling totally inadequate to the task. Thérèse remembers how she sought "a little way" to God that resembled an "elevator" suited to her inability to climb the traditional "rough stairway of perfection." Searching scripture, Thérèse recognized herself in Proverbs 9:4 and Isaiah 66: 13, 12 (she reversed the verses) in which God invites persons into the divine embrace. Her elevator, then, was "your arms, O Jesus," and for this she "had to remain *little* and become this more and more" (208). This life in Jesus sustained her as she initiated the newest members into community life.

Coughing up blood on Good Friday 1896 had been a consolation because her unquestioning faith affirmed that soon she would be in heaven with Jesus. Then, on Easter, Thérèse was invaded by a profound darkness which initiated her into awareness that there really could be unbelievers. Inner voices mocked her earlier confidence in heaven. They proclaimed that death would usher her not into the presence of her Creator but only into "nothingness." Thérèse resisted these voices "by more acts of faith in this past year than all through my whole life" (213). Nevertheless, Thérèse welcomed unbelievers as "brothers" and agreed to "eat the bread of sorrows" with them as long as God desired this trial (212).

Thérèse offered to transfer to the Saigon Carmel in the French colony of Vietnam. Her prioress confirmed her capacities for this kind of "exile"; however, Thérèse's declining health made this journey impossible. She remained peaceful because "for a long time I have not belonged to myself since I delivered myself totally to Jesus" (218).

New insight into the meaning of charity graced her final year. She came to believe that beyond simply loving your neighbor as yourself, Jesus makes it possible for us to love others as Jesus has loved us by himself loving others through us. Thérèse felt it was Jesus acting in her that enabled her to let people take not only her paintbrushes but also her thoughts for use as their own. Union with Jesus even enabled her to give her most genuine smile to a person who "has the faculty of displeasing me in everything" (222).

Thérèse imagines herself as God's small brush used for painting God's image in the novices and the two missionaries who were given to her as spiritual brothers. Prayer and sacrifice are her means for helping her novices and her spiritual brothers develop greater maturity. For her, prayer is an expansive cry of the heart which unites her to Jesus, and her sacrifice is that of letting go of self-interest for the sake of loving all.

In this book already filled with biblical material, the final pages are meditations on the Canticle of Canticles and John 17. Both reveal Thérèse's dying desire to "pray for all," especially her novices and spiritual brothers. She understands Canticle 3:1 to mean that having plunged herself into God's ocean of love, she draws with her all those entrusted to her. Identifying herself with Jesus as he approached death, Thérèse appropriates phrases from John 17:4–24 as her own prayer. Finally, she declares that even if she had great sins on her conscience she would, with "loving audacity, go to God with confidence and love" (259). Too weak to hold even a pencil, Thérèse can write no more; these are her final words in *Story of a Soul*.

The Epilogue includes some material from the original edition's chapter XII that dealt with Thérèse's death. Three appendices include a letter to Jesus that Thérèse carried on her heart; the Oblation of Merciful Love; and her explanation of her "coat of arms" created for her "titles of nobility . . . of the Child Jesus and of the Holy Face" (278).

INFLUENCE

Although the Lisieux nuns wondered how they would ever dispose of the first printing of two thousand copies of *Story of a Soul*, to everyone's amazement the book was almost immediately a success. Copies were passed among so many sisters and priests and their friends that it soon sold out and had to be reprinted every year. The first translation was into English in 1901; by 1905 the book was available in eight additional languages including Japanese and Russian. By 1915 the Carmel had sent out over two hundred thousand copies and its influence continued to spread. In less than twenty years this book by an obscure young French nun was known and loved by millions all over the world.

Story of a Soul inspired many people to pray asking Thérèse to be their sister in Christ and, with them, "ask . . . search . . . knock," as Jesus taught (Mt 7:7–11). Thousands of people attested to favors they believed were received through her intercession with God. Testimony to her spiritual influence and to the power of her message came from all over the world, resulting in her canonization as a saint in 1925. By that time *Story of a Soul* had crossed geographical and cultural boundaries through translation into twenty languages. Religious congregations all over the world have been established under Thérèse's patronage. Thousands of churches or chapels on almost every continent are dedicated to her, or have a statue of her in a place of honor.

Story of a Soul testified to Thérèse's partnership in ministry with two missionaries and revealed her vocation to bear apostolic fruit through the transforming power of contemplative love. This influenced Pope Pius XI to proclaim her Patroness of the Missions in 1927, making her comparable to the sixteenth-century Jesuit, Saint Francis Xavier, who evangelized in the Far East. Her theological influence resulted in the 1997 declaration of Thérèse as a Doctor of the Universal Church, a title given to only two other women in the Catholic Church: Teresa of Avila and Catherine of Siena.

People in all walks of life have been drawn to Thérèse's message. Jean Francois-Six, professor at the Catholic Institute of Paris, withstood his colleagues' scorn and devoted fifteen years to a scholarly study of the personality and theology revealed in *Story of a Soul*. Dorothy Day, social activist and co-founder of The Catholic Worker movement, wrote a biography intended for young people based on *Story of a Soul*. Edith Piaf, the popular French entertainer of the 1940s and 50s, claimed she was healed from a childhood illness through Thérèse's intercession.

READING THE TEXT TODAY

Story of a Soul appeals today because it fiercely pursues questions central to mature spiritual life: How can an ordinary person become holy? How can one satisfy the desire to serve everyone? How can challenges to faith become openings to love? *Story of a Soul* explicitly addresses each of these questions in ways that disclose new spiritual meaning and expand experiential possibilities.

How can an ordinary person become holy?

Thérèse's desire to be close to God—"to be a saint," in her language— becomes a genuine quest because she cannot match her sense of her- self with her image of a saint. How can she who feels so "imperfect," so like a "grain of sand," possibly measure up to a "mountain"? How can she deal with being "too small to climb the rough stairway of perfection" which is the traditional way of holiness? Trusting her desire, Thérèse thinks creatively. Unable to climb, she needs a kind of spiritual "elevator"; that is, "a means of going to heaven by a little way that is very straight, very short, and totally new" (207).

New meaning and experiential possibilities emerged. Holiness now could mean not striving to climb up to God but, rather, receiving God, in Jesus, reaching out to us. If holiness means abiding in God's loving arms, then the experience of smallness, of inadequacy and vul- nerability, has new potential. "And for this [enclosure in the elevator of Jesus's arms], I had no need to grow up, but rather I had to remain *little* and become this more and more" (208). What is littleness that it could be experienced with anticipation? The text gives several clues. "I am . . . resigned to see myself always imperfect and in this I find my joy" (158). "For a long time I have not belonged to myself since I delivered myself totally to Jesus." (218). Littleness welcomes vulnerability as an opening to intimate relationship. It is the self- forgetfulness, born from confidence in Divine Love, that generates inner freedom and joy. It is awareness of one's inadequacy before the gaze of God's merciful love enabling one to pray, "I beg you, O my God! to be Yourself my *Sanctity!*" (276) Thus, *Story of a Soul* discloses holiness not as human accomplishment, but as trust in God's transforming love.

How can one satisfy the desire to serve everyone?

Puzzled by new dissatisfaction with limits she feels in her cherished vocation as a Carmelite, Thérèse is exhausted by desiring other vocations: warrior, priest, apostle, doctor, martyr. She prays urgently, "O Jesus, my Love, my Life, how can I combine these contrasts . . . the desires of my poor *little soul?*" (192).

Following her usual pattern when raising a profound question, Thérèse first trusts that her desires reveal God's invitation. Then she searches scripture for inspired words that match her experience and answer her question. In this case, she opens the First Epistle to the Corinthians, chapter 12, in which Paul teaches that the body of Christ has many members, many vocations that cannot all be exercised by one person. Not yet satisfied, Thérèse interprets verse 31, "*I point out to you a yet more excellent way*" (194) as an incentive to examine chapter 13, where she is consoled by Paul's revelation that "*the most PERFECT gifts* are nothing without LOVE" (194). Integrating these two chapters, Thérèse recognizes the answer to her question and desires: love comprises all vocations. Although dying and in profound spiritual darkness, she can still cry in "delirious joy . . . O Jesus, my Love . . . *my vocation*, at last I have found it . . . MY VOCATON IS LOVE!" (194). In the body of Christ it is the loving heart that can energize all the members for the service of everyone.

How can challenges to faith become openings to love?

Story of a Soul discloses how experiencing challenges to faith can allow new understanding of others and expand possibilities for relating to them. Before Easter 1896, Thérèse believed that "people who had no faith" meant persons who were "actually speaking against their own inner convictions"; they were somehow not real to her. She discovers their reality through a challenge to her own faith that she accepted as a grace intended to expand her awareness. "Jesus made me feel" there were unbelievers. "He permitted my soul to be invaded by . . . darkness" so that "the thought of heaven" and "*eternal* possession of the Creator" became "no longer anything but the cause of struggle and torment" (211). Not only did unbelievers become persons feeling a darkness that Thérèse recognized in herself, they were claimed as "her brothers" (212). Her experience of prayer also expanded into identification with them in praying Luke 18:13, "*Have pity on us, O Lord, for we are poor sinners*" (212).

Another transformation emerging from this challenge to faith was movement from Thérèse's teenage "desire to snatch [great sinners] from the eternal flames" (99) to a mature "desire to eat this bread of trial at the table [with sinners]" as long as God desires it (212). From an experience of reaching down to sinners, Thérèse expanded into sisterly feelings of mutuality.

True to the potential of a classic text, *Story of a Soul* challenges conventional understandings and invites readers into a world of spiritual freedom. There one can not only discover Thérèse's new meanings and experiential possibilities but also find the invitation to do as she did: notice one's own urgent questions and confidently seek adequate answers.

TRANSLATION

(1996) *Story of a Soul: The Autobiography of Saint Thérèse of Lisieux*, 3rd edn, trans. J. Clarke, Washington, DC: Institute of Carmelite Studies.

FURTHER READING

Frohlich, M. (ed.) (2003) *St. Thérèse of Lisieux: essential writings*, Maryknoll, NY: Orbis Books, puts *Story of a Soul* into the context of Thérèse's other writings.

de Meester, C. (2002) *The Power of Confidence: genesis and structure of the "Way of Spiritual Childhood" of Saint Thérèse of Lisieux*, trans. S. Conroy, New York: Alba House, is a masterly study of the heart of *Story of a Soul*, though Thérèse never identified her way as one of "spiritual childhood."

Payne, S. (2002) *Saint Thérèse of Lisieux: doctor of the universal church*, New York: Alba House, explains the background to obtaining the critical edition of *Story of a Soul* and its significance for the declaration of Thérèse as a Doctor of the Universal Church.

Schmidt, J.F. (2007) *Everything is Grace: the life and way of Thérèse of Lisieux*, Ijamsville, MD: The Word Among Us Press, reveals how the inner weaknesses of Thérèse were the precise places of God's transforming action in her.

Six, J.F. (1998) *Light of the Night: the last eighteen months in the life of Thérèse of Lisieux*, trans. J. Bowden, Notre Dame, IN: University of Notre Dame Press, clarifies the nature and significance of Thérèse's spiritual darkness and counters misconceptions that are associated with *Story of a Soul*.

27

EVELYN UNDERHILL
(1875–1941)
Mysticism

DANA GREENE

Mysticism: A Study of the Nature and Development of Man's Spiritual Consciousness appeared in 1911, published by Methuen and Company, a major London publishing house. It was an immediate success. Widely reviewed, new editions continued to be made, twelve in all. Until the late 1970s this 500-page book served as the best single introduction in English to the subject of mysticism, a research tool for scholars and a survey for the general reader. Based on more than one thousand sources, the book was also eminently accessible, full of apt quotations and written with an energy and elegance that engaged the reader. It has continued in print since its original publication and can be found on the shelves of university and community libraries throughout the Anglophone world.

The author of *Mysticism* was largely unknown, a married woman, author of three novels of limited literary quality, a "lady scribbler" of a somewhat otherworldly bent. Some people assumed this Evelyn Underhill must be male; since it was unthinkable that a woman, a person with no academic or ecclesial appointment, could produce a volume so simultaneously erudite and compelling. *Mysticism* was the seminal book of Underhill's life; all of her subsequent writing derived from it. Its immediate popularity is explained in part by a new interest in the ancient phenomenon of mysticism that arose at the beginning of the twentieth century. But its sustained success over decades resulted from the author's ability to enter into her subject, both intellectually and emotionally. *Mysticism* provides not merely information, provocative conceptualization, and elegant prose, but wisdom handed down, integrated, and offered to those who open its covers. It creates a space for the reader's personal engagement and even transformation. In this sense it is truly a classic text.

After the seventeenth century, interest in the phenomenon of mysticism abated, particularly in the Protestant world. The Enlightenment and the spread of scientific explanation ensured that religious experience, with its attendant enthusiasm, was suspect, even dangerous. But in the early years of the twentieth century cracks began to appear in the positivistic and empiricist worldview that dominated intellectual life. The new science of psychology placed emphasis on human experience, the philosophy of Henri Bergson expounded a vitalism at the heart of reality, and some religious thinkers began to broaden out from the standard religious scholarship of church history and biblical exegesis. William Inge's *Christian Mysticism* appeared in 1899; William James's *Varieties of Religious Experience* came out in 1902; Friedrich von Hügel's *Catherine of Genoa* was published in 1908. But there was a lacuna. James's bent was psychological, Inge's work was narrow, and von Hügel offered an interpretation of a single mystic. It was Underhill who attempted a broad treatment of the subject, defining its elements, setting it off from other phenomena, venturing a schema of stages, and illustrating her ideas with abundant references to actual mystic texts. She did what had not been done before—lay out the contribution of the mystics, a daring and provocative expression of human consciousness. Underhill's genius lay in her ability to clarify and conceptualize, but also to convince the reader that these "great pioneers" represented the highest and best examples of human consciousness and that to ignore their contribution was perilous. Whatever the limits of *Mysticism*, it established its subject as a worthy one. It served as a mediator, reclaiming and preserving the treasures of the past and offering them as a beginning point for the creation of modern spirituality. Although Underhill could not have known it, she had carved out an original insight which she would continue to elaborate throughout her life.

AUTHOR AND AUDIENCE

On every count the author of *Mysticism* was an anomaly—a married woman, attracted to Roman Catholicism but not a Catholic, a writer of novels and poetry and a few essays on esoteric subjects. Evelyn Underhill (1875–1941) lived a "quiet" life with her barrister husband, one block from her parents in the lovely Kensington area of London. She had no children. She began writing her "big book" in 1907, the year she married at age thirty-two, and the year Pope Pius X issued his condemnation of Modernism. As a Modernist herself, Underhill concluded she could not enter the Roman church. Her alternative was to make no institutional commitment but rather to write, to pour out her insights about the phenomenon of mysticism. Like Luther, it was as if she could do no other. In the next three years she produced a torrent of writing. By 1910 the manuscript of *Mysticism* was complete. When Friederich von Hügel reviewed it and offered to correct what he believed were her errors, she declined to accept his input. This was an inauspicious beginning of what would prove to be the most profound relationship of her life.

Underhill was a prolific writer, and although *Mysticism* was her seminal work, she went on to edit or author many more books. In all she produced thirty-nine, along with 350 articles and reviews. She published several editions of mystic texts and biographies of mystics, both English and continental.

After many years of living outside institutional religion, in 1919 she returned to the Anglican Communion in which she was baptized and confirmed, and petitioned Friederich von Hügel, the most prominent Catholic theologian in England, to be what would now be known as her spiritual director. This relationship lasted until von Hügel's death in 1925. Underhill attested, somewhat hyperbolically, that von Hügel saved her life; her gratitude to him was inestimable.

Underhill's relationship to the Anglican Church was tenuous until she attended a retreat at the diocesan retreat house in Pleshey. It was there that she came to understand that she could make a contribution to religious life. Beginning in 1925 and continuing for a decade, she nurtured the incipient retreat movement within Anglicanism by giving retreats throughout England. These retreats were subsequently published, extending her influence and augmenting her literary corpus. In 1936 she published her last major work, *Worship*, another classic which defined the elements of worship and explored the forms of worship in Judaism, the Roman and Orthodox traditions, and a variety of Protestant expressions. She claimed that each of these was a "chapel in the cathedral of the Spirit." In 1939, as World War II exploded over Europe, Underhill became a pacifist, one of the few in the Anglican Church. As the war raged on, she wrote for the Anglican pacifist fellowship about the vocation of the pacifist, one that followed from the love of God. She died in June 1941 at the age of sixty-seven, hailed by her contemporaries. Her friend T.S. Eliot acknowledged her as a writer attuned to the great spiritual hunger of her times. He saw her not so much as a scholar, but as one conscious of the "grievous need of the contemplative element in the modern world." The *Times Literary Supplement* claimed Underhill was unmatched in understanding the gropings of the soul in her times, and Michael Ramsey, Archbishop of Canterbury, attested that more than anyone else Evelyn Underhill kept the spiritual life alive in the Anglican Church in the period between the wars.

SYNOPSIS

As a writer, Underhill's reputation rested principally on *Mysticism*. Its subtitle—"the study of the nature and development of man's spiritual consciousness"—illustrates the parameters of the subject and how it is to be considered. Although she studied history and art, and was influenced by the developments in modern psychology, philosophy, and science, Underhill's focus was on human experience and the possibility it offered for the development of a consciousness of the transcendent. She asks the question so often ignored: What is the deepest human longing? She found her answer in the experience of Western mystics who claimed that it was to behold Love itself—that is, God—and to respond with awe and gratitude to that Love.

Mysticism was a serious book. The language, tone, and pace of the book are related to her purpose, which was to convince the reader of the importance of the mystics, the "forerunners" of a higher human consciousness toward which all of the "race" aims. Urgent and compelling, her intent was to show the riches of an uncharted world that lay within the reach of every human. In its first half, "The Mystic Fact," Underhill defines mysticism, sets out its characteristics, and shows its relationship to vitalism, psychology, theology, symbolism, and magic. The remainder of the text, "The Mystic Way," describes the stages of mystic consciousness. A brief historical sketch of European mysticism and an impressive bibliography are included.

The mystic fact

Underhill's starting point is the "mystic fact," the existence of texts describing mystical experience. Her intent is to makes these experiences intelligible and hence to show them in relationship to truth. Consequently, she largely ignored their historical context, claiming that all mystics "speak the same language and come from the same country."

Her "point of departure" is a definite type of personality, one that "craves absolute truth" and for whom the whole meaning of life is found in this passionate quest. She first clears away philosophical obstacles to this understanding. Naturalism, idealism, and skepticism are each found inadequate for understanding this subject. Vitalism is examined as an alternative scheme, but is rejected as presenting only half the truth. In defining her subject she focuses on the two great psychic cravings: the desire to know, expressed in magic and science, and the desire to love, which is associated with mysticism. This distinction, which is central to her book, is reflected in her dismissal of the attempt to control reality by magical or scientific means. The highest human effort was not to control reality, but to participate in it through love.

Underhill defines mysticism variously, but at its core it is a movement of the heart, an attempt to transcend one's individual standpoint and to surrender to ultimate Reality, not for personal gain, or curiosity, or to obtain joy, but purely from the instinct of love. Above all mysticism is a life process, driven forward by the desire to attain Reality itself. This organic movement was the highest form of human consciousness, one consummated in the Love of God. Although each human had the "little buried talent" to achieve this consciousness, the mystics were the great exemplars of it, those who had been "transfigured" by their experience. In short, for Underhill mysticism was a way of life, open to all, achieved by the few whose lives were transformed by that which they loved. Each person was "kin" to the mystics, separated from them only in degree, not kind.

One of the most important aspects of *Mysticism* was the setting out and illustrating of four characteristics of the phenomenon. She first rejects William James's four marks of the mystic state (ineffability, noetic quality, transiency, passivity) and then defines her own. She claimed mysticism was active and practical, not passive and theoretical. It was an organic life process, something done by the whole self. It was a spiritual activity undertaken not to gain or achieve anything for its own end, not from a desire to be transformed (although that was the inevitable outcome), and not for any moral or ethical reason. The mystic's method and purpose was love—that is, a total dedication of the will toward its source.

The mystic way

The first section of *Mysticism* is analytical and definitional, but the second catapults the reader into the process of the mystic life itself. Underhill maps out five stages of the mystical way, illustrating each from mystical writings. She names these stages as awakening, purgation, illumination, dark night of the soul, and union. Passage through these stages results in a gradual and complete change in the self, a turning from the unreal world of sense to a union with Absolute Reality and surrender to it. The great adventure of humanity is to enter into this process, this winning over of the will. The mystics show the way through their genius and passion, which is connected to a particular psychological make-up, a natural capability of extraordinary concentration, an intensity of love and will, and the capacity for self-discipline, steadfastness, and courage.

In the beginning stage of awakening to the Divine, the field of consciousness begins to shift subtly from the self to the Divine and one experiences a certain joy. The second stage is one of purification, self-simplification, and stripping. Having awakened to the Perfect, there is the desire to eliminate what stands between the self and the Divine. This stage is marked by pain. Illumination, the third stage, provides a kind of clarity of vision different from normal life. This is "the first mystic life"; many artists achieve this level of consciousness, and many mystics never move beyond it. The fourth stage, "dark night of the soul," is filled with disharmony and strain and a sense of abandonment, sinfulness, despair, powerlessness, and temptation.

In this stage one is being remade through participation in the life of "Reality" itself. At times abnormal psychic phenomena—rapture, ecstasy, voices, and visions—may appear, but Underhill makes it clear that these are not central to the mystic life. What is central is the movement of increasing participation in the life of the Absolute. The final state, union, is known only by the great mystics. It is a state of vitality, of unification of personality, of freedom and heroic activity. The result of this life is what she calls "divine fecundity." Although she used the insights of psychology and philosophy to hone her defense of mysticism, in the end her "big" book was above all a personal defense of the achievements of the mystics, one she was able to understand because she lived intimately with their texts.

INFLUENCE

Mysticism was original: it redefined what it was to be both human and religious. It was compensatory: it aimed to illustrate the highest form of human consciousness, that embodied in mystic expression. It was iconoclastic: it posited the mystical element as essential to religion, giving less importance to doctrinal adherence, scriptural fidelity, or institutional allegiance.

Mysticism was not theology, but psychology, history, and a compendium of literature. It lived up to its subtitle, "a study of the nature and development of man's spiritual consciousness." Its appeal was to the ardent, those who saw religion as a quest. Although grounded in substantial research, its tone was not scholarly, but engaging and compelling. It invited the reader not only to honor the much-neglected mystic contribution, but to seek it for oneself.

When the text was published there were those who criticized it, most notably the venerable von Hügel who claimed, with good reason, that it was anti-historical, anti-institutional, and monistic. Others commented on its equating the "God of Christianity" with the "World-Soul of Pantheism" and the "Absolute of Philosophy." William Inge praised the book publicly, but privately indicated that its orthodoxy was suspect. But John Chapman, future abbot of Downside Abbey, hailed it as the "most enlightening" book on mysticism available. Its appeal was not to theologians, but to those interested in the life of the spirit in all its pastoral complexity.

Mysticism's flowery Edwardian prose, poetic argumentation, and lack of specific ethical and moral implications were seen as limitations. When Underhill revised the text for its twelfth and last edition, published in 1930, she made it more congruent with Christian doctrine. Her new preface acknowledged a significant increase in interest in the transcendent, and the works of Rudolf Otto and Karl Barth were mentioned specifically. But the changes she made to *Mysticism* were minimal. Its central insight was unchanged: the most important human experience was personal engagement with Reality, God, the Absolute—words which continued to be used interchangeably.

Mysticism's influence on theological discourse was indirect. It spawned neither a school of thought nor disciples. However, its implications were very much in keeping with theological developments emanating before and after Vatican II. For example, although there was no direct influence between the insights of *Mysticism* and those of Karl Rahner's "mysticism of everyday faith" or his claim for the necessity of the mystic element in Christianity's future, there was in the two a convergence of sympathies.

One of the most important influences of *Mysticism* was that it provided the scaffolding for a spate of accessible books on the "devotional life." In these writings the insights of the mystics were translated into a practical mysticism for "normal people." Without this grounding in the experience of the great mystics, this translation to quotidian life would have been much less credible. In this sense, one of *Mysticism*'s greatest contributions was the connection it established between the experience of the mystics and that of the ordinary Christian. This connection was appreciated by Thomas Merton, T.S. Eliot, Alan Watts, Charles Williams, and Michael Ramsey.

The continual republication of *Mysticism* for almost a century offers irrefutable evidence of its influence. Its popular appeal is explained by its compelling prose which invited the reader to experience first vicariously, and then personally, an encounter with God. In short, it stimulated a desire and fulfilled it simultaneously. Late twentieth-century historians of religious thought such as John Macquarrie, Horton Davies, John Booty, Martin Thornton, and Urban Holmes acknowledge the book's significance, even while criticizing some of its assumptions.

READING THE TEXT TODAY

The twenty-first century offers a vantage point from which to appreciate the groundbreaking nature of *Mysticism*. It unleashed a dynamic, pent-up desire to appropriate the life of the spirit for oneself. It fueled a movement which over the decades produced thousands of new publications, spawned the renewal of spiritual practices, and appropriated a creative dimension of human life that had previously seemed inaccessible to the ordinary Christian. *Mysticism* has a confirmed place in the history of Christian spirituality.

Mysticism as experience of the love of God

But the text is not merely a historical document; it has relevance for the contemporary reader. *Mysticism* gives pride of place to the experience of God as the defining characteristic of both mystic and human life lived to its fullest. The text's underlying psychology is positive. Every human has a "capacity for God"; the mystic realizes that capacity by becoming "a pure capacity for God." As one needs to reclaim the mystic contribution to human consciousness, one needs to assert as well the capacity for God inherent in each person.

Mysticism relies on mystic literature for illustration, offering quotations from hundreds of mystics organized around the stages of mystic life. Underhill had a particular genius for selecting quotes that appropriately demonstrated her points. As a result, the book serves as a compendium, an introduction to a literature that has been largely inaccessible to the public until quite recently. The inclusion of a historical sketch on mysticism and an extensive bibliography make available resources for further exploration.

One of the goals of the book is to define what mysticism is not. The phenomenon is discussed in relationship to theology, symbolism, magic, philosophy, and psychology. In this sense the text is an early example of how religious experience can be placed in dialogue with other disciplines and bodies of knowledge. This aspect of the text is more fully developed in one of Underhill's later volumes, *The Life of the Spirit and the Life of Today* (1922), in which the classic expressions of the spiritual life are explored in light of modern psychology. *Mysticism* encourages the contemporary reader to be inclusive in bringing to bear all forms of knowledge in examining this unique human phenomenon.

In the past and currently, there has been a tendency to characterize mysticism by its abnormal expressions of visions and voices. Underhill's text includes an entire chapter on this topic, dismissing the notion that these phenomena are constitutive of the mystic experience. Using the witness of the mystics themselves, mysticism is defined as the experience of the love of God. It is understood both as a desire for God and a transformation of the self through love which results in "a form of enhanced life" characterized by a "divine fecundity." Mysticism is "an organic life-process" that influences the whole of one's being and life. Although the full implications of this definition are not worked out in this text, they become the subject of Underhill's later writing on the spiritual life, which she says is "a life in which all that we do comes from the centre where we are anchored in God."

Although *Mysticism* has been criticized for not emphasizing the moral life, it does raise the important question of the relationship between the experience of the love of God and the transformed life, an important consideration for Christian spirituality. What the text makes very explicit is the priority of the love of God, which inevitably must result in what Underhill elsewhere describes as becoming the "parent of new life." Although only addressed cryptically, the relationship between love of God and love of neighbor is clearly established. As she indicates later, the best way to teach the second commandment is to focus on the first. Her final writing on pacifism, which she defines as a corollary of the love of God, is illustrative of this point.

The aim of *Mysticism* was to define the phenomenon, illustrate it through quotation, and codify a process. The second half of the book details the stages of the mystic life. While codification is a powerful instructive tool, it can inadvertently give the impression of a formulaic developmental process. As Underhill's later writings indicate, the spiritual life has great fluidity and suppleness, operating not in some straightforward manner, but in circular or spiraling movements. While the setting out of stages of mystic consciousness is one of the marks of genius of *Mysticism*, it must be cautiously examined. A reading of Underhill's *Letters* gives ample testimony of her sensitivity to the variety of ways the Spirit worked in the lives of those who came to her for spiritual direction. For the mystic and the ordinary Christian, the path to the fullness of life was never direct.

Mysticism as universal phenomenon

Because *Mysticism* is a tour de force, a defense of a much under-appreciated aspect of human achievement, the text leans heavily toward defining mysticism as a universal phenomenon, minimizing the historical particularity of its various individual expressions. This limitation is corrected by the author in her later writings, where she gives more weight to the influence of history and culture in explaining the phenomenon. Nonetheless, the effort to universalize mysticism allowed for her text to include at least some non-Christian expressions, especially those of Sufism and Judaism. Although these inclusions are minimal, they illustrate a willingness to explore the broad spectrum of mystical experience. Again, Underhill develops this line of thought in her last important book, *Worship*, in which she examines the origins of Christian worship in earlier cultic practice, especially Judaism, and explores its myriad expressions in Western history, each arising to meet a particular historic need.

As a stand-alone text *Mysticism* has appeal for many who may not define themselves within the Christian tradition. It can easily be read as a book about religious experience illustrated with Christian examples. While this widens the influence of the book, today it sometimes causes consternation, as it did in the past, among some orthodox Christians who object to the lack of consideration of subjects such as sin, grace, atonement, Christ, sacraments, and the church; these are barely mentioned, if at all. But this is to fault the book for what it is not: an apologetic for Christianity. *Mysticism*'s genius is that it is a pioneering effort to reclaim the contribution of those "giants" and "heroes" of the race who are seen as "brethren" and fellow travelers.

Mysticism can also be understood as a beginning point, a seed-bed, from which sprung Underhill's subsequent writings, which were increasingly more Christian in focus, but nonetheless derivative from this important classic text. Implicit in *Mysticism* are all the elements of the spiritual life—the importance of desire, of prayer, of transformation, of the relationship of the love of God and one's fellows, of the organic and integrated responsiveness of the person to life in its entirety. In this sense, *Mysticism* is the broadest, most inclusive, and most provocative of the writings of Evelyn Underhill; it continues to compel and engage readers, establishing her as a foremother of contemporary Christian spirituality.

EDITION

Underhill, E. (2002) *Mysticism: A Study in the Nature and Development of Spiritual Consciousness*, Mineola, NY: Dover Publications.

FURTHER READING

Greene, D. (1990) *Evelyn Underhill: artist of the infinite life*, New York: Crossroad, is a biography that provides a full discussion of Underhill's works.

Griffin, E. (2003) *Evelyn Underhill: essential writings*, Maryknoll, NY: Orbis Press, is an anthology with selections from a wide range of Underhill's writings.

28

DIETRICH BONHOEFFER
(1906–45)
Life Together

LISA E. DAHILL

For two millennia Christians have faced questions of how to sustain authentic and life-giving faith in the face of powers hostile to the subversive energy of the gospel. For sheer savagery and the pervasive betrayal of values central to human culture and the Christian church, however, few contexts in those two thousand years can match Nazi Germany. Out of the post-war trauma and humiliating economic disaster of the Treaty of Versailles, Hitler's rise to power fed on national instability and promised order, hope, and pride for Germany—but at the cost of humanity, in every sense. By the mid 1930s, Nazi chaos had begun to dissolve German society by eroding truth, stability, peace, trust, and the basic coherence of shared communal reality. By 1940, this chaos had overtaken every dimension of life in full-blown war and the Holocaust itself. This was life in hell: a totalitarian police state ruled by madmen, where those who tell the truth are put to death and those who lie to save their lives risk losing their souls. It was a state with neither free speech of any kind nor any way to communicate with allies, where any slip could mean death for oneself or torture for one's companions. And it was a state that was not just devastating its own citizens but visiting chaos on its neighbors in every direction: invading Poland, the Sudetenland, France, and Holland, bombing England, and occupying Scandinavia.

For Dietrich Bonhoeffer, participation in the conspiracy to overthrow Hitler's government had led him even further into this chaos. He was imprisoned for years in a Gestapo prison in Berlin, under direct Nazi control and interrogation, under heavy Allied bombing. It is hard to think how things could have been worse—until July of 1944, when the process began that would sentence him to death. A person living in this situation might understandably be overwhelmed by rage, panic, or despair. Yet Bonhoeffer's prison letters reveal a faith deepening into radiance, joy, hope, even gratitude. What underlies such faith? What nourishes it over the long haul in a resistance that risks and faces death? What sustains an authentic costly discipleship radiant enough to inspire contemporaries and later generations in their own Christ-conforming lives? For Bonhoeffer, the origin and heart and goal of Christian life is participation in the reality of Jesus Christ, the fullness of God embracing the world. And such participation is inherently communal: as Christ is Body, only in his Body can Christians be sustained in this alternative reality. This is the life of prayer and communal formation he describes in his classic, *Life Together*.

AUTHOR AND AUDIENCE

Dietrich Bonhoeffer was born in Breslau, Germany, in 1906. He and his twin sister Sabine were the sixth and seventh of the eight children of Dr. Karl and Paula (von Hase) Bonhoeffer. In 1912 the family moved to Berlin as Karl accepted the chair of psychiatry and neurology of the University of Berlin. Dietrich studied theology in Tübingen and Berlin and received his doctorate in 1927 with his dissertation, *Sanctorum Communio* (*The Communion of Saints*). Following a parish internship in Barcelona, Spain, he wrote and defended his habilitation thesis, entitled *Act and Being*, in 1930, then spent a post-doctoral year in New York at Union Theological Seminary. That year was formative in exposing Bonhoeffer to the vibrant faith of African American Christians in the face of racism, in drawing him into pacifist convictions, and in opening him to encounter with Jesus Christ through the Sermon on the Mount. He returned to Germany, was ordained to the Lutheran pastorate in 1931, and began lecturing in theology at the University of Berlin. Following Hitler's rise to power in 1933, Bonhoeffer attempted to rouse his church to non-violent resistance of Nazi policies. This proved unsuccessful, though he helped prepare the way for the Confessing Church, which in 1934 seceded from the Nazi-controlled state church. During that time Bonhoeffer served as a pastor in London, where he strengthened his ecumenical connections and visited Anglican monasteries and other communities for inspiration regarding forms of common Christian life.

In 1935 the Confessing Church called Bonhoeffer to lead a newly formed seminary in east Prussia. Eventually located in the town of Finkenwalde, the school housed two "courses" of seminarians over its two years of operation. At Finkenwalde Bonhoeffer created a rule of regular prayer and personal meditation, silence, communal meals, service, worship, study, and recreation. Here too he presented the lectures later gathered into the well-known book *Discipleship* (published in 1938, originally translated into English as *The Cost of Discipleship*). Following the Gestapo's closure of the seminary in 1937, he wrote *Life Together* (published in 1939) as a record of Finkenwalde practice and an invitation to such common life for the church more broadly.

Post-Finkenwalde, Bonhoeffer attempted to continue the illegal formation of Confessing Church pastors via underground "collective pastorates" in present-day Poland. As Nazi scrutiny bore down ever harder on him, Bonhoeffer eventually fled to New York in late spring 1939. There, however, he sensed that this was a mistake; God was calling him back to Germany to share in his church's need and fate. Returning in July 1939, he soon joined the conspiracy against Hitler. Here Bonhoeffer used his ecumenical and international connections to communicate with the Allies on behalf of the resistance, and in his unfinished *Ethics* (first published in 1949) he reflected on the theological groundings of Christian thought and action in ambiguous times. Arrested in 1943, he was held in Tegel Prison, Berlin, for nearly two years. The letters he wrote from prison (published in 1951) have become classic texts of Christian witness and post-Christendom faithfulness in the "world come of age." Along with several other conspirators, Bonhoeffer was executed on April 9, 1945, at Flossenbürg Concentration Camp in Bavaria.

Emerging out of the heart of this intense life trajectory, *Life Together* received almost immediate acclaim. Written for the church and in disarmingly simple language, this short book has been reprinted dozens of times in German and twenty-three times in its original English-language translation. It has been translated into many languages and is among Bonhoeffer's most widely read works.

SYNOPSIS

Bonhoeffer divided *Life Together* into five chapters. While each chapter contains both theological exposition and practical guidelines for communal life, the book as a whole moves from the predominantly theoretical first chapter ("Community") into a sketch of concrete recommendations under various headings in the later chapters.

Community

In this first chapter Bonhoeffer outlines his working theology of Christian community. He begins with a reminder of the profound gift, easily taken for granted, of such community. Writing after the Finkenwalde community had been scattered by the Gestapo and foreseeing further diaspora as the alumni of that community would soon be conscripted into Hitler's army, he speaks poignantly of longing for "the physical presence of other Christians [as] a source of incomparable joy and strength to the believer" (p. 29). The community is distinguished from other human groups by its formation "only through Jesus Christ and in Jesus Christ" (p. 31).

This christological foundation of the community safeguards against two dangers. The first is the "unhappy desire for something more" (p. 34)—that is, despising the *reality* of Christian community in which one lives in favor of some ideal. How often, he notes, do members of family, seminary, parish, or other communities judge and condemn one another on the basis of some lofty-seeming ideal of what a Christian community "should" be? To reject the real to the extent it falls short of an abstract ideal destroys community and places the idealist in the position of accuser (p. 36). Such an approach— most insidious when cloaked in pious rhetoric—must be unmasked, its arrogant judgments stripped away, and the bare reality of *this* community, *these* people, *this* brother and sister, received as the gift and miracle of God they are.

Such humility also helps safeguard against the second danger Bonhoeffer notes: the creation of "emotional" (*seelisch*) or "psychic" (*psychisch*) community rather than the "spiritual" (*pneumatisch*) community that God desires. Here Bonhoeffer is warning against basing community on unmet needs, projection, or other irresistible urges of the human psyche "for immediate contact with other human souls. . . . the complete intimate fusion of I and You" (p. 41). What contemporary theorists refer to as boundary violation or enmeshment is a recurring danger in communities marked by the vulnerability, intensity, and depth that religious experience can evoke. To safeguard the mystery and worth of every member of the community (especially the weakest), Bonhoeffer points to the illusion of "immediacy," or non-mediated relationship. Because Jesus Christ is the One through whom all relationship takes place, standing always between every I and You, spiritual community is marked not by emotional drama or by acolytes surrounding an adored leader, but by a shared orientation to Jesus Christ alone. Spiritual love "will respect the other as the boundary that Christ establishes between us" (p. 44). Thus rather than the coercion of ideals or unconscious projections, what marks authentic Christian community is radical freedom and the space for each person to be who he or she fully is in Jesus Christ. In such a community

> individuals will make an amazing discovery. They will be able to stop constantly keeping an eye on others, judging them, condemning them, and . . . thus doing violence to them. . . . The view of such persons expands and, to their amazement, they recognize for the first time the richness of God's creative glory shining over their brothers and sisters.
>
> (Bonhoeffer, *Life Together*, 95)

The day together

How does such a community order its life? Those oriented to Jesus Christ need to learn to listen to him in and as the living Word of God coming to the community and each individual anew each day. The day begins and ends with communal prayer immersed in this Word. As in Christian monasticism, for Bonhoeffer morning and evening prayer is centered in the Psalms as the church's primary prayer book. His characteristic interpretive step is to see both human words and God's Word in their fullness united in Jesus' own praying of the Psalms, to which Christians' prayer with the Psalms joins them. By encountering the rest of scripture through whole chapters read out loud in *lectio continua* (continuous reading), participants enter God's story ever more fully. Thus Christians must get to know scripture—God's love letter to the world—in intimate depth and familiarity, in all its complexity and strangeness. Prayer also includes hymn-singing as a form of communal breath and praise; intercessions offered on behalf of all and for the needs of the world; and, in the evening, the confession of the day's sins so as to rest in the One who prays in us even as we sleep.

The day alone

Bonhoeffer's centering on "life together" does not slight individuals' need for solitude. In fact, a central paradox unfolds: "Whoever cannot be alone should beware of community. . . . [and] [w]hoever cannot stand being in community should beware of being alone" (p. 82). As Bonhoeffer realizes, healthy community depends on authentic selfhood, solitude, personal encounter with God. Both solitude and community begin with the call of Jesus Christ (p. 83). Thus a healthy Christian community includes intentional preservation of time and space for solitude as a human need, to be defended against untoward claims of others (p. 91). This solitude includes extended personal meditation on the Word, a depth of encounter balancing the communal breadth of scriptural immersion and clearly echoing monastic *lectio divina*. The practice of silence before the Word helps people "manage [their] silence and speech during the day" (p. 85), fostering an essentially contemplative stance toward all things and all people. Bonhoeffer teaches his seminarians to let go of their accustomed exegetical, homiletical, or pastoral approaches to the Word and learn to listen for thirty minutes each day to the depth of God's address *to them personally.* Prayer and intercessions—especially for people from whom one feels alienated—emerge from this encounter with the Word, as does the rest of the day's life.

Service

In moving from prayer into his chapter on "Service," Bonhoeffer suggests discernment criteria regarding the quality of communal and personal prayer (pp. 91–2): Has the community's prayer made people "free, strong, and mature," or "insecure and dependent"? Has personal prayer invited pray-ers into an "unreal world" from which life in the world shocks them as a "fright," or ever more fully, joyfully, and courageously into "the real world of God"? He concludes, "Only the day can decide."

The practice of love begins in community members' treatment of one another. In fact, a central practice of the Finkenwalde community is found in Bonhoeffer's "decisive rule of all Christian community life that each individual is prohibited from talking about another Christian in secret" (p. 94). Concerns are to be expressed directly to the other in question; persons are obliged to face those community members who seem most irritating or difficult to them—indeed, to come to see in them the very image and goodness of God (p. 95).

Rather than talking about others, Bonhoeffer proposes listening, the primary practice of mutual hospitality. Those who are unable to listen to others are demonstrating their underlying inability to listen to God. "The death of the spiritual life starts here" (p. 98). From the capacity for listening flow other gifts: helpfulness and willingness to be bothered by others; bearing with others, particularly in their freedom before God, their otherness from oneself, and their sin; forgiving one another; and (only after all these) speaking the Word of God in comfort, challenge, or admonishment when needed. The capacity for such admonishment underlies healthy community in Christ, since without it no one can learn of his or her blind spots and grow free of them; the community must be able to speak the truth in love. This requires clear and free personhood, good self-differentiation, and humility toward the mystery and humanity of one another.

Confession and the Lord's Supper

The capacity for truth-telling must extend to one's own life as well. In his final chapter Bonhoeffer develops an apologia for the restoration among Protestants of personal confession. Practiced here between confession partners, rather than with one pastor or priest hearing the confessions of the community, this aspect of shared life makes possible the deep humility of grace and the fullest expression of Christian community in the sacrament of the Lord's Supper. What is confessed is one's *real* sins in their humiliating particularity, not vague abstractions. In confession the human being faces the truth of oneself, both in shattering encounter with one's sin and in the encounter (impossible apart from such exposure) with the One whose love embraces even this fullness of one's reality: "God wants you as you are . . . desiring you alone" (p. 108).

For Bonhoeffer such truth-telling in every dimension of one's life—as breakthrough into the fullest possible encounter with the One who is the Truth—not only marks the Christian community but is impossible apart from such community. Authentic confession opens many breakthroughs (p. 111–13): "to community," as opposed to the pseudo-intimacy and alienation of false selves; "to the cross," where all illusions are stripped; "to new life," the "renewal of the joy of baptism"; and "to assurance," the firm ground of reality between persons, within oneself, and with God. From this grounding in baptismal reality, the members of the community are able to experience together the consummate gift of God: the Body and Blood of Jesus Christ.

INFLUENCE

As noted earlier, *Life Together* is one of Bonhoeffer's most widely read works, with more copies in print than any other of his books. The work's engaging style and multiple layers of access open it to a broad readership. Roommates, couples, families, or other groupings of Christians seeking practical guidance for their common life; clergy and laity in congregations, seminarians, or leaders of church camps, retreats, or agencies exploring the meaning, structure, and healthy nurture of Christian community for their contexts; social service or political activists around the world seeking a depth of spiritual practice and communal accountability to ground their ministry or resistance; bishops and housewives and teenagers and office workers desiring growth in personal prayer—all these and many others continue to turn to *Life Together*.

Two particular areas of the text's influence are as a prototypical "rule" for Protestant monastic or quasi-monastic communities, and an invitation for individuals longing for a greater depth of spiritual practice than many (still anti-Catholic) Protestant pieties of the mid-twentieth century tolerated. Seeing in Bonhoeffer a testimony to the power of life formed deeply in prayer and community, Christians desiring a similarly authentic discipleship in their own contexts embraced the book's invitation to reclaim these in the intentionally structured communal life of prayer Bonhoeffer found so essential for sustained resistance. Along with the legacy of the Finkenwalde experience itself, *Life Together* contributed to a renaissance of Protestant monasticism and other forms of communal living following World War II in Germany and beyond. In the United States, *Life Together* has helped nourish the "New Monasticism" emerging—often within peace church or evangelical Protestant circles—in urban and rural contexts of poverty, as well as Catholic, Lutheran, Mennonite, and other urban volunteer corps.

In the area of prayer and discipline, *Life Together* provided a similarly important witness to twentieth-century Protestants about the need for Christian discipleship in the world to reclaim practices long feared to be "Catholic." Extended daily solitude, the structuring of one's life around prayer, and even personal confession receive sympathetic advocacy in this book. Of course none of these practices is un-Protestant in itself, any more than reading the Bible is un-Catholic. But *Life Together*—with the witness of its martyr author—transcended this division and granted permission for Protestants to explore spiritual practices and forms of common life unthinkable earlier. Ultimately, it gave all Christians an invitation to think deeply about the meaning and forms of their shared life.

READING THE TEXT TODAY

Life Together takes seriously the relational nature of Christian faith, indeed of all life. It invites readers to ponder the nature of the communities to which they belong, the power those communities exercise in forming their members' experiences of God, and the readers' own personal contributions to the health or disease of a given community. As readers encounter this text today, several issues are of particular importance.

Monasticism vs. virtuality?

Life Together intends not the seclusion of Christians safely away from the world's messiness but a life oriented always toward and into one's public vocation in the world. As Bonhoeffer notes on the first page of his book, "Jesus Christ lived in the midst of his enemies" (p. 27). Thus disciples of Christ live and participate in the real world too, even Nazi Germany. The conviction that such discipleship can be sustained best by patterns of communal prayer and ordered life represents the core purpose of Christian monasticism; it is not a new insight of Bonhoeffer's. Yet his book confronts both Protestant and Catholic stereotypes with this conviction. Bonhoeffer's witness and martyrdom first undermine traditional Protestant objections to monasticism as a naïve withdrawal from the world. From within one of the most demonic socio-political contexts of human history, Bonhoeffer demonstrates that it is only by means of such intentional and prayerful "Catholic" life together that authentic "Protestant" obedience to the Word and worldly Christian faith can be lived at all. His explication of quasi-monastic patterns and practices as compatible with—or even necessary for—the fullness of Christian life has served as a salutary challenge for post-war Protestant churches, as the expanding interest in Protestant or ecumenical forms of monasticism reveals. Simultaneously, his insistence on the indivisibility of contemplative life from fearless strategic political action reminds contemporary monastic communities to take seriously the public dimensions of their witness as well.

In the present context of growing reliance on "virtual" communities for human relating, however, it may be Bonhoeffer's grounding of Christian life in the ongoing physical presence of other believers that is most countercultural today. In other words, his insistence on the priority of the real might find a new resonance in challenging not only the hegemony of ideals but also the pervasiveness of "virtuality." Of course in extraordinary places and times, remote forms of connection may well be better than nothing. But lest Christians be seduced into thinking virtual is somehow always or inherently better, slicker, spiffier, Bonhoeffer reminds them that ordinary, flawed, unadorned reality is where the incarnate God lives. "Life together" means literally that. The life of faith is meant to be lived in the real body, with other real bodies, real persons, in real presence with Jesus Christ.

Listening

This life of faith is grounded in listening: to God, to the Word, to one another. In hearing broad stretches of scripture, Christians are drawn into the contours of God's story; meditating in depth on a single verse, they gradually learn the subtle echoes of the voice of Love itself in the Word. In hearing one another, persons are invited into the gift of another's experience, feelings, reality. These facets of listening are interwoven in the community, yet there is one curious omission. Bonhoeffer takes for granted the capacity to listen to oneself, one's own body or needs or desires. He tends to give priority to the other over the self; others' "demands and requests" come before one's own priorities (p. 99), and "it is good for [Christians'] own will to be broken in their encounter with" others (p. 96). In this he presupposes a community of peers, equal in relative power and equally able to serve or be served. In other contexts—where sexism, racism, abuse, privilege, or other forms of structural or psychic imbalance distort persons' perceptions of themselves and others—Bonhoeffer's instructions could reinforce submission on the part of readers who need instead to defend or assert themselves vis-à-vis others. Thus the importance of listening to God's desires for oneself, and negotiating those desires in community, needs to complement the listening and sacrifice toward others that Bonhoeffer develops so beautifully.

Ecological community

A contemporary appropriation of *Life Together* must surely take account of the unprecedented ecological crisis facing humanity. As the atmosphere warms, oil supplies peak, and water and food become increasingly scarce for increasingly large numbers of human beings, the underpinnings of contemporary economies and civilization itself grow increasingly fragile. The changes needed on every level of global life together are overwhelming at best. If these changes fail or are never attempted, the planet faces grave degradation; the human race, possible extinction.

Just as Christian monasticism began in the collapse of a dominant civilization, preserving a remnant of order in chaotic times, so the wisdom of *Life Together*—itself not coincidentally born out of the twentieth century's greatest chaos—may be precisely what the church and humanity need in the greater catastrophes the species almost surely faces. What if the forms of life outlined in *Life Together*, like the earliest Christian monastic rules, are in fact a survival manual for soul, body, and social order in disintegrating times? Even more broadly, what if the volume were read not for Christians only but expanding the circle of those with whom they live together to include all earth's creatures, all its people, all its ecosystems and inhabitants, and their descendants? Sacrificial service of the weakest, listening to every other precisely in its alterity, shared endless orientation to the will and ways of the Word permeating the entire cosmos and attentiveness to the call of the Spirit in courageous, creative intervention at the heart of the world's danger—this is a "life together" that could ease the ravaged planet and bring to deeper awareness its lament and pain and needs. Whether or not future generations will have life in abundance may depend on the quality of this ultimate spiritual capacity: an ever more radically incarnational "life together," or none at all.

TRANSLATION

Dietrich Bonhoeffer (1996) *Life Together/Prayerbook of the Bible*, ed. G.L. Müller and A. Schönherr (German), and G.B. Kelly (English), trans. D.W. Bloesch and J.H. Burtness, Minneapolis: Fortress Press.

FURTHER READING

Barnett, V.J. (1992) *For the Soul of the People: Protestant protest against Hitler*, Oxford: Oxford University Press, provides historical context for the Nazi church struggle and the Confessing Church.

Bethge, E. (2000) *Dietrich Bonhoeffer: a biography*, rev. edn, trans. and rev. V.J. Barnett, Minneapolis: Fortress Press, is still the most encompassing Bonhoeffer biography, written by Bonhoeffer's closest friend.

De Gruchy, J.W. (ed.) (1999) *The Cambridge Companion to Dietrich Bonhoeffer*, Cambridge: Cambridge University Press, contains essays tracing central aspects of Bonhoeffer's context, biography, formation, theology, and legacy.

Green, C.J. (1999) *Bonhoeffer: a theology of sociality*, rev. edn, Grand Rapids, MI: Wm. B. Eerdmans Publishing Co., explores Bonhoeffer's understanding of Christian community, the formation of the human person, and social ethics.

Kelly, G.B. and Nelson, F.B. (2003) *The Cost of Moral Leadership: the spirituality of Dietrich Bonhoeffer*, Grand Rapids, MI: Wm B. Eerdmans Publishing, provides a chronological tracing of Bonhoeffer's spirituality, including a wealth of primary quotations.

29

HOWARD THURMAN
(1899–1981)
Jesus and the Disinherited

LUTHER E. SMITH, JR.

Few books inspire both spiritual formation and social transformation. *Jesus and the Disinherited* is one of them. Since its publication in 1949, the book has challenged readers to rethink how the social status of Jesus, as a poor Jew living under Roman occupation and oppression, had bearing on his message and mission. It was a creative interpretation of Jesus's status as one of the disinherited whose ministry empowered the disinherited to overcome their plight.

Howard Thurman analyzed Jesus's social circumstances and compared them to his own oppressive context of racial injustice. Thurman concluded that "the striking similarity between the social position of Jesus in Palestine and that of the vast majority of American Negroes is obvious to anyone who tarries long over the facts" (p. 34). The parallels Thurman saw were deeply personal. These parallels spoke to his identity as an African American who suffered the traumas of prejudice, discrimination, and humiliation that occur in a segregated society.

The most quoted passage from the book is the question: "What, then, is the word of the religion of Jesus to those who stand with their backs against the wall?" (p. 108). This question presents the vivid image of desperation and the saving possibility in the religion of Jesus. Delineating Jesus's ethic and practices as intended for the physical and spiritual survival of the disinherited, Thurman argues that God's saving message is given directly to them. No intermediary is required. The disinherited are worthy and capable of hearing from God without the intervention of those with social prestige, political power, and wealth. Thurman lifts up Jesus, who is one of the disinherited and the message bearer, as evidence of this truth.

Jesus and the Disinherited was a bold social application of Thurman's biblical interpretation. It undermined the religious justifications for a segregated society—including segregated churches. To the disinherited, the book asserted their worth and capacity to challenge the injustices perpetrated against them. To the advantaged, it confronted their complicity in structures and practices of privilege as a failure in moral and religious commitment. And to the Christian church came the invitation to consider the implications of Jesus as one of the disinherited whose message and ministry were given to empowering those "who stand with their backs against the wall."

Jesus and the Disinherited illumined how issues of race and race relations define Christian discipleship. It became a major influence on the leadership of the modern civil rights movement and others who sought to eliminate the scourge of racism. Its significance and impact, however, extend far beyond Thurman's time and context to wherever and whenever Christians look to Jesus for wisdom on relating to the disinherited.

AUTHOR AND AUDIENCE

Howard Thurman was born in Daytona, Florida, in 1899. His leaving Daytona to attend high school in Jacksonville, Florida revealed two harsh realities of his early life: racism and poverty. The segregated Daytona school system provided neither eighth-grade classes nor a high school for African Americans. Thurman was so intent on getting an education that his school principal tutored him on the eighth-grade curriculum so that he could pass the exam that qualified him for high school. Since there was no public high school for African Americans in the Daytona area, he applied and was accepted to the church-sponsored Florida Baptist Academy in Jacksonville. As he waited for the train to Jacksonville, he was told that he had to pay for shipping his luggage. His mother was not able to contribute to his education, nor did she even have money for the additional shipping charge.

The payment for shipping came from a generous stranger at the train station who wanted Thurman to pursue his educational dream.

His early life was also influenced by nurture and trauma from his local church. The nurture came through inspiring worship and supportive members. The trauma was when he heard the preacher at his father's funeral condemn his father to hell for not belonging to any church. The assurance and crises from church experiences were complemented by a profound nature-mysticism (especially from experiences of the Atlantic Ocean, the Halifax River, storms, star-lit nights, and a particular oak tree) that gave Thurman a sense of grounding and wonder. This mysticism would influence his convictions about the importance of religious experience as the means to religious knowledge, and the limitations of the institutional church and dogma as the arbiters of faith.

As valedictorian of his Academy class, he earned a tuition scholarship to Morehouse College in Atlanta, Georgia. At Morehouse he majored in economics, was a leader in many school organizations, read every book in the Morehouse library, and in 1923 graduated as valedictorian. He then went to Rochester Theological Seminary in Rochester, New York. After completing his bachelor of divinity degree in 1926, he married Kate Kelley and became pastor of a Baptist church in Oberlin, Ohio. In 1929, because his wife's health required that they move to a milder climate, he accepted a joint teaching position in religion and philosophy at Morehouse and Spelman colleges. After his first wife's death in 1930 and his subsequent marriage to Sue Bailey in 1932, Thurman became professor of Christian Theology at Howard University's School of Religion in Washington, DC. He was later appointed dean of Rankin Chapel where he continued his leadership of university worship and religious programming.

Long before the book's publication, Thurman worked on the themes of *Jesus and the Disinherited* in lectures and articles. Basic tenets of his argument were in a 1928 article entitled "Peace Tactics and a Racial Minority." His early years at Howard University were a period of expansion and refinement on its themes. In 1935, his address on "Good News for the Underprivileged" was given at a convocation on preaching and then published that same year. His 1938 series of lectures in Canada entitled "The Significance of Jesus" put forth the major arguments later found in the book. The themes were part of his many speaking engagements to racially diverse audiences. From these events he received soundings that indicated his ideas were compelling.

While on a "Pilgrimage of Friendship" in 1936, Thurman and his wife met with Mohandas K. Gandhi. Upon returning to the United States, through newspaper publicity and extensive lecturing, Thurman stirred national interest about the relevance of Gandhi's philosophy and nonviolent methods to overcoming racism in the United States.

His dream to create an interracial and intercultural religious fellowship was fulfilled in 1944 when he co-founded The Church for the Fellowship of All Peoples in San Francisco. This was the first inter-racial church, in both membership and leadership, in the USA. It became internationally known as a prophetic example for how the church could end its segregated membership and worship.

In 1953, Thurman was invited to become professor of Spiritual Resources and Disciplines and dean of Marsh Chapel at Boston University. He believed this deanship at a large and predominately white university, which was an unprecedented position for an African American, would enable him to continue his dream to establish inclusive community on a larger scale. As throughout his career, Thurman preached and lectured extensively in conferences, churches, synagogues, and universities. A 1953 issue of the popular *Life* magazine listed him as one of the twelve greatest preachers in the United States. Many of his twenty-three books were written during and after the Boston years. Upon retirement in 1965, Thurman returned to San Francisco and founded the Howard Thurman Educational Trust that provided need-based financial assistance to college students, sponsored seminars on spirituality, and distributed his books and audiotapes. He died on April 11, 1981.

SYNOPSIS

Jesus and the Disinherited is an apologetic that defends the Christian faith's capacity to overcome social injustice—especially racial prejudice and discrimination. The failure of Christian churches and individuals to advocate in significant numbers against racial prejudice and discrimination in society and the church was perplexing. Thurman asked: "Is this impotency due to the betrayal of the genius of the religion, or is it due to a basic weakness in the religion itself?" (p. 7).

Thurman was adamant that Christians have the capacity to overcome social injustice but have either misunderstood or retreated from Jesus's message and example that call his followers to live in loving community with others regardless of their racial, economic, national, and religious differences.

Thurman believed that Christians must rediscover Jesus's social standing as one of the disinherited and Jesus's commitment to challenge dehumanizing interpersonal and social dynamics. This rediscovery is fundamental to empowering Christians as advocates for a loving community. Thurman's corrective had two primary approaches. First, understanding Jesus as a poor and oppressed Jew meant that Jesus was one of the disinherited. To be a disciple of Jesus, therefore, is to identify with the disinherited, their plight, and how God's truth (especially in the example of Jesus) comes directly to the disinherited. The corrective's second approach distinguished "the religion of Jesus" from "religion about Jesus." Thurman argued that when Christians comprehend what Jesus believed about God and God's will for humanity, they are closer to a more accurate interpretation of Jesus's mission. Jesus's beliefs and practices were rooted in Judaism's sacred scriptures and his personal experiences of God's presence. What comes from the religion *of* Jesus is the awareness that all humanity is embraced as God's beloved children.

Religion *about* Jesus, however, is more likely to incorporate theological constructions informed by believers' personal fears, cultural prejudices, and ecclesial biases. The constructions may be sincere endeavors to capture Jesus's personal and cosmic meaning. Still, without attention to the social dimensions of Jesus's life, religion about Jesus is prone to reflect what persons and institutions want Jesus to be. Thurman believed that in the religion about Jesus the true significance of the disinherited is often ignored or diminished.

His interpretation of Jesus's historical context drew heavily upon Vladimir G. Simkhovitch's *Toward the Understanding of Jesus* (1921). He agreed with Simkhovitch's conclusion that Jesus sought to challenge oppressive conditions by announcing that the reality of salvation is within human beings. But Simkhovitch believed the disinherited of Jesus's day were incapable of understanding his profound spiritual message. He depicted Jesus as a spiritual and intellectual genius whose insights were missed by the very oppressed who needed them most. Thurman, however, interpreted Jesus's message as being comprehensible good news to the disinherited. They embraced his message that spoke to their plight, and they experienced the enlivenment that flows from understanding it.

Thurman's sources for *Jesus and the Disinherited* reinforced his conviction about the capacity and significance of the disinherited. The Bible (which is quoted throughout the book) and the religious genius of black slaves (as found in black spirituals) were primary source material. And resonant with the mystic tradition of privileging experience as the means to spiritual truth, Thurman's own life was major source material. Nearly a fourth of the book's pages present Thurman reflecting upon his life experience to illumine the point being made. He believed that his life, as one of the disinherited, was a fundamental source of meaning.

The hounds of hell

After the first chapter on "Jesus—An Interpretation," the next three chapters identify and explicate "the three hounds of hell that track the trail of the disinherited" (p. 29). These hounds are simultaneously forces that pursue to destroy as well as useful survival tactics for the disinherited. *Fear* emerges in a pervasive climate of threat, humiliation, and violence that dehumanizes the disinherited and consumes their energies. As a survival tactic, fear keeps them alert to situations and interactions that could result in harm—especially to their children. *Deception* distorts the possibility for relationships that are characterized by sincerity and honesty. At the same time, it protects the disinherited from exposing their hearts and bodies to the privileged who deny and disrespect their dignity. *Hate* keeps the disinherited and privileged in a relationship of enemy-status. Hate also lessens dangerous contact with the enemy because it relieves the disinherited from a sense of moral obligation to have concern or care for their oppressors.

Thurman concluded that Jesus recognized the value of these hounds of hell as coping techniques; but whatever their immediate benefit, they kill the inner self that God calls to a higher ethic. Jesus insisted that the disinherited had the power to respond creatively to their oppressors who pushed them against the wall, but only if they retained control over their inner attitude. Thurman wrote that "no external force, however great and overwhelming, can at long last destroy a people if it does not first win the victory of the spirit [inner attitude] against them" (p. 21). The book's last chapter focused on love as the force empowering resistance to the hounds and fostering creative options for living life with a sense of worth, meaning, and joy.

The love-ethic

The love-ethic, according to Thurman, was central to the religion of Jesus. When Jesus said "love thy neighbor as thyself," he dismissed all barriers of race, religion, and social standing that prevented the exercise of love from one human being to another. The question was no longer *if* one had a moral and religious responsibility to love adversaries, but *how* to overcome the normal urges of fear, deception, and hate so that love governed all relationships. Overcoming these urges is possible when there is "a common sharing of a sense of mutual worth and value" (p. 98) between the privileged and disinherited. Jesus's teaching to "love your enemy" began with this fundamental effort that acknowledges another as a child of God.

Crucial to the work of love is the necessity to forgive. If past and current injuries imprison the heart, the love-ethic is kept at bay until forgiveness breaks cycles of distrust and retaliation. Always the ethical demand of love is on both the privileged and disinherited. Each has responsibility for creating a climate that represents God's intent for loving relationships. The love-ethic is not only a survival technique for the disinherited but also a survival technique for God's dream of community.

INFLUENCE

The civil rights movement not only forever changed the United States; it is also credited with inspiring freedom movements around the world. African leaders transforming their countries from colonial control or apartheid, the efforts of South American protesters to end dictatorships and military juntas, the singing of "We Shall Overcome" by demonstrators in Eastern Europe declaring independence from the Soviet bloc, and countless other freedom efforts at local and national levels have found the civil rights movement to be instructive and energizing. Less known is the important fact that *Jesus and the*

Disinherited was a source of instruction and inspiration for leaders of the civil rights movement.

During the Montgomery bus boycott, the protest that launched the modern civil rights movement in 1955–6, Martin Luther King, Jr. carried a copy of *Jesus and the Disinherited* with him. Leaders of the Nashville student movement, one of the most defining and successful protests of the era, studied two books that spiritually grounded their activism: the Bible and *Jesus and the Disinherited*. Other civil rights leaders identified this book as seminal reading for their involvement. The book's description of the oppressed being against the wall portrayed what these leaders and participants in the movement felt as their reality. The civil rights leaders did not have to strain to derive connections between their efforts to end segregation and Thurman's writing about Jesus's relationship to the disinherited. The relevance to their battleground was explicit.

The book also dealt explicitly with the importance of nonviolence as a religious method of social transformation. The emphasis on non-violence as a way of life that represents Christian discipleship, rather than utilizing nonviolence only because it is strategically effective, was consistent with Martin Luther King, Jr.'s rationale for the method. And just as King cited Jesus and Gandhi as his major inspirations for nonviolence, Thurman's focus on Jesus and his visit with Gandhi were well-known to King and other civil rights leaders. The appeal to common sources reinforced Thurman's credibility and the book's relevance to these leaders.

Another clear link with the goals of the movement was Thurman's emphasis upon social action having as its primary objective a new relatedness with the enemy. Although the common goals of Thurman and the movement were to affirm self-worth and one's capacity to effect change, more was at stake than just the acquisition of rights by the disinherited. Love of neighbors, especially neighbors who were the enemy, meant that movement participants would come to a more selfless and ultimate vision of their activism.

Thurman's status, as one of the disinherited who had the added authority of a theological education, gave validity to his arguments. He wrote as a Christian who stood with his back against the wall. His historical analysis of Jesus contributed substantive conclusions born of scholarship and discipleship. The enthusiastic reception of *Jesus and the Disinherited*, however, went beyond the veracity of Thurman's writing. He was one of the most popular and revered preachers in the nation. Long before the publication of the book, Howard Thurman was respected for his mystic orientation, intellectual rigor, and pastoral presence. The publication of the book was eagerly awaited and welcomed by thousands who had already experienced Thurman as a trustworthy interpreter of the spiritual life.

The book remained in publication and continued to inspire laity, clergy, and social activists. It had a major influence on James Cone, the leading exponent of black liberation theology, who credits *Jesus and the Disinherited* as influencing his thesis that the religion of Jesus was focused on the poor with particular contemporary significance to black people. Thurman's theological orientation, especially his convictions about reconciliation, is different from Cone's theology that stresses God's favor for liberation and blackness. The point remains that it was an influential book in the development of a major twentieth-century liberation theology.

The book's influence on the civil rights movement and black theology should not overshadow its impact as a source for personal spiritual formation. Individuals have discovered insights on Jesus's ministry for confronting "the wall" and the "hounds of hell" that have informed their renewed sense of self and the possibilities for reconciliation. The text is required reading in many seminaries and spiritual formation retreats. It extends the influence of *Jesus and the Disinherited* to seminarians, retreat participants, and those whose lives are affected by these readers.

READING THE TEXT TODAY

Jesus and the Disinherited continues to have an increasing number of readers because its insights speak to contemporary issues of faith and community. The disinherited remain central to perspectives of Christian identity and faithfulness in Christian discipleship. In the era and for the context that Thurman wrote, African Americans were the disinherited. Although much has changed in the United States, African Americans continue to suffer discrimination, poverty, incarceration, healthcare disparities, and unemployment at high levels that are disproportionate to their percentage of the population. But as Thurman would attest, African Americans are not the only disinherited. The definition of who are the disinherited is determined by the political and social realities of context. Refugees, illegal immigrants, migrant workers, prisoners, the poor, and all who endure political oppression and human rights abuses are the disinherited of whatever race, gender, or ethnicity in whatever country.

Solidarity with the disinherited

Thurman is unequivocal in asserting that to take Jesus seriously requires one to take seriously the suffering of the disinherited. A Christology that diminishes or ignores the plight of the disinherited distorts the message and ministry of Jesus. A Christology that declares poverty as a sign of spiritual failings and prosperity as a sign of spiritual faithfulness contradicts Jesus. Wherever these types of Christology flourish in churches and missionary endeavors, *Jesus and the Disinherited* confronts them as betrayals of Jesus and his vision of God's reconciling community. The challenge for the privileged is not to transform Jesus into one of them, but to enter into solidarity with the disinherited.

As a basic element of such solidarity, the book calls for a sustained personal fellowship with the disinherited that is characterized by a sympathetic understanding of their plight. Thurman's emphasis on personal responsibility and initiative diminishes the tendency to transfer all social transformation possibilities to institutions and systems. Solidarity with the disinherited is intimidating to many because overcoming convictions formed by privilege means confessing that one has benefited from systems of oppression. Solidarity is also risky because one faces powerful people and systems that are threatened by demands for justice. Sustained fellowship with the disinherited, however, should lead to confronting the people and structures of their oppression.

A reconciling community

The challenge for the disinherited is to claim their God-given power to resist the hounds of hell through forgiveness and the love-ethic. With the disinherited already feeling the burdens of oppression, placing on them the requirement of loving the enemy could feel like another burdensome expectation. Thurman interprets Jesus's insistence on the love-ethic as a *release* from the crushing burdens of fear, deception, and hate. The commitment to love even their enemies frees the disinherited from strategies of survival that are in fact the means of spiritual imprisonment. This capacity to love even in the crisis of being against the wall is God's empowerment of the disinherited. Sustained by a right inner attitude, they are never bereft of the hope to give expression to God's call upon their lives. Their capacity for forgiveness and faithfulness is not dependent on the initiatives of the privileged to grant them favors. The love-ethic has the promise of eventually creating the experience of reconciling community. The ethic, however, has the immediate effect of freeing the mind and heart from imprisonment by the hounds of hell.

The book challenges disinherited and privileged alike in ways relevant to contemporary injustices. The particular circumstances of oppression differ from place to place, but the fundamental dynamics that cause individuals and groups to relate inhumanely to others are common to them all. *Jesus and the Disinherited* focuses on these dynamics. Instead of a blueprint that provides a step-by-step approach to a reconciling community, Thurman identifies and analyzes the spiritual issues that must be considered by all communities seeking reconciliation with the disinherited. His insistence that the disinherited and the privileged have the option to resist an oppressive status quo also means there are no excuses for failing to work on behalf of reconciling community.

An invitation to be with Jesus at the wall

The book is more than a prophetic analysis or an indictment against inaction. *Jesus and the Disinherited* is an invitation to deepen one's Christian discipleship. Perhaps as challenging as his invitation to take the initiative to interact with enemies and oppressive systems is his invitation to follow Jesus's example of experiencing God with a certainty that inspires radical social witness. A fierce attention to one's inner landscape is related to practicing the spiritual disciplines that fuel the love ethic—humility, forgiveness, hospitality, and sympathetic fellowship. Jesus is the exemplar for relatedness to the disinherited and for the cultivation of the spiritual life that makes such relatedness possible.

Howard Thurman enjoins readers who follow Jesus to engage the particulars of race, poverty, ethnicity, religion, and oppression that shaped Jesus and his mission. Following Jesus takes readers to the wall where he and the other disinherited stand with their backs pressed against it. Thurman's interpretation of Jesus does not eradicate enemies even when some enemies become caring neighbors. What changes at the wall is the realization that Jesus's love-ethic frees the disinherited and their oppressors from a present and future determined by the hounds of hell. God empowers the disinherited and their oppressors with the ability to take initiatives that affirm each other's worth and to establish relationships of loving justice.

The wall is a place to encounter fear, deception, and hate. The wall is also a place of revelation where God's empowerment is experienced. The wall is a place of reconciliation where repentance and forgiveness transform enemies into sisters and brothers. Most of all, the wall is where Christians must be if they are faithful to their commitment to be disciples of Jesus. Howard Thurman's *Jesus and the Disinherited* is an invitation to be with Jesus at the wall, to know the saving power of love, and to experience the fulfillment that comes from trusting in Jesus.

EDITION

Thurman, H. (1996) *Jesus and the Disinherited*, Boston, MA: Beacon Press.

FURTHER READING

Fluker, W. (1989) *They Looked for a City: a comparative analysis of the ideal of community in the thought of Howard Thurman and Martin Luther King, Jr.*, Lanham, MD: University Press of America, focuses on the religious bases for their social vision.

Johnson, A. (1997) *Good News for the Disinherited: Howard Thurman on Jesus of Nazareth and human liberation*, Lanham, MD: University Press of America, examines Christology from the African American tradition and themes of *Jesus and the Disinherited*.

Smith, L. (2007) *Howard Thurman: the mystic as prophet*, Richmond, IN: Friends United Press, is a comprehensive study of his biography, theology, and social witness.

30

THOMAS MERTON (1915–68)

New Seeds of Contemplation

BRUCE H. LESCHER

Rainer Maria Rilke, in one of his poems, proclaims, "I live my life in widening circles." That sentence exquisitely captures the life and the writing of Thomas Merton. Orphaned as a teenager, Merton believed that without the burden of parental controls he could become a free and sophisticated "man of the world." Instead, in his first year of college in England, he ended up enslaving himself to his own selfish desires, placing himself and some of those closest to him in moral jeopardy. Later, as a college student at Columbia University in New York City, he converted to Catholicism and then, in an astounding turn, sought his freedom not by becoming a well-traveled and sophisticated intellectual, but by living within the confines of a strict monastic community at the Trappist Abbey of Gethsemani in Kentucky. His abbot, recognizing Merton's talent, encouraged him to keep writing. And write he did! Caught up in the fervor of a convert, Merton first produced books reflecting a jingoistic Catholicism: the church, and especially the monastery, stood as a beacon of truth and sanity in a world lost in lies and confusion.

Yet as he matured, both as a person and an author, Merton outgrew this smugness and narrowness and entered into a profound and loving dialogue with his contemporaries, his American culture, and indeed his world. This is the Merton one encounters in *New Seeds of Contemplation*. A crucial "epiphany" happened to Merton in 1958, as he records in his journal:

Yesterday, in Louisville, at the corner of 4th and Walnut, suddenly realized that I loved all the people and that none of them were, or, could be totally alien to me. As if waking from a dream—the dream of separateness, of the "special" vocation to be different. My vocation does not really make me different from the rest of men or put me is a special category except artificially, juridically. I am still a member of the human race—and what more glorious destiny is there for man, since the Word was made flesh and became, too, a member of the Human Race!

(*The Intimate Merton*, p. 124)

As he matured, Merton engaged in a wide written correspondence with artists, intellectuals, religious thinkers, and ordinary people from all around the world. This dialogue stretched and opened him. Rather than being "different," he now appreciated his solidarity with the average man or woman trying to get by in a complicated world. He began to challenge the rigidity and intellectual shallowness of his church and his own monastic training. Since the Reformation, Catholic theology had been dominated by the scholasticism developed in the medieval universities. Merton fostered the rediscovery of a more ancient style of theological reflection, one that took personal transformation as seriously as intellectual acumen: the theology carried on in monasteries. At the height of the Cold War, he questioned the morality of using nuclear weapons and argued the validity of nonviolence as a strategy. All of these developments within Merton inform the issues which he explores in *New Seeds*.

AUTHOR AND AUDIENCE

Thomas Merton's youth was colorful, unusual, and not without its problems. He was born in Prades, France, on January 31, 1915. His father, Owen Merton was from New Zealand; his mother, Ruth Jenkins Merton was from the United States. Both Owen and Ruth were painters who met in Paris while studying art. Since living in southern France during World War I proved to be dangerous, in 1917 they moved to Flushing, New York, near Ruth's parents. In 1920, Ruth became very ill; she was diagnosed with stomach cancer and died a year later at the age of thirty-four. Tom was six years old. From then on, Merton sometimes lived with his grandparents and sometimes traveled with his father, who went to Cuba, France, and England seeking landscapes to paint.

Tom's education included grade school in France and England, high school in England, and undergraduate studies at Clare College, Cambridge University. On January 18, 1931, during Merton's senior year of high school, his father died of a brain tumor, and Tom was orphaned at age sixteen. Merton entered his freshman year at Cambridge in October 1933 and soon went into a moral tailspin, neglecting his studies and spending his time drinking, gambling, and carousing. He was sent back to New York in autumn of 1934 after a young woman became pregnant by him. In January 1935, he enrolled in Columbia University, majoring in English. Here he thrived under the tutelage of professors like Mark Van Doren and Daniel Walsh and made deep and lasting friendships with several of his classmates, especially the poet Robert Lax.

While at Columbia, Merton and some of his friends began a serious study of Catholicism. Reacting to the rootlessness and confusion of the "lost generation" between the two World Wars, they sought a solid spiritual foundation upon which to base their lives. Merton read Étienne Gilson's *The Spirit of Medieval Philosophy*, which introduced him to an intellectually solid concept of God, and Aldous Huxley's *End and Means*, which argued for the reality of experiential contact with God. A visiting Hindu monk, Bramachari, told Merton to explore the Christian mystical tradition before seeking answers in Eastern religions. Merton was baptized into the Catholic Church in November 1938. He finished his M.A. thesis in January 1939, writing on the poetry of William Blake, who critiqued the spiritual emptiness of England during the early Industrial Revolution. He began teaching English at St. Bonaventure's College (now University) in Olean, New York, in the fall of 1940. During Holy Week 1941, he made a retreat at Gethsemani Abbey, the Trappist monastery in Kentucky, and fell in love with the lifestyle he encountered there. After much soul-searching, he entered the monastery on December 10, 1941.

Merton thought that entering the monastery would put an end to his ambitions to be a writer, but his abbot wisely instructed him to keep writing. He was a prolific author, publishing dozens of books and numerous essays on monasticism, prayer, Zen, poetry, nuclear weapons, nonviolence, and racism. He died on December 10, 1968, at age 53, when he was accidentally electrocuted while attending an interreligious conference on monasticism in Bangkok, Thailand. Several other books have been posthumously published, including five volumes of his letters and seven volumes of his journals. His best known publications are his autobiography, *The Seven Storey Mountain* (1948), and *New Seeds of Contemplation* (1961).

Merton had a genius for exploring religious concepts in language that captured the imagination of his contemporaries, and he became one of the bestselling spiritual writers in the English language. Perhaps because his own life started in a rootless fashion, he had a gift for speaking to an audience much wider than Roman Catholics. *The Seven Storey Mountain* addressed the spiritual hunger which haunted many people in post-World War II America and, to the amazement of the publishing world, became a *New York Times* bestseller. In the "Author's Note" to *New Seeds of Contemplation* Merton says that "the kind of considerations written in these pages ought to be something for which everybody, not only monks, would have a great hunger in our time" (p. xix).

SYNOPSIS

New Seeds of Contemplation (1961) is a rewrite and expansion of Merton's earlier work, *Seeds of Contemplation* (1949). *Seeds* had been written while Merton was still studying for the priesthood and, in his words, "was written in a kind of isolation, in which the author was alone with his own experience of the contemplative life" (p. xv). Subsequent to its publication Merton was named Master of Scholastics (1951), teaching the monks studying for the priesthood, and later Master of Novices (1955), teaching all the young men who entered the monastery. Merton notes, then, that for *New Seeds* "the author's solitude has been modified by contact with other solitudes . . ." (pp. xv–xvi), both the "solitudes" of the young monks whom he mentored and the "solitudes" of the many people who wrote him letters in response to the popularity of *Seven Storey Mountain*.

Merton excelled at the essay. Many of the individual chapters of *New Seeds of Contemplation* shimmer as literary gems. Merton probes the human spirit with remarkable insight, so the reader responds, "Oh yes, that captures my experience exactly!" His prose often bends toward poetry, as when he writes:

The special clumsy beauty of this particular colt on this April day in this field under these clouds is a holiness consecrated by God. . . . The little yellow flowers that nobody notices on the edge of the road are saints looking up into the face of God.

(p. 30)

He is not a systematic thinker, so *New Seeds* can be viewed as a string of pearls rather than a tightly reasoned treatise.

Contemplation

Merton's explorations of contemplation serve as bookends in the text: the opening chapters lay out fundamental categories for understanding contemplative prayer, while the closing chapters explore the journey from active meditation to contemplative prayer.

In the Preface to *New Seeds*, Merton writes that *Seeds* may have misled some readers: "the worst disadvantage of the word [contemplation] is that it sounds like 'something,' an objective quality, a spiritual commodity that one can procure; something which, when possessed, liberates one from problems and unhappiness" (p. xvi). The first three chapters of *New Seeds*, then, explore more deeply the experience of contemplative prayer. Contemplation is "a sudden gift of awareness, an awakening to the Real within all that is real" (p. 3). Yet, placing himself firmly in the Christian apophatic tradition, Merton says that this awakening leads one "beyond our own knowledge, beyond our own light, beyond systems, beyond explanations, beyond discourse, beyond dialogue, beyond our own self" (p. 2). Contemplation is above all a response to a call, "a call from Him Who has no voice, and Who speaks in everything that is, and Who, most of all, speaks in the depths of our own being" (p. 3).

Merton seeks to disabuse people of popular misunderstandings of "contemplation." It is not a product of an "I" thinking about myself; it is not a form of "psychic peace," nor "a tendency to find peace and satisfaction in liturgical rites," nor a "trance or ecstasy," nor "the ability to read the secrets" of other people's hearts (pp. 9–10). Especially, contemplation is not "an escape from conflict, from anguish or from doubt" (p. 12). Indeed, contemplation goes beyond intellectual knowledge and leads to the anguish that one *"no longer knows what God is"* (p. 13, italics in original).

Chapter three is entitled "Seeds of Contemplation." Here Merton explores God's immanence: "the love of God seeks us in every situation, and seeks our good. His inscrutable love seeks our awakening" (p. 15). The challenge, then, is to become aware of these seeds or "germs of spiritual vitality" (p. 14) that God sends, and then to respond. As one responds, one draws ever closer to the Divine. God's will is not an inscrutable puzzle which people must try to figure out; rather, "the very nature of each situation usually bears written in itself some indication of God's will" (p. 18). Implicit here is Merton's concern to show that all people, not only monastics, are called to contemplation. God seeks to awaken people in every circumstance of their lives.

Having laid the groundwork for understanding contemplative prayer, Merton returns to this theme in chapters 29–38, which explore the journey from beginning prayer, in which one uses one's mental faculties, to infused contemplation, in which God takes the initiative. At this depth of prayer, rather than an "I" who revels in "my" religious experience there is rather "God living in God and identifying a created life with His own Life" (p. 284). This journey involves a renunciation of one's attachments (especially those which are unconscious), a shedding of false images of the self and of God, a refusal to be trapped by one's taste for religious experience. Throughout these chapters Merton's indebtedness to John of the Cross, whom he had previously studied in *The Ascent to Truth* (1951), is obvious.

Identity

Identity comprises a theme to which Merton returns frequently in his writing. *New Seeds* contains the most thorough development of his thought on this topic. Each person faces a struggle between the "true self" and the "false self." Merton says, "For me to be a saint means to be myself. Therefore the problem of sanctity is in fact the problem of finding out who I am and of discovering my true self" (p. 31). The "false self" is "the tenacious need to maintain our separate, external, egotistical will" (p. 21). This is the external self that glories in its own achievements and loves to pit these achievements against those of other people: if one has more, the other has less. The "true self" is that image of God hidden in the depths of each person—the person, so to speak, that God intends one to be. Each woman or man is ultimately grounded in the Divine. "The secret of my full identity is hidden in Him. He alone can make me who I am, or rather who I will be when at last I fully begin to be" (p. 33).

Human beings are free: they have the choice of embracing the "seeds" of each moment and moving closer to their deepest identity or not accepting these "seeds" and creating a false, ego-centered image. In the choices they make, people become co-creators of their identity: "Our vocation is not simply to *be*, but to work together with God in the creation of our own life, our own identity, our own destiny" (p. 32).

Solitude and community

Merton clearly understood that the Christian vocation is a call to love, that is, to be in communion with others. "Love is my true identity. Selflessness is my true self. Love is my true character. Love is my name" (p. 60). At the same time, he understood that "physical solitude, exterior silence and real recollection are all morally necessary for anyone who wants to lead a contemplative life" (p. 80). Solitude and community, rather than being opposed to each other, are two facets of an integrated life. He sought to counteract an erroneous understanding of solitude as an attempt to get away from other people. The contemplative enters solitude to love others more deeply: "Go into the desert not to escape other men but in order to find them in God" (p. 53). The great temptation of his contemporaries, he believed, was to immerse oneself in the illusions of mass society, surrendering one's identity to society's expectations of power and success. Time spent in solitude would provide a buffer against this tendency.

A closely related issue which Merton explores in these chapters is the difference between a "person" and an "individual." Here Merton engages in a critique of American culture by drawing upon Roman Catholic theological anthropology. A "person," grounded in the image of a Trinitarian God, realizes his or her profound connection to others. A "person" is shaped by nuclear family, ethnicity, and culture; he or she is a product of relationships. An "individual" imagines oneself to be a monad, an independent subject, and enters into relationship with others through a social contract, an agreement which governs relationships. A person, then, can be connected to others even in solitude, while an individual can be disconnected even when in the presence of others.

Tradition and revolution

"The biggest paradox about the Church is that she is at the same time essentially traditional and essentially revolutionary" (p. 142). Between the bookend chapters on contemplation, Merton addresses a number of topics from the Christian mystical tradition, including asceticism, humility, faith, Christ, Mary, obedience, and detachment. In addressing these topics he demonstrates how deeply rooted he is in this tradition. In his own words, "Everything taught in the Gospel of Christ and the Rule of St.. Benedict, everything accepted by Catholic tradition about the self-discipline of Christian asceticism is here taken for granted" (p. xx).

Yet Merton addresses these topics in a refreshing manner that is accessible to people who are not theologians or perhaps not "religious" at all. He mentions cigarettes, alcohol, and television in his treatment of asceticism; he talks about humility in terms of personal integrity. Mary, for him, is an exemplar not because of her exalted status as Queen of Heaven but because of her emptiness, poverty, and obscurity. Obedience is not the opposite of freedom because "the simplest definition of freedom is this: it means the ability to do the will of God" (p. 201). Obedience involves our "patience and humility" in loving others and "sympathizing with their most unreasonable needs and demands" (p. 191). Merton's discussion of detachment focuses not on letting go of material possessions but rather on the spiritual "possessions" that hold people back from God, whether these be favored spiritual practices leading to rigidity or a desire for "a constant sense of achievement" (p. 206) in ministry.

READING THE TEXT TODAY

Thomas Merton died just a half century ago, so the cultural distance between him and the contemporary reader is not so great. Nonetheless, like any human being, he is a product of his time. Some readers will be challenged opening themselves to this text. Merton wrote before the growing awareness of the harm inflicted by sexist language. He consistently refers to human beings and to God using masculine imagery and pronouns (later in his life this would change as he opened himself to the divine feminine—see his lovely poem "Hagia Sophia"). Also, Merton, while critical of the sterile theological training he received, could not completely escape the confines of the Roman Catholic Neoscholastic theology of the 1950s. Indeed, he needed ecclesiastical approval to have his writings published. So in exploring existential issues faced by modern people, he sometimes turned to categories drawn from medieval Scholasticism (such as intellect, memory, and will)—an approach that some readers may find jarring. Nevertheless, Merton offers a wealth of riches to the reader who engages him.

The turn to spirituality

In 1953 Merton published a journal entitled *The Sign of Jonas*. In the prologue he noted an important insight:

> I found in writing *The Ascent to Truth* that technical language, though it is universal and certain and accepted by theologians, does not reach the average man and does not convey what is most personal and most vital in religious experience. Since my focus is not upon dogmas as such, but only on their repercussions in the life of a soul in which they begin to find a concrete realization, I may be pardoned for using my own words to talk about my own soul.
>
> (pp. 8–9)

Implicit here is a turn toward the subject, a movement away from "dogmas as such" to "what is most personal and most vital in religious experience." It is not too much to see this as a turn toward what scholars today call "spirituality." Merton here anticipates the explosion of interest in spirituality that occurred in the 1960s and beyond. His focus on the "repercussions" of doctrine in "the life of the soul" continues to draw many people, both those identified with a religion and those who are not, to his writings.

Broadening the tradition

Merton read monastic authors both widely and deeply, and he remained profoundly rooted in Western monasticism. Yet he had a genius for addressing traditional topics in language accessible to the laity and even to people with no religious commitment. In Merton's hands, monastic concerns broaden to human concerns: the question of identity, the relationship between solitude and community, the practices that support one on the journey of spiritual growth. In the preface to *New Seeds* he opined that "there are perhaps people without formal religious affiliations who will find in these pages something that appeals to them" (xvii). And that has indeed proven to be the case.

Merton contended that the gift of contemplative prayer was available to all people. "Every moment and every event of every man's life on earth plants something in his soul" (p. 14). Here he entered a debate that surfaced in Catholic theology in the early twentieth century: are only a few chosen souls called to contemplation, or is contemplation the flowering of the graces of baptism and hence available to all? While most Catholics at mid century believed the former position, Merton forcefully argued the latter. His writing revolutionized the way many people understood contemplation and opened them to this form of prayer.

Merton remains a solid spiritual teacher even as he broadens the tradition. Using the tradition as a fulcrum upon which to base his cultural critique, he avoids some of the pitfalls that occur in an overly privatized approach to spiritual practice. The paradoxical nature of his writing holds the tensions that might easily be collapsed. One enters solitude not to be alone but to love others more deeply; one devotes oneself to prayer, but becoming attached to a prayer method can lead one astray; contemplation is an intuitive grasp of the Divine, but the Divine remains ungraspable and beyond all concepts; one seeks one's true self, yet also remains in dialogue with religious authority. Finally, the fruits of contemplation are not for the contemplative alone but are to be shared: "If we experience God in contemplation, we experience Him not for ourselves alone but for others" (p. 269).

Honoring nature

While not a major theme in *New Seeds*, Merton's love of nature is manifest in two chapters and resonates with current ecological concern. In "Things in Their Identity," he builds on Gerard Manly Hopkins's notion of "inscape," the particular beauty of each being in its uniqueness, to revel in the natural world: "The forms and individual characters of living and growing things, of inanimate beings, of animals and flowers and all nature, constitute their holiness in the sight of God" (p. 30). In the last chapter, "The General Dance," Merton celebrates the presence of God in the cosmos: "The world was made as a temple, a paradise, into which God himself would descend to dwell familiarly with the spirits He had placed there to tend it for Him" (p. 290). Readers interested in Merton's celebration of nature will especially enjoy reading his journals, which frequently record his delight in observing animals and plants.

Contemplation and prophecy

Finally, in *New Seeds* Merton connects contemplation to a prophetic social critique, a connection that he explored more thoroughly in his later writings. Merton believed that the contemplative was called to address social problems precisely from one's perspective as a contemplative.

Criticism of popular culture in the United States surfaces frequently in the text. As noted above, Merton saw the temptation faced by modern people to be losing their true selves in mass culture. One is tempted to develop a self based on social norms of power, popularity, and wealth rather than to develop into the person intended by God. Thus the journey toward contemplation involves standing against cultural trends to embark upon a journey of shedding false images of self and of God.

Further, in two striking chapters, "The Root of War is Fear" and "He Who is Not with Me Is against Me," Merton explores the scapegoating dynamic of projecting one's own faults onto another to create an enemy. He wrote this at the time of heightened tension between the United States and the Soviet Union, when each nation threatened to destroy the other with a nuclear arsenal. In the popular imagination, the United States was engaged in a battle of good versus evil. Merton responds, "When I pray for peace, I pray not only that the enemies of my country may cease to want war, but above all that my own country will cease to do the things that make war inevitable" (p. 121). He would later develop these thoughts in writing about the commitment to nonviolence as well as in a critique of race relations in the United States.

Merton's writing gives witness to his own broadening and deepening, and the reader who engages *New Seeds of Contemplation* is invited to explore the widening circles of his or her own life.

EDITION

Thomas Merton (2007) *New Seeds of Contemplation*, with an introduction by Sue Monk Kidd, New York: New Directions.

FURTHER READING

Carr, A.E. (1988) *A Search for Wisdom and Spirit: Thomas Merton's theology of the self*, Notre Dame, IN: University of Notre Dame Press, is a thorough study of Merton's approach to identity.

Cunningham, L.S. (1999) *Thomas Merton and the Monastic Vision*, Grand Rapids, MI: W.B. Eerdmans, provides an excellent study of the centrality of Merton's commitment to monasticism and how his vision evolved.

Cunningham, L.S. (1992) *Thomas Merton: spiritual master*, New York, NY: Paulist Press, contains a helpful introduction and provides a sampling of his writing in different genres.

Merton, T. (1999) *The Intimate Merton: his life from his journals*, San Francisco: HarperSanFrancisco, provides an excellent overview of Merton's personal growth, the story behind his published texts.

Mott, M. (1984) *The Seven Mountains of Thomas Merton*, Boston: Houghton Mifflin Company, is a thorough and well-researched biography.

Shannon, W.H., Bochen, C.M., and O'Connell, P.F. (eds) (2002) *The Thomas Merton Encyclopedia*, Maryknoll, NY: Orbis Books, provides articles on themes in Merton's writing, places of importance in his life, and people with whom he interacted.

INDEX

Aaron, vestments of 78
abandonment *see* self-abandonment
Abelard, Peter 102
Adam 152
affections, definition of 272; distinct
    from passions 273; genuine signs
    275–7, 278–9; and intellect 121–2;
    and love 273; and spirituality
    272–4; unreliable signs of 274–5
affirmative theology 51
African Americans 349
Akyndinos, Gregory 140
Albert the Great 53, 58
Alcuin 81
Alexander, bishop of Alexandria 14–15
Alexander of Hales 112
Alexandria 4
Alfred the Great 81
Alighieri, Dante *see* Dante
allegory 6–7, 9–10, 28
Alumbrados 216
Ambrose 9, 42, 64
American Tract Society 277
Amvrosii of Optino 294, 295
anchorites/esses 150
Andronikos III 138, 140
annihilation 133
Anonymous texts *see Cloud of*
    Unknowing, The; Way of a
    Pilgrim, The

Anselm 117, 157
Antony of Egypt 13; calling 16–17, 21
apophatic mysticism 162–3; Dionysius
    the Areopagite 52, 54, 57; Gregory
    Palamas 141–2; Marguerite Porete
    127–8
Applewhite, Marshall 270
Apponius 9
Aquinas, Thomas 43, 44, 49, 53, 56, 57,
    92, 112, 119, 161; in Dante's
    Paradiso 111
Arianism 15, 26
Aristotle 40, 49, 116, 137, 138, 189
art 20
asceticism 17–18, 238–9, 280, 360; and
    theology 144–5
Athanasios the Athonite 137
Athanasius 13–15
    Life of St. Antony: audience 14–15;
        and Christian monasticism 20;
        influence 19–20; modern readings
        on 20–3; synopsis 15–19
Athonite monasticism 137
atonement 154
Augustine of Hippo 37–9, 64, 82, 113,
    116, 156, 161; exegesis of Genesis
    42–3; odyssey 40–2; *Soliloquies*
    44
    Confessions 19, 37–8, 238; audience
        38–9; influence 43–4; modern